Fundamentals of Financial Management

O.S. Deol

ATLANTIC
PUBLISHERS & DISTRIBUTORS (P) LTD

Published by
ATLANTIC
PUBLISHERS & DISTRIBUTORS (P) LTD
7/22, Ansari Road, Darya Ganj,
New Delhi-110002
Phones : +91-11-40775252, 23273880, 23275880, 23280451
Fax : +91-11-23285873
Web : www.atlanticbooks.com
E-mail : orders@atlanticbooks.com

Branch Office
5, Nallathambi Street, Wallajah Road,
Chennai-600002
Phones : +91-44-64611085, 32413319
E-mail : chennai@atlanticbooks.com

Printed in India at Nice Printing Press, A-33/3A, Site-IV,
Industrial Area, Sahibabad, Ghaziabad, U.P.

Syllabus

University of Delhi
B.Com.: Semester V
Paper No. BC 5.2(a)
Fundamentals of Financial Management

Duration: 3 Hrs. Maximum Marks: 75

Objective: To familiarise the students with the principles and practices of Financial Management.

Unit I: Introduction

Nature, Scope and Objectives of Financial Management. Time Value of Money, Risk and Return (including Capital Asset Pricing Model).

Unit II: Long-Term Investment Decisions

The Capital Budgeting Process, Cash Flow Estimation, Payback Period Method, Accounting Rate of Return, Net Present Value (NPV), Net Terminal Value, Internal Rate of Return, Profitability Index.

Unit III: Financing Decisions

Sources of Long-Term Financing, Estimation of Components of Cost of Capital, Methods for Calculating Cost of Equity, Cost of Retained Earnings, Cost of Debt and Cost of Preference Capital, Weighted Average Cost of Capital (WACC). Capital Structure—Theories of Capital Structure (Net Income, Net Operating Income, MM Hypothesis, Traditional Approach), Operating and Financial Leverages, Determinants of Capital Structure.

Unit IV: Dividend Decisions

Theories of Relevance and Irrelevance of Dividend Decision for Corporate Valuation: Walter's Model, Gordon's Model, MM Approach, Cash and Stock Dividends, Dividend Policies in Practice.

Unit V: Working Capital Decisions

Concepts of Working Capital, Operating and Cash Cycles, Sources of Short-Term Finance, Working Capital Estimation, Cash Management, Receivables Management, Inventory Management.

> Spread sheet is the recommended software for doing basic calculations in Finance and hence can be used for giving students subject related assignments for their internal assessment purpose.

Preface

This book, *Fundamentals of Financial Management*, has been written with the main objective of imparting basic knowledge of financial management to undergraduate students. Efforts have been made to develop the contents of the book in such a way that the concepts and techniques to solve financial problems can be comprehended easily. The book discusses the concepts, assumptions, theories and techniques relating to financial decision making. It covers financing, investment, dividend and working capital management decisions. A chapter on "Time Value of Money" has been included to explain the mathematical tools which are generally used in the study of financial management.

The book has been written in lucid style, simple and unambiguous manner so that the students can easily understand the concepts and techniques used in solving the financial problems. It will provide a foundation to the students interested in pursuing advanced studies in the area of finance.

Contents of the book evolved during the teaching of the subject and discussions with the students in the college. Due care has been given in devising the framework of the book to the level of difficulty faced by the students. In addition to examples and solved problems, the practical problems have been provided at the end of each chapter for further exercise by the students.

The book is comprised of thirteen chapters. Chapter 1 deals with meaning, nature, objectives, functions, and organisation of financial management. It also deals with the concept of return and risk in common stocks. Chapter 2 deals with mathematical techniques which are generally used in assessing the time value of money.

Chapters 3, 4, and 5 are concerned with capital budgeting and cost of capital. Chapter 3 explains the concept of capital budgeting and estimation of cash flows associated with a project. The capital budgeting techniques are discussed in detail in chapter 4. Chapter 5 explains how to measure the cost of capital of various sources of funds.

Chapters 6 and 7 are concerned with financing decisions of a firm. Chapter 6 deals with the concept of leverage and its importance in the functioning of a firm. The theories of capital structure and valuation of the firm have been discussed in chapter 7.

Theories of dividend and dividend policies are discussed in chapters 8 and 9. Chapter 8 is concerned with dividend policies. The models relating to dividend and its impact on the value of a firm have been discussed in chapter 9.

The working capital management is explained in four chapters 10, 11, 12, and 13. Chapter 10 explains the working capital management of a firm. Cash management of a firm has been dealt with in chapter 11. Chapter 12 explains the management of receivables in a firm. The inventory management of a firm has been discussed in chapter 13.

I am sincerely grateful to all my colleagues for their constant support and encouragement. I am thankful to my wife, Asha and my son, Shubhankar for their support and inspiration.

Finally, I express my gratitude to Atlantic Publishers and Distributors (P) Ltd., New Delhi and its team of editors for designing, editing and improving the format and presentation of the book.

I am confident that the book would be useful to the students and teachers working on financial management.

O.S. Deol

Contents

Preface v

List of Abbreviations ix

1. Introduction 1
2. Time Value of Money 19
3. Capital Budgeting: Estimation of Cash Flows 36
4. Capital Budgeting Techniques 58
5. Cost of Capital 102
6. Financing Decisions: Leverage 135
7. Capital Structure: Valuation of Firm 174
8. Dividend Policy 207
9. Dividend and Valuation of Firm 216
10. Working Capital Management 243
11. Cash Management 267
12. Receivables Management 284
13. Inventory Management 301

Appendix 1: University Question Paper 2016 316

Appendix 2: Mathematical Tables 319

List of Abbreviations

ARR: Accounting rate of return
β: Systematic risk of stock
C: Cash flow
CFAT: Cash flows after tax
CVF: Compound value factor
CVFA: Compound value factor for annuity
D: Dividend
EBIT: Earnings before interest & tax
EPS: Earnings per share
g: Growth rate in dividend
IRR: Internal of return
k_d: Cost of debt
k_e: Cost of equity capital
k_o: Overall cost of capital
k_p: Cost of preference shave capital
n: Number of periods
NI: Net income
NOI: Net operating income
NPV: Net present value
P: Present value
P_o: Issue price of capital stock
PVF: Present value factor
PVFA: Present value factor for annuity

r: Rate of interest, Rate of return of stock

R: Regular cash flow, Rate of return of stock

r_e: Effective rate of interest

S: Compound value (Future value)

W.C.: Working capital

WACC: Weighted average cost of capital

Introduction

1

Chapter Outline

1.1 Meaning
1.2 Nature
1.3 Scope
1.4 Objectives
1.5 Finance Functions or Decisions
1.6 Role of Financial Manager
1.7 Organisation of Finance Functions
1.8 Concept of Risk and Return

1.1 Meaning

Financial management is concerned with financial decision-making of a firm. It deals with procurement of funds and their effective utilisation in the business of the firm to attain the objectives of the firm.

According to Solomon Ezra, "financial management is concerned with the efficient use of an important economic resource, namely capital fund".

In words of Wheeler A.H., "financial management is the activity which is concerned with the acquisition and administration of capital funds in meeting the financial needs and overall objectives of business enterprise".

According to Bradlay, "financial management is the area of business management devoted to a judicious use of capital and careful selection of source of capital in order to enable a firm to move in the direction of reaching its goals".

Thus, financial management is a functional area of business management of a firm that is concerned with the acquisition and optimum utilisation of funds to meet the goals of the firm. Financial management is interlinked with all other functions of the business. The main financial decisions are concerned with the procurement of funds, application of funds, and distribution of funds.

1.2 Nature

The nature of financial management has changed and its scope has widened over the years. Now, financial management function is different from accounting function. It has become a continuous business function. According to modern approach, the main features of financial management can be identified as given below:

1. Different from accounting function: The accounting function is concerned basically with the recording of transactions and maintaining the accounts. While, financial management is concerned the procurement of funds, application of funds, and distribution of funds. The basic objective of financial management is the maximisation of shareholders' wealth. Accounting information is used by financial managers in performing the financial management function. It is said that "Accounting is an input to finance".

2. Continuous business management function: The nature of financial management has changed. In traditional approach, financial management was an occasional activity. It was basically concerned with the procurement of funds in most economical method. The modern approach has widened the scope of financial management. Now, it concerned with the procurement of funds, application of funds, and distribution of funds. This nature of financial management has made financial management a continuous business management function.

3. Centralised nature: Financial management function is a centralised function catering the needs of different departments and attaining the objectives of the firm as well. It performs centralised function in procuring funds and distributing funds as well in other financial functions in the firm.

4. Analytical function: A lot of analytical work is performed in financial management. Modern mathematical and statistical tools are used in financial analysis. All decisions are taken on the basis of financial analysis.

5. Interlinked with other business functions: Financial management is inter-linked with all the departments of business organisation. Financial planning is made after getting inputs on requirements and forecasts made by other departments, like marketing, purchase, production, personnel, etc. Financial decisions are taken on the basis of other business functions. Thus, financial management of a firm is dependent on all other business functions.

6. Essential part of every organisation: Whatever be the size, nature, control and ownership of a business organisation, financial management is an essential part of it. Every organisation needs finance for its operation. The nature of financial management required for may vary from organisation to organisation, but financial management is a must for each organisation. Financial management makes the operations of organisation economical and efficient.

1.3 Scope

The scope of financial management has widened over the years. Traditionally, the scope of financial management was limited to the procurement of funds. But, modern approach has widened the scope of financial management. The modern approach incorporates the three major decisions of financial management as given below:

(i) Investment decision
(ii) Financing decision
(iii) Dividend decision

Investment decision: Investment decision comprises both investment in long-term assets and investment in short-term assets. The technique of deciding the investment in long-term assets of a firm is called "Capital Budgeting". Separate method or technique is used assessing the working capital requirements (short-term assets) of the firm.

The following decisions are taken regarding the investment in long-term assets:

(i) What would be the size of the firm?

(ii) Which are the assets or projects for the investment?

(iii) Projects to be discontinued.

(iv) Which project provides best returns after taking into consideration risk involved?

The efficient management of working capital affects the profitability of a firm and is vital for the continued existence of business. There should be neither paucity nor excess of working capital. Working capital requirement should be assessed after taking all relevant factors into consideration, like credit policy, cash management, stock requirements etc.

The investment decision is the most crucial decision of a firm. It affects the value of a firm. The investment in fixed assets and current assets should be evaluated in relation to their expected return and the risk involved therein. Since the objective of financial management is to maximise shareholders' wealth, the investment decision is foremost decision in attaining the objective.

Financing decision: Financing decision of a firm is concerned with deciding the capital structure and its sources of fund to meet the investment requirements. In other words, financing decision involves selection of optimum proportion of debt and equity. A capital structure with a reasonable mix of debt and equity capital is called optimum capital structure.

The cost of capital affects the optimum capital structure. Since debt is paid before equity capital, risk involved is lower for investors and they demand lower return on investment. But, higher level of debt in capital structure raises the risk in the business. Thus, there is risk return trade off involved in capital structure. The optimum capital structure is presumed where the average cost of capital is minimum as far as possible.

Dividend decision: Dividend decision is concerned with the distribution of profit earned by the firm to stockholders. The proportion of profit distributed to stockholders as dividend is called the dividend-payout ratio and undistributed portion of profit is called the retention ratio. The financial manager has to decide that how much portion of profit should be distributed. A number of factors, like profitable investment opportunities, firm's financial needs, expectations of shareholders, legal requirements etc. affect the dividend decision of a firm.

If the firm has investment opportunities, it should finance this by some retained earnings keeping in mind the cost of external financing, the value of firm and shareholders' expectations. Since the basic objective of financial management is to maximise shareholders' wealth, the optimum dividend policy is the one that maximises the value of firm. Thus, a firm should maintain a balance between distributed and undistributed profits, and also satisfying the expectations of shareholders.

1.4 Objectives

Some objective or standard must be set for efficient financial management so that a financial decision could be judged in the light of set standard. Following are the two widely discussed objectives of financial management:

1. Profit maximisation
2. Shareholders' wealth maximisation.

Traditionally profit maximisation was considered basic objective of financial management. But, certain drawbacks made this objective unrealistic. Now, it is generally agreed in theory that shareholders' wealth maximisation should be the financial objective of the firm.

Profit maximisation: Generally, profit maximisation is offered as the basic objective of the firm. In pursuance of this objective, the investment, financing and dividend policy decisions of the firm should be slanted towards to the maximisation of profit. This objective of the firm leads to efficient allocation of resources, since uses of resources are assessed in terms of profitability. If all firms in the society follows the objective, there will be optimum allocation of resources in the society. But, increase in profit can be shown by some manipulations. Maximising earnings per share is often supported as an improved version of profit maximisation. The maximisation of earnings per share also inherit the main shortcomings of profit maximisation. There are certain limitations that make profit maximisation an unrealistic objective. The limitations are mentioned below:

(i) **No consideration for time value of money:** The profit maximisation is not an appropriate goal because it does not specify the timings and duration of expected returns. All monetary benefits and costs are considered in the absolute value terms without adjusting for time value. Example given below will clear the concept:

Profit Pattern of a Firm

Year	Proposal I	Proposal II
I	10,000	–
II	10,000	–
III	10,000	30,000
Total	**30,000**	**30,000**

The above example makes it clear that according to profit maximisation criteria, both the proposals are equally good. But, if time value of money is considered proposal I is better.

(ii) **No consideration for risk:** Two firms may have similar profit pattern, but different degree of risk involved. This situation may result in wrong selection of a project. The capital structure also has bearing on the degree of risk involved. Higher the proportion of debt in total capital of a firm, higher the risk involved. The profit maximisation criteria does not take these factors into consideration. The market price of share of a firm having the lesser degree of risk will be higher, while earning profit equal to that of another firm. In this situation, maximisation of shareholders' wealth is a better yardstick to judge a financial decision.

(iii) **Ineffective dividend policy:** If profit maximisation is the objective of a firm, it will never allow to pay dividend to shareholders. In such a situation, both the profit and earnings per share would increase year after year, whether the quantum is small or large. The payment of dividend affects the value of a firm. Thus, profit maximisation would not be a satisfactory objective of financial management of a firm.

Wealth maximisation: The profit maximisation objective has been criticised because it does not consider time value of money, ignores risk involved in expected earnings and does not take care of social responsibilities of a business firm. The wealth maximisation objective is a better alternative to profit maximisation. The wealth maximisation implies the maximisation of value of a firm to its shareholders, in other words maximising market price of share of the firm. The market price of share takes into consideration present and future earnings per share, the timing and the risk of these earnings, the dividend policy of the firm and other relevant factors affecting the market price of shares of the firm.

In wealth maximisation approach, net present value of benefit from the project has to be maximised. The net present value is calculated by subtracting the amount of investment required from the present value of benefits earned from the project. Shareholders' wealth includes value of shares, reserves and surplus. But, more emphasis is laid on market value of shares of a company. Thus, shareholders' wealth is represented by market value of shares of a firm.

Superiority of wealth maximisation: Wealth maximisation objective of a firm is superior to profit maximisation. The following points support the superiority of wealth maximisation objective:

(i) It measures benefits in terms of cash flows, which is a better measure as compared to accounting profits.

(ii) It considers time value of money by discounting the expected cash flows by a proper discount rate.

(iii) It analyses the risk and uncertainty to find the best available option of investment.

(iv) It ensures efficient utilisation of resources. The resources are allocated to projects which provides maximum value to shareholders.

In nutshell, we can say that shareholders' wealth maximisation is better objective of financial management of firm.

1.5 Finance Functions or Decisions

The functions of raising funds, investing in assets and distributing returns to shareholders are main financial functions or financial decisions in a firm. The finance functions are divided into long-term and short-term decisions as mentioned below:

(a) Long-term finance decisions
   - (i) Investment decision
   - (ii) Financing decision
   - (iii) Dividend decision

(b) Short-term finance decisions
   - (i) Liquidity decision

Investment decision: To take a long-term investment decision, various capital budgeting techniques are used. Risk return trade-off is involved in capital budgeting decision. For a given degree of risk, project giving the maximum net present value is selected. The objective of financial management is to maximise shareholders' wealth. Hence, investment decision is most crucial in attaining the objective. After a careful analysis of risk return trade-off, the size of plant should be determined.

Financing decision: Financing decision is concerned with the capital structure of the firm. The decision is basically taken about proportion of equity capital and debt capital in total capital of the firm. Higher the proportion of debt in capital of the firm, higher is the risk. A capital structure having a reasonable mix of equity capital and debt capital is called optimum capital structure.

Financing should be from sources having lowest cost of capital. A number of factors affect the capital structure of a firm. Debt has lower cost of capital, but it increases risk in the business of the firm. A leveraged firm carries higher degree of risk in business. A reasonable mix of debt and equity capital should be selected to maintain the balance between risk and return.

Dividend decision: The third major decision is concerned with the distribution of profit to shareholders. A finance manager has to decide how much proportion of profit should be distributed to shareholders. If a firm needs funds for investment in available projects and the cost of external financing is higher, then it is better to retain profit to meet the requirement. The payment of dividends also affect the value of firms. These factors should be taken into consideration while deciding the optimal dividend policy of the firm.

Liquidity decision: A firm needs working capital to manage the day-to-day affairs smoothly. Working capital means firm's total investment in current assets. Net working capital is equal to difference between the total current assets and current liabilities. In working capital management, a finance manager has to take decision on following issues:

(i) What should be the total investment in working capital of the firm?
(ii) What should be the level of individual current assets?
(iii) What should be the relative proportion of different sources to finance the working capital requirement?
(iv) What should be the firm's credit policy while selling to customers?

Management of working capital involves risk-return trade-off. If the level of current assets of the firm is very high, it has excess liquidity. When the firm does so its rate of return will decline as more funds are tied up in idle cash. If the firm's level of current assets is low, it would result in interrupted production and sales. This would lead to reduction in profit. Thus a firm should maintain optimum level of current assets.

1.6 Role of Financial Manager

Traditionally, finance manager was concerned with the procurement of funds required by the firm. The modern approach has changed and widened the role of a finance manager. All activities in a business firm, be it purchase, production or marketing has financial implications. Hence, finance function is inter-linked with other business functions as well. A finance manager has to focus on the following tenets:

- Procurement of funds at the lowest cost, as and when required by the firm,
- Investing the procured funds in most profitable approach,
- Distributing the returns among shareholders as per the rational approach.

Taking into consideration the above mentioned tenets, a finance manager has to perform the following functions:

(i) Overall financial planning and control
(ii) Procurement of funds from different sources
(iii) Investment in fixed assets
(iv) Management of working capital
(v) Other financial function related to the above.

To perform these functions, a finance manager should have clear understanding of capital markets. The role of finance manager is intermediary because of two-way cash flows between the firm and the investors. Firm raises the fund through the capital markets. The funds raised are utilised in the investment projects of the firm. The investment project generate profits which are either distributed to the shareholders or retained in the business for reinvestment in future projects of the firm.

While performing his duties, a finance manager faces the following tasks:

(i) What should be the size of the firm and what are its growth prospects?
(ii) What are the various types of assets to be required?
(iii) What should be the capital structure of the firm?

In performing the above tasks, finance manager has to take following decisions:

(i) Investment decision
(ii) Financing decision
(iii) Dividend decision.

In fact, investment, financing and dividend decision are all inter-related. In capital budgeting, present values are calculated by applying an appropriate discount rate to discount the future cash flows. The appropriate discount rate is the cost of capital which is given by the capital structure of the firm. Thus, investment and financing are inter-related. Operating profitability affects the dividend decision of the firm. Further, operating profitability of the firm depends on the capital budgeting decision (investment). Thus, dividend and investment are inter-related. In nutshell, all the three financial decisions are inter-related.

Depending on the size and nature of the firm, the finance manager has to perform all or some of these functions from time to time. From the above discussion, it is evident that role of finance manager is very crucial for continued existence of the firm.

1.7 Organisation of Finance Functions

For efficient decision-making and smooth running of business operations, it is important to have well defined organisation of finance functions. A department to organise finance activities in generally created under the direct control of top management (Board of Directors, CEO), which is ultimately responsible to carry out finance functions.

The organisational chart of finance functions is given below in figure 1. A company may adopt a variation of this format of organisation of finance functions depending upon nature of business and the needs of the company.

The designation of chief executive officer may vary from organisation to organisation. The chief finance officer may be designated as vice president (finance), director (finance), general manager (finance). The chief finance officer (CFO) has both line and staff responsibilities. The chief finance officer is member of top management. The CFO is associated with the formulation of policies and taking decisions for the firm. The treasurer and controller of the firm work under supervision of the CFO. The CFO have to supervise and guide the staff of finance department for smooth and effective working of the department.

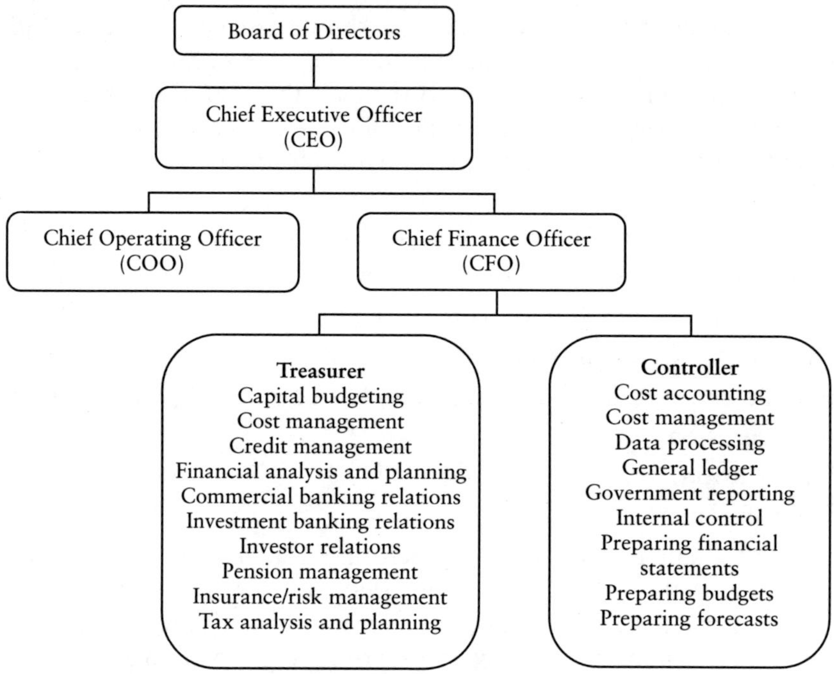

Fig. 1: Organisation of Financial Management Functions

The finance functions of the firm are placed under direct control of top management due to following factors:

1. The objective of financial management of the firm is to maximise shareholders' wealth. The financial decisions are crucial to maximise shareholders' wealth.
2. Financial decisions are crucial for continued existence of the business firm.
3. A number of economies can be achieved by centralising the finance functions in a firm.
4. The market value depends on earnings of the firm, which in turn depend on capital structure and investment of the firm. Being so important, it is essential to put the financial decisions in the hand of top management.

The controller's responsibilities are primarily accounting in nature. Cost accounting, cost management, data processing, and general ledger are the functions, the controller has to perform. Internal control is carried out by the controller. External reporting is provided to concerned government agencies and shareholders. The preparation of budget, and providing the forecasts are responsibilities of the controller.

The treasurer's responsibilities fall into the decision areas generally associated with financial management, like—investment (capital budgeting and pension management), financing (commercial banking and investment banking relationships, investor relations, dividend disbursement), and asset management (cash management, credit management).

The controller and treasurer are interlinked. Information flows simply between the both officers. In small firms, the functions of controller and treasurer are merged and put under one position.

1.8 Concept of Risk and Return

Return on a stock is defined as earnings on the stock divided by the purchase price of the stock or price at the beginning of the period. The earnings include both the capital gain and dividend.

Risk is defined as the variation of actual return from the expected return. The risks usually faced by a firm can be divided into two broad categories as given below:

1. Unsystematic Risk
2. Systematic Risk.

1. Unsystematic Risk: Unsystematic risk arises due to the particular factors related to the firm. These factors can be controlled so as to avoid the risk. For example, factors like, change in the demand of products of the firm, labour strike, management inefficiency, increase in the competition in the market etc. Unsystematic risk can be averted by diversifying the investment portfolio.

Unsystematic risk can be of two types as given below:

(i) Business risk

(ii) Financial risk

Business risk arises due to fluctuation in the operations of the firm. The reasons causing the fluctuations in operation of the firm may be internal or external to the firm.

Financial risk is caused by the presence of debt in the capital structure of the firm. Higher the degree of debt (leverage) in the capital structure of the firm, higher is the financial risk.

The rate of return is total sum of capital gain and dividend yield. The risk of return of a stock is measured by standard deviation of rates of returns on the stock:

$$\sigma = \sqrt{\frac{1}{n}\sum_{t=1}^{n}(R_t - \bar{R})^2}$$

Where, n = Number of periods

R = Rate of return

σ = Risk of return.

Example 1. Compute the annual rates of return and average return of a firm on the basis of data given below:

Year	1	2	3	4	5	6	7	8	9	10
Share price (₹)	100	110	114	120	115	118	130	125	130	136
Dividend (₹)	8	10	6	8	10	9	6	10	6	8

Solution: Calculation of annual rates of return:

Year	Share price (₹)	Capital gain (%)	DPS (₹)	Dividend yield (%)	Rate of return
1	100	–	8	–	–
2	110	10.0	10	10.0	20.0
3	114	3.6	6	5.5	9.1
4	120	5.3	8	7.0	12.3
5	115	– 4.2	10	8.3	4.1
6	118	2.6	9	7.8	10.4
7	130	10.2	6	4.6	14.8
8	125	– 3.8	10	7.7	3.9
9	130	4.0	6	4.8	8.8
10	136	4.6	8	6.2	10.8

$$\text{Average return} = \frac{20.0+9.1+12.3+4.1+10.4+14.8+3.9+8.8+10.8}{9}$$

Average return = 10.5%.

Example 2. Find the risk of return on stock for the data given in the example 1.

Solution: Calculation of risk of return:

Year	Return (%)	$(R-\bar{R})$	$(R-\bar{R})^2$
2	20.0	9.5	90.25
3	9.1	–1.4	1.96
4	12.3	1.8	3.24
5	4.1	–6.4	40.96
6	10.4	–0.1	0.01
7	14.8	4.3	18.49
8	3.9	–6.6	43.56
9	8.8	–1.7	2.89
10	10.8	0.3	0.09
Sum			**201.45**

The risk of return of a stock is measured by standard deviation of rates of returns on the stock.

$$\sigma = \sqrt{\frac{1}{n}\sum_{t=1}^{n}(R_t-\bar{R})^2}$$

Substituting the values,

$$\sigma = \sqrt{\frac{201.45}{9}}$$

$$\sigma = 4.78\%$$

The rates of return shows moderate degree of variability in returns of the firm.

2. Systematic Risk: The risk that is not diversifiable and linked to the system is called systematic risk. This type of risk affects the whole market. For example, economic down turn in the economy, political changes affect the whole system. This risk is also known as market risk. Since the risk is related to the system, it is not possible for an individual firm to avert this risk.

The Capital Asset Pricing Model (CAPM) is a model that provides a framework to determine the expected rate of return on an asset and indicates a positive and linear relationship between expected return and the systematic risk. CAPM is based on the assumption that there is no unsystematic risk in the investment portfolio because it is efficiently diversified portfolio.

Capital market line (CML) shows relationship between expected return and risk on a stock portfolio and all investors would choose to remain on this line (frontier). The figure 2 shows the capital market line.

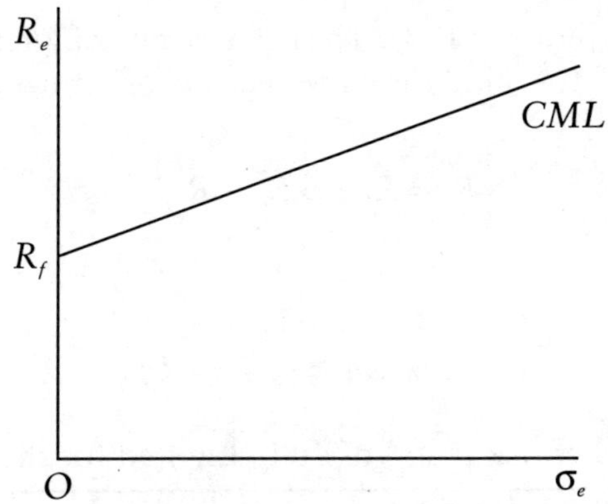

Fig. 2: The Capital Market Line

The equation for capital market line is given below:

$$R_e = R_f + \beta(R_m - R_f)$$

Where, R_e = Expected rate of return on efficient portfolio
R_f = Risk free rate of return
R_m = Rate of return on market portfolio
β = measure of systematic risk (Beta coefficient)

β can be directly calculated with the help of following formula:

$$\beta = \frac{\text{cov}_{e,m}}{\sigma_m^2} = \frac{\sigma_e}{\sigma_m} \times \text{cor}_{e,m}$$

Where, $cov_{e,m}$ = Covariance between security returns and market returns

$cor_{e,m}$ = Correlation between security returns and market returns

σ_m = standard deviation of market returns

σ_e = standard deviation of security returns.

Assumptions: The model is based on following assumptions:

(i) All the investors hold efficiently diversified portfolios having no unsystematic risk. The systematic risk is the only relevant risk in estimating returns.

(ii) There is perfect competition in the capital market.

(iii) Investors are risk averse.

(iv) There are no transaction costs or taxes. The capital market is efficient.

Limitations: The CAPM model has following limitations:

(i) The model is based on unrealistic assumptions.

(ii) Beta does not remain stable over the time.

(iii) It is difficult to test the validity of capital asset pricing model.

Example 3. The market rate of return is 12%. The risk free rate of interest of government securities is 6%. A company has beta of 1.4. Find the expected rate of return on the stock of company.

Solution: We know that:

$$R_e = R_f + \beta(R_m - R_f)$$

Substituting the values,

$$R_e = 6\% + 1.4(12\% - 6\%)$$
$$R_e = 6\% + 8.4\% = 14.4\%.$$

Example 4. Calculate the market risk (beta) of Tulip Limited for the following data:

Year	Return of Tulip (%)	Market return (%)
1	6	5
2	6	6
3	5	6
4	8	5
5	9	7
6	4	4
7	8	6
8	9	7
9	7	6
10	6	8

Solution: Calculation of beta of Tulip Limited:

Year	R_m	R_t	$(R_m - \bar{R}_m)$	$(R_t - \bar{R}_t)$	$(R_m - \bar{R}_m)(R_t - \bar{R}_t)$	$(R_m - \bar{R}_m)^2$
1	5	6	–1	1	–1	1
2	6	6	0	–1	0	0
3	6	7	0	0	0	0
4	5	8	–1	1	–1	1
5	7	9	1	2	2	1
6	4	4	–2	–3	6	4
7	6	8	0	1	0	0
8	7	9	1	2	2	1
9	6	7	0	0	0	0
10	8	6	2	–1	–2	4
Total	**60**	**70**			**6**	**12**

$$\bar{R}_m = \frac{60}{10} = 6$$

$$\bar{R}_t = \frac{70}{10} = 7$$

$$\text{cov}_{t,m} = \frac{6}{10} = 0.6$$

$$\sigma_m^2 = \frac{12}{10} = 1.2$$

We know that:

$$\beta = \frac{\text{cov}_{t,m}}{\sigma_m^2}$$

Substituting the values,

$$\beta = \frac{0.6}{1.2} = 0.5$$

Thus, market risk coefficient (beta) is 0.5.

SOLVED PROBLEMS

Problem 1. Compute the annual rates of return and average return of a firm on the basis of data given below:

Year	1	2	3	4	5	6	7	8	9	10
Share price (₹)	100	105	112	110	115	118	120	125	128	132
Dividend (₹)	6	7	6	8	4	5	6	7	6	8

Solution: Calculation of annual rates of return:

Year	Share price (₹)	Capital gain (%)	DPS (₹)	Dividend yield (%)	Rate of return (%)
1	100	–	6	–	–
2	105	5.0	7	7.0	12.0
3	112	6.7	6	5.7	12.4
4	110	– 1.8	8	7.1	5.3
5	115	4.5	4	3.6	8.1
6	118	2.6	5	4.4	7.0
7	120	1.7	6	5.1	6.8
8	125	4.2	7	5.8	10.0
9	128	2.4	6	4.8	7.2
10	132	3.1	8	6.3	9.4

$$\text{Average return} = \frac{12.0+12.4+5.3+8.1+7.0+6.8+10.0+7.2+9.4}{9}$$

$$\text{Average return} = \frac{78.2}{9}$$

Average return = 8.7%.

Problem 2. Find the risk of return on stock for the data given in the problem 1.

Solution: Calculation of risk of return:

Year	Return (%)	$(R-\bar{R})$	$(R-\bar{R})^2$
2	12.0	3.3	10.89
3	12.4	3.7	13.69
4	5.3	– 3.4	11.56
5	8.1	– 0.6	0.36
6	7.0	– 1.7	2.89
7	6.8	– 1.9	3.61
8	10.0	1.3	1.69
9	7.2	– 1.5	2.89
10	9.4	0.7	0.49
Sum			48.07

The risk of return of a stock is measured by standard deviation of rates of returns on the stock.

$$\sigma = \sqrt{\frac{1}{n}\sum_{t=1}^{n}(R_t - \bar{R})^2}$$

Substituting the values,

$$\sigma = \sqrt{\frac{48.07}{9}}$$

$$\sigma = 2.31\%.$$

The rates of return shows low degree of variability in returns of the firm.

Problem 3. The market rate of return is 10%. The risk free rate of interest of government securities is 4%. A company has beta of 1.2. Find the expected rate of return on stock of the company.

Solution: We know that:

$$R_e = R_f + \beta(R_m - R_f)$$

Substituting the values,

$$R_e = 4\% + 1.2(10\% - 4\%)$$
$$R_e = 4\% + 7.2\% = 11.2\%.$$

Thus, the expected return on stock is 11.2%.

Problem 4. Calculate the market risk (beta) of Trump Limited for the following data:

Year	Return of Trump (%)	Market return (%)
1	10	6
2	8	7
3	12	8
4	10	9
5	9	7
6	11	6
7	13	6
8	9	7
9	11	8
10	7	6

Solution: Calculation of beta of Tulip Limited:

Year	R_m	R_t	$(R_m - \bar{R}_m)$	$(R_t - \bar{R}_t)$	$(R_m - \bar{R}_m)(R_t - \bar{R}_t)$	$(R_m - \bar{R}_m)^2$
1	6	10	–1	0	0	1
2	7	8	0	–2	0	0
3	8	12	1	2	2	1

4	9	10	2	0	0	4
5	7	9	0	–1	0	0
6	6	11	–1	1	–1	1
7	6	13	–1	3	–3	1
8	7	9	0	–1	0	0
9	8	11	1	1	1	1
10	6	7	–1	–3	3	1
Total	**70**	**100**			**2**	**10**

$$\overline{R}_m = \frac{70}{10} = 7$$

$$\overline{R}_t = \frac{100}{10} = 10$$

$$\text{cov}_{t,m} = \frac{2}{10} = 0.2$$

$$\sigma_m^2 = \frac{10}{10} = 1$$

We know that:

$$\beta = \frac{\text{cov}_{t,m}}{\sigma_m^2}$$

Substituting the values,

$$\beta = \frac{0.2}{1} = 0.2$$

Thus, market risk coefficient is 0.2.

THEORETICAL QUESTIONS

1. Comment on the following statements:
   (a) "Wealth maximisation is superior criteria than profit maximisation." Do you agree? Give reasons.
   (b) "The Modern Approach is an improvement over the Traditional Approach of Financial Management." Do you agree? *(D.U., B.Com. 2009)*
2. What are the major types of financial management decisions that business firms make? Describe each one of them. *(D.U., B.Com. 2010)*

3. "Financial management is more than procurement of funds." What do you think are the responsibilities of a Finance Manager? *(D.U., B.Com. 2011)*
4. "Financial Management is concerned with the solution of three major decisions a firm must take." What are these three decisions and how are they interrelated? *(D.U., B.Com. 2012)*
5. "Profit maximisation should be the objective of the Financial Management." Do you agree? Give reasons. *(D.U., B.Com. 2012)*
6. "The profit maximisation is not an operationally feasible criteria." Do you agree? Give reasons. *(D.U., B.Com. 2013)*
7. What are basic financial decisions? How do they involve risk return trade-off? *(D.U., B.Com. 2013)*
8. What do you understand by Financial Management? Discuss its significance in business management. *(D.U., B.Com. 2015)*
9. Briefly discuss major financial decisions with which a finance manager is confronted? *(D.U., B.Com. 2016)*
10. The role of finance manager has evolved over time? Discuss. *(D.U., B.Com. 2016)*
11. Differentiate between "Business Risk" and "financial risk". Outlining the main causes of each type of risk. *(D.U., B.Com. 2012)*
12. Explain the risk-return trade-off in the context of financial decision-making.

PRACTICAL PROBLEMS

1. Compute the annual rates of return and average return of a firm on the basis of data given below:

Year	1	2	3	4	5	6	7	8	9	10
Share price (₹)	50	55	60	55	75	80	78	85	88	92
Dividend (₹)	3	4	3	5	6	5	7	7	3	4

[**Ans.** Annual returns: 18.0%, 14.6%, 0.0%, 47.3%, 13.4%, 6.3%, 18.0%, 7.0%, 9.1%, average return: 14.9%]

2. Find the risk of return on stock for the data given in below:

Year	1	2	3	4	5	6	7	8	9	10
Share price (₹)	50	55	60	55	75	80	78	85	88	92
Dividend (₹)	3	4	3	5	6	5	7	7	3	4

[**Ans.** = 15.64%]

3. The market rate of return is 5%. The risk free rate of interest of government securities is 3%. A company has beta of 1.3. Find the expected rate of return on stock of the company.

[**Ans.** 5.6%]

4. Calculate the market risk (beta) of Mahan Limited for the following data:

Year	Return of Mahan (%)	Market return (%)
1	5	3
2	4	3
3	5	4
4	7	4
5	3	3
6	4	4
7	6	5
8	3	4
9	7	5
10	6	5

[**Ans.** β = 1.17]

Time Value of Money

2

Chapter Outline

2.1 Introduction
2.2 Time Preference for Money
2.3 Compound Value of an Amount
2.4 Compound Value of an Annuity
2.5 Compound Value of an Annuity Due
2.6 Present Value of an Amount
2.7 Present Value of an Annuity
2.8 Present Value of Annuity Due
2.9 Present Value of a Perpetuity
2.10 Net Present Value

2.1 Introduction

What would be your preference—₹ 1,000 today or ₹ 1,000 five years from today? The obvious answer is ₹ 1,000 today because it involves time value to money. If we receive ₹ 1,000 today, it provides us opportunity to our money to work and earn interest. Thus, in time value of money, the interest rate is important factor that allows us to adjust the value of cash flows, whenever they occur, to a particular point in time. Once the mechanism to adjust the value of cash flows to a single point in time by using the rate of interest is developed, we will be in position to answer most difficult questions, like: Should a debenture providing income of ₹ 100 per annum for infinite number of years be purchased, if its offer price is ₹ 1000?

The interest rate allows us to adjust the value of cash flows, whenever they occur, to a particular point in time. The particular point in time is called focal point. The fair comparison can be made of various time adjusted cash flows at the focal point. The process helps in making financial decisions.

Most financial decisions, personal or business, involve time value of money considerations. Maximisation of shareholder's wealth is the prime objective of financial management. In this regard, financial manager takes decisions relating to financing, investment and dividend. In taking these decisions, a financial manager has to take into account the 'time factor'. Here, financial manager needs to know the various valuation concepts, i.e., present value concept, compound value concept and annuity concept etc.

Much of the development of financial management depends on the concepts of time value of money. You will never really understand finance until you understand the time value of money. In this Chapter, we first discuss how to find the compound values (future values) of cash flows at a particular point in time. The technique of finding future values is called 'compounding'. Then, we discuss the ways to find the present values of cash flows. The technique of finding the present values is called 'discounting'. In fact, this is not discounting. It is reverse compounding. The present value is calculated in such a way that if present value is compounded it becomes equal to the future value. In last, the process to find the net present value of a project or investment is discussed.

2.2 Time Preference for Money

The money has a time value because of the following reasons:

1. **Investment opportunities.** This is the basic fundamental reason for time value of money. Money can be employed productively to earn positive returns. If an individual receives money today, he can invest it in project. He will able to earn some profit by selling the products. Thus, if he is given opportunity, he would prefer money today to receive the same after some time. Further, if an individual receives ₹ 1,000 today and deposit it in a bank offering interest rate of 10% p.a., his money grows to ₹ 1,100 in a year. Hence, the individual will obviously prefer ₹ 1,000 today as compared to receiving the same after one year.

   The time value of money is adjusted by the rate of interest prevailing in the market.
2. **Preference for current consumption.** People have a general tendency to prefer current consumption to future consumption. They have perception that they can buy more goods and services with the money received today in comparison of purchases made with the same amount received later on.
3. **Risk.** The present is more certain than future, hence, there is a general preference to receive money at present than at a future date. There are number of factors causing the uncertainty. There is risk of dishonour on part of other party. There are chances that a person may fall ill. Like these factors, there a number of unforeseen events that involve the elements of risk in deferring the receiving the money today. Due to these reasons, individuals prefer receiving the money today to receiving the money in future.

Therefore, the essential principle behind the concept of 'time value of money' is that a sum of money received today is worth more than if the same is received after some time. The rate of interest adjust the time value of money. Projects and investment proposals are selected on the basis of time value of money.

There are two techniques to find the time value of money. (i) Compounding is used to find the future value of money. (ii) Reverse Compounding (Discounting in finance terminology) is used in finding the present value of money to be received in future.

The both techniques are explained below:

2.3 Compound Value of an Amount

In compound interest computation, interest calculated for a given period is added to principal amount before calculating the interest for next period. The interest for next period is calculated on both the initial principal and interest amount of the preceding period. The same process is applied for calculating the interest in subsequent periods. The period may be a year, quarter, month, etc.

2.3.1 Interest Compounded Once in a Period

Let P be the principal amount and r rate of interest per period. The interest amount is compounded once in the period. The sum of amount to be received after the period(s) is computed as given below:

Amount after one period $S_1 = P + Pr = P\ (1 + r)$

Amount after two periods $S_2 = P\ (1 + r) + P\ (1 + r)r = P\ (1 + r)^2$

Amount after three periods $S_3 = P\ (1 + r)^2 + P\ (1 + r)^2\ r = P\ (1 + r)^3$

Amount after n periods $S_n = P\ (1 + r)^{n-1} + P\ (1 + r)^{n-1}\ r = P\ (1 + r)^n$

Thus, if an amount P is put at compound interest for n periods at rate of interest r per period, the amount (S) received at the end of n periods is calculated by applying the following formula:

$$S = P\ (1 + r)^n$$

The term $(1 + r)^n$ is called compound value factor (CVF) and it implies that the sum to be received on depositing ₹ 1 for n periods at rate of interest r% per period. The CVF value can be read from the CVF tables.

Example 1. A sum of ₹ 10,000 is put at compound interest for three years at 4% per year. Find the sum received at the end of three years.

Solution: We know that the sum received at the end of n years:

$$S = P\ (1 + r)^n$$

By substituting the values, we get:

$$S = 10{,}000\ (1+ 0.04)^3$$

$$S = 11{,}248.6$$

Thus, the amount to be received at the end of three years is ₹ 11,248.6.

We can use CVF table to find the sum by applying the following formula:

$$S = P \times \text{CVF}\ (r\%, n)$$

Substituting the values:

$$S = 10{,}000 \times 1.125$$

$$S = ₹\ 11{,}250$$

The difference in two sums calculated above due to rounding off.

2.3.2 Interest Compounded Regularly

When interest is compounded more than once in a period, the following formula is applied to find the sum received at the end of n periods:

$$S = P\left(1+\frac{r}{m}\right)^{mn}$$

Where,

P = Principal

S = Sum at the end of n periods

r = Rate of interest per period

n = Number of periods

m = Number of times, interest is compounded in a period.

For instance, if an amount is deposited for 10 years and interest is compounded quarterly, then $n = 10$ and $m = 4$.

The term $\left(1+\frac{r}{m}\right)^{mn}$ is compound value factor. We can read it its value from the compound value factor table at CVF (r/m%, mn).

Example 2. Compute compound interest on ₹ 10,000 deposited for three years at the rate of 4% per year, if interest is compounded quarterly.

Solution: Interest is compounded quarterly for three years, so $n = 3$ and $m = 4$.

We know that sum to be received after n periods:

$$S = P\left(1+\frac{r}{m}\right)^{mn}$$

Substituting the values, we get:

$$S = 10{,}000\left(1+\frac{0.04}{4}\right)^{4\times 3}$$

$$S = 10{,}000(1.01)^{12}$$

$$S = ₹\ 11{,}268.25$$

Interest earned in three years, $I = S - P = 11{,}268.25 - 10{,}000 =$ ₹ 1,268.25.

We can also use compound value factor table.

$$S = P \times \text{CVF}\ (r/m\%,\ mn)$$

Substituting the values,

$$S = 10{,}000\ (1.127)$$

$$S = ₹\ 11{,}270$$

Interest earned in three years, $I = S - P = 11{,}270 - 10{,}000 =$ ₹ 1,270.

2.3.3 Interest Compounded Continuously

When interest is compounded continuously in a period, the following formula is applied to find the sum received at the end of n periods:

$$S = Pe^{rn}$$

Example 3. Compute compound interest on ₹ 10,000 deposited for three years at the rate of 4% per year, if interest is compounded continuously.

Solution: We know that the sum to be received after n periods by compounding the interest continuously is:

$$S = Pe^{rn}$$

Substituting the values, we get:

$$S = 10{,}000\ e^{0.04\times3}$$

$$S = 10{,}000\ e^{1.2}$$

Taking log on both sides,

$$\log S = \log 10{,}000 + 1.2 \log e$$

$$\log S = 4 + 1.2\ (0.4343) = 4.052116$$

Taking anti-log on both sides,

$$S = \text{Anti log } 4.0521 = ₹\ 11{,}280$$

Interest earned in three years, $I = S - P = 11{,}280 - 10{,}000 =$ ₹ 1,280.

2.3.4 Effective Interest Rate

The announced rate of interest for period is called nominal interest rate. The rate by which financial obligation grows actually is called the effective interest rate. If interest is compounded more than once in a period, the effective interest rate for the period will be higher than the nominal rate of interest for the period. For example, if the nominal rate of interest is r per year and interest is compounded quarterly, the effective rate of interest per year r_e will be higher than r. During the period, interest rate may be compounded regularly at intervals or continuously.

The following formula is used to find effective rate of interest:

$$r_e = \left(1+\frac{r}{m}\right)^m - 1$$

Where,

r_e = Effective interest rate for the period

r = Nominal interest rate for the period

m = Number of times, interest is compounded in the period.

Example 4. If per annum interest rate of 6% is compounded quarterly, find the effective rate of interest.

Solution: We know that effective rate of interest is calculated by the formula given below:

$$r_e = \left(1+\frac{r}{m}\right)^m - 1$$

Substituting the values, we get:

$$r_e = \left(1+\frac{0.06}{4}\right)^4 - 1$$

$$r_e = (1.015)^4 - 1$$

$$r_e = 1.0614 - 1$$
$$r_e = 0.0614$$

Thus, effective rate of interest is 6.14%.

2.4 Compound Value of an Annuity

An annuity is sequence of equal deposits/payments made for equal intervals at the end of each interval. In ordinary annuity, deposits/payments are made at end of each period.

Amount (S) of the annuity = $R + R(1 + r) + R(1 + r)^2 + \ldots\ldots + R(1 + r)^{n-1}$

The sum of annuity (S) is computed by the following formula:

$$S = R\left[\frac{(1+r)^n - 1}{1}\right]$$

Where,

R = Amount of regular payment

r = Nominal interest rate per interval

n = Number of intervals

Mathematical tables for annuity can be used to compute the future sum (S) of an annuity. Term $\left[\frac{(1+r)^n - 1}{1}\right]$ is called compound value factor for annuity (CVFA) and it implies that the amount (sum) of an ordinary annuity consisting payments of ₹ 1 regularly for n periods at the rate i per period. This value can be found from the annuity tables (CVFA $_{r\%,\, n}$).

Thus, the future sum of an annuity (S) is given by the following formula:

$$S = R \times \text{CVFA}_{(r\%,\, n)}.$$

Example 5. Mr. X deposited 10,000 every year for 10 years at interest rate of 8% per year. Find the value of his deposits at the end of 10 years.

Solution: We know the value of an annuity is calculated by the following formula:

$$S = R \times \text{CVFA}_{(r\%,\, n)}$$

Here, R = 10,000, n = 10 years, r = 0.08 and CVFA $_{(8\%,\, 10)}$ = 14.487 (from annuity table).

Substituting the values, we get:

$$S = 10{,}000 \times 14.487 = 14{,}487$$

Thus, value of deposits at the end of ten years is ₹ 14,487.

2.5 Compound Value of an Annuity Due

If the cash flow occurs at the beginning of each period, the annuity is an annuity due. Since each cash flow occurs one period earlier, the compound value of annuity due is equal to compound value of ordinary annuity multiplied by $(1 + r)$. The following formula is used to find the compound value of annuity due:

$$S_{\text{due}} = S_{\text{ordinary}}\,(1 + r)$$

Where, S_{due} = Compound value of annuity due

$S_{ordinary}$ = Compound value of ordinary annuity

r = Rate of interest

Thus, $S_{due} = R \times \text{CVFA}_{(r\%, n)} \times (1 + r)$.

Example 6. Mr. Ramesh receives ₹ 10,000 in the beginning of each year for 10 years from an investment made earlier. Find the future value of all cash inflows at the end of 10 years, if the rate of interest is 6%.

Solution: This is a case of annuity due. Here, R = ₹ 10,000, r = 8% and n = 10 years. Then,

$$S_{due} = 10{,}000 \times \text{CVFA}_{(6\%, 10)} \times (1 + 0.06)$$
$$= 10{,}000 \times 13.181 \times (1.06)$$
$$= 1{,}38{,}718.6$$

Thus, the future value of cash inflows is ₹ 1,38,718.6.

2.6 Present Value of an Amount

Present value is found by the process of reverse compounding. The compound interest rate (discount rate in finance terminology) is applied to make present value equal to future sum. Technically, discount rate is different from compound interest rate. In fact cash flows are not discounted, present value of cash flows is compounded to make it equal to cash flows.

2.6.1 Present Value When Interest Compounded Once

The present value of a future sum (S) compounded periodically for n periods is given by the following formula:

$$P = \frac{S}{(1+r)^n}$$

Where,

P = Present value

S = Future sum

r = Rate of interest

n = number of periods

The factor $\frac{1}{(1+r)^n}$ in the above formula is called the present value factor (PVF). This represents the present value of ₹ 1 due after n periods if rate of interest is r. The PVF values can be read from PVF tables.

Thus present value (P) of a future sum (S) can be computed by applying the following formula:

$$P = S \times \text{PVF}_{(r\%, n)}.$$

Example 7. Find the present value of ₹ 600 due after 20 years at 5% compounded annually.

Solution: We can apply the following formula to find the present value:

$$P = \frac{S}{(1+r)^n}$$

By substituting the values,

$$P = \frac{600}{(1+0.05)^{20}}$$

$$P = \frac{600}{2.665}$$

$$P = 225.98$$

We can also find the present value by applying the PVF table.

$$P = S \times \text{PVF}_{(r\%,\, n)}$$

Here, the value of PVF (5%, 20) is 0.377. Substituting the values,

$$P = 600 \times 0.377$$

$$P = ₹\, 226.2$$

2.6.2 Present Value When Interest Compounded Regularly

The present value of a future sum compounded more than one time in a period is computed as given below:

$$P = \frac{S}{\left(1+\frac{r}{m}\right)^{mn}}$$

Where,

P = Present value

S = Future sum

r = Rate of interest per period

n = Number of periods

m = Number of times, the interest is compounded in a period.

The factor $\frac{1}{\left(1+\frac{r}{m}\right)^{mn}}$ in the above formula is called the present value factor (PVF). This represents the present value of ₹ 1 due after $m \times n$ periods if rate of interest is $r/m\%$. The PVF values can be read from PVF tables.

Thus present value (P) of a future sum (S) can be computed by applying the following formula:

$$P = S \times \text{PVF}_{(r/m\%,\, mn)}.$$

Example 8. Find the present value of ₹ 5,000 due in 10 years, when interest of 10% per annum is compounded semi-annually.

Solution: We can apply the following formula:

$$P = S \times \text{PVF}_{(r/m\%,\ mn)}$$

Here, S = ₹ 5,000, $m = 2$, $n = 10$ and $\text{PVF}_{(5\%,\ 20)} = 0.377$.

After substituting the values:

$$P = 5{,}000 \times 0.377$$

$$P = ₹\ 1{,}885$$

Thus, the present value of ₹ 5,000 due in 10 years is ₹ 1,885.

2.6.3 Present Value When Interest Compounded Continuously

The present value of a future sum compounded continuously in a period is computed as given below:

$$P = \frac{S}{e^{rn}}$$

Where,

P = Present value

S = Future sum

r = Rate of interest per period

n = Number of periods.

Example 9. Find present value of ₹ 5,000 due in 10 years, when interest of 10% per annum is compounded continuously.

Solution: The present value is calculated by the formula:

$$P = \frac{S}{e^{rn}}$$

Here, S = ₹ 5,000, $r = 10\%$, $n = 10$ years.

Substituting the values, we get:

$$P = \frac{5{,}000}{e^{0.1 \times 10}}$$

$$P = \frac{5{,}000}{e}$$

$$P = \frac{5{,}000}{2.7183}$$

$$P = ₹\ 1{,}839$$

Thus, the present value of ₹ 5,000 due in 10 years is ₹ 1,839.

2.7 Present Value of an Annuity

An annuity is sequence of equal deposits/payments made at equal intervals. The deposit/payments are made at the end of each interval/period. The present value of annuity (P) is computed by the following formula:

$$P = R\left[\frac{1-(1+r)^{-n}}{r}\right]$$

Where,

R = Amount of regular payment

r = rate of interest per interval/period

n = number of intervals/periods

Mathematical tables can be used to compute the present value (P) of an annuity. The term $\left[\frac{1-(1+r)^{-n}}{r}\right]$ is called present value factor for annuity (PVFA) and it represents the present value of an ordinary annuity consisting payments of ₹ 1 regularly at the Interest rate r per period. The present value factor for annuity (PVFA) can be read by annuity tables.

Thus, present value of an annuity can be computed by applying following formula:

$$P = R \times \text{PVFA } (r\%, n).$$

Example 10. Mr. *X* deposits ₹ 10,000 every year for 10 years at interest rate of 10% per year. Find the present value of his deposits.

Solution: We know that:

$$P = R \times \text{PVFA } (r\%, n)$$

Here, R = ₹ 10,000, r = 10%, n = 10 years and $\text{PVFA}_{(10\%,\ 10)} = 6.145$

Substituting the values,

$$P = 10{,}000 \times 6.145$$

$$P = ₹\ 61{,}450$$

Thus, the present value of ₹ 10,000 deposited every year for 10 years is ₹ 61,450.

2.8 Present Value of an Annuity Due

Since cash flow occurs in the beginning of each period with an annuity due, first cash flow will have full present value. The present value of annuity due is equal to present value of ordinary annuity multiplied by $(1 + r)$. The following formula is used to find the present value of annuity due:

$$P_{due} = P_{ordinary}\ (1 + r)$$

Where, P_{due} = Present value of annuity due

$P_{ordinary}$ = Present value of ordinary annuity

r = Rate of interest

Thus, $P_{due} = R \times \text{PVFA}_{(r\%,\ n)} \times (1 + r).$

Example 11. Mr. *X* receives ₹ 10,000 in the beginning of each year for 10 years from an investment made earlier. Find the present value of all cash inflows, if the rate of interest is 6%.

Solution: This is a case of annuity due. Here, R = ₹ 10,000, r = 8% and n = 10 years. Then,

$$P_{due} = 10{,}000 \times \text{PVFA}_{(6\%,\ 10)} \times (1 + 0.06)$$

$$= 10{,}000 \times 7.36 \times (1.06)$$
$$= 78{,}016$$

Thus, the present value of cash inflows is ₹ 78,016.

2.9 Present Value of a Perpetuity

Perpetuity is an infinite series of equal cash flows occurring at regular intervals for infinite time period. The present value (P) of series of cash flows can be represented by the following formula:

$$P = \frac{C}{(1+r)} + \frac{C}{(1+r)^2} + \frac{C}{(1+r)^3} + \dots\dots\dots + \frac{C}{(1+r)^\infty}$$

Where, r = Interest rate

C = Cash flow

This is a geometric progression series having infinite terms. On simplification, the sum of the series (P) can be calculated as given below:

$$P = \frac{C}{r}$$

Thus, present value of a perpetuity is equal to the cash flow divided by rate of interest.

Example 12. A finance company has launched a scheme which requires an initial investment of ₹ 1,00,000. The company will pay the investor ₹ 10,000 every year for infinite time period. If the rate of interest is 11%, should a person invest in the scheme? If the rate of interest is 9%, will there be a change in the decision?

Solution: The present value of cash inflows is calculated by the following formula:

$$P = \frac{C}{r}$$

In this case, C = ₹ 10,000 and $r = 0.11$

Substituting the values,

$$P = \frac{10{,}000}{0.11}$$

P = ₹ 90,909

Since the present value of cash inflows is less than the initial investment, it is advisable not to invest in the scheme.

When rate of interest is 9%, the present value of cash inflows will be:

$$P = \frac{10{,}000}{0.09}$$

P = ₹ 1,11,111

Now, the present value of cash inflows is more than the initial investment. Hence, it is beneficial to invest in the scheme.

Example 13. A company is selling a debenture which will provide annual interest payment of ₹ 1,100 for indefinite number of years. Should the debenture be purchased if it is being quoted in the market ₹ 10,100 and the required rate of return is 11 percent? What will be your answer if the required rate of return is 10 percent?

Solution: We know that:

$$\text{Present value of perpetuity} = \frac{\text{Annual cash flow}}{r}$$

Substituting the values, we get:

$$\text{Present value of cash flows} = \frac{₹1,100}{0.11} = ₹10,000$$

Thus, the present value of cash inflows, ₹ 10,000 is less than the price of debenture. So, it is advisable not to purchase the debenture.

If the rate of return is 10%,

$$\text{Present value of cash inflows} = \frac{₹1,100}{0.10} = ₹11,000$$

Now, the present value of cash inflows, ₹ 11,000 is more than the price of debenture i.e., ₹ 10,100. Thus, it is advisable to purchase the debenture.

2.10 Net Present Value

The concept of net present value is very important for decision-making in finance. The cash flows must be adjusted for time to find their present value. The net present value is calculated by subtracting the initial investment cash flow from the present value of subsequent cash inflows generated by the investment. An investment proposal or project is profitable if its net present value is positive. If there are a number of projects or investment proposals, the project or proposal having highest positive net value is opted for. Thus,

Net present value (NPV) = present value of cash inflows – cash outflow (investment)

$$NPV = -C_0 + \frac{C_1}{(1+r)^1} + \frac{C_2}{(1+r)^2} + ... + \frac{C_n}{(1+r)^n}$$

Where, r = rate of interest (required rate of return)

C = cash flow

n = Number of periods.

Example 14. A company is offering a debenture at ₹ 1000. The debenture will provide annual interest of ₹ 120 for infinite number of years. If the required rate of return 13%, will it be profitable to purchase the debenture?

Solution: Present value of cash inflows is calculated by following formula:

$$P = \frac{C}{r}$$

In this case, C = ₹ 120, $r = 13\%$. Substituting the values,

$$P = \frac{120}{0.13}$$

$$P = ₹\ 923$$

Hence, NPV = ₹ 923 – ₹ 1000 = – ₹ 77.

Because the net present value of debenture is negative, it not profitable to purchase the debenture.

SOLVED PROBLEMS

Problem 1. *X* financed a car by taking a loan of ₹ 4,00,000 at 10% p.a.. The loan is to be repaid in four equal annual instalments starting from the end of the first year. Calculate the amount of equal annual instalment. *(D.U., B.Com. 2016)*

Solution: We know that:

Present Value = Annuity × PVFA (10%, 4 years)

Substituting the values,

4,00,000 = Annuity × 3.170

Hence,

Annuity = 1,26,183

Thus, the amount of equal annual instalment is ₹ 1,26,183.

Problem 2. A company is selling a debenture which will provide annual interest payment of ₹ 1,200 for indefinite number of years. Should the debenture be purchased if it is being quoted in the market ₹ 10,500 and the required rate of return is 12 percent? What will be your answer if the required rate of return is 10 percent? *(D.U., B.Com. 2011)*

Solution: We know that:

$$\text{Present value of perpetuity} = \frac{\text{Annual cash flow}}{r}$$

Substituting the values, we get:

$$\text{Present value of cash flows} = \frac{1,200}{0.12} = 10,000$$

Thus, the present value of cash inflows, ₹ 10,000 is less than the price of debenture. So, it is advisable not to purchase the debenture.

If the rate of return is 10%,

$$\text{Present value of cash inflows} = \frac{₹1,200}{0.10} = ₹12,000$$

Now, the present value of cash inflows, ₹ 12,000 is more than the price of debenture i.e., ₹ 10,500. Thus, it is advisable to purchase the debenture.

Problem 3. Vijay borrows from a bank an amount of ₹ 10,00,000 @12% per annum on 1-4-2012. As per agreement, repayment including interest is to be made in five equal annual instalments with first instalment falling due after three years, i.e., on 31-3-2015. What would be the amount of each instalment? *(D.U., B.Com. 2012)*

Solution: We know that:

$$\text{Present value of an amount} = \text{Amount} \times PVF_{(r,\, n)}$$

If the amount of annual instalment is A, the present value of all instalments will be:

$$PV = A \times PVF_{(12\%,\, 3)} + A \times PVF_{(12\%,\, 4)} + A \times PVF_{(12\%,\, 5)} + A \times PVF_{(12\%,\, 6)} + A \times PVF_{(12\%,\, 7)}$$

Substituting the values, we get:

$$₹\ 10{,}00{,}000 = A\,(0.712) + A\,(0.636) + A\,(0.567) + A\,(0.507) + A\,(0.452)$$

$$\Rightarrow \quad ₹\ 10{,}00{,}000 = A\,(2.874)$$

$$\Rightarrow \quad A = ₹\ 3{,}47{,}947$$

Thus, the amount of each instalment should be ₹ 3,47,947.

Problem 4. Mr. Ramesh is borrowing ₹ 20 lacs from a bank for expanding his business. Bank is giving him two options. Option one is to return this money in five equal instalments at rate of interest of 10% p.a. Option two is to return this money in equal half-yearly instalments over a period of five years at annual rate of interest of 9.8% p.a. Which option should be selected and why? *(D.U., B.Com. 2013)*

Solution: Here the comparison can be made on the basis of effective rate of interest.

In option I, annual effective rate of interest is 10%.

In option II, annual effective rate of interest can be calculated by applying the formulae given below:

$$r_e = \left(1 + \frac{r}{m}\right)^m - 1$$

By substituting the values, we get:

$$r_e = \left(1 + \frac{0.098}{2}\right)^2 - 1$$

$$r_e = 0.1004$$

Thus, the annualised effective rate of interest is 10.04% in option II. Mr. Ramesh should opt for option I.

Problem 5. *X* deposited ₹ 1,50,000 in a fixed deposit account at 8% p.a. compounded quarterly for three years. How much amount he will get on maturity? *(D.U., B.Com. 2015)*

Solution: We know that compound amount is given by:

$$S = P\left(1 + \frac{r}{m}\right)^{m.n}$$

In this case n = 3 years, m = 4 , r = 0.08 and P = ₹ 1,50,000.

Substituting the values we get:

$$S = 1{,}50{,}000\left(1+\frac{0.08}{4}\right)^{4\times 3}$$

$$S = 1{,}50{,}000(1.02)^{12}$$

$$S = 1{,}90{,}235.86$$

Thus, X will get ₹ 1,90,235.86 on maturity of deposit.

Problem 6. X took an educational loan of ₹ 3,00,000 at 12% p.a. The loan is to be repaid in five equal annual instalments starting from the end of first year. Calculate the amount of each equal annual instalment. *(D.U., B.Com. 2015)*

Solution: We know that:

Present Value = Annuity × PVFA (12%, 5 years)

Substituting the values,

3,00,000 = Annuity × 3.605

Hence,

Annuity = 83,217.75

Thus, the amount of equal annual instalment is ₹ 83,217.75.

THEORETICAL QUESTIONS

1. What is meant by time value of money? Explain the techniques which are used for time adjustment in cash flows.
2. Why is consideration of time important in financial decision-making? How can time be adjusted? *(D.U., B.Com. 2009)*
3. "Cash flows occurring at different points of time are not comparable." Explain the reasons and how can they be made comparable? *(D.U., B.Com. 2010)*
4. "A rupee of today is not equal of the rupee tomorrow." Explain. *(D.U., B.Com. 2011)*
5. What is a perpetuity? How can the present value of a perpetuity be calculated?
6. What is annuity? Give three examples of an annuity. *(D.U., B.Com. 2016)*
7. Why time value of money is important in financial decision-making? *(D.U., B.Com. 2016)*
8. What is the difference between Annuity and Annuity Due? How can the present value of an Annuity Due be calculated?
9. Write short notes on:
   (i) Effective rate of interest
   (ii) Present value of a growing annuity.

PRACTICAL PROBLEMS

1. Mr. *X* wants to go on a world tour after 10 years. This tour is expected to cost him ₹ 7,00,000. How much should he save annually to a have a sum of ₹ 7,00,000 after 10 years if rate of return is:
   (i) 10% p.a.
   (ii) 12% p.a. (*D.U., B.Com. 2012, Corres.*)
   [**Ans.** (i) ₹ 43,923; (ii) ₹ 39,888]
2. Mr. *X* purchased a house under a housing scheme valued at ₹ 24 lacs. Under the provisions of scheme, *X* agreed to pay a part of the amount through ten equal annual instalments of ₹ 2,50,000 involving effective rate of interest of 12%. Find the cash down payment required to be made by *X* to pay the total price of the house.
   (*D.U., B.Com. 2013, Corres.*)
   [**Ans.** ₹ 9,87,500]
3. Mr. *X* wants ₹ 5,00,000 at the end of 8 years from now. Find the amount to be deposited each year in an account offering 10% interest compounded per annum.
   (*D.U., B.Com. 2013, Corres.*)
   [**Ans.** ₹ 43,721.58]
4. A company is selling a debenture which will provide annual interest payment of ₹ 1,000 for indefinite number of years. Should the debenture be purchased if it is being quoted in the market for ₹ 10,000 and the rate of interest is 12%? What will be your answer in the above case in the rate of interest is 8%? (*D.U., B.Com. 2014, Corres.*)
   [**Ans.** At 12% PV = ₹ 8,333, No: At 8% PV = ₹ 12,500, Yes]
5. A machine costs ₹ 1,00,000 and its effective life is estimated to be 12 years. If the scrap value is ₹ 5,000, what should be retained out of profit at the end of each year to accumulate at compound interest rate of 5% p.a. so that a new machine can be purchased after 12 years? (*D.U., B.Com. 2015, N.C.*)
   [**Ans.** ₹ 5,968.46]
6. Find out the present value of ₹ 10,000 receivable after 8 years if the discount rate is 10%. (*D.U., B.Com. 2015, Corres.*)
   [**Ans.** ₹ 4,670]
7. Mr. *X* will make five equal annual payments of ₹ 20,000 each in his deposit account that pays 15% interest compounded annually. Find out the future value of the series at the end of 5 years. (*D.U., B.Com. 2015, Corres.*)
   [**Ans.** ₹ 1,34,840]
8. A finance company makes an offer to deposit a sum of ₹ 35,000 and then receive a return of ₹ 3,960 p.a. perpetually. Should the offer be accepted if the rate of interest is (i) 12% p.a., (ii) 11% p.a.? (*D.U., B.Com. 2016, N.C.*)
   [**Ans.** (i) PV = ₹ 33,000; (ii) ₹ 36,000 Offer should be accepted if rate of interest is 11%]

9. A company is selling a debenture which will provide annual interest payment of ₹ 1,500 for an indefinite number of years. Should the debenture be purchased if it is being quoted in the market for ₹ 14,000 and the rate of interest is 10%? What will be your answer if the rate interest is 13%? *(D.U., B.Com. 2016, Corres.)*
[**Ans.** At 10% PV = ₹ 15,000, Yes; At 13% PV = ₹ 11,538, No]

Capital Budgeting: Estimation of Cash Flows

3

Chapter Outline

3.1 Introduction
3.2 Features of Capital Budgeting Decisions
3.3 Importance of Capital Budgeting
3.4 Types of Capital Budgeting Decisions
3.5 Types of Capital Projects
3.6 Capital Budgeting Process
3.7 Estimation of Cash Flows
3.8 Additional Aspects in Cash Flow Estimation

3.1 Introduction

Capital budgeting is the process of evaluating and selecting investments in capital assets or fixed assets in a firm. Capital budgeting is vital in achieving the shareholders' wealth maximisation objective of a firm. In capital budgeting, we estimate the future cash flows and make the investment, only if the present value of cash inflows exceeds the investment's cost or cash inflows yield a return equal to the required rate of return on the capital. The capital budgeting may involve selecting investments in starting of business, modernisation of business, replacement of existing fixed assets, expansion of business or in diversification of business. Merger and acquisition is also a capital budgeting decision for the acquiring firm.

For example, investing in a cycle manufacturing unit involves a capital budgeting decision. Here, future cash flows are estimated and if they yield a return required to meet the cost of capital (the return required by those financing the project) the investment in the cycle manufacturing unit is desirable.

Capital budgeting may involve evaluating a number of projects simultaneously and selecting the most suitable from these projects. The cost of capital (the return required by those financing the project) and estimation of future cash inflows are two main considerations in making capital budgeting. The capital budgeting is also known as capital expenditure decision, capital expenditure management, management of fixed assets, long-term decision etc.

3.2 Features of Capital Budgeting Decisions

Capital budgeting has some special features as mentioned below:

1. **Long-term investment.** Capital budgeting is concerned with evaluation and selection of long-term investment in a firm. Long-term investment creates the production capacity of the firm and consequently the benefits occur over a long period of time.
2. **Cash flows over a long period of time.** Capital budgeting takes into consideration the cash inflows occurring in future for many years from the long-term investment made. Cash flows are estimated after taking into consideration a number of factors. Cash flows are different from the accounting profit. In estimating cash flows, non-cash expenditures are excluded.

   In capital budgeting, initial cash flows, interim cash flows and terminal cash flows from the project are estimated and decision is taken on the basis of these flows and the cost of capital. The cost of capital is the required rate of return on the capital i.e., the discount rate. The appropriate discount rate is also known as 'cut off rate' or 'hurdle rate'.
3. **Risk.** The actual cash flows of a firm may be different from the estimated cash flows as the future is uncertain. Thus, the risk is involved in evaluation and selection of investments. If future cash flows and cost of capital are not properly estimated, the firm may suffer losses and risk is involved therein. Thus, an error in capital budgeting may ruin a firm.

3.3 Importance of Capital Budgeting

Capital budgeting decisions are of paramount importance in financial decision-making, since they affect the working and profitability of the firm in the future. The basic objective of financial management is to maximise shareholders' wealth and it cannot be accomplished without a diligent capital budgeting decision. The meticulous estimation of future cash flows is a must for the survival of the firm.

The need for capital budgeting in a firm arise due to following reasons:

1. **Survival of business.** The financial position and profitability are main concern of a business firm. A firm cannot survive if it is incurring losses for year after year. The future cash inflows are estimated in the capital budgeting process. Thus, efficient capital budgeting is a necessity for the survival of a business.
2. **Irreversible decision.** Once implemented, the capital budgeting decisions cannot be reversed. The losses once suffered by a firm on part of inefficient capital budgeting cannot be recovered. Hence, efficient capital budgeting becomes of immense importance for a firm.
3. **Growth of business.** The shareholders' wealth cannot be maximised without the growth of the business. The growth of the business depends on future cash inflows of a firm and estimation of cash flows for coming years is dependent on capital budgeting.
4. **Heavy investment.** The capital budgeting decision is concerned with evaluating and selecting the long-term investments in fixed assets. The fixed assets creates the productive capacity of the firm and involves heavy investment. Thus, any error in capital budgeting decision can be devastating for a firm and consequently, heavy losses may be incurred by the firm. The risk is involved in making capital budgeting decision.
5. **Long-term implications.** The results of capital budgeting decision are felt over the years to come. The growth of business and maximisation of shareholders' wealth on the capital

budgeting decision. The wrong capital budgeting decision have implications for a long-term.

6. **Maintaining the competitiveness.** To remain in competition, upgradation and modernisation of business is necessary for every firm. These acts involve capital expenditure and capital budgeting is required to make a decision in this regard.

3.4 Types of Capital Budgeting Decisions

Capital budgeting decisions are concerned with a number of issues related to a firm. It may be set up of a new business, modernisation of business or the other. The following types of capital budgeting decisions are taken by a firm:

1. **Set up of new business.** The setting up of a business involves large capital investment. The decision to start a business is simply a capital budgeting decision.
2. **Modernisation.** To remain in business, a firm may require modernisation from time to time. Modernisation may involve huge investment in long-term assets. Capital budgeting decision is taken in such a case.
3. **Replacement.** A capital budgeting decision may be related to replacement of an existing machinery or equipment in a firm. The replacement of machinery or equipment may be needed on account of a number of factors, like to increase the efficiency, obsolescence, cost saving etc.
4. **Expansion.** A firm doing good business may be interested in expanding the production capacity to capture more market share. Capital budgeting is necessary to evaluate the expansion and decide about the execution of expansion.
5. **Diversification.** The existing firms may be interested in diversifying their business by introducing new product lines to increase their product base. Before the execution any such move, a firm has to take capital budgeting decision.
6. **Acquisition.** In an acquisition, one firm buys another one. This is different from buying a machinery or starting a new firm. The same principles of capital budgeting are involved in acquisition analysis.

3.5 Types of Capital Projects

1. Independent projects. Independent projects do not compete with each other and serve the same purpose. Each independent project is evaluated separately by applying the capital budgeting criteria. Independent projects can be selected simultaneously if they fulfil the required capital budgeting criteria. For example, if a firm is planning to set up one cement manufacturing unit and one steel manufacturing unit, it can select both the projects depending on the capital budgeting decision.

2. Mutually exclusive projects. Mutually exclusive projects serve the same purpose and compete with each other. After the evaluation of projects, if one project is selected, other projects are excluded. For example, if a company is planning to set up a plant that needs a semiautomatic or fully automatic machinery to produce the items, the company will evaluate both the projects. If the company selects semiautomatic machinery on basis of some criteria, it will exclude selection of the fully automatic machinery.

3. Contingent projects. When the choice of one project is dependent on the selection of one or more projects, the former project is called contingent project. For example, Project B is to be selected if Project A is undertaken, then Project B is contingent project. The selection of Project B is dependent on the undertaking of Project A.

3.6 Capital Budgeting Process

In capital budgeting decisions, costs and benefits of a project are measured in terms of cash flows. The values of cash flows are compared at a focal point by applying the required rate of return (discount rate) in order to take the financial decision. Three steps are involved in capital budgeting process.

1. Estimation of cash flows. In capital budgeting, the first step is forecasting of future cash flows related to the project. There is difference between cash flows and profits arising out from a project. First, in measuring profit, revenues and expenditures are considered on accrual basis rather than realisation basis. Second, in measuring profit of a firm all revenue expenditures including non-cash expenditures are considered. The non-cash expenditures are not considered in measuring the cash flows of a firm. The cash flows are divided in three categories on the basis of time of their occurrence, i.e. initial flows, interim cash flows and terminal cash flows.

2. Estimation of required rate of return. The project has to be financed by raising the funds from capital market. The rate at which the funds can be raised from the market is the required rate of return or the opportunity cost of capital. This rate should be used in computing the present values of cash flows so as the comparison can be made on the focal point for cash inflows and out flows.

3. Evaluation of capital projects by applying some technique. After estimating the cash flows arising from the investment, the present values are computed by applying the appropriate discount rate. A number of capital budgeting techniques (investment criteria) are used in taking a capital investment decision. These techniques can be grouped in the two categories as mentioned below:

(i) Non-discounted cash flow techniques
  (a) Payback Period Method
  (b) Accounting Rate of Return
(ii) Discounted cash flow techniques
  (a) Net Present Value Method
  (b) Internal Rate of Return Method
  (c) Profitability Index

These capital budgeting techniques are discussed in the next chapter.

3.7 Estimation of Cash Flows

The cost and benefit analysis of a project can be done on the basis of profit or cash flows. In the case of replacement of an asset, incremental cash inflows are estimated and compared with the incremental investment. The estimation of cash flows and profits is explained below:

1. **Accounting profits.** In computing the accounting profits, non-cash expenses are taken into consideration. Depreciation is a non-cash expense and is taken into account while

calculating the accounting profit of a firm. Thus, profit is measured by applying following equation:

$$\text{Profit} = \text{Revenues} - \text{Expenses} - \text{Depreciation}$$

Cash flows are considered to be superior to accounting profits in evaluating a capital project. The reasons for non-appropriateness of accounting profits in capital budgeting decision are given below:

(i) Consideration of non-cash expenses
(ii) Calculation on 'accrual basis'
(iii) Effect of company policies
(iv) Inconsistent with 'Shareholders' wealth maximisation' objective.

2. **Cash flows.** One of the most important tasks in capital budgeting is the estimation of future cash flows for a project. Cash, not accounting income, is central to all decisions of the firm and all benefits from a project are expected in term of cash flows rather than income flows.

For each investment proposal we need to provide information on operating, not the financial cash flows. Financial cash flows such as interest payments, principal payments, and cash dividends are excluded from cash flow analysis in capital budgeting.

All the forecasted cash flows are expressed in after-tax terms. Cash flows from a project are divided into three categories i.e., initial cash outflows, interim cash flows and terminal cash flows.

(i) *Initial cash flows.* Initial investment in a project is a cash outflow. Initial cash flows also include installation charges, insurance, freight cost, and increase in working capital. If firm already doing business and old machinery is sold, the value of scrap is a cash inflow. Tax payments on profit on sale of old asset is an outflow of cash. Tax savings on loss on sale of old assets is inflow of cash. The initial cash flows of a project are calculated as given below in the table:

Computation of Initial Cash outflows

Particulars	Amount
Purchase price of assets	—
Add: Insurance, Freight and Installation charges	—
Increase in working capital	—
Tax on profit on sale of old assets	—
Less: Salvage value of old assets	—
Loss on sale of old assets	—
Initial cash outflow	—

Example 1. From the following information find out initial cash flows:

Cost of machine	₹ 1,25,000
Salvage value	₹ 10,000
Installation cost	₹ 5,000

Freight	₹ 2,000
Increase in working capital	₹ 20,000
Life	5 years
Expected annual sales	10,000 units
Sales price per unit	₹ 40
Variable cost per unit	₹ 16
Tax rate	50%

Solution: Computation of Initial cash outflows

Particulars	Amount (₹)
Purchase price of assets	1,25,000
Add: Freight and Installation charges	7,000
Increase in working capital	20,000
Initial cash outflow	1,52,000

The initial cash outflow is ₹ 1,52,000.

(ii) *Interim cash flows*. The initial investment in a project is expected to generate periodic cash inflows over the life of project. These periodic inflows may be same every period during the life of the project or may vary from period to period. These periodic inflows are also known as net annual cash flows or operating cash flows. These cash flows are after tax cash flows. The earnings before interest, depreciation and tax are calculated over the life of the project. Then, amount of depreciation charged is deducted. The tax is calculated and deducted from earnings after depreciation. After deducting the tax, we get income after tax and depreciation amount is added back to this amount. The resultant figure is cash flow after tax (CFAT). The CFAT is used in capital budgeting. The format for estimation of cash flows after tax (CFAT) is given below:

Computation of interim/annual cash flows

Particulars	Amount
Revenue	—
Less: Operating expenses	—
Earnings before Depreciation, Interest and Tax (EBIT)	—
Less: Depreciation	—
Earnings before Interest and Tax (EBIT)	—
Less: Tax	—
Earnings after tax (EAT)	—
Add: Depreciation	—
Cash Flows After Tax (CFAT)	—

The important items to be adjusted in the calculation of cash flow after tax (CFAT) are given below:

(a) **Depreciation.** Depreciation has to be charged as per the policies of the firm.

(b) **Tax.** Tax is deducted from earnings after depreciation as per the rate applicable.

Example 2. Krishna Ltd. is considering to purchase a new machine which will cost ₹ 1,20,000. The cost of installation will amount to ₹ 25,000. The increase in working capital requirement will be ₹ 25,000. The machine is expected to provide cash inflows before depreciation and taxes of ₹ 70,000 for a period of five years after which it can be sold for ₹ 50,000. The firm applies straight-line method of depreciation. The tax rate on income is 35%. Calculate interim/annual cash flows associated with the machine.

Solution: Computation of annual cash flows

Particulars	Year 1–4 (₹)
Earnings Before Depreciation, Interest and Tax	70,000
Less: Depreciation[1]	19,000
Profit before tax	51,000
Less: Tax	17,850
Profit after tax	33,150
Add: Depreciation	19,000
CFAT (₹)	52,150

Working Note:

1. Depreciation per year = 95,000 ÷ 5 = ₹ 19,000.
   Total cost = ₹ 1,20,000 + ₹ 25,000 = ₹ 1,45,000.
   Salvage value = ₹ 50,000.
   Life of machine: 5 years.

(iii) *Terminal cash flows*. The cash flows expected in the last year of economic life of the project are called terminal cash flows. In the calculation of terminal cash flows, some additional cash flows relating to scrap value, tax profit/loss on sale of assets, release of working capital are included in the annual cash flows. Usually, depreciation is charged till last year of economic life of the assets and then capital gain/loss is calculated based on scrap value. However, as per Income Tax Act, 1961, no depreciation is provided in the last year if there is a single asset in the block of assets of the firm. The format for calculation of terminal cash flows is given below:

Computation of terminal cash flows

Particulars	Amount
Revenue	—
Less: Operating expenses	—
Earnings before Depreciation, Interest and Tax (EBIT)	—

Less: Depreciation	—
Earnings before Interest and Tax (EBIT)	—
Less: Tax	—
Earnings after tax(EAT)	—
Add: Depreciation	—
Add: Release of working capital	—
Add: Salvage value	—
Add: Tax savings on STCL	—
Cash Flows After Tax (CFAT)	—

Example 3. Find out the initial, subsequent annual and terminal cash flows from the following data:

Cost of machine: ₹ 40,000

Life expectancy: 5 years

Salvage value: ₹ 10,000

Earnings: ₹ 20,000 per year

Installation cost: ₹ 5,000

Tax rate: 30%.

Depreciation is charged on straight-line basis.

Solution: Computation of cash flows

Particulars	Year 0 (₹)	Year 1 – 4 (₹)	Year 5 (₹)
Cost of machine	–40,000		
Installation cost	–5,000		
PBDT		20,000	20,000
Less: Depreciation[1]		7,000	7,000
Profit before tax		13,000	13,000
Less: Tax		3,900	3,900
Profit after tax		9,100	9,100
Add: Depreciation		7,000	7,000
Add: Salvage value			10,000
CFAT (₹)	–45,000	16,100	26,100

Working Notes:

1. Depreciation per year = 35,000 ÷ 5 = ₹ 7,000.

   Total cost = ₹ 40,000 + ₹ 5,000 = ₹ 45,000.

   Salvage value = ₹ 10,000.

3. **Incremental cash flows.** The preceding examples were simple as they related to starting of business and no replacement of assets took place during the economic life of the firm.

Now, we turn to some more complicated cases where some asset(s) are replaced in order to create more efficiency in the production. In such a case, we compute incremental cash flows. The financial decision is taken by comparing the incremental cost with the incremental cash flows. The format of computation of incremental cash flows is given below:

Computation of Incremental Cash Flows

Particulars	Year 0	Year 1 – *n*	Terminal Year
Cost of new machine	---		
Add: Salvage value of old machine	---		
Add: Tax savings on sale of old machine	---		
Savings on operating cost		---	---
Less: Incremental Depreciation		---	---
Incremental Profit Before Tax		---	---
Less: Tax		---	---
Incremental Profit After Tax		---	---
Add: Incremental Depreciation		---	---
Add: Incremental Salvage Value			---
Incremental cash flow	---	---	---

Example 4. PQR Ltd. purchased a special machine one year ago at a cost of ₹ 24,000. The annual cash operating cost is approximately ₹ 40,000. At present, book value of machine is ₹ 20,000 and it is estimated to have additional useful life of 5 years after which its salvage value will be nil. A new machine has just come in the market which will do the same job but with an annual cash operating cost of only ₹ 30,000. The new machine costs ₹ 50,000 and has an estimated life of 5 years with zero salvage value. The old machine can be sold now for ₹ 18,000. Straight-line method of depreciation is used. Assume the tax rate of 30% on income and capital gains both. Calculate all incremental cash flows after taxes associated with this replacement decision.

Solution: Computation of incremental cash flows

Particulars	Year 0 (₹)	Year 1 – 4 (₹)	Year 5 (₹)
Cost of new machine	–50,000		
Add: Salvage value	18,000		
Add: Tax savings on sale of old machine[1]	600		
Savings on operating cost		10,000	10,000
Less: Incremental Depreciation[2]		6,000	6,000
Incremental Profit Before Tax		4,000	4,000
Less: Tax		1200	1200
Incremental Profit After Tax		2800	2800

Add: Incremental Depreciation		6,000	6,000
Add: Incremental Salvage Value			0
Incremental cash flow	–31,400	8,800	8,800

Notes: 1. 30% of (₹ 20,000 – 18,000)

2. Incremental depreciation = ₹ 10,000 – ₹ 4,000 = ₹ 6,000.

3.8 Additional Aspect in Cash Flow Estimation

There are some additional items which can be countered in the cash flow analysis of a project. The treatments to be given for such items in cash flow analysis of a project are given below:

1. **Opportunity costs.** Sometimes firms use their existing resources for proposed project. If explicit cash outlays do not exists for such resources, their opportunity costs should be considered in cash flow analysis. Opportunity costs are the expected benefits, which the company would have derived from those resources if they were not devoted to the proposed project. For example, if a company has an existing building which may be used for the proposed project, then the market price of the building is its opportunity cost. Opportunity costs are considered in the computation of cash flows of a project.
2. **Allocated overheads.** In general, there are general overheads in a firm allocated to existing projects. These general overheads will be incurred whether or not the new project is undertaken. The allocated overheads in such a case should be ignored in the computation of cash flows of new project.

   For example, a firm has five machines and its general overheads are ₹ 15,000. Thus, ₹ 3,000 are allocated to each machine. Further, a new machine is purchased and total number of machines is six. Now, the question is: should the general overheads be allocated to new machine? Because the general overheads of ₹ 15,000 would be incurred whether new machine is purchased or not, the general overheads should not be allocated to new machine.
3. **Sunk costs.** A sunk cost is an outlay that was incurred in the past and cannot be recovered in the future regardless of whether the project under consideration is accepted. Because the sunk costs were incurred in the past and cannot be recovered regardless of whether the project is accepted or rejected, they are not relevant in capital budgeting analysis. Thus, these costs are not included in the computation of cash flows of the project.

   For example, if ₹ one lac were spent to investigate the potential site for a new project. That amount would be a sunk cost—the money is gone, and would not be recovered regardless of whether or not the new project undertaken.

Example 5. ABC Ltd. is considering to purchase a machine. Two machines are available in the market to serve the purpose. Details of machines are given below:

Particulars	Machine A	Machine B
Capital cost	60,000	60,000
Sales	1,00,000	80,000

Expected life	2	3
	Cost	
Labour	10,000	6,000
Material	8,000	10,000
Factory overhead	12,000	10,000
Administrative cost	4,000	2,000
Selling cost	2,000	2,000

Other information:

(a) The costs shown above relates to annual expenditure resulting from each machine.

(b) Tax to be paid may be assumed at 50% of net earnings.

Find the annual cash flows.

Solution: Computation of annual cash flows

Particulars	**Machine A**	**Machine B**
Sales	1,00,000	80,000
Cost of Sales		
Labour	10,000	6,000
Material	8,000	10,000
Factory overheads	12,000	10,000
Depreciation[1]	30,000	20,000
Administrative cost	4,000	2,000
Selling cost	2,000	2,000
Total cost	66,000	50,000
Profit before tax	34,000	30,000
Less: tax	17,000	15,000
Profit after tax	17,000	15,000
Add: Depreciation	30,000	20,000
Cash Flow After Tax	47,000	35,000

Notes: 1. Depreciation machine (A) = 60,000 ÷ 2 = ₹ 30,000

2. Depreciation machine (B) = 60,000 ÷ 3 = ₹ 20,000

Example 6. A company is considering to install a new project costing ₹ 7,20,000 with life of 6 years and no salvage value. The tax rate is 30% and it uses straight-line method of depreciation. The estimated cash flows before depreciation and tax are as follows:

Year	Amount (₹)
1	1,50,000
2	2,00,000
3	2,25,000
4	2,50,000
5	3,00,000
6	3,00,000

You are required to calculate annual cash flows after tax.

Solution: Computation of earnings after tax

Year	Cash flows before depreciation	Depreciation	Earnings before tax	Tax	Earnings after tax	Cash flow after tax
1	1,50,000	1,20,000	30,000	9,000	21,000	1,41,000
2	2,00,000	1,20,000	80,000	24,000	56,000	1,76,000
3	2,25,000	1,20,000	1,05,000	31,500	73,500	1,93,500
4	2,50,000	1,20,000	1,30,000	39,000	91,000	2,11,000
5	3,00,000	1,20,000	1,80,000	54,000	1,26,000	2,46,000
6	3,00,000	1,20,000	1,80,000	54,000	1,26,000	2,46,000

Example 7. Murari Ltd. purchased a special machine one year ago at a cost of ₹ 6,000. The annual cash operating cost is approximately ₹ 10,000. At present, book value of machine is ₹ 5,000 and it is estimated to have additional useful life of 5 years after which its salvage value will be nil. A new machine has just come in the market which will do the same job but with an annual cash operating cost of only ₹ 8,000. The new machine costs ₹ 12,000 and has an estimated life of 5 years with zero salvage value. The old machine can be sold now for ₹ 4,000. Straight-line method of depreciation is used. Assume the tax rate of 40% on income and capital gains both. Calculate all incremental cash flows after taxes associated with this replacement decision.

Solution: Computation of incremental cash flows

Particulars	Year 0 (₹)	Year 1 – 4 (₹)	Year 5 (₹)
Cost of new machine	–12,000		
Add: Salvage value	4,000		
Add: Tax savings on sale of old machine[1]	400		
Savings on operating cost		2,000	2,000
Less: Incremental Depreciation[2]		1,400	1,400
Incremental Profit Before Tax		600	600

Less: Tax		240	240
Incremental Profit After Tax		360	360
Add: Incremental Depreciation		1,400	1,400
Add: Incremental Salvage Value			0
Incremental cash flow	–7,600	1,760	1.760

Notes: 1. 40% of (₹ 5,000 – 4,000).

2. Incremental depreciation = ₹ 2,400 – ₹ 1,000 = ₹ 1,400.

SOLVED PROBLEMS

Problem 1. From the following information find out initial, subsequent annual and terminal cash flows:

Cost of machine	₹ 5,25,000
Salvage value	₹ 30,000
Installation cost	₹ 5,000
Life	5 years
Expected annual sales	10,000 units
Sales price per unit	₹ 40
Variable cost per unit	₹ 16
Tax rate	50%

(*D.U., B.Com. 2011*)

Solution: Computation of cash flows

Particulars	Year 0	Year 1 – 4	Year 5
Cost of machine	–5,25,000		
Installation cost	–5,000		
Annual contribution		2,40,000	2,40,000
Less: Depreciation		1,00,000	1,00,000
Profit before tax		1,40,000	1,40,000
Less: Tax		70,000	70,000
Profit after tax		70,000	70,000
Add: Depreciation		1,00,000	1,00,000
Salvage value			30,000
CFAT (₹)	–5,30,000	1,70,000	2,00,000

Working Notes:

1. Contribution per year: ₹ 2,40,000
   Contribution per unit = ₹ 40 – ₹ 16 = ₹ 24.
2. Depreciation per year = 5,00,000 ÷ 5 = ₹ 1,00,000
   Total cost = ₹ 5,25,000 + ₹ 5,000 = ₹ 5,30,000
   Salvage value: ₹ 30,000
   Life of machine: 5 years.

Problem 2. Laxman Ltd. purchased a special machine one year ago at a cost of ₹ 12,000. The annual cash operating cost is approximately ₹ 20,000. At present, book value of machine is ₹ 10,000 and it is estimated to have additional useful life of 5 years after which its salvage value will be nil. A new machine has just come in the market which will do the same job but with an annual cash operating cost of only ₹ 16,000. The new machine costs ₹ 25,000 and has an estimated life of 5 years with zero salvage value. The old machine can be sold now for ₹ 8,000. Straight-line method of depreciation is used. Assume the tax rate of 40% on income and capital gains both. Calculate all incremental cash flows after taxes associated with this replacement decision.

(D.U., B.Com. 2010, Corres.)

Solution: Computation of incremental cash flows

Particulars	Year 0 (₹)	Year 1 – 4 (₹)	Year 5 (₹)
Cost of new machine	–25,000		
Add: Salvage value	8,000		
Add: Tax savings on sale of old machine[1]	800		
Savings on operating cost		4,000	4,000
Less: Incremental Depreciation[2]		3,000	3,000
Incremental Profit Before Tax		1,000	1,000
Less: Tax		400	400
Incremental Profit After Tax		600	600
Add: Incremental Depreciation		3,000	3,000
Add: Incremental Salvage Value			0
Incremental cash flow	–16,200	3,600	3,600

Notes: 1. 40% of (₹ 10,000 – 8,000).
2. Incremental depreciation = ₹ 5,000 – ₹ 2,000 = ₹ 3,000.

Problem 3. Atul Ltd. is considering to purchase a new machine which will cost ₹ 1,20,000. The cost of installation will amount to ₹ 25,000. The increase in working capital requirement will be ₹ 25,000. The machine is expected to provide cash inflows before depreciation and taxes of ₹ 70,000 for a period of five years after which it can be sold for ₹ 50,000. The firm applies straight-line method of depreciation. The tax rate on income is 35%. Calculate all the cash flows associated with the machine.

Solution: Computation of cash flows

Particulars	Year 0 (₹)	Year 1 – 4 (₹)	Year 5 (₹)
Cost of machine	–1,20,000		
Installation cost	–25,000		
Increase in working capital	–25,000		
PBDT		70,000	70,000
Less: Depreciation[1]		19,000	19,000
Profit before tax		51,000	51,000
Less: Tax		17,850	17,850
Profit after tax		33,150	33,150
Add: Depreciation		19,000	19,000
Add: Release of working capital			25,000
Salvage value			50,000
CFAT (₹)	–1,70,000	52,150	1,27,150

Working Notes:

1. Depreciation per year = ₹ 95,000 ÷ 5 = ₹ 19,000.
   Total cost = ₹ 1,20,000 + ₹ 25,000 = ₹ 1,45,000.
   Salvage value = ₹ 50,000.
   Life of machine: 5 years.

Problem 4. XYZ Ltd. is evaluating an investment proposal with the following information:

Cost of machine	₹ 8,00,000
Installation charges	₹ 1,00,000
Life of machine	5 years
Salvage value	₹ 50,000
Increase in working capital	₹ 60,000
Annual profit before depreciation and taxes	₹ 4,00,000
Tax rate	30%

Calculate the relevant cash flows associated with the above proposal.

Solution: Computation of cash flows

Particulars	Year 0 (₹)	Year 1 – 4 (₹)	Year 5 (₹)
Cost of machine	–8,00,000		
Installation cost	–1,00,000		
Increase in working capital	–60,000		
PBDT		4,00,000	4,00,000

Less: Depreciation[1]		1,70,000	1,70,000
Profit before tax		2,30,000	2,30,000
Less: Tax		69,000	69,000
Profit after tax		1,61,000	1,61,000
Add: Depreciation		1,70,000	1,70,000
Add: Release of working capital			60,000
Salvage value			50,000
CFAT (₹)	–9,60,000	2,31,000	3,41,000

Working Notes:

1. Depreciation per year = ₹ 8,50,000 ÷ 5 = ₹ 1,70,000.
   Total cost = ₹ 8,00,000 + ₹ 1,00,000 = ₹ 9,00,000.
   Salvage value = ₹ 50,000.

Problem 5. Find out the initial, subsequent and terminal cash flows from the following data:

Cost of machine: ₹ 10,00,000
Life of machine: 5 years
Salvage value: ₹ 2,00,000
EBDT: ₹ 4,00,000
Additional working capital requirement: ₹ 1,00,000.

Depreciation is charged @ 20% p.a. on written down value basis. Income tax rules apply and the tax rate for income and short-term capital gains is 20%.

Solution: Computation of cash flows

Particulars	Year 0 (₹)	Year 1 (₹)	Year 2 (₹)	Year 3 (₹)	Year 4 (₹)	Year 5 (₹)
Cost of machine	–10,00,000					
Increase in working capital	–1,00,000					
PBDT		4,00,000	4,00,000	4,00,000	4,00,000	4,00,000
Less: Depreciation[1]		2,00,000	1,60,000	1,28,000	1,02,400	
Profit before tax		2,00,000	2,40,000	2,72,000	2,97,600	4,00,000
Less: Tax		40,000	48,000	54,400	59,520	80,000
Profit after tax		1,60,000	1,92,000	2,17,600	2,38,080	3,20,000
Add: Depreciation		2,00,000	1,60,000	1,28,000	1,02,400	
Add: Release of working capital						1,00,000
Add: Salvage value						2,00,000
Add: Tax savings on STCL						41,920
CFAT (₹)	–11,00,000	3,60,000	3,52,000	3,45,600	3,40,480	6,61,920

Working Note: 1. Calculation of depreciation:

Year	Cost of machine	Depreciation	Written down value
1	10,00,000	2,00,000	8,00,000
2		1,60,000	6,40,000
3		1,28,000	5,12,000
4		1,02,400	4,09,600

2. Loss on sale of machine = 4,09,600 – 2,00,000 = ₹ 2,09,600.
3. Tax savings on STCL @ 20% = ₹ 41,920.

Problem 6. Find out the initial, subsequent annual and terminal cash flows from the following data:

Cost of machine: ₹ 40,000

Life expectancy: 5 years

Salvage value: ₹ 10,000

Contribution per unit: ₹ 20

Expected annual sales: 1000 units

Installation cost ₹ 5,000

Tax rate: 30%.

Depreciation is charged on straight-line basis.

Solution: Computation of cash flows

Particulars	Year 0 (₹)	Year 1 – 4 (₹)	Year 5 (₹)
Cost of machine	–40,000		
Installation cost	–5,000		
PBDT		20,000	20,000
Less: Depreciation[1]		7,000	7,000
Profit before tax		13,000	13,000
Less: Tax		3,900	3,900
Profit after tax		9,100	9,100
Add: Depreciation		7,000	7,000
Salvage value			10,000
CFAT (₹)	–45,000	16,100	26,100

Working Notes:

1. Depreciation per year = 35,000 ÷ 5 = ₹ 7,000.
   Total cost = ₹ 40,000 + ₹ 5,000 = ₹ 45,000.
   Salvage value = ₹ 10,000.

Problem 7. From the following information find out initial, subsequent annual and terminal cash flows:

Cost of machine	₹ 5,00,000
Salvage value	₹ 50,000
Installation cost	₹ 10,000
Life	5 years
Expected annual sales	10,000 units
Sales price per unit	₹ 40
Variable cost per unit	₹ 16
Tax rate	50%

(D.U., B.Com. 2011)

Solution: Computation of cash flows

Particulars	Year 0	Year 1 – 4	Year 5
Cost of machine	–5,00,000		
Installation cost	–10,000		
Annual contribution		2,40,000	2,40,000
Less: Depreciation		92,000	92,000
Profit before tax		1,48,000	1,48,000
Less: Tax		74,000	74,000
Profit after tax		74,000	74,000
Add: Depreciation		92,000	92,000
Salvage value			50,000
CFAT (₹)	–5,10,000	1,66,000	2,16,000

Working Notes:

1. Contribution per year: ₹ 2,40,000
   Contribution per unit = ₹ 40 – ₹ 16 = ₹ 24.
2. Depreciation per year = 4,60,000 ÷ 5 = ₹ 92,000
   Total cost = ₹ 5,00,000 + ₹ 10,000 = ₹ 5,10,000
   Salvage value: ₹ 50,000
   Life of machine: 5 years.

Problem 8. XYZ Ltd. purchased a special machine one year ago at a cost of ₹ 24,000. The annual cash operating cost is approximately ₹ 40,000. At present, book value of machine is ₹ 20,000 and it is estimated to have additional useful life of 5 years after which its salvage value will be nil. A new machine has just come in the market which will do the same job but with an annual cash operating cost of only ₹ 32,000. The new machine costs ₹ 50,000 and has an estimated life of 5 years with zero salvage value. The old machine can be sold now for ₹ 16,000. Straight-line method of depreciation is used. Assume the tax rate of 30% on income and capital gains both. Calculate all incremental cash flows after taxes associated with this replacement decision.

Solution: Computation of incremental cash flows

Particulars	Year 0 (₹)	Year 1 – 4 (₹)	Year 5 (₹)
Cost of new machine	–50,000		
Add: Salvage value	16,000		
Add: Tax savings on sale of old machine[1]	1,200		
Savings on operating cost		8,000	8,000
Less: Incremental Depreciation[2]		6,000	6,000
Incremental Profit Before Tax		2,000	2,000
Less: Tax		600	600
Incremental Profit After Tax		1,400	1,400
Add: Incremental Depreciation		6,000	6,000
Add: Incremental Salvage Value			0
Incremental cash flow	–32,800	7,400	7,400

Notes: 1. 30% of (₹ 20,000 – 16,000)

2. Incremental depreciation = ₹ 10,000 – ₹ 4,000 = ₹ 6,000.

Problem 9. Rohan Ltd. is evaluating an investment proposal with the following data:

Cost of machine	₹ 4,00,000
Installation charges	₹ 50,000
Life of machine	5 years
Salvage value	₹ 25,000
Increase in working capital	₹ 30,000
Annual profit before depreciation and taxes	₹ 2,00,000
Tax rate	30%

Calculate the relevant cash flows associated with the above proposal.

Solution: Computation of cash flows

Particulars	Year 0 (₹)	Year 1 – 4 (₹)	Year 5 (₹)
Cost of machine	–4,00,000		
Installation cost	–50,000		
Increase in working capital	–30,000		
PBDT		2,00,000	2,00,000
Less: Depreciation[1]		85,000	85,000
Profit before tax		1,15,000	1,15,000
Less: Tax		34,500	34,500

Profit after tax		80,500	80,500
Add: Depreciation		80,500	80,500
Add: Release of working capital			30,000
Add: Salvage value			25,000
CFAT (₹)	–4,80,000	1,70,000	2,25,000

Working Notes:

1. Depreciation per year = 4,25,000 ÷ 5 = ₹ 85,000.
   Total cost = ₹ 4,00,000 + ₹ 50,000 = ₹ 4,50,000.
   Salvage value = ₹ 25,000.

Problem 10. Ramesh Ltd. is evaluating an investment proposal with the following information:

Cost of machine	₹ 10,00,000
Installation charges	₹ 1,00,000
Life of machine	5 years
Salvage value	₹ 50,000
Increase in working capital	₹ 60,000
Annual profit before depreciation and taxes	₹ 4,00,000
Tax rate	40%

Calculate the relevant cash flows associated with the above proposal.

Solution: Computation of cash flows

Particulars	Year 0 (₹)	Year 1 – 4 (₹)	Year 5 (₹)
Cost of machine	–10,00,000		
Installation cost	–1,00,000		
Increase in working capital	–60,000		
PBDT		4,00,000	4,00,000
Less: Depreciation[1]		2,10,000	2,10,000
Profit before tax		1,90,000	1,90,000
Less: Tax		76,000	76,000
Profit after tax		1,14,000	1,14,000
Add: Depreciation		2,10,000	2,10,000
Add: Release of working capital			60,000
Salvage value			50,000
CFAT (₹)	–11,60,000	3,24,000	4,34,000

Working Notes:

1. Depreciation per year = 10,50,000 ÷ 5 = ₹ 2,10,000.
   Total cost = ₹ 10,00,000 + ₹ 1,00,000 = ₹ 11,00,000.
   Salvage value = ₹ 50,000.

THEORETICAL QUESTIONS

1. How is cash flow different from accounting profit? Which one is better for capital budgeting decision? Why? *(D.U., B.Com. 2011)*
2. What is capital budgeting decision? Why is it significant for a firm?
3. In determining the expected cash flows from a new investment project, why should past sunk costs be ignored in the estimates?
4. What are three types of cash flows calculated for evaluating a capital project? Discuss in brief.
5. Explain the treatment of depreciation and taxes in estimating cash flows from point of view of capital budgeting.
6. What is difference between independent and contingent investments?

PRACTICAL PROBLEMS

1. A firm is considering to purchase a new machine which will cost ₹ 1,20,000. The cost of installation will amount to ₹ 25,000. The increase in working capital requirement will be ₹ 15,000. The machine is expected to provide cash inflows before depreciation and taxes of ₹ 70,000 for a period of five years after which it can be sold for ₹ 50,000. The firm applies straight-line method of depreciation. The tax rate on income is 35%. Calculate all the cash flows associated with the machine. *(D.U., B.Com. 2009, Corres.)*
   [**Ans.** Initial cash flow: ₹ –1,60,000, Interim cash flows: ₹ 52,150, Terminal cash flow: ₹ 1,17,150]
2. PQR Ltd. is evaluating an investment proposal with the following information:

Cost of machine	₹ 18,00,000
Installation charges	₹ 1,00,000
Life of machine	5 years
Salvage value	₹ 1,50,000
Increase in working capital	₹ 1,00,000
Annual profit before depreciation and taxes	₹ 6,00,000
Tax rate	40%

   Calculate the relevant cash flows associated with the above proposal.
   (D.U., B.Com. 2012, Corres.)
   [**Ans.** Initial cash flow: ₹ –20,00,000, Interim cash flows: ₹ 5,00,000, Terminal cash flow: ₹ 7,50,000]

3. ABC Ltd. is evaluating an investment proposal with the following information:

Cost of machine	₹ 36,00,000
Installation charges	₹ 2,00,000
Life	5 years
Salvage value	₹ 3,00,000
Increase in working capital	₹ 2,00,000
Annual profit before depreciation and taxes	₹ 12,00,000
Tax rate	40%

Calculate the relevant cash flows associated with the investment proposal.

(D.U., B.Com. 2015, N.C.)

[**Ans.** Initial cash flow: ₹ –40,00,000, Interim cash flows: ₹ 10,00,000, Terminal cash flow: ₹ 15,00,000]

4. A firm is considering to purchase a new machine costing ₹ 1,20,000. The installation charges will be ₹ 25,000. This decision will result in increase in working capital requirement by ₹ 15,000. The machine is expected to provide cash inflows before depreciation and taxes amounting to ₹ 70,000 for a period of five years after which it can be sold for ₹ 50,000. The firm uses straight-line method of depreciation. The income tax applicable is 35%. Calculate all cash flows associated with the machine.

(D.U., B.Com. 2015, Corres.)

[**Ans.** Initial cash flow: ₹ –1,60,000, Interim cash flows: ₹ 52,150, Terminal cash flow: ₹ 1,17,150]

Capital Budgeting Techniques

4

Chapter Outline

4.1 Introduction
4.2 Investment Evaluation Criteria
4.3 Accounting Rate of Return Method
4.4 Payback Period Method
4.5 Net Present Value Method
4.6 Internal Rate of Return Method
4.7 Profitability Index Method

4.1 Introduction

Capital budgeting is the most important decision in financial management. Capital budgeting is concerned with long-term investment of funds to create production capacity of a firm in anticipation of an expected flow of benefits over a long period of time.

According to Charles T. Horngren and George Foster, "Capital budgeting is as the making of long-term planning decisions for investments and their financing."

Capital budgeting is an important technique widely used for the evaluation of various capital investment proposals and selecting the most appropriate source of finance for the chosen investment proposal. In general, investing in long-term fixed assets is called capital budgeting.

In capital budgeting, we forecast a set of cash flows, find the present value of these cash flows, and make the investment only if the present value of the inflows is greater than the investment's cost.

4.2 Investment Evaluation Criteria

A number of capital budgeting techniques (investment criteria) are used in taking a capital investment decision. These techniques can be grouped in the two categories as mentioned below:

1. Non-discounted cash flow techniques
   (a) Payback Period Method
   (b) Accounting Rate of Return Method
2. Discounted cash flow techniques
   (a) Net Present Value Method

(b) Internal Rate of Return Method

(c) Profitability Index Method

The Net Present Value (NPV) is the best method, primarily because it addresses directly the central goal of financial management-maximising the shareholders' wealth. However, all of the methods provide useful information, and all are used in practice at least to some extent.

4.3 Accounting Rate of Return Method

The accounting rate of return, also known as the return on investment, is calculated on the basis of accounting statements. The accounting rate of return is equal to the average net operating profit divided by the average investment. It is calculated by applying the following formula:

$$\text{Accounting rate of return} = \frac{\text{Average profit after tax}}{\text{Average investment}} \times 100$$

Where,

$$\text{Average investment} = \frac{(\text{Initial cost} - \text{Salvage value})}{2} + \text{Salvage value} + \text{Increase in W.C.}$$

The project is accepted, if the accounting rate of return is more than the required rate of return.

Example 1. A firm is considering to install a new project costing ₹ 7,00,000 with life of 6 years and salvage value ₹ 1,00,000. The tax rate is 30% and it uses straight-line method of depreciation. The estimated cash flows before depreciation and tax are as follows:

Year	Amount (₹)
1	1,50,000
2	2,00,000
3	2,25,000
4	2,50,000
5	3,00,000
6	3,00,000

(i) Calculate Average/Accounting rate of return

(ii) What will be average rate of return, if the installation of the plant also requires increase in net working capital requirement by ₹ 1,00,000.

Solution: (i) Computation of earnings after tax

Year	Cash flows before depreciation	Depreciation	Earnings before tax	Tax	Earnings after tax
1	1,50,000	1,00,000	50,000	15,000	35,000
2	2,00,000	1,00,000	1,00,000	30,000	70,000
3	2,25,000	1,00,000	1,25,000	37,500	87,500
4	2,50,000	1,00,000	1,50,000	45,000	1,05,000

5	3,00,000	1,00,000	2,00,000	60,000	1,40,000
6	3,00,000	1,00,000	2,00,000	60,000	1,40,000
Total					**5,77,500**

Depreciation = (7,00,000 – 1,00,000) ÷ 6 = ₹ 1,00,000

Average earnings after tax = 5,77,500 ÷ 6 = 96,250

We know that:

$$\text{Average investment} = \frac{(\text{Initial cost} - \text{Salvage value})}{2} + \text{Salvage value} + \text{Increase in W.C.}$$

Substituting the values,

$$\text{Average investment} = \frac{(7{,}00{,}000 - 1{,}00{,}000)}{2} + 1{,}00{,}000 + 0.$$

Average Investment = 4,00,000.

We know that:

$$\text{Average investment} = \frac{\text{Average profit after tax}}{\text{Average investment}} \times 100$$

Substituting the values,

$$\text{Accounting rate of return} = \frac{96{,}250}{4{,}00{,}000} \times 100$$

Accounting Rate of Return = 24.1%

(ii) we know that:

$$\text{Average investment} = \frac{(\text{Initial cost} - \text{Salvage value})}{2} + \text{Salvage value} + \text{Increase in W.C.}$$

Substituting the values,

$$\text{Average investment} = \frac{(7{,}00{,}000 - 1{,}00{,}000)}{2} + 1{,}00{,}000 + 1{,}00{,}000$$

Average investment = 5,00,000

Thus,

$$\text{Accounting rate of return} = \frac{96{,}250}{5{,}00{,}000} \times 100$$

Accounting rate of return = 19.25%.

Example 2. Tulip Ltd. is planning to purchase a machine for ₹ 1,50,000 which is likely to generate the following earnings in the next five years:

Year	1	2	3	4	5
Earnings (₹)	50,000	55,000	60,000	62,000	65,000

The purchase of machine has resulted in increase of working capital by ₹ 15,000. The machine will be depreciated on SLM basis and has salvage value of ₹ 25,000. The company is subject to at the tax rate of 50%. Find the average rate of return.

Solution: Statement of earnings after tax

Particulars	Year 1	Year 2	Year 3	Year 4	Year 5
Earnings	50,000	55,000	60,000	62,000	65,000
Less: Depreciation[1]	25,000	25,000	25,000	25,000	25,000
Profit before tax	25,000	30,000	35,000	37,000	40,000
Less: tax @ 50%	12,500	15,000	17,500	18,500	20,000
Profit after tax	12,500	15,000	17,500	18,500	20,000

Average earnings after tax = (12,500 + 15,000 + 17,500 + 18,500 + 20,000) ÷ 5 = 16,700.

We know that:

$$\text{Average Investment} = \frac{(\text{Initial cost} - \text{Salvage value})}{2} + \text{Salvage value} + \text{Increase in W.C.}$$

Substituting the values,

$$\text{Average Investment} = \frac{(1{,}50{,}000 - 25{,}000)}{2} + 25{,}000 + 15{,}000$$

Average Investment = 1,02,500

We know that:

$$\text{According rate of return} = \frac{\text{Average profit after tax}}{\text{Average investment}} \times 100$$

Substituting the values,

$$\text{According rate of return} = \frac{16{,}700}{1{,}02{,}500} \times 100$$

Accounting rate of return = 16.29%

Note: 1. Depreciation = ₹ 25,000

Price of machine ₹ 1,50,000 and salvage value = ₹ 25,000.

1. Merits of average rate of return method. The average rate of return method has the following merits:

(i) **Simplicity:** This method of capital budgeting is simple to understand and use.

(ii) **Accounting profitability:** In this method, accounting profits over the economic life of the project are considered in evaluating the project. The required data are easily available from the firm's financial statements.

2. Demerits of average rate of return method. The average rate of return method has the following demerits:

(i) **No consideration of time value:** This method ignores time value of the earnings.

(ii) **Overlook of cash flows:** Accounting profit is taken into consideration instead of cash flows from the project.

(iii) **Inconsistent with the objective:** This method is inconsistent with the objective of maximising shareholders' wealth.

(iv) **Arbitrary cut-off:** Firms using average rate of return use arbitrary cut-off rate in taking a decision about a project.

4.4 Payback Period Method

Payback period method is traditional and simple most method of capital budgeting. It is defined as the length of time that is required for a stream of cash inflows from the investment to recover the original cash outlay invested in the project.

When periodic cash inflows from the investment are equal, the following formula is used to compute payback period:

$$\text{Payback Period} = \frac{\text{Initial investment}}{\text{Annual cash inflow}}$$

Example 3. A firm invests ₹ 5,00,000 in a project and expects cash inflow of ₹ 80,000 per annum. Find the payback period for the investment made.

Solution: We know that:

$$\text{Payback Period} = \frac{\text{Initial investment}}{\text{Annual cash inflow}}$$

Substituting the values, we get:

$$\text{Payback Period} = \frac{5,00,000}{80,000}$$

$$\text{Payback Period} = 6.25 \text{ years.}$$

When periodic cash inflows from the investment are not equal, payback period will be calculated by taking cumulative total of each period's cash inflows and the exact payback period will be calculated by interpolation. The following formula is used in finding the payback period:

$$\text{Payback Period} = n^{\text{th}} \text{ period} + \frac{\text{Original cost} - \text{Cumulative CFAT for } n^{\text{th}} \text{ period}}{\text{CFAT for } (n+1)^{\text{th}} \text{ period}}$$

Where, n^{th} period is equal to the number of periods immediately preceding the period of final recovery. CFAT is cash flow after tax.

Example 4. A company requires an initial investment of ₹ 5,00,000. The estimated net cash flows are as follows:

Year	Net cash flow (₹)
1	80,000
2	70,000

3	70,000
4	70,000
5	60,000
6	60,000
7	60000
8	50000
9	50,000
10	50,000

Determine the Payback Period.

Solution: Cumulative cash flow

Year	Net cash flow (₹)	Cumulative cash flow (₹)
1	80,000	80,000
2	70,000	1,50,000
3	70,000	2,20,000
4	70,000	2,90,000
5	60,000	3,50,000
6	60,000	4,10,000
7	60,000	4,70,000
8	50,000	5,20,000
9	50,000	5,70,000
10	50,000	6,20,000

Payback Period: We know that payback period is calculated by following formula:

$$\text{Payback Period} = n^{\text{th}} \text{ period} + \frac{\text{Original cost} - \text{Cumulative CFAT for } n^{\text{th}} \text{ period}}{\text{CFAT for } (n+1)^{\text{th}} \text{ period}}$$

₹ 4,70,000 of the investment is recovered by 7th year. Substituting the values, we get:

$$\text{Payback Period} = 7 + \frac{5,00,000 - 4,70,000}{50,000}$$

Payback period = 7.6 years

Thus, the payback period is 7.6 years.

Example 5. A company is considering to install a new project costing ₹ 7,00,000 with life of 7 years and no salvage value. The tax rate is 30% and it uses straight-line method of depreciation. The estimated cash flows before depreciation and tax are as follows:

Year	Amount (₹)
1	2,00,000
2	2,00,000
3	3,00,000
4	2,00,000
5	3,00,000
6	2,00,000
7	2,00,000

You are required to calculate payback period.

Solution: Computation of cash flow after tax

Year	Cash flows before depreciation	Depreciation	Earnings before tax	Tax	Earnings after tax	Cash flow after tax	Cum. CFAT
1	2,00,000	1,00,000	1,00,000	30,000	70,000	1,70,000	1,70,000
2	2,00,000	1,00,000	1,00,000	30,000	70,000	1,70,000	3,40,000
3	3,00,000	1,00,000	2,00,000	60,000	1,40,000	2,40,000	5,80,000
4	2,00,000	1,00,000	1,00,000	30,000	70,000	1,70,000	7,50,000
5	3,00,000	1,00,000	2,00,000	60,000	1,40,000	2,40,000	9,90,000
6	2,00,000	1,00,000	1,00,000	30,000	70,000	1,70,000	11,60,000
7	2,00,000	1,00,000	1,00,000	30,000	70,000	1,70,000	13,30,000

We know:

$$\text{Payback Period} = n^{\text{th}} \text{ period} + \frac{\text{Original cost} - \text{Cumulative CFAT for } n^{\text{th}} \text{ period}}{\text{CFAT for } (n+1)^{\text{th}} \text{ period}}$$

₹ 5,80,000 of the investment is recovered by 3rd year. Substituting the values, we get:

$$\text{Payback Period} = 3 + \frac{7,00,000 - 5,80,000}{1,70,000}$$

Payback period = 3.71 years

Thus, the payback period is 3.71 years.

Merits of Payback Period Method

Payback period method has following merits:

1. **Simplicity:** It is simple to understand and easy to calculate.
2. **Emphasis on early returns:** This method lays emphasis on early returns. Investments with shorter payback period will be less risky.
3. **Based on cash flows:** The evaluation of capital expenditures is carried out on the basis of cash inflows arising from the investments.

Limitations of Payback Period Method

Though the payback period method is simple and lays emphasis on liquidity and risk, it has following limitations:

1. **No consideration of time value:** This method ignores time value of the earnings.
2. **Overlook of remaining cash flows:** Cash flows from the project after the recovery of cost are ignored.
3. **Inconsistent with the objective:** This method is inconsistent with the objective of maximising shareholders' wealth as it does not take into consideration all cash flows.
4. **Supplementary technique:** Payback period method does not say anything about selection or rejection of projects. It can be used as supplementary technique to discounted techniques.

4.5 Net Present Value Method

Net present value technique is most popular and most widely used technique of capital budgeting. This technique lays emphasis on time value of money. This method is consistent with the objective of shareholders' wealth maximisation. In this method, present values of all cash flows are computed. Cost of capital (required rate of return) is employed as discount rate. The excess of present value of all inflows over present value of initial investment is equal to net present value of the investment made in the project.

Net Present Value = Present Value of Cash Inflows – Cost of Initial Investment

$$NPV = \frac{C_1}{(1+k)} + \frac{C_1}{(1+k)^2} + \frac{C_1}{(1+k)^3} + \ldots\ldots\ldots + \frac{C_N}{(1+k)^n} - C_0$$

Where, NPV: Net Present Value

C_0: Initial cost of investment

$C_1, C_2, \ldots$ Cash inflows in period 1, 2, ...

k: Cost of capital

If the net value of a project is more than zero, project is selected. In case of mutually exclusive projects, the project with highest net present value is accepted. The amount of net present value is the addition to the wealth of shareholders.

Example 6. A company is considering to install a new project costing ₹ 14,00,000 with life of 7 years and no salvage value. The tax rate is 40% and it uses straight-line method of depreciation. The estimated cash flows before depreciation and tax are as follows:

Year	Amount (₹)
1	4,50,000
2	4,50,000
3	3,50,000
4	3,50,000
5	3,00,000

6	3,00,000
7	3,00,000

You are required to calculate net present value at 12% discount rate. Interpret the result.

Solution: Computation of net present value

Year	EBDT	Depreciation	Earnings before tax	Tax	Earnings after tax	CFAT	PVF (12%, n)	Present value
1	4,50,000	2,00,000	2,50,000	1,00,000	1,50,000	3,50,000	0.893	3,12,550
2	4,50,000	2,00,000	2,50,000	1,00,000	1,50,000	3,50,000	0.797	2,78,950
3	3,50,000	2,00,000	1,50,000	60,000	90,000	2,90,000	0.712	2,06,480
4	3,50,000	2,00,000	1,50,000	60,000	90,000	2,90,000	0.636	1,84,440
5	3,00,000	2,00,000	1,00,000	40,000	60,000	2,60,000	0.567	1,47,420
6	3,00,000	2,00,000	1,00,000	40,000	60,000	2,60,000	0.507	1,31,820
7	3,00,000	2,00,000	1,00,000	40,000	60,000	2,60,000	0.452	1,17,520
Total								**13,79,180**

Net present value = 13,79,180 – 14,00,000 = ₹ –20,820

Since the net present value of investment is negative, the project is not profitable.

Example 7. Kalptaru Ltd. is considering the following investment projects:

Project	Cash flows (₹)			
	Year 0	Year 1	Year 2	Year 3
A	–20000	20,000	–	–
B	–20000	15,000	15,000	–
C	–20000	4,000	8,000	24,000
D	–20000	20,000	6,000	6,000

1. Rank the projects according to: (i) Payback period method and (ii) NPV method assuming discounting rate of 10%.
2. Assuming that the projects are mutually exclusive, which one should be accepted?

Solution: (i) Cumulative cash flows

Year	Project A		Project B		Project C		Project D	
	Cash flow	Cumulative cash flow	Cash flow	Cumulative cash flow	Cash flow	Cumulative cash flow	Cash flow	Cumulative cash flow
1	20,000	20,000	15,000	15,000	4,000	4,000	20,000	20,000
2	0	20,000	15,000	30,000	8,000	12,000	6,000	26,000
3	0	20,000	0	30,000	24,000	36,000	6,000	32,000

We know that:

$$\text{Payback Period} = n^{\text{th}}\ \text{period} + \frac{\text{Original cost} - \text{Cumulative CFAT for } n^{\text{th}} \text{ period}}{\text{CFAT for } (n+1)^{\text{th}} \text{ period}}$$

Substituting the values,

Project A,

$$\text{Payback period} = 1 + \frac{20{,}000 - 20{,}000}{0} = 1\,\text{year}$$

Project B,

$$\text{Payback period} = 1 + \frac{20{,}000 - 15{,}000}{15{,}000} = 1.33\,\text{years}$$

Project C,

$$\text{Payback period} = 2 + \frac{20{,}000 - 12{,}000}{12{,}000} = 2.33\,\text{years}$$

Project D,

$$\text{Payback period} = 1 + \frac{20{,}000 - 20{,}000}{6{,}000} = 1\,\text{year}$$

Net Present Value of cash flows

Year	$PVF_{(10\%, n)}$	Project A		Project B		Project C		Project D	
		Cash flow	PV	Cash flow	PV	Cash flow	PV	Cash flow	PV
1	0.909	20,000	18,180	15,000	13,635	4,000	3,636	20,000	18,180
2	0.826			15,000	12,390	8,000	6,608	6,000	4,956
3	0.751					24,000	18,024	6,000	4,506
Total PV			18,180		26,025		28,268		27,642
Investment									
NPV									

Evaluation of projects

Particulars	Project			
	A	B	C	D
Payback period	1 year	1.33 years	2.33 years	1 year
Ranking	2	3	4	1
NPV	–1,820	6,025	8,268	7,642
Ranking	4	3	1	2

(ii) Project C has better net present value. It should be selected.

Merits of Net Present Value Method

Net Present Value method has following merits:

1. **Recognition of time value of money:** In net present value method, present values of all cash inflows are computed. Decision is taken on the basis of excess of present value of all cash flows over present value of cash outflows.
2. **Consideration of all cash flows:** This method considers cash inflows rather than accounting profits. All cash flows are considered.
3. **Consistent with objective:** Net present value method is consistent with the objective of maximisation of shareholders' wealth. Net present value of the project is addition to the shareholders' wealth.

Demerits of Net Present Value Method

Net Present value method has following limitations:

1. **Difficult to compute:** Net present value method is difficult to understand and calculation of net present value is difficult and requires skills.
2. **Work out of appropriate cost of capital difficult:** Net present value cannot be computed if cost of capital is unknown. Weight average of capital is used to find the present values of cash inflows. It is particularly difficult to measure cost of equity.
3. **Not suitable in capital rationing:** Net present value method is not suitable for evaluating capital expenditure when funds are limited.
4. **Misleading result in case of mutually exclusive projects:** If projects having different life span and capital size are to be evaluated, net present value method can give the misleading results. In such situation, profitability index is more suitable.

4.6 Internal Rate of Return Method

A project's internal rate of return is the discount rate that makes the present value of its inflows equal to its cost. This is equivalent to forcing the net present value to equal to zero. The internal rate of return is an estimate of the project's rate of return. The internal rate of return is also known as yield on investment and marginal efficiency of capital.

A project is selected if the internal rate of return is more than the required rate of return (cost of capital). Net present value method is preferred in evaluating the capital projects. In small project, the internal rate of return may be higher, but its net present value may be lower than the net present value of large project. Since the objective in financial management is to maximise the shareholders' wealth, net present value method is preferred to the internal rate of return method of capital expenditure evaluation.

1. Calculation of IRR when cash inflows are equal. When cash inflows are equal, the concept of present value of an annuity is applied. We know that:

$$P = C \times PVFA\ (r\%, n)$$

Where, P = present value of an annuity

C = annual cash inflow

PVFA = present value factor for annuity

After finding PVFA, we can read the rate of interest corresponding to the calculated PVFA and the life of the project (number of years) from PVFA table. This rate of interest is the internal rate of return of the project.

The following steps are needed in computing the internal rate of return of a project:

(i) Calculate payback period as given below and treat it as PVFA.

$$\text{Payback period} = \frac{\text{Initial investment}}{\text{Annual cash inflow after tax}}$$

(ii) In PVFA table, move in the row which is equal to the life of the project and find the value which is equal to the payback period calculated above. If we get the exact value, the rate of interest corresponding to this value in the PVFA table is equal to the internal rate of return of the project.

(iii) In case we do not find the exact value in the PVFA table, we note down two values from the table, one lower than calculated payback period and another higher than payback period. Then, we find corresponding interest rates to the values from PVFA table. These interest rates are treated as lower discount rate (L) and higher discount rate (H). The following formula is used to find exact internal rate of return by interpolation:

$$\text{IRR} = \text{L} + \frac{\text{PV of CFAT at L} - \text{PV of Initial Invesment}}{\text{PV of CFAT at L} - \text{PV of CFAT at H}} \times (\text{H–L})\%$$

Where, IRR = Internal rate of return
L = Lower discount rate
H = Higher discount rate
PV = Present value
CFAT = Cash flows after tax

Example 8. A firm is investing ₹ 4,10,000 in a project. It is expected that the project will generate annual cash inflow of ₹ 1,00,000 for a period of 5 years. Calculate the internal rate of interest of the project.

Solution: Since annual cash inflows are equal, annuity concept of evaluation of project can be employed here.

$$\text{Payback period} = \frac{\text{Initial investment}}{\text{Annual cash inflow after tax}}$$

Substituting the values, we get:

$$\text{Payback period} = \frac{4,10,000}{1,00,000} = 4.100$$

Now, moving in the PVFA table against $n = 5$ years, we get corresponding interest rate as 7%.

Thus, internal rate of return of the project is 7%.

Example 9. A firm is investing ₹ 8,00,000 in a project. It is expected that the project will generate annual cash inflow of ₹ 1,00,000 for a period of 10 years. Calculate the internal rate of interest of the project.

Solution: We know that:

$$\text{Payback period} = \frac{\text{Initial investment}}{\text{Annual cash inflow after tax}}$$

Substituting the values, we get:

$$\text{Payback period} = \frac{8,00,000}{1,00,000} = 8.000$$

Now, moving in the PVFA table against $n = 10$ years, we get two values 7.722 (<8) and 8.111 (>8). The corresponding interest rate as 5% (H) and 4% (L). We can use these as discount rates.

Present value of cash inflows at 5% discount rate is

$$1,00,000 \times 7.722 = 7,72,200$$

Present value of cash inflows at 4% discount rate is

$$1,00,000 \times 8.111 = 8,11,100$$

The following formula is used to find exact internal rate of return by interpolation:

$$\text{IRR} = \text{L} + \frac{\text{PV of CFAT at L} - \text{PV of Initial Invesment}}{\text{PV of CFAT at L} - \text{PV of CFAT at H}} \times (\text{H–L})\%$$

Substituting the values, we get:

$$\text{IRR} = 4 + \frac{8,11,100 - 8,00,000}{8,11,100 - 7,72,200} \times (5 - 4)\%$$

$$\text{IRR} = 4.26\%$$

Thus, internal rate of return of the project is 4.26%.

2. Calculation of IRR when cash inflows are unequal. When cash inflows are unequal, the trial and error approach is used to find the discount rate that makes present value of cash inflows from the project equal to the initial investment. This discount rate is the internal rate of return. The following steps are used to find the internal rate of return:

(i) Find the fake payback period by dividing the initial investment by average cash inflows.

$$\text{Fake payback period} = \frac{\text{Initial investment}}{\text{Average cash inflow after tax}}$$

(ii) Move in the row which is equal the life of the project in PVFA table, and find the value which is equal to the fake payback period. If exact value is not found, look for the value approximate to fake payback period. Note down the corresponding interest rate to the approximate value from PVFA table.

(iii) Compute the present value of cash inflows at discount rate equal to rate of interest noted above. If the present value is greater than initial investment, designate this as lower discount rate (L). Now, move to higher discount rate and repeat this process until we get the discount rate which makes the present value of cash inflows lower than the initial investment. Designate this rate as higher discount rate (H).

If the present value is lower than initial investment, designate this as higher discount rate (H). Now, move to lower discount rate and repeat this process until we get the discount rate which makes the present value of cash inflows higher than the initial investment. Designate this rate as lower discount rate (L).

(iv) The following formula is used to find exact internal rate of return by interpolation:

$$\text{IRR} = \text{L} + \frac{\text{PV of CFAT at L} - \text{PV of Initial Invesment}}{\text{PV of CFAT at L} - \text{PV of CFAT at H}} \times (\text{H–L})\%$$

Where, IRR = Internal rate of return
L = Lower discount rate
H = Higher discount rate
PV = Present value
CFAT = Cash flows after tax.

Example 10. A company is considering to install a new project costing ₹ 14,00,000 with life of 7 years and no salvage value. The tax rate is 40% and it uses straight-line method of depreciation. The estimated cash flows before depreciation and tax are as follows:

Year	Amount (₹)
1	4,50,000
2	4,50,000
3	3,50,000
4	3,50,000
5	3,00,000
6	3,00,000
7	3,00,000

You are required to calculate the internal rate of return. Interpret the result.

Solution: Computation of CFAT

Year	EBDT	Depreciation	Earnings before tax	Tax	Earnings after tax	CFAT
1	4,50,000	2,00,000	2,50,000	1,00,000	1,50,000	3,50,000
2	4,50,000	2,00,000	2,50,000	1,00,000	1,50,000	3,50,000
3	3,50,000	2,00,000	1,50,000	60,000	90,000	2,90,000
4	3,50,000	2,00,000	1,50,000	60,000	90,000	2,90,000
5	3,00,000	2,00,000	1,00,000	40,000	60,000	2,60,000
6	3,00,000	2,00,000	1,00,000	40,000	60,000	2,60,000
7	3,00,000	2,00,000	1,00,000	40,000	60,000	2,60,000
Total						**20,60,000**

Average earnings after tax = 20,60,000 ÷ 7 = ₹ 2,94,285

We know that:

$$\text{Fake payback period} = \frac{\text{Initial investment}}{\text{Average cash inflow after tax}}$$

Substituting the values,

$$\text{Fake payback period} = \frac{14,00,000}{2,94,285} = 4.757$$

From PVFA table, for 7 = 5, approximate value to fake payback period is 4.564. At PVFA 4,564 corresponding interest rate is 12%.

Computation of Present value

Year	CFAT	PVF (12%, n)	Present value	PVF (11%, n)	Present value
1	3,50,000	0.893	3,12,550	0.901	3,15,350
2	3,50,000	0.797	2,78,950	0.812	2,84,200
3	2,90,000	0.712	2,06,480	0.731	2,11,990
4	2,90,000	0.636	1,84,440	0.659	1,91,110
5	2,60,000	0.567	1,47,420	0.593	1,54,180
6	2,60,000	0.507	1,31,820	0.535	1,39,100
7	2,60,000	0.452	1,17,520	0.482	1,25,320
Total			**13,79,180**		**14,21,250**

The present value of cash inflows is lower than the initial investment. Thus, lower discount rate, 11% should be tried to make present value greater than initial investment.

We know that:

$$\text{IRR} = \text{L} + \frac{\text{PV of CFAT at L} - \text{PV of Initial Invesment}}{\text{PV of CFAT at L} - \text{PV of CFAT at H}} \times (\text{H–L})\%$$

Substituting the values,

$$\text{IRR} = 11 + \frac{14,21,250 - 14,00,000}{14,21,250 - 13,79,180} \times (12 - 11)\%$$

$$\text{IRR} = 11 + 0.51 = 11.51\%$$

Thus, internal rate of return is 11.51%.

Example 11. Mahesh Ltd. is considering the introduction of a new product for which two alternative machines are available in the market. Cash flows after taxes (in ₹) associated with the machines are given below:

Year	0	1 – 5
Machine A	–10,000	3,000
Machine B	–55,000	17,000

Compute NPV at 10% p.a. and IRR for both the machines and advise the company which machine should be purchased. State the reason for your advice also.

Solution: Computation of net present value

Year	$PVFA_{(10\%, 5)}$	Machine A		Machine B	
		Cash flow	PV	Cash flow	PV
1 – 5	3.791	3,000	11,373	15,000	56,865
Investment			10,000		55,000
NPV			1,373		1,865

Computation of IRR:

Both machines have present values higher than initial cost. Higher discount rate should be used to make present values lower than initial cost.

Let's try 16% discount rate to make present values lower than initial investment.

Year	$PVFA_{(16\%, 5)}$	Machine A		Machine B	
		Cash flow	PV	Cash flow	PV
1 – 5	3.274	3,000	9,822	15,000	49,110
Investment			10,000		55,000
NPV			–178		–5,890

We know that:

$$IRR = L + \frac{\text{PV of CFAT at L} - \text{PV of Initial Invesment}}{\text{PV of CFAT at L} - \text{PV of CFAT at H}} \times (H–L)\%$$

Substituting the values,

$$IRR(A) = 10 + \frac{11{,}373 - 10{,}000}{11{,}373 - 9{,}822} \times (16 - 10)\%$$

IRR(A) = 10 + 5.31 =15.31%

$$IRR(B) = 10 + \frac{56{,}865 - 55{,}000}{56{,}865 - 49{,}110} \times (16 - 10)\%$$

IRR(B) = 10 + 1.44 = 11.44%

Machine B has more net present value. Thus, purchase of machine B should be preferred if required rate of return is 10%.

Merits of Internal Rate of Return Method

Internal rate of return method of capital budgeting has following merits:

1. **Recognition of time value of money.** In internal rate of return method, present values of all cash inflows are computed. Decision is taken on the basis of equality of present value of all cash flows to present value of cash outflows.

2. **Consideration of all cash flows.** This method considers cash inflows rather than accounting profits. All cash flows are considered.
3. **No requirement of cost of capital.** There in no pre-requirement of knowledge of cost of capital. Internal rate of return can be calculated without the required rate of return. However, the decision is taken by comparing the internal rate of return with the cost of capital of investment.
4. **Consistent with the objective:** In the selected project, internal rate of return is more than cost of capital. So, there is net present value of the project, which is addition to the wealth of shareholders.

Demerits of Internal Rate of Return Method

The internal rate of return method has following limitations:

1. **Difficult to calculate:** The calculation of internal rate of return is complicated.
2. **Unrealistic reinvestment assumption:** It is assumed that cash flows generated by the project can be reinvested at its internal rate of return. This assumption is unrealistic.
3. **Negative or multiple results:** In some cases, IRR may be negative. In non-conventional projects there is possibility of multiple internal rate of returns.

4.7 Profitability Index Method

Profitability index method of capital expenditure evaluation is a version of net present value method. In this method, the ratio of present value of cash inflows to present value of cash outflow is calculated and the decision is taken on the basis of this.

$$\text{Profitability index} \quad \frac{\text{Present value of cash inflows}}{\text{Present value of cash outflows}}$$

In situation of capital rationing, profitability index method is preferred to net present value method. If unlimited capital is available, the net present value method is suitable. In case of limited capital, net present method may give misleading decision. Profitability index method removes this limitation of net present value method.

A project is selected if its profitability ratio is greater than one. The profitability index of less than one indicates loss in undertaking the project. In this situation, firm's cost of capital exceeds the rate of return.

Example 12. A company is considering to install a new project costing ₹ 14,00,000 with life of 7 years and no salvage value. The tax rate is 40% and it uses straight-line method of depreciation. The estimated cash flows before depreciation and tax are as follows:

Year	Amount (₹)
1	4,50,000
2	4,50,000
3	3,50,000
4	3,50,000
5	3,00,000

6	3,00,000
7	3,00,000

You are required to calculate profitability index at 12% discount rate. Interpret the result.

Solution: Computation of Net Present Value

Year	EBDT	Depreciation	Earnings before tax	Tax	Earnings after tax	CFAT	PVF (12%, n)	Present value
1	4,50,000	2,00,000	2,50,000	1,00,000	1,50,000	3,50,000	0.893	3,12,550
2	4,50,000	2,00,000	2,50,000	1,00,000	1,50,000	3,50,000	0.797	2,78,950
3	3,50,000	2,00,000	1,50,000	60,000	90,000	2,90,000	0.712	2,06,480
4	3,50,000	2,00,000	1,50,000	60,000	90,000	2,90,000	0.636	1,84,440
5	3,00,000	2,00,000	1,00,000	40,000	60,000	2,60,000	0.567	1,47,420
6	3,00,000	2,00,000	1,00,000	40,000	60,000	2,60,000	0.507	1,31,820
7	3,00,000	2,00,000	1,00,000	40,000	60,000	2,60,000	0.452	1,17,520
Total								**13,79,180**

We know that:

$$\text{Profitability index} = \frac{\text{Present value of cash inflows}}{\text{Present value of cash outflows}}$$

Substituting the values,

$$\text{Profitability index} = \frac{13,79,180}{14,00,000} = 0.96$$

Since the profitability index is less than one, the project is not profitable.

Example 13. A company is considering the replacement of an existing machine. It is faced with two alternatives:

(i) To buy machine A which is similar to the existing machine.

(ii) To buy machine B which is more expensive and has higher capacity.

(iii) The cash flows after taxes (in lakhs of ₹) at present level of operations are as under:

Year	0	1	2	3	4	5
Machine A	– 30	8	10	20	14	14
Machine B	– 40	15	28	32	34	30

Cost of capital is 10%. Depreciation is calculated on straight-line basis. Calculate Profitability Index.

Advise the company about the better alternative.

Solution: Computation of present value of cash flows after tax

Year	$PVF_{(10\%, n)}$	Machine A		Machine B	
		CFAT	PV	CFAT	PV
1	0.909	14	12.726	23	20.907
2	0.826	16	13.216	36	29.736
3	0.751	26	19.526	40	30.040
4	0.683	20	13.660	42	28.686
5	0.621	20	12.420	38	23.598
Total PV			71.548		132.967
Investment			30		40
NPV			41.548		92.967

(i) Both machines have positive net present values.

(ii) The profitability index:

Machine A = 71.548 ÷ 30 = 2.39

Machine B = 132.967 ÷ 40 = 3.22

Purchasing of machine B is better option.

Merits of Profitability Index Method

The profitability index method of capital budgeting has following merits:

1. **Consideration of time value of money:** The profitability index method considers time value of money.
2. **Consideration of all cash flows:** It considers all cash flows generated during the economic life of the project.
3. **Useful in capital rationing:** When funds are limited, the profitability index method is better than net present value method in selecting the projects.
4. **Consistent with the objective:** The profitability index of selected projects is greater than 1 and it results in net present value of projects. The net present value is an addition to the wealth of shareholders. Thus, profitability index method is consistent with the objective of maximisation of shareholders' wealth.

Demerits of Profitability Index Method

The profitability index method has following limitations:

1. **Requirement of cost of capital:** The cost of capital must be known before the computation of present values of cash inflows. An error in calculation of cost of capital (discount rate) can result in making wrong decision.
2. **Unrealistic assumption:** It is presumed that all immediate cash flows can be reinvested at the discount rate being used. This assumption is unrealistic.

SOLVED PROBLEMS

Problem 1. A company is considering to install a new project costing ₹ 7,00,000 with life of 7 years and no salvage value. The tax rate is 30% and it uses straight-line method of depreciation. The estimated cash flows before depreciation and tax are as follows:

Year	Amount (₹)
1	1,50,000
2	2,00,000
3	2,25,000
4	2,50,000
5	3,00,000
6	4,00,000
7	4,00,000

You are required to calculate:

(i) Average/Accounting rate of return

(ii) Net present value at 12% discount rate

(iii) Profitability index at 12%.

Solution: (i) Computation of Earnings after Tax

Year	Cash flows before depreciation	Depreciation	Earnings before tax	Tax	Earnings after tax
1	1,50,000	1,00,000	50,000	15,000	35,000
2	2,00,000	1,00,000	1,00,000	30,000	70,000
3	2,25,000	1,00,000	1,25,000	37,500	87,500
4	2,50,000	1,00,000	1,50,000	45,000	1,05,000
5	3,00,000	1,00,000	2,00,000	60,000	1,40,000
6	4,00,000	1,00,000	3,00,000	90,000	2,10,000
7	4,00,000	1,00,000	3,00,000	90,000	2,10,000
Total					8,57,500

Average earnings after tax = 8,57,500 ÷ 7 = 1,22,500

Average investment = 7,00,000 ÷ 2 = 3,50,000

We know that:

$$\text{Accounting rate of return} = \frac{\text{Average profit after tax}}{\text{Average investment}} \times 100$$

Substituting the values,

$$\text{Accounting rate of return} = \frac{1,22,500}{3,50,000} \times 100$$

Accounting Rate of Return = 35%.

(ii) Computation of Net Present Value

Year	Earnings after tax	Depreciation	Cash flows after tax	PVF (12%, n)	Present value
1	50,000	1,00,000	1,50,000	0.893	1,33,950
2	1,00,000	1,00,000	2,00,000	0.797	1,59,400
3	1,25,000	1,00,000	2,25,000	0.712	1,60,200
4	1,50,000	1,00,000	2,50,000	0.636	1,59,000
5	2,00,000	1,00,000	3,00,000	0.567	1,70,100
6	3,00,000	1,00,000	4,00,000	0.507	2,02,800
7	3,00,000	1,00,000	4,00,000	0.452	1,80,800
Total					**11,66,250**

Net present value = 11,66,250 – 7,00,000 = ₹ 4,66,250

(iii) We know that:

$$\text{Profitability index} = \frac{\text{Present value of cash inflows}}{\text{Present value of cash outflows}}$$

Substituting the values,

$$\text{Profitability index} = \frac{11,66,250}{7,00,000}$$

Profitability index = 1.67.

Problem 2. A company is considering to install a new project costing ₹ 7,20,000 with life of 6 years and no salvage value. The tax rate is 30% and it uses straight-line method of depreciation. The estimated cash flows before depreciation and tax are as follows:

Year	Amount (₹)
1	1,50,000
2	2,00,000
3	2,25,000
4	2,50,000
5	3,00,000
6	3,00,000

You are required to calculate:

(i) Average/Accounting rate of return
(ii) Net present value at 12% discount rate
(iii) Profitability index at 12%.

Solution: (i) Computation of Earnings after Tax

Year	Cash flows before depreciation	Depreciation	Earnings before tax	Tax	Earnings after tax
1	1,50,000	1,20,000	30,000	9,000	21,000
2	2,00,000	1,20,000	80,000	24,000	56,000
3	2,25,000	1,20,000	1,05,000	31,500	73,500
4	2,50,000	1,20,000	1,30,000	39,000	91,000
5	3,00,000	1,20,000	1,80,000	54,000	1,26,000
6	3,00,000	1,20,000	1,80,000	54,000	1,26,000
Total					**4,93,500**

Average earnings after tax = 4,93,500 ÷ 6 = 82,250
Average investment = 7,20,000 ÷ 2 = 3,60,000

We know that:

$$\text{Accounting rate of return} = \frac{\text{Average profit after tax}}{\text{Average investment}} \times 100$$

Substituting the values,

$$\text{Accounting rate of return} = \frac{82{,}250}{3{,}60{,}000} \times 100$$

Accounting Rate of Return = 22.8%.

(ii) Computation of Net Present Value

Year	Earnings after tax	Depreciation	Cash flows after tax	PVF (12%, n)	Present value
1	21,000	1,20,000	1,41,000	0.893	1,25,913
2	56,000	1,20,000	1,76,000	0.797	1,40,272
3	73,500	1,20,000	1,93,500	0.712	1,37,772
4	91,000	1,20,000	2,11,000	0.636	1,34,196
5	1,26,000	1,20,000	2,46,000	0.567	1,39,482
6	1,26,000	1,20,000	2,46,000	0.507	1,24,722
Total					**8,02,357**

Net present value = 8,02,357 – 7,20,000 = ₹ 82,357

(iii) We know that:

$$\text{Profitability index} = \frac{\text{Present value of cash inflows}}{\text{Present value of cash outflows}}$$

Substituting the values,

$$\text{Profitability index} = \frac{8,02,357}{7,20,000}$$

Profitability index = 1.11.

Problem 3. Ram Ltd. is considering the introduction of a new product for which two alternative machines are available in the market. Cash flows after taxes (in ₹) associated with the machine are given below:

Year	0	1 – 5
Machine A	– 10,000	3,000
Machine B	– 50,000	15,000

Compute NPV at 10% p.a. and IRR for both the machines and advise the company which machine should be purchased. State the reason for your advice also.

Solution: Computation of net present value

Year	$PVFA_{(10\%, 5)}$	Machine A		Machine B	
		Cash flow	PV	Cash flow	PV
1 – 5	3.791	3,000	11,373	15,000	56,865
Investment			10,000		50,000
NPV			1,373		6,865

Computation of IRR:

Both machines have present values higher than initial cost. Higher discount rate should be used to make present values lower than initial cost.

We know that:

$$\text{Payback period} = \frac{\text{Initial investment}}{\text{Annual cash inflow after tax}}$$

Substituting the values, we get:

$$\text{Payback period (A)} = \frac{10,000}{3,000} = 3.333 \text{ years}$$

$$\text{Payback period (B)} = \frac{50,000}{15,000} = 3.333 \text{ years}$$

From PVFA table, for n = 5, at PVFA = 3.333 interest rate should be higher than 15% to make present values lower than initial investment.

Year	$PVFA_{(16\%, 5)}$	Machine A		Machine B	
		Cash flow	PV	Cash flow	PV
1 – 5	3.274	3,000	9,822	15,000	49,110
Investment			10,000		50,000
NPV			–178		–890

We know that:

$$\text{IRR} = \text{L} + \frac{\text{PV of CFAT at L} - \text{PV of Initial Investment}}{\text{PV of CFAT at L} - \text{PV of CFAT at H}} \times (\text{H}-\text{L})\%$$

Substituting the values,

$$\text{IRR (A)} = 10 + \frac{11{,}373 - 10{,}000}{11{,}373 - 9{,}822} \times (16-10)\%$$

$$\text{IRR (A)} = 10 + 5.31 = 15.31\%$$

$$\text{IRR (B)} = 10 + \frac{56{,}865 - 50{,}000}{56{,}865 - 49{,}110} \times (16-10)\%$$

$$\text{IRR (B)} = 10 + 5.31 = 15.31\%.$$

Machine B has more net present value. Thus, purchase of machine B should be preferred if required rate of return is 10%.

Problem 4. A company is planning to buy a machine. Machine A and machine B are available in the market. The cash flows associated with the purchase are given below:

Year	Machine A	Machine B
0	–25,000	–30,000
1	7,000	2,500
2	6,600	3,600
3	5,500	5,000
4	4,000	8,000
5	2,000	11,000

Cost of capital is 10%.

Rank these machines on the basis of:

(a) Payback period;

(b) Net present value.

Solution: (a) Payback period

Computation of cumulative cash flows

Year	Machine A		Machine B	
	Cash flows	Cum. Cash flows	Cash flows	Cum. Cash flows
1	7,000	7,000	2,500	2,500
2	6,600	13,600	3,600	6,100
3	5,500	19,100	5,000	11,100
4	4,000	23,100	8,000	19,100
5	2,000	25,100	11,000	30,100

We know that payback period is calculated by following formula:

$$\text{Payback period} = n^{\text{th}} \text{ period} + \frac{\text{Original cost} - \text{Cumulative CFAT for } n\text{th period}}{\text{CFAT for } (n+1)^{\text{th}} \text{ period}}$$

Substituting the values, we get:

$$\text{Payback period (A)} = 4 + \frac{25{,}000 - 23{,}100}{2{,}000}$$

$$\text{Payback period (A)} = 4.95 \text{ years}$$

$$\text{Payback period (B)} = 4 + \frac{30{,}000 - 19{,}100}{11{,}000}$$

$$\text{Payback period (B)} = 4.99 \text{ years}$$

Rankings of machines are: machine (A), rank 1 and machine (B) rank 2.

(b) Computation of net present value

Year	$PVF_{(10\%, n)}$	Machine A		Machine B	
		Cash flows	PV	Cash flows	PV
1	0.909	7,000	6,363	2,500	2,273
2	0.826	6,600	5,452	3,600	2,974
3	0.751	5,500	4,131	5,000	3,755
4	0.683	4,000	2,732	8,000	5,464
5	0.621	2,000	1,242	11,000	6,831
Total			19,921		21,297
Investment			25,000		30,000
Net present value			–5,079		–8,703

Rankings of machines are: machine (A) rank 1 and machine (B) rank 2.

Problem 5. A company is considering to purchase a machine. Two machines A and B are available each costing ₹ 8,00,000. In comparing the profitability of machines a discount rate of 10% is to be used. Earnings after tax are expected to be as follows:

Year	Machine A	Machine B
1	3,00,000	1,00,000
2	4,00,000	3,00,000
3	4,00,000	3,00,000
4	3,00,000	6,00,000
5	2,00,000	4,00,000

You are required to indicate which of the machine would be profitable using the following methods of ranking investment proposals:

(i) ARR method

(ii) Net present value method.

Solution: (i) ARR Method

Average profit (A) = (3,00,000 + 4,00,000 + 4,00,000 + 3,00,000 + 2,00,000) ÷ 5 = ₹ 3,20,000

Average profit (B) = (1,00,000 + 3,00,000 + 3,00,000 + 6,00,000 + 4,00,000) ÷ 5 = ₹ 3,40,000

We know that:

$$\text{Average Rate of Return} = \frac{\text{Average profit after tax}}{\text{Average investment}} \times 100$$

Substituting values,

$$\text{Average Rate of Return (A)} = \frac{3,20,000}{4,00,000} \times 100 = 80\%$$

$$\text{Average Rate of Return (B)} = \frac{3,40,000}{4,00,000} \times 100 = 85\%$$

Machine B will be profitable.

(ii) Computation of net present value

Year	$PVF_{(10\%, n)}$	Machine A		Machine B	
		EAT	PV	EAT	PV
1	0.909	3,00,000	2,72,700	1,00,000	90,900
2	0.826	4,00,000	3,30,400	3,00,000	2,47,800
3	0.751	4,00,000	3,00,400	3,00,000	2,25,300
4	0.683	3,00,000	2,04,900	6,00,000	4,09,800
5	0.621	2,00,000	1,24,200	4,00,000	2,48,400
Total			12,32,600		12,22,200
Investment			8,00,000		8,00,000
NPV			4,32,600		4,22,200

Machine A will be profitable.

Problem 6. A company requires an initial investment of ₹ 75,000. The estimated net cash flows are as follows:

Year	Net cash flow
1	8,000
2	8,000
3	8,000
4	8,000
5	11,000
6	16,000
7	20,000
8	18,000
9	15,000
10	10,000

Using 10% as cost of capital (rate of discount), determine:

(a) Payback Period;

(b) Net Present Value. *(D.U., B.Com. 2009)*

Solution: Cumulative cash flow

Year	Net cash flow	Cumulative cash flow
1	8,000	8,000
2	8,000	16,000
3	8,000	24,000
4	8,000	32,000
5	11,000	43,000
6	16,000	59,000
7	20,000	79,000
8	18,000	97,000
9	15,000	1,13,000
10	10,000	1,23,000

(a) Payback Period: We know that payback period is calculated by following formula:

$$\text{Payback period} = n^{\text{th}} \text{ period} + \frac{\text{Original cost} - \text{Cumulative CFAT for } n^{\text{th}} \text{ period}}{\text{CFAT for } (n+1)^{\text{th}} \text{ period}}$$

₹ 59,000 of the investment is recovered by 6th year. Substituting the values, we get:

$$\text{Payback period} = 6 + \frac{75{,}000 - 59{,}000}{20{,}000}$$

Payback period = 6.8 years

Thus, the payback period is 6.8 years.

(b) Net Present Value Method:

Year	Net Cash Flow	$PVF_{(10\%, n)}$	Present Value
1	8000	0.909	7,272
2	8000	0.826	6,608
3	8000	0.751	6,008
4	8000	0.683	5,464
5	11000	0.621	6,831
6	16000	0.564	9,024
7	20000	0.513	10,260
8	18000	0.467	8,406
9	15000	0.424	6,360
10	10000	0.386	3,860
Total			**70,093**

We know that:

Net Present Value = Total Present Value – Investment

Substituting the values,

Net Present Value = ₹ 70,093 – ₹ 75,000

= – ₹ 4,907

Thus, the net present value is – ₹ 4,907.

Problem 7. X Ltd. is planning to purchase a machine for ₹ 1,50,000 which is likely to generate the following earnings in the next five years:

Year	1	2	3	4	5
Earnings (₹)	50,000	55,000	60,000	62,000	65,000

The purchase of machine has resulted in increase of working capital by ₹ 15,000. The machine will be depreciated on SLM basis and has salvage value of ₹ 25,000. The company is subject to tax rate of 50%. Should the machine be purchased if the cost of capital is 10% (use NPV method)?

(D.U., B.Com. 2010)

Solution: Statement of present value of cash flows after tax

Particulars	Year 1	Year 2	Year 3	Year 4	Year 5
Earnings	50,000	55,000	60,000	62,000	65,000
Less: Depreciation[1]	25,000	25,000	25,000	25,000	25,000
Profit before tax	25,000	30,000	35,000	37,000	40,000

Less: tax @ 50%	12,500	15,000	17,500	18,500	20,000
Profit after tax	12,500	15,000	17,500	18,500	20,000
Add: Depreciation	25,000	25,000	25,000	25,000	25,000
Add: Release of working capital					15,000
Add: Salvage value					25,000
Cash flow after tax	37,500	40,000	42,500	43,500	85,000
$PVF_{(10\%, n)}$	0.909	0.826	0.751	0.683	0.621
Present value of cash flows	34,087.5	33,040	31,917.5	29,710.5	52,785

Total Present value of all cash flows = ₹ 1,81,540.5

Initial investment = Price of machinery + increase in working capital

= 1,50,000 + 15,000 = ₹ 1,65,000

Net Present Value = ₹ 1,81,540.5 – ₹ 1,65,000 = ₹ 16,540.5

Since Net Present Value (NPV) is positive, machine should be purchased.

Note 1. Depreciation = ₹ 25,000

Price of machine ₹ 1,50,000 and salvage value = ₹ 25,000.

Problem 8. A company is considering the following investment projects:

Project	Cash flows (₹)			
	Year 0	Year 1	Year 2	Year 3
A	–10,000	10,000	–	–
B	–10,000	7,500	7,500	–
C	–10,000	2,000	4,000	12,000
D	–10,000	10,000	3,000	3,000

1. Rank the projects according to (i) Payback period method and (ii) NPV method assuming discounting rate of 10%.
2. Assuming that the projects are mutually exclusive, which one should be accepted?

(D.U., B.Com. 2011)

Solution: (i) Cumulative Cash Flows

Year	Project A		Project B		Project C		Project D	
	Cash flow	Cumulative cash flow	Cash flow	Cumulative cash flow	Cash flow	Cumulative cash flow	Cash flow	Cumulative cash flow
1	10,000	10,000	7,500	7,500	2,000	2,000	10,000	10,000
2		10,000	7,500	15,000	4,000	6,000	3,000	13,000
3		10,000		15,000	12,000	18,000	3,000	16,000

We know that:

$$\text{Payback period} = n^{\text{th}} \text{ period} + \frac{\text{Original cost} - \text{Cumulative CFAT for } n^{\text{th}} \text{ period}}{\text{CFAT for } (n+1)^{\text{th}} \text{ period}}$$

Substituting the values,

Project A,

$$\text{Payback period} = 1 + \frac{10{,}000 - 10{,}000}{0} = 1 \text{ year}$$

Project B,

$$\text{Payback period} = 1 + \frac{10{,}000 - 7{,}500}{7{,}500} = 1.33 \text{ years}$$

Project C,

$$\text{Payback period} = 2 + \frac{10{,}000 - 6{,}000}{12{,}000} = 2.33 \text{ years}$$

Project D,

$$\text{Payback period} = 1 + \frac{10{,}000 - 10{,}000}{3{,}000} = 1 \text{ year}$$

Net Present Value of cash flows

Year	$PVF_{(10\%, n)}$	Project A		Project B		Project C		Project D	
		Cash flow	PV	Cash flow	PV	Cash flow	PV	Cash flow	PV
1	0.909	10,000	9,090	7,500	6,817.5	2,000	1,818	10,000	9,090
2	0.826			7,500	6,195	4,000	3,304	3,000	2,478
3	0.751					12,000	9,012	3,000	2,253
Total PV			9,090		13,012.5		14,134		13,821
Investment			10,000		10,000		10,000		10,000
NPV			–910		3,012.5		4,134		3,821

Evaluation of projects

Particulars	Project			
	A	B	C	D
Payback period	1 year	1.33 years	2.33 years	1 year
Ranking	1	2	3	1
NPV	–910	3,012.5	4,134	3,821
Ranking	4	3	1	2

Project C has better net present value. It should be selected.

Problem 9. XYZ Ltd. is planning to start a project which requires an initial outlay of ₹ 1,00,000 on the purchase of a machine having a life of 5 years. It is expected to generate year ending profits (before depreciation and taxes), of ₹ 50,000, ₹ 30,000, ₹ 20,000, ₹ 30,000 and ₹ 40,000 from the end of first year to the end of fifth year. Assuming that the company pays Income tax @ 40% and uses straight-line method of depreciation with no salvage value, you are required to calculate:

(a) Payback Period,

(b) Average Rate of Return. *(D.U., B.Com. 2012)*

Solution: Statement of cash flows after tax

Particulars	Year 1	Year 2	Year 3	Year 4	Year 5
Profits	50,000	30,000	20,000	30,000	40,000
Less: Depreciation[1]	20,000	20,000	20,000	20,000	20,000
Profit before tax	30,000	10,000	0	10,000	20,000
Less: Tax @ 40%	12,000	4,000	0	4,000	8,000
Profit after tax	18,000	6,000	0	6,000	12,000
Add: Depreciation	20,000	20,000	20,000	20,000	20,000
Cash flow after tax	38,000	26,000	20,000	26,000	32,000
Cumulative cash flow after tax	38,000	64,000	84,000	1,10,000	1,42,500

(a) Payback period is calculated as given below:

$$\text{Payback period} = n^{\text{th}} \text{ period} + \frac{\text{Original cost} - \text{Cumulative CFAT for } n^{\text{th}} \text{ period}}{\text{CFAT for } (n+1)^{\text{th}} \text{ period}}$$

Substituting the values,

$$\text{Payback period} = 3 + \frac{1,00,000 - 84,000}{26,000}$$

Payback period = 3.62 years

(b) We know that:

$$\text{Average rate of return} = \frac{\text{Average profit}}{\text{Average investment}} \times 100$$

Here, Total profit = 18,000 + 6,000 + 0 + 6,000 + 12,000 = ₹ 42,000

Average profit = ₹ 42,000 ÷ 5 = ₹ 8,400

Average investment = 1,00,000 ÷ 2 = ₹ 50,000

By substituting the values,

$$\text{Average rate of return} = \frac{8,400}{50,000} \times 100$$

ARR = 16.8%.

Problem 10. Dayal Ltd. is presently having a manually operated machine which was purchased ten years ago. It has a book value of ₹ 1,40,000 and remaining life of ten years. Salvage value after 10 years is ₹ 40,000. The machine has recently begun causing problems with frequent breakdowns and is costing the company ₹ 20,000 per year in maintenance expenses. The company is considering replacing the old machine with a fully automatic machine. It has been offered ₹ 1,00,000 for old machine as a trade-in on the automatic model which has a list price (before allowance for trade-in) of ₹ 2,20,000. It is expected to have a ten-year life and a salvage value of ₹ 20,000. The new machine will require installation modifications costing ₹ 40,000, but it is estimated to have a cost savings of ₹ 80,000 per year. Maintenance costs of new machine are included in the purchase contract and are borne by the machine manufacturer. The tax rate is 40% (applicable to revenue income as well as capital gain/loss). Straight-line depreciation over ten years will be used. The company expects a minimum return of 12% per annum on new/additional investments. Should the machine be replaced? *(D.U., B.Com. 2012)*

Solution: Statement of incremental cash flows

Particulars	Year 0	Year 1 – 9	Year 10
Cost of new machine	–2,20,000		
Add: Installation cost	–40,000		
Less: Salvage value of old machine	1,00,000		
Less: Tax savings on sale of old machine	16,000		
Cost savings		80,000	80,000
Add: Savings on maintenance		20,000	20,000
Less: Incremental depreciation		14,000	14,000
Profit before tax		86,000	86,000
Less: Tax		34,400	34,400
Profit after tax		51,600	51,600
Add: Incremental depreciation		14,000	14,000
Add: Incremental salvage value			–20,000
Incremental cash flow	–1,44,000	65,600	45,600

Calculation of net present value of incremental cash flow

Particulars	Year 0	Year 1 – 9	Year 10
Cash flow	–1,44,000	65,600	45,600
$PVF_{(12\%, n)}$	1.00	5.328	0.322
Present value	–1,44,000	3,49,517	14,683

Net present value = –1,44,000 + 3,49,517 + 14,683 = 2,20,200

Since present value of incremental cash flow is positive machinery should be purchased.

Notes: Depreciation on new machine = (2,60,000 – 20,000) ÷ 10 = ₹ 24,000
Depreciation on old machine = (1,40,000 – 40,000) ÷ 10 = ₹ 10,000
Incremental depreciation = ₹ 14,000
Loss on sale of old machine = 1,40,000 – 1,00,000 = ₹ 40,000.

Problem 11. Banani Ltd. purchased a machine three years ago at a cost of ₹ 35,000. At that time machine was expected to have a life of 7 years and nil scrap value after its economic life. Its annual cash inflow before taxation and depreciation are ₹ 22,000. Finance manager wants to replace it with a new machine having annual cash inflow before depreciation and taxes of ₹ 30,000. Cost of the new machine is ₹ 50,000 and its estimated life is 4 years with scrap value of ₹ 2,000. Present scrap value of old machine is ₹ 10,000. Straight-line method of depreciation is used by the company. Corporate tax rate is 35%. Cost of capital is 12%. Find out different cash flows associated with this replacement proposal. Advise finance manager regarding the acceptability of this proposal on the basis of NPV method. *(D.U., B.Com. 2013)*

Solution: Computation of incremental cash flow

Particulars	Year 0	Year 1 - 3	Year 4
Cost of new machine	–50,000		
Less: Scrap value of old machine	10,000		
Less: Capital loss on sale of old machine	3,500		
Incremental cash flow		8,000	8,000
Less: Incremental depreciation		7,000	7,000
Cash flow before tax		1,000	1,000
Less: Tax		350	350
Net Cash flow		650	650
Add: Incremental depreciation		7,000	7,000
Salvage value of new machine			2,000
Cash flow after tax	–36,500	7,650	9,650
$PVF_{(12\%, n)}$	1	2.402	0.636
	–36,500	18,375	6,137

Net present value = –36,500 + 18375 + 6137 = ₹ –11988

Since the net present value of project is negative, it should not be accepted.

Notes: Depreciation on new machine = (50,000 – 2,000) ÷ 4 = ₹ 12,000
Depreciation on old machine = 35,000 ÷ 7 = ₹ 5,000
Capital loss on sale of old machine = 20,000 – 10,000 = ₹ 10,000.

Problem 12. A project requires an initial outlay of ₹ 20,000 and having life of 5 years. It generates year ending profits before depreciation and taxes of ₹ 12,000, ₹ 10,000, ₹ 8,000, ₹ 6,000 and ₹ 5,000. It is depreciated on a straight-line method. Tax rate is 35%. Compute the following:

(i) Payback period,

(ii) Accounting Rate of Return,

(iii) Acceptability of this period if project should satisfy both the criteria of standard payback period of 3 years and standard accounting rate of return of 20%. *(D.U., B.Com. 2013)*

Solution: Computation of cash flows after tax

Particulars	Year1	Year 2	Year 3	Year 4	Year 5
Profits	12,000	10,000	8,000	6,000	5,000
Less: Depreciation	4,000	4,000	4,000	4,000	4,000
Profits before tax	8,000	6,000	4,000	2,000	1,000
Less: Tax	2,800	2,100	1,400	700	350
Profit after tax	5,200	3,900	2,600	1,300	650
Add: Depreciation	4,000	4,000	4,000	4,000	4,000
Cash flow after tax	9,200	7,900	6,600	5,300	4,650
Cumulative	9,200	17,100	23,700	29,000	33,650

(i) We know that:

$$\text{Payback period} = n^{\text{th}} \text{ period} + \frac{\text{Original cost} - \text{Cumulative CFAT for } n^{\text{th}} \text{ period}}{\text{CFAT for } (n+1)^{\text{th}} \text{ period}}$$

Substituting the values,

$$\text{Payback period} = 2 + \frac{20{,}000 - 17{,}100}{6{,}600}$$

$$= 2.44 \text{ years.}$$

(ii) We know that:

$$\text{Accounting rate of return} = \frac{\text{Average profit ater tax}}{\text{Average investment}} \times 100$$

Here, Total profit = 5,200 + 3,900 + 2,600 + 1,300 + 650 = ₹ 13,650

Average profit = ₹ 13,650 ÷ 5 = ₹ 2,730

Average investment = 20,000 ÷ 2 = ₹ 10,000

By substituting the values,

$$\text{Accounting rate of return} = \frac{2{,}730}{10{,}000} \times 100$$

ARR = 27.3%.

(iii) The project satisfies both the criteria. Hence, the project is acceptable.

Problem 13. A company is considering the replacement of an existing machine. It is faced with two alternatives:

(i) To buy machine A which is similar to the existing machine.
(ii) To buy machine B which is more expensive and has higher capacity.
(iii) The cash flows after taxes (in lakhs of ₹) at present level of operations are as under:

Year	0	1	2	3	4	5
Machine A	–25	–	10	20	14	14
Machine B	–40	20	28	32	34	30

Cost of capital is 10%. Depreciation is charged on straight-line basis. Calculate:
(i) Net Present Value
(ii) Profitability Index.
Advise the company about the better alternative. *(D.U., B.Com. 2015)*

Solution: Computation of present value of cash flows after tax

Year	$PVF_{(10\%, n)}$	Machine A		Machine B	
		CFAT	PV	CFAT	PV
1	0.909	5	4.545	28	25.452
2	0.826	15	12.390	36	29.736
3	0.751	25	18.775	40	30.040
4	0.683	19	12.977	42	28.686
5	0.621	19	11.799	38	23.598
Total PV			60.486		137.512
Investment			25		40
NPV			35.486		97.512

Cash flows after tax = Earnings after tax + depreciation
(i) Both machines have positive net present values.
(ii) The profitability index:
Machine A = 60.486 ÷ 25 = 2.42
Machine B = 137.512 ÷ 40 = 3.44
Purchasing of machine B is better option.

Problem 14. A company is considering to purchase a machine. Two machines A and B are available each costing ₹ 50,000. Earnings after taxation are expected to be as follows:

Year	Machine A	Machine B
1	15,000	5,000
2	20,000	15,000
3	25,000	20,000
4	15,000	30,000
5	10,000	20,000

You are required to indicate which of the machines would be profitable using:

(i) Payback Method,

(ii) Return on Investment Method. *(D.U., B.Com. 2016)*

Solution: Computation of cash flows

Year	Machine A			Machine B		
	EAT	CFAT	Cu. CFAT	EAT	CFAT	Cu. CFAT
1	15,000	25,000	25,000	5,000	15,000	15,000
2	20,000	30,000	55,000	15,000	25,000	40,000
3	25,000	35,000	90,000	20,000	30,000	70,000
4	15,000	25,000	1,15,000	30,000	40,000	1,10,000
5	10,000	20,000	1,35,000	20,000	30,000	1,40,000
Total	85,000			90,000		

Depreciation (A) = 50,000 ÷ 5 = ₹ 10,000

Depreciation (B) = 50,000 ÷ 5 = ₹ 10,000

(i) Payback Period is calculated by:

$$\text{Payback period} = n^{\text{th}}\ \text{period} + \frac{\text{Original cost} - \text{Cumulative CFAT for } n^{\text{th}}\ \text{period}}{\text{CFAT for } (n+1)^{\text{th}}\ \text{period}}$$

Substituting the values in the formula,

$$\text{Payback period (A)} = 1 + \frac{50{,}000 - 25{,}000}{30{,}000}$$

Payback period (A) = 1.833 years

$$\text{Payback period (B)} = 2 + \frac{50{,}000 - 40{,}000}{30{,}000}$$

Payback period (B) = 2.333 years

Purchasing of machine A is better.

(ii) Return on Investment method:

$$\text{Return on investment} = \frac{\text{Average profit after tax}}{\text{Average investment}} \times 100$$

Substituting values,

$$\text{Accounting rate of return (A)} = \frac{17{,}000}{25{,}000} \times 100 = 68\%$$

$$\text{Accounting rate of return (B)} = \frac{18{,}000}{25{,}000} \times 100 = 72\%$$

Purchasing of machine B is better.

Problem 15. A choice is to be made between two proposals which require an equal investment of ₹ 50,000 each and are expected to generate net cash flows as under:

Year	Project A	Project B
1	25,000	10,000
2	15,000	12,000
3	10,000	18,000
4	Nil	25,000
5	12,000	8,000
6	6,000	4,000

Which project should be chosen under:

(a) Payback period,

(b) Average rate of return method? *(D.U., B.Com. 2016)*

Solution: Computation of cash flows

Year	Machine A		Machine B	
	CFAT	Cu. CFAT	CFAT	Cu. CFAT
1	25,000	25,000	10,000	10,000
2	15,000	40,000	12,000	22,000
3	10,000	50,000	18,000	40,000
4	0	50,000	25,000	65,000
5	12,000	62,000	8,000	73,000
6	6,000	68,000	4,000	77,000

(a) Payback Period is calculated by:

$$\text{Payback period} = n^{\text{th}} \text{ period} + \frac{\text{Original cost} - \text{Cumulative CFAT for } n^{\text{th}} \text{ period}}{\text{CFAT for } (n+1)^{\text{th}} \text{ period}}$$

Substituting the values in the formula,

Payback period (A) = 3 years

$$\text{Payback period (B)} = 3 + \frac{50{,}000 - 40{,}000}{25{,}000}$$

Payback period (B) = 3.4 years

The Project A should be chosen.

(b) Return on Investment method:

EAT = CFAT – Depreciation

Computation of cash flows after tax

Year	Machine A		Machine B	
	CFAT	EAT	CFAT	EAT
1	25,000	16,667	10,000	1,667
2	15,000	6,667	12,000	3,667
3	10,000	1,667	18,000	9,667
4	0	–8,333	25,000	16,667
5	12,000	3,667	8,000	–333
6	6,000	–2,333	4,000	–4,333
Total		**18,002**		**27,002**

Depreciation (A) = 50,000 ÷ 6 = ₹ 8,333

Depreciation (B) = 50,000 ÷ 6 = ₹ 8,333

$$\text{Average rate of return} = \frac{\text{Average profit after tax}}{\text{Average investment}} \times 100$$

Substituting values,

$$\text{Average rate of return (A)} = \frac{3{,}000}{25{,}000} \times 100 = 12\%$$

$$\text{Average rate of return (B)} = \frac{4{,}500}{25{,}000} \times 100 = 18\%$$

The Project B should be chosen.

Problem 16. A company is considering to purchase a machine. Two machines X and Y are available each costing ₹ 1,50,000. Earnings after taxation are expected to be as follows:

Year	Machine X	Machine Y
1	40,000	15,000
2	50,000	50,000
3	85,000	60,000
4	55,000	80,000
5	40,000	80,000

You are required to indicate which of the machines would be profitable using:

(i) Payback Method,

(ii) Return on Investment Method.

Solution: Computation of cash flows

Year	Machine X			Machine Y		
	EAT	CFAT	Cu. CFAT	EAT	CFAT	Cu. CFAT
1	40,000	70,000	70,000	15,000	45,000	45,000
2	50,000	80,000	1,50,000	50,000	80,000	1,25,000
3	85,000	1,15,000	2,65,000	60,000	90,000	2,15,000
4	55,000	85,000	3,50,000	80,000	1,10,000	3,25,000
5	40,000	70,000	4,20,000	80,000	1,10,000	4,35,000
Total	2,70,000			2,85,000		

Depreciation (X) = 1,50,000 ÷ 5 = ₹ 30,000

Depreciation (Y) = 1,50,000 ÷ 5 = ₹ 30,000

(i) Payback Period is calculated by:

$$\text{Payback period} = n^{\text{th}} \text{ period} + \frac{\text{Original cost} - \text{Cumulative CFAT for } n^{\text{th}} \text{ period}}{\text{CFAT for } (n+1)^{\text{th}} \text{ period}}$$

Substituting the values in the formula,

$$\text{Payback period (X)} = 2 + \frac{1{,}50{,}000 - 1{,}50{,}000}{1{,}15{,}000}$$

Payback period (X) = 2 years

$$\text{Payback period (Y)} = 2 + \frac{1{,}50{,}000 - 1{,}25{,}000}{90{,}000}$$

Payback period (Y) = 2.278 years

Purchasing of machine X is better.

(ii) Return on Investment method:

$$\text{Return on investment} = \frac{\text{Average profit after tax}}{\text{Average investment}} \times 100$$

Substituting values,

$$\text{Accounting rate of return (X)} = \frac{54{,}000}{75{,}000} \times 100 = 72\%$$

$$\text{Accounting rate of return (Y)} = \frac{57{,}000}{75{,}000} \times 100 = 76\%$$

Purchasing of machine Y is better.

THEORETICAL QUESTIONS

1. What are the various techniques of capital budgeting decisions? Explain them briefly. *(D.U., B.Com. 2009)*
2. What is meant by capital budgeting decisions? What are its main features? Explain the payback period method and profitability index method of capital budgeting. *(D.U., B.Com. 2010)*
3. Distinguish between 'Net Present Value' and 'Internal Rate of Return' methods of evaluating a capital budgeting proposal. *(D.U., B.Com. 2012)*
4. Explain the significance of capital budgeting for a firm.
5. "The payback period is more a method of liquidity rather than profitability." Examine the statement explaining the payback period method of capital budgeting.
6. What is payback period? What are the advantages and limitations of payback period method of capital budgeting?
7. Why does the net present value method favour larger projects over smaller ones when used to choose between mutually exclusive projects? Is this a problem?

PRACTICAL PROBLEMS

1. Rama Ltd. is considering two mutually exclusive machines to meet the rapidly rising demand for its product. The cash flows after taxes (in ₹ Lakhs) under two alternatives are as follows:

Year	0	1 – 5
Machine A	–25	10
Machine B	–40	14

The company's cost of capital is 10%. Compute net present value and profitability index for both the machines and advise the company which machine should be brought. Specify the reason also for your advice. *(D.U., B.Com. 2009, Corres.)*
[**Ans.** NPV (A) = ₹ 12,91,000, NPV (B) = ₹ 13,07,400, PI (A) = 1.516, PV (B) = 1.326]

2. Shakti Ltd. is considering the introduction of a new product for which two alternative machines are available in the market. Cash flows after taxes (in ₹) associated with the machine are given below:

Year	0	1 – 5
Machine A	–10,000	3,343
Machine B	–50,000	15,629

Compute NPV and IRR for both the machines and advise the company which machine should be purchased. State the reason for your advice also. *(D.U., B.Com. 2010, Corres.)*
[**Ans.** NPV (A)@10% = ₹ 2,673, NPV(B) = ₹ 9,250, IRR(A) = 20%, IRR (B) =17%]

3. PQR Ltd. is evaluating the following two mutually exclusive proposals:

Particulars	Project P	Project R
Outlay	₹ 50,000	₹ 70,000
Annual net inflows	₹ 18,000	₹ 21,000
Life	8 years	8 years
Scrap value	₹ 5,000	₹ 4,000

Evaluate the proposals if the discount rate is 12% using Net Present Value and Profitability Index for both the projects and advise the company which project should be bought? Specify the reasons for your advice. *(D.U., B. Com. 2011, Corres.)*

[**Ans.** NPV (A) = 41,444, NPV (B) = 35,944, PI (A) = 1.83, PI (B) =1.51]

4. A company is planning to buy a machine. Machine A and machine B are available in the market. The cash flows associated with the purchase are given below:

Year	Machine A	Machine B
0	–20,000	–32,000
1	7,000	2,500
2	6,600	3,600
3	5,500	5,000
4	4,000	8,000
5	2,000	11,000

Cost of capital is 10%.

Rank these machines on the basis of:

(a) Payback period;

(b) Net present value. *(D.U., B.Com. 2011, Corres.)*

[**Ans.** PB (A) = 2.97 years, PB (B) = 4.46 years, NPV (A) = 80.9, NPV(B) = 10,703.9]

5. A company is considering to purchase a machine. Two machines A and B are available each costing ₹ 10,00,000. In comparing the profitability of machines a discount rate of 10% is to be used. Earnings after tax are expected to be as follows:

Year	Machine A	Machine B
1	3,00,000	1,00,000
2	4,00,000	3,00,000
3	5,00,000	4,00,000
4	3,00,000	6,00,000
5	2,00,000	4,00,000

You are required to indicate which of the machines would be profitable using the following methods of ranking investment proposals:

(i) ARR method

(ii) Net present value method (*D.U., B.Com. 2012, Corres.*)

[**Ans.** ARR (A) = 68%, ARR (B) = 72%, NPV (A) = ₹ 3,07,700, NPV (B) = ₹ 2,97,300]

6. Machine A costs ₹ 1,00,000 and machine B costs ₹ 1,20,000. The expected cash flows after tax (CFAT) are as follows:

Year	Machine A (₹)	Machine B (₹)
1	20,000	–
2	60,000	60,000
3	40,000	60,000
4	30,000	80,000
5	20,000	–

At 10% opportunity cost, which machine should be selected on the basis of profitability Index method. (*D.U., B.Com. 2013, Corres.*)

[**Ans.** PI (A) = 1.30, PI (B) = 1.24]

7. From the following information, calculate payback period and NPV at 10% for the two machines X and Y costing ₹ 50,000 and ₹ 75,000 respectively. The cash flows (₹) after tax are as follows:

Year	Machine X	Machine Y
1	7,000	15,000
2	8,000	30,000
3	10,000	20,000
4	15,000	30,000
5	20,000	20,000

Which machine should be preferred and why? (*D.U., B.Com. 2013, Corres.*)

[**Ans.** PB (X) = 4.5 years, PB (Y) = 3.33 years, NPV (X) = ₹ –6,854, NPV (Y) = ₹ 11,345]

8. The cost of a machine is ₹ 90,000 with installation of ₹ 10,000. Its expected life is 5 years. It is expected to generate profits before depreciation and tax of ₹ 30,000 annually for 5 years. Tax rate is 30%. Calculate IRR. Find out whether project is acceptable or not if the cost of capital is 10%. (*D.U., B.Com. 2013, Corres.*)

[**Ans.** IRR = 10.93, Project should be accepted]

9. A company is considering the following investment projects:

Project	Cash flows (₹)			
	Year 0	Year 1	Year 2	Year 3
A	–10,000	10,000	–	–
B	–10,000	7,500	7,5000	–

C	–10,000	2,000	4,000	12,000
D	–10,000	10,000	3,000	3,000

(a) Rank the projects according to payback method and NPV method assuming discount rate of 10%.

(b) Assuming that the projects are mutually exclusive, which one should be accepted?

(D.U., B.Com. 2014, Corres.)

[**Ans.** NPV (A) = ₹ –910, NPV (B) = ₹ 3,013, NPV(C) = ₹ 4,134, NPV (D) = ₹ 3,821]

10. A company is considering an investment proposal to purchase a machine costing ₹ 2,50,000. The machine has a life expectancy of 5 years and no salvage value. The company's tax rate is 40%. The company uses straight-line method of providing depreciation. The estimated earnings after taxes from the machine are as follows:

Year	Earnings after taxes (₹)
1	6,000
2	12,000
3	24,000
4	30,000
5	60,000

You are required to calculate:

(i) Average/Accounting Rate of Return

(ii) Payback Period

(iii) Internal Rate of Return. *(D.U., B.Com. 2015, N.C.)*

[**Ans.** ARR = 21.1%, PB = 3.73 Years, IRR = 14.2%]

11. A company is considering to install a new project costing ₹ 7,50,000 with life of 6 years and no salvage value. The tax rate is 40% and it uses straight-line method of depreciation. The estimated cash flows before depreciation and tax are as follows:

Year	Amount (₹)
1	1,50,000
2	2,00,000
3	2,25,000
4	2,50,000
5	3,00,000
6	4,00,000

You are required to calculate:

(i) Average/Accounting rate of return

(ii) Net present value at 12% discount rate

(iii) Profitability index at 12%. *(D.U., B.Com. 2015, Corres.)*

[**Ans.** ARR = 20.67%, NPV = ₹ 46,870, PI = 1.06]

12. A Ltd. is considering two machines P and Q to meet the increasing demand for its product. The cash flows (₹ Lakhs) after taxes of two machines are as follows:

Year	Machine P	Machine Q
0	–50	–80
1 – 5	20	28

The company's cost of capital is 10%. Calculate net present value and profitability index for both the machines and advise the company which machine should be bought. Also provide the reasons for your advice. *(D.U., B.Com. 2016, N.C.)*

[**Ans.** [NPV (P) = ₹ 25,82,000, NPV (Q) = ₹ 26,14,800, PI (P) = 1.52, PI (Q) = 1.33]

13. A machine costs ₹ 1,80,000 and is expected to produce profit after depreciation and tax during its useful life as follows:

Year	1	2	3	4	5
Amount (₹)	15,000	22,000	30,000	28,000	20,000

The machine will have a scrap value of ₹ 20,000 after its useful life of 5 years. Calculate:
(i) Average rate of return
(ii) Profitability index at a discount rate of 18% and
(iii) Payback Period. *(D.U., B.Com. 2016, N.C.)*

[**Ans.** ARR = 23%, PI = 0.99, Payback = 3.28 years]

14. A project costing ₹ 1,20,000 is expected to produce annual cash flows of ₹ 40,000 over a period of four years. Calculate the internal rate of return of the project. *(D.U., B.Com. 2016, Corres.)*

[**Ans.** 12.59%]

15. A project having a life of 5 years will cost ₹ 10,00,000. It is expected to provide the following income stream before depreciation and taxes during its life:

Year	Amount (₹)
1	2,50,000
2	3,50,000
3	5,00,000
4	4,00,000
5	2,50,000

Depreciation is charged on SLM basis and applicable tax rate is 40%. You are required to calculate (i) Average/Accounting rate of return (ii) payback period. *(D.U., B.Com. 2016, Corres.)*

[**Ans.** ARR = 18%, PB = 3.31 years]

Cost of Capital

5

Chapter Outline

5.1 Introduction
5.2 Concept of Cost of Capital
5.3 Capital Components
5.4 Factors Affecting Cost of Capital
5.5 Importance of Cost of Capital
5.6 Cost of Debt
5.7 Cost of Preference Shares
5.8 Cost of Equity Shares
5.9 Cost of Retained Earnings
5.10 Weighted Average of Cost of Capital

5.1 Introduction

An important element of capital budgeting techniques evaluating a project is cost of capital. Cost of capital is used as discount rate to compute the present values of cash flows. Cost of capital is the required rate of return on various types of financing. Thus, cost of capital is the rate of return the firm has to pay to various suppliers of funds in the firm.

The basic objective of a business firm is to maximise shareholders' wealth in the long run. The return earned in excess of cost of capital creates net present value of the firm. This net present value is an addition to shareholders' wealth. Thus, in the process of shareholders' wealth creation, the computation of cost of capital is a pre-requirement. In this chapter, computation of cost of capital for various sources of funds has been discussed.

5.2 Concept of Cost of Capital

The cost of capital of an asset is the rate of return which asset must produce to justify raising the funds for the asset.

According to Ezra Solomon, "The cost of capital is the minimum required rate of earnings or the cut-off rate for capital expenditures."

According to M.J. Gordon, "The cost of capital is the rate of return a company must earn on an investment to maintain the value of the company."

Thus, cost of capital is the minimum required rate of return on the invested funds so that the company can pay the compensation required by financial markets.

The cost of capital can be classified in several ways. Some of the classifications on the basis of comparability of costs of capital are described below:

1. **Specific and composite cost.** A firm raises financial resources for a project from various sources. Each source of finance has its own cost of capital. The cost of capital of a particular source is known as specific cost of capital. It is also known as component cost.

   Composite cost of capital refers to the combined cost of various sources of finance. This is also called overall cost of capital. It is generally calculated as weighted average of cost of capital (WACC). In evaluating a project weighted average cost of capital is used.

2. **Explicit and implicit cost.** Explicit cost of capital involves cash outflow as payment. In common jargon, explicit cost is basically the cost of raising the funds. When a firm pays interest of loan, dividend on equity shares, these interest and dividends are referred to as explicit cost of capital.

   Implicit cost of capital does not involve any outflow of cash. The cost of retained earnings is an implicit cost i.e., opportunity cost. The firm not declaring the dividend to its shareholders and retaining earnings has on its obligatory part to generate sufficient return on these retained earnings so as to compensate the shareholders. Thus, retained earnings have no explicit cost but they do have implicit cost.

5.3 Capital Components

The investor-supplied finance—debt, preferred stock, and common equity—are called capital components. Increases in asset have to be financed by increases in these capital components. The cost of each component is called its component cost. These costs are then combined to form a weighted average cost of capital, which is used in the company's capital budgeting analysis.

Thus, capital of a project comprises of following components:

1. Debt
2. Preferential stock
3. Equity stock
4. Retained earnings.

5.4 Factors Affecting Cost of Capital

A number of factors affect cost of capital of a firm. The important factors are given below:

1. **Risk free interest rate**: The risk free interest rate is the interest rate on the risk free and default free securities. The securities issued by governments are considered as risk free and default free in respect of periodic interest payments and principal payment at the time of maturity of the security. The risk free interest rate is the minimum cost of capital that firms can expect when raising the funds from the market. If a risk is involved in the project, a sum, known as risk premium, compensating for risk involved is added to the minimum cost of capital. Higher the degree of risk involved in the project, higher will be the cost of capital.

2. **Nature of business:** The nature of business affects cost of capital for a firm. Projects requiring heavy investment in fixed assets would incur a higher cost of capital as compared to those requiring small investment in fixed assets. Firms requiring funds for longer period of time would bear higher cost of capital.
3. **Business risk:** Business risk is very important factor affecting the cost of capital. Business risk is concerned with the firm's promise to pay interest and dividend to the investors. Business risk is measured by the response of profit before tax and interest to changes in sales of the firm. More risky businesses would have to bear higher cost of capital.
4. **Financial risk:** Financial risk is associated with fixed financial costs. Financial risk is caused by debt financing by a firm. Higher the proportion of debt in the firm's capital structure, higher the degree of financial risk involved. The increased financial risk raises the cost of capital for a firm.
5. **Goodwill of the firm:** The goodwill of a firm affects the cost of capital required by an existing firm. Good reputation of firm and its management reduces the cost of capital of the funds raised.
6. **Requirement of the firm:** The amount of funds required by a firm affects the cost of capital. A firm requiring large amount of funds bear a higher cost of capital in comparison of those firms which require less amount of funds. For large amount of funds external borrowing is almost necessity, which increases the cost of capital.

5.5 Importance of Cost of Capital

The concept of cost of capital is very important for several reasons mentioned below:

1. **Used in capital budgeting:** In the capital budgeting, the investment decisions are taken. To take an investment decision, net present value of cash inflows is compared with the cash outflow. The cost of Capital is used as discount rate in computing the present value of cash inflows of a firm. Thus, cost of capital is an integral part of investment decisions and provides a good measure of judging the relative worth of investment proposals. The capital budgeting is based on the cost of capital of a project.
2. **Useful in designing the capital structure of the company:** The capital structure of a firm may comprise various sources of funds such as equity shares, preferential shares, debt and retained earnings. Each source of fund has its own cost of capital and the financial risk associated with it. For example, debt has minimum cost of capital, but the more financial risk is associated with it. As the proportion of debt in capital structure increases, the degree of financial risk also increases. On the other hand, equity capital has highest cost of capital and the minimum financial risk. Thus, capital structure of a firm should be such that maximum return is provided and involves minimum risk. The specific costs of capital helps in deciding the suitable mix of different sources of funds. The minimisation of overall cost of capital results in the maximisation of shareholders' wealth.
3. **Helpful in comparative study of various sources of finance:** The cost of capital helps in comparative analysis of various sources of funds. The cost of capital helps in selecting a source of funds to finance the requirements of a firm.

5.6 Cost of Debt

A security or instrument which bears a fixed financial charge is generally known as debt. For example, debentures, bonds, long-term loan etc. bear a fixed interest rate. The interest rate a firm pays on its new debt is defined as its before tax cost of debt. Thus, cost of debt is the rate of return demanded by the lenders or debenture holders of the firm who lend the money to the firm.

The basic purpose is to maximise the value of the firm. Since stock price depends on after tax cash flows, we should consider after tax cash flows. We adjust the interest rate downward due to debt's preferential tax treatment.

The after tax cost of debt is calculated as given below:

$$\text{After tax cost of debt} = \text{interest rate on debt} - \text{tax savings}$$
$$= i - \text{it}$$
$$= i\,(1 - t)$$

Where, i is interest rate of debt, and t is tax rate.

The rate at which the firm has borrowed in the past is irrelevant when cost of new capital is concerned. For these reasons, the yield to maturity on outstanding debt (which reflects the current market conditions) is a better measure of the cost of debt than coupon rate.

Debt is considered to be the cheapest source of finance due to preferential treatment given to it in regard to tax and payments. The cost of debt should be adjusted for floatation costs associated with issuing new debt.

The debt may be of two types:

1. Irredeemable debt
2. Redeemable debt.

1. Irredeemable debt. Irredeemable debt is also known perpetual debt. The calculation of cost of irredeemable debt is very simple as explained below:

(i) *Before tax cost of irredeemable debt*. The before tax cost of irredeemable debt is calculated by applying the following formula:

$$k_d = \frac{I}{B_0}$$

Where, k_d = cost of debt

B_0 = Issue Price (Net of discount, floatation cost and other costs) or market price

I = Annual Interest Payment.

Example 1. P Ltd. issued irredeemable debenture of ₹ 100 at discount rate of 10% carrying interest rate of 18%. Calculate the before tax cost of debt.

Solution: The issue price of debenture = ₹ 100 – ₹ 10 = ₹ 90

Annual interest = 18% of 100 = ₹ 18.

We know that:

$$k_d = \frac{I}{B_0}$$

Substituting the values,

$$k_d = \frac{18}{90} = 0.2$$

$$k_d = 20\%$$

(ii) *After tax cost of irredeemable debt.* The after tax cost of irredeemable debt is calculated by applying the following formula:

$$k_d = \frac{I}{B_0}(1-t)$$

Where, k_d = cost of debt

B_0 = Issue Price (Net of discount, premium, floatation cost and so on) or market price

I = Annual Interest Payment

t = Tax Rate.

Example 2. Rama Ltd. issued irredeemable perpetual debentures of ₹ 100 each carrying interest rate of 12%. The tax rate is 30%. Compute the cost of the debt:

(i) When debentures are issued at par.
(ii) When debentures are issued at 10% discount.
(iii) When debentures are issued at 10% premium.

Solution: Computation of cost of capital

Particulars	At par	10% discount	10% premium
Annual interest	12	12	12
Issue price	100	90	110
Before tax cost of capital	12%	13.33%	10.91%
After tax cost of capital	8.4%	9.33%	7.64%

2. Redeemable Debt. The time of maturity of redeemable debt is specified and at the time of maturity the principal amount is repaid back to the lender or bondholder.

The rate of discount which makes present value of cash inflows from the debt equal to the present value of cash outflows (issue price) is cost of debt. In case of bonds, it is known as Yield to Maturity (YTM) of the bond.

Present value of cash inflows = Present value of cash outflows

The cost of debt can be calculated by following equation:

$$B_0 = \sum_{i=1}^{n} \frac{I(1-t)}{(1+k_d)} + \frac{RV_n}{(1+k_d)^n}$$

Where, k_d = cost of debt

B_0 = Issue Price (Net of discount, premium, floatation cost and other costs) or market price

I = Annual Interest Payment

t = Tax Rate

RV = Redemption Value

n = life of debt in years

In approximation, the cost of debt can be calculated by following formula:

$$k_d = \frac{I(1-t) + \dfrac{(f + d + p_r - p_i)}{n}}{\dfrac{(RV + B_0)}{2}}$$

Where,
k_d = cost of debt

B_0 = Issue Price (Net of discount, premium, floatation cost and other costs)

I = Annual Interest Payment

t = Tax Rate

RV = Redemption Value

n = life of debt in years

f = floatation cost

d = discount on issue of debt

p_r = premium on redemption of debt

p_i = premium on issue of debt

Another form of above formula is given below:

$$k_d = \frac{I(1-t) + \dfrac{(RV - B_0)}{n}}{\dfrac{(RV + B_0)}{2}}$$

Where,
k_d = cost of debt

B_0 = Issue Price (Net of discount, premium, floatation cost and other costs) or market price

I = Annual Interest Payment

t = Tax Rate

RV = Redemption Value

n = life of debt in years.

Example 3. Avon Ltd. issues 12% debentures of ₹ 100 each to be redeemed after 10 years. The debenture is expected to be sold at 5% discount. Floatation cost of 1% is also incurred. The applicable tax rate is 40%. Compute the cost of debt.

Solution: We know that cost of debt:

$$k_d = \frac{I(1-t) + \dfrac{(RV - B_0)}{n}}{\dfrac{(RV + B_0)}{2}}$$

Substituting the values, we get:

$$k_d = \frac{12(1-0.4) + \dfrac{(100-94)}{10}}{\dfrac{(100+94)}{2}}$$

$$k_d = \frac{7.2+0.6}{97} = 0.0804$$

$k_d = 8.04\%$

$B_0 = 100 - 5 - 1 = 94$

Thus, cost of debt is 8.04%.

Example 4. A company issues 16% debentures of face value ₹ 100 redeemable after 5 years at a premium of 10%. The floatation cost is 7% and the tax rate is 40%. Find the cost of debt.

Solution: We know that cost of debt:

$$k_d = \frac{I(1-t) + \dfrac{(RV - B_0)}{n}}{\dfrac{(RV + B_0)}{2}}$$

Substituting the values, we get:

$$k_d = \frac{16(1-0.4) + \dfrac{(110-93)}{5}}{\dfrac{(110+93)}{2}}$$

$$k_d = \frac{9.6+3.4}{101.5} = 0.1281$$

$k_d = 12.81\%$

$B_0 = 100 - 7 = 93$

Thus, cost of debt is 12.81%.

Example 5. Damini Ltd. is planning to raise ₹ 100 crore by the issue of 14% debentures of ₹ 100 each at 10% discount. The underwriting expenses are expected to be 5%. Find out the cost of debentures in each of the following cases:

(i) If debentures are irredeemable.

(ii) If debentures are redeemable at the end of 10th year at 15% premium. Use short-cut method.

Assume tax rate is 40%.

Solution: (i) If debentures are irredeemable:

Issue price = 100 – 10 – 5 = ₹ 85

We know that:

P_0 = Issue Price (Net of discount, premium, floatation cost and so on) or market price

D = Annual Preference Dividend

RV = Redemption Value

n = Life of preference share capital in years.

There is an approximation formula for calculating cost of preference share.

$$k_p = \frac{D + \frac{(RV - P_0)}{n}}{\frac{(RV + P_0)}{2}}$$

Where, k_p = cost of preference share capital

P_0 = Issue Price (Net of discount, premium, floatation cost and so on) or market price

D = Annual Preference Dividend

RV = Redemption Value

n = Life of preference share capital in years.

The examples given below will clear the concept of calculation of cost redeemable preference shares:

Example 7. A company issues 12% redeemable shares having face value of ₹ 100 at a discount of 10% to be redeemed after 10 years at par. Find the cost of preference shares.

Solution: We know that:

$$k_p = \frac{D + \frac{(RV - P_0)}{n}}{\frac{(RV + P_0)}{2}}$$

Substituting the values,

$$k_p = \frac{12 + \frac{(100 - 90)}{10}}{\frac{(100 + 90)}{2}}$$

$$k_p = 0.1368 = 13.68\%.$$

Example 8. A company issues 14% preference shares (face value ₹ 100) with maturity of 10 years. The floating cost of 3% was incurred. Find the cost of preference shares.

Solution: We know that:

$$k_p = \frac{D + \frac{(RV - P_0)}{n}}{\frac{(RV + P_0)}{2}}$$

Substituting the values,

$$k_p = \frac{14 + \frac{(100-97)}{10}}{\frac{(100+97)}{2}}$$

$$k_p = 0.1452 = 14.52\%.$$

5.8 Cost of Equity Shares

The cost of equity shares is most difficult to compute as it involves measuring what the equity shareholders expect from the firm. It is also argued that the equity capital is cost free because the firm is not legally bound to pay the dividend to equity shareholders. This is not true because the investors invest in the equity share capital of the firm with the expectations of getting the dividend. The market value of equity share capital depends on the dividend expected, growth of firm and book value of firm. Thus, the rate of discount which equates the present value of expected dividends with the market value of equity share is the cost of equity share capital.

In brief, the cost of equity is equal to minimum rate of return that must be earned by the firm on new share capital financed investment in order to maintain its share price to the satisfaction of its equity shareholders.

There are two approaches to calculate the cost of equity share capital:

(i) Dividend approach

(ii) Capital asset pricing model (CAPM).

1. Dividend approach. The cost of capital depends on the future streams of dividends which the shareholders expects to receive from the firm. The viewpoint of this method is that equity shareholders expect not only a certain dividend per share but also an increase every year in such dividend. The following formula is used to find the cost of capital:

$$k_e = \frac{D_1}{P_0} + g$$

Where, k_e = Cost of equity share capital

P_0 = Issue Price (Net of discount, floatation cost and so on) or market price

D_1 = Expected dividend in next year

g = Constant growth rate in dividend.

The main limitation of the approach is that the cost of equity capital cannot be determined if the company is not paying the dividend.

Example 9. Find the cost of equity capital in the following cases:

(i) An ordinary share currently selling at ₹ 110 and paying dividend of ₹ 10 which is expected to grow at a rate of 10 percent.

(ii) A company's share is being quoted at ₹ 20 in the market. The company pays dividend of ₹ 2 per share and investors expect growth of 10 percent in dividends per year. Compute the cost of equity.

Solution:

(i) We know that:

$$k_e = \frac{D_1}{P_0} + g$$

Substituting the values,

$$k_e = \frac{10(1+0.1)}{110} + 0.10 = 0.10 + 0.10 = 0.20 = 20\%$$

(ii) We know that:

$$k_e = \frac{D_1}{P_0} + g$$

Substituting the values,

$$k_e = \frac{2(1+0.1)}{20} + 0.10 = 0.11 + 0.10 = 0.21 = 21\%$$

Example 10. The share of a company currently sells for ₹ 25. It is expected that the company will pay a dividend of ₹ 3 per share which will grow at 7% per year. Find the cost of equity.

Solution: We know that:

$$k_e = \frac{D_1}{P_0} + g$$

Substituting the values,

$$k_e = \frac{3}{25} + 0.07 = 0.12 + 0.07 = 0.19 = 19\%$$

2. Capital asset pricing model approach. The CAPM was originated by Professor William F. Sharpe in his article: "Capital Asset Prices: A Theory of Market Equilibrium under Conditions of Risk" in *Journal of Finance*, 1964. The CAPM is an extremely important theory in finance. The CAPM provides an alternative approach for the calculation of the cost of equity.

There are two types of risks associated with any equity stock:

(i) Systematic risk

(ii) Unsystematic risk.

(i) Systematic risk: This risk arises due to systematic factor such as change in government policy, change in trade policy, political issues. The risk that is not diversifiable and linked to the system is called systematic risk. This type of risk affects the whole market. For example, economic down turn in the economy, political changes affect the whole system. This risk is also known as market risk. Since the risk is related to the system, it is not possible for an individual firm to avert this risk.

(ii) Unsystematic risk: Unsystematic risk arises due to the particular factors related to the firm. These factors can be controlled so as to avoid the risk. For example, factors like, change in the demand of products of the firm, labour strike, management inefficiency, increase in the competition in the market etc. Unsystematic risk can be averted by diversifying the investment portfolio.

The CAPM is based on the proposition that any stock's required rate of return is equal to the risk-free rate of return plus a risk premium that reflects only the risk remaining after diversification.

The cost of equity capital is calculated by applying the following formula:

$$k_e = R_f + (R_m - R_f)\beta$$

Where, k_e = cost of equity share capital

R_f = Risk free rate

R_m = Market rate of return

β = Beta coefficient of company's share capital (measure of systematic risk of share capital in relation to the market).

β can be directly calculated with the help of following formulae:

$$\beta = \frac{\text{Cov}_{e,m}}{\sigma_m^2} = \frac{\sigma_e}{\sigma_m} \times \text{Cor}_{e,m}$$

Where, $\text{Cov}_{e,m}$ = Covariance between security returns and market returns

$\text{Cor}_{e,m}$ = Correlation between security returns and market returns

σ_e = Standard deviation of security returns

σ_m = Standard deviation of market returns

Capital Asset Pricing Model is an equilibrium model used to forecast expected return on a capital stock. It is assumed that in market portfolio there is no unsystematic risk as it is fully diversified portfolio. According to this model, only systematic risk is priced in the capital market.

The following three parameters are required to estimate a firm's cost of equity:

(i) Risk free rate of return

(ii) The market risk premium

(iii) The beta of the firm's share.

(i) Risk free rate of return: The rate of return on securities which carry no risk of default on payments is known as risk free rate of return. The yields on the government Treasury securities are used as risk free rate of return. The interest rate on 91 days Treasury bills is usually used as risk free rate of return. To determine the cost of capital, current risk free rate of return is used rather than historical risk free rate of return. The risk free rate of return is a compensation paid for time factor.

(ii) The market risk premium: $R_m - R_f$ is market risk premium. The market risk premium is calculated as the difference between the long-term, historical arithmetical average of market returns and long-term, historical arithmetic average of risk free rate of returns. There should be consistency in respect of the time horizon of returns. The market risk premium is compensation for investing in the market rather than in risk free securities.

(iii) The beta of the firm's share: Beta is a measure of systematic risk of returns on a specific stock in relation to the market returns. This risk cannot be eliminated through diversification. Beta shows the sensitivity of a company's returns in relation to market returns.

Beta can be measured by regressing stock returns to the market returns. The stock risk premium is calculated by multiplying beta with the market risk premium.

Assumptions: The model is based on following assumptions:

(i) All the investors hold efficiently diversified portfolios having no unsystematic risk. The systematic risk is the only relevant risk in estimating returns.

(ii) There is perfect competition in the capital market.

(iii) Investors are risk averse.

(iv) There are no transaction costs or taxes. The capital market is efficient.

Limitations: The CAPM model has following limitations:

(i) The model is based on unrealistic assumptions.

(ii) Beta does not remain stable over the time.

(iii) It is difficult to test the validity of capital asset pricing model.

Example 11. Find the cost of equity capital of a company by using CAPM approach. The beta coefficient of the company is 0.82. The average return in the capital markets is 9%. The risk free return on government securities is 5%.

Solution: We know that:

$$k_e = R_f + (R_m - R_f)\,\beta$$

Here, $R_f = 5\%,\ R_m = 9\%,\ \beta = 0.82$

Substituting the values,

$$k_e = 5\% + (9\% - 5\%)\ (0.82)$$

$$k_e = 5\% + 3.28\%$$

$$k_e = 8.28\%.$$

Thus, the cost of equity capital is 8.28%.

Example 12. Calculate the market risk (beta) of Trump Limited for the following data:

Year	Return of Tulip (%)	Market return (%)
1	7	6
2	7	5
3	5	6
4	8	5
5	7	6
6	6	5
7	8	6
8	9	7
9	7	6
10	6	8

Solution: Calculation of beta of Trump Limited

Year	R_m	R_t	$(R_m - \bar{R}_m)$	$(R_t - \bar{R}_t)$	$(R_m - \bar{R}_m)(R_t - \bar{R}_t)$	$(R_m - \bar{R}_m)^2$
1	6	7	0	0	0	0
2	5	7	–1	0	0	1
3	6	5	0	–2	0	0
4	5	8	–1	1	–1	1
5	6	7	0	0	0	0
6	5	6	–1	–1	1	1
7	6	8	0	1	0	0
8	7	9	1	2	2	1
9	6	7	0	0	0	0
10	8	6	2	–1	–2	4
Total	60	70			0	8

$$\bar{R}_m = \frac{60}{10} = 6$$

$$\bar{R}_t = \frac{70}{10} = 7$$

$$\text{Cov}_{t,m} = \frac{0}{10} = 0$$

$$\sigma_m^2 = \frac{8}{10} = 0.8$$

We know that:

$$\beta = \frac{\text{Cov}_{t,m}}{\sigma_m^2}$$

Substituting the values,

$$\beta = \frac{0}{0.8} = 0$$

Thus, market risk coefficient (beta) is 0.

5.9 Cost of Retained Earnings

The companies generally do not distribute the entire profit as dividend to the shareholders. The portion of profit which remains undistributed is called retained earnings. The retained earnings are also termed as "internal equity". The retained earnings are used for development and future expansion of the company.

The retained earnings, like equity funds, have no accounting cost but have an opportunity cost. The opportunity cost of retained earnings is the dividend foregone by the shareholders. If retained earnings had been distributed to the shareholders then they would have invested it somewhere and earned profit on it.

Thus, retained earnings are like fresh capital provided by the shareholders. Hence, the shareholders' required rate of return would be the same whether they supply the capital by purchasing the shares of the company or by foregoing the dividend in the form of retained earnings. In other words, cost of retained earnings is the same as the cost of equity capital except the other charges incurred in raising the equity capital.

The following formula is used to calculate the cost of retained earnings.

$$k_r = \frac{D_1}{P_0} + g$$

Where, k_r = Cost of retained earnings

P_0 = Issue Price or market price

D_1 = Expected dividend in next year

g = Constant growth rate in dividend

Thus, the cost of retained earnings, k_r is slightly lower than cost of equity, because the issue of equity share capital involves floatation charges, commission etc.

Example 13. A company's shares are currently selling for ₹ 100 each. The company is interested in financing its capital expenditure of ₹ 60,00,000. The company has two options: first, by issuing new shares or second, by using retained earnings. If the company issues new shares, the issue will incur 5% floating charges. The face value of share is ₹ 100. The expected dividend is ₹ 5 per share and it is expected to grow at 6%. Find the cost of equity in both the cases.

Solution: The cost of internal equity (retained earnings) is calculated by the following formula:

$$k_r = \frac{D_1}{P_0} + g$$

Substituting the values,

$$k_r = \frac{5}{100} + 0.06 = 0.05 + 0.06 = 0.11 = 11\%$$

The cost of external equity is calculated by the following formula:

$$k_e = \frac{D_1}{P_0} + g$$

Substituting the values,

$$k_r = \frac{5}{95} + 0.06 = 0.0526 + 0.06 = 0.1126 = 11.26\%$$

Thus, the cost of retained earnings is lower than the cost of equity (new issue).

Example 14. The current market price of a company's share is ₹ 100 and the expected dividend per share in next year is ₹ 8. If the dividend are expected to grow at a constant rate of 8%, find the cost of retained earnings.

Solution: We know that:

$$k_e = \frac{D_1}{P_0} + g$$

Substituting the values,

$$k_e = \frac{8}{100} + 0.08 = 0.08 + 0.08 = 0.16 = 16\%$$

Thus, the cost of retained earnings is 16%.

5.10 Weighted Average of Cost of Capital

In capital budgeting, to evaluate a project the overall cost of capital or the average cost of capital is employed. After ascertaining the specific cost of each source of capital, the average or overall cost of all the sources of capital has to be determined. To determine the average cost of capital, the cost of each component of the capital is weighted by the relative proportion of that type of component in the capital structure of the firm. The cost of capital arrived in such manner is called weighted average cost of capital.

The following formula is used in computing weighted average cost of capital.

$$\text{WACC} = \begin{pmatrix} \% \\ \text{of} \\ \text{debt} \end{pmatrix}\begin{pmatrix} \text{after-tax} \\ \text{cost of} \\ \text{debt} \end{pmatrix} + \begin{pmatrix} \text{\% of} \\ \text{preferred} \\ \text{stock} \end{pmatrix}\begin{pmatrix} \text{cost of} \\ \text{preferred} \\ \text{stock} \end{pmatrix} + \begin{pmatrix} \text{\% of} \\ \text{common} \\ \text{quity} \end{pmatrix}\begin{pmatrix} \text{cost of} \\ \text{common} \\ \text{equity} \end{pmatrix}$$

Thus,

$$\text{WACC} = W_d \times k_d + W_p \times k_p + W_e \times k_e$$

Where, W_d = Weight of debt

W_p = Weight of preferential capital

W_e = Weight of equity capital

k_d = Cost of debt

k_p = Cost of preferential capital

k_e = Cost of equity capital.

The following steps are involved in the calculation of weighted average cost of capital:

1. Calculate the cost of each specific source of capital.
2. Multiply each specific cost by its corresponding weight in the capital structure.
3. Add the weighted cost of all sources of capital.

Weights can be assigned on the following basis:

(i) Book value

(ii) Market value.

Book value weights: The use of book value weights is preferred in computing the average cost of capital because of the following reasons:

1. Book value weights are easily available from the published statements of the firms.
2. The firms generally set their target capital structure in terms of book values.
3. Investors carry out capital structure analysis in terms of debt equity ratio on the basis of book values.

Market value weights: It is very difficult to use market value weights as the market prices of securities fluctuate widely and frequently. However, the use of market value weights has following advantages:

1. The market value weights are theoretically superior to book value weights.
2. The market value weights reflect economic values and are not influenced by accounting policies.
3. The cost of specific sources of capital in the capital structure are normally calculated using prevailing market prices.

Importance of weighted average cost of capital. The simple average cost of capital is not appropriate to use in capital budgeting because firms generally use various sources of capital in varying proportion in the capital structure. The basic objective of financial management is to maximise the shareholders' wealth. If weighted average cost is used as the criterion in selecting the projects, generally the projects will result in increasing the share prices. It is logical and practical to use the weighted average cost of capital in evaluating the investment projects.

Example 15. The following information is available from the balance sheet of a company:

Equity share capital (800 share of ₹ 100 each)	₹ 4,00,000
14% Debentures	₹ 4,00,000
16% Term loan	₹ 12,00,000
Total	₹ 20,00,000

Determine the weighted average cost of capital of the company. Company had been paying dividends at a rate of ₹ 20 per share (g = 0). Income tax rate is 40%. *(D.U., B.Com. 2010)*

Solution: Computation of weighted average cost of capital

Particulars	Amount (₹)	W	k	WACC
Equity shares	4,00,000	0.2	20%	4.00%
14% Debentures	4,00,000	0.2	8.4%	1.68%
16% Term Loan	12,00,000	0.6	9.6%	5.76%
Total	20,00,000			11.44%

Thus, the weighted cost of capital is 11.44%.

Notes: 1. Cost of equity capital:

$$k_e = \frac{D_1}{P_0} + g$$

$$k_e = \frac{20}{100} + 0 = 0.2 = 20\%$$

2. Cost of debentures:

$$k_d = \frac{I}{B_0}(1-t)$$

$$k_d = \frac{14}{100}(1-0.4) = 0.084 = 8.4\%$$

3. Cost of Term-Loan

$$k_d = \frac{I}{B_0}(1-t)$$

$$k_d = \frac{16}{100}(1-0.4) = 0.96 = 9.6\%.$$

SOLVED PROBLEMS

Problem 1. The following information is available from the balance sheet of a company:

Equity share capital (800 shares of ₹ 100 each)	₹ 8,00,000
12% Debentures	₹ 8,00,000
18% Term loan	₹ 24,00,000
Total	₹ 40,00,000

Determine the weighted average cost of capital of the company. Company had been paying dividends at a rate of ₹ 20 per share ($g = 0$). Income tax rate is 40%. *(D.U., B.Com. 2010)*

Solution: Computation of average weighted cost of capital

Particulars	Amount (₹)	W	k	WACC
Equity shares	8,00,000	0.2	20%	4.00%
12% Debentures	8,00,000	0.2	7.2%	1.44%
18% Term Loan	24,00,000	0.6	10.8%	6.48%
Total	40,00,000			11.92%

Thus, the weighted cost of capital is 11.92%.

Notes: 1. Cost of equity capital:

$$k_e = \frac{D_1}{P_0} + g$$

$$k_e = \frac{20}{100} + 0 = 0.2 = 20\%$$

2. Cost of debentures:

$$k_d = \frac{I}{B_0}(1-t)$$

$$k_d = \frac{12}{100}(1-0.4) = 0.072 = 7.2\%$$

3. Cost of Term-Loan

$$k_d = \frac{I}{B_0}(1-t)$$

$$k_d = \frac{18}{100}(1-0.4) = 0.108 = 10.8\%$$

Problem 2. From the balance sheet of a company, following information is available:

Equity share capital ₹ 5,00,000
12% Preference Shares ₹ 5,00,000
10% Debentures ₹ 10,00,000

Determine weighted cost of capital of the company. It had been paying dividend at a rate of ₹ 20 per share (g = 0), income tax rate is 50% and the current price of ₹ 100 share is ₹ 160.

(D.U., B.Com. 2011)

Solution: Computation of weighted cost of capital

Particulars	Amount (₹)	W	k	WACC
Equity shares	5,00,000	0.25	12.5%	3.125%
12% Pref. shares	5,00,000	0.25	12.0%	3.0%
10% Debentures	10,00,000	0.50	5.0%	2.5%
Total	20,00,000			8.625%

Thus, the weighted cost of capital is 11.92%.

Notes: 1. Cost of equity capital:

$$k_e = \frac{D_1}{P_0} + g$$

$$k_e = \frac{20}{160} + 0 = 0.125 = 12.5\%$$

2. Cost of preference shares:

$$k_p = \frac{D}{P_0}$$

$$k_p = \frac{12}{100} = 0.12 = 12\%$$

3. Cost of debentures:

$$k_d = \frac{I}{B_0}(1-t)$$

$$k_d = \frac{10}{100}(1-0.5) = 0.05 = 5\%$$

Problem 3. XYZ Ltd. has the following capital structure:

Equity shares (Face value of ₹ 10 per share)	₹ 10,00,000
10% preference shares (Face value of ₹ 100 per share)	₹ 2,00,000
12% Debentures (Face value of ₹ 100 per debenture)	₹ 8,00,000

All these securities are traded in the capital market. Recent prices are:

Debentures @ ₹ 110 per debenture

Preference shares @ ₹ 120 per share

Equity shares @ ₹ 25 per share

The company expects to pay dividend of ₹ 2 on the equity shares at the end of year which is expected to grow @ 7% p.a. The company pays Income Tax @ 30%. Calculate the company's cost of capital using market value weights. *(D.U., B.Com. 2012)*

Solution: Computation of weighted cost of capital

Particulars	Market value (₹)	W	k	WACC
Equity shares	25,00,000	0.69	15%	10.35%
10% Pref. Shares	2,40,000	0.066	8.33%	0.55%
12% Debentures	8,80,000	0.243	7.64%	1.86%
Total	36,20,000			12.76%

Thus, the weighted cost of capital is 12.76%.

Notes: 1. Cost of equity capital:

$$k_e = \frac{D_1}{P_0} + g$$

$$k_e = \frac{2}{25} + 0.07 = 0.15 = 15\%$$

2. Cost of preference shares:

$$k_p = \frac{D}{P_0}$$

$$k_p = \frac{10}{120} = 0.0833 = 8.33\%$$

3. Cost of debentures:

$$k_d = \frac{I}{B_0}(1-t)$$

$$k_d = \frac{12}{110}(1-0.3) = 0.0764 = 7.64\%$$

Problem 4. Equity shares of Avon Ltd. is currently selling in the market at ₹ 100. Dividends paid in the last 5 years are ₹ 4, ₹ 4.25, ₹ 4.60, ₹ 4.85 and ₹ 5.05. The company wants to issue new equity shares and has been advised to price the share at ₹ 90. Floatation costs are likely to be ₹ 8 per share. Calculate the growth rate, cost of existing shares and cost of new equity shares.

Solution:

(i) Calculation of growth rate:

$$D_5 = D_1 (1 + g)^4$$

Substituting the values,

$$5.05 = 4 (1 + g)^4$$

Then, $(1 + g)^4 = 1.2625$

From the compound value table, the corresponding growth rate for 4 years is 6%. Thus, the growth rate is 6%.

(ii) We know that:

$$k_e = \frac{D_1}{P_0} + g$$

For the existing share capital, substituting the values,

$$k_e = \frac{(5.05)(1+0.06)}{100} + 0.06$$

$$k_e = 0.05353 + 0.06 = 0.11353 = 11.35\%.$$

(iii) We know that:

$$k_e = \frac{D_1}{P_0} + g$$

For the existing share capital, substituting the values,

$$k_e = \frac{(5.05)(1+0.06)}{90-8} + 0.06$$

$$k_e = 0.06528 + 0.06 = 0.12528 = 12.53\%.$$

Problem 5. A company has following capital structure:

Capital	Amount (₹)
Equity shares (4,00,000)	80,00,000
10% Preference shares	20,00,000

14% Debentures	60,00,000
Total	1,60,00,000

The share of company is currently selling for ₹ 25. It is expected that the company will pay a dividend of ₹ 2 per share which will grow at 7% forever. Tax rate is 50%. Find the weighted average cost of capital on the existing structure.

Solution: Computation of weighted cost of capital

Particulars	Amount (₹)	W	k	WACC
Equity shares	80,00,000	0.5	15%	7.5%
12% Pref. shares	20,00,000	0.125	10%	1.25%
10% Debentures	60,00,000	0.375	7%	2.625%
Total	1,60,00,000			11.375%

Thus, the weighted cost of capital is 11.375%.

Notes: 1. Cost of equity capital:

$$k_e = \frac{D_1}{P_0} + g$$

$$k_e = \frac{2}{25} + 0.07 = 0.15 = 15\%$$

2. Cost of preference shares:

$$k_p = \frac{D}{P_0}$$

$$k_p = \frac{10}{100} = 0.10 = 10\%$$

3. Cost of debentures:

$$k_d = \frac{I}{B_0}(1-t)$$

$$k_d = \frac{14}{100}(1-0.5) = 0.07 = 7\%.$$

Problem 6. The following is the capital structure of a company:

Capital	Amount (₹)
Equity share capital (₹ 10 each)	5,00,000
12% Preference share capital (₹ 100 each)	4,00,000
8% Debentures (₹ 100 each)	6,00,000
Total	15,00,000

Equity shares are currently selling at ₹ 15 each. The company paid a dividend of ₹ 2 per share for the last year. The dividends are expected to increase at 5% p.a. The preference shares and debentures are being traded at 90% and 80%. Tax rate is 40%. Find the weighted average cost of capital of the company using:

(a) Book value weights, and

(b) Market value weights

Solution:

1. Cost of equity capital:

$$k_e = \frac{D_1}{P_0} + g$$

$$k_e = \frac{2.10}{15} + 0.05 = 0.19 = 19\%$$

2. Cost of preference shares:

$$k_p = \frac{D}{P_0}$$

$$k_p = \frac{12}{90} = 0.1333 = 13.33\%$$

3. Cost of debentures:

$$k_d = \frac{I}{B_0}(1-t)$$

$$k_d = \frac{8}{80}(1-0.4) = 0.06 = 6\%$$

(a) Using book value weights

Particulars	Amount (₹)	W	k	WACC
Equity shares	5,00,000	0.333	19%	6.33%
12% Pref. shares	4,00,000	0.267	13.33%	3.56%
8% Debentures	6,00,000	0.400	6%	2.4%
Total	15,00,000			12.29%

(b) Using market value weights

Particulars	Amount (₹)	W	k	WACC
Equity shares	7,50,000	0.472	19%	8.97%
12% Pref. shares	3,60,000	0.226	13.33%	3.01%
8% Debentures	4,80,000	0.302	6%	1.81%
Total	15,90,000			13.79%

Problem 7. The following information is available for a company:

Capital	Amount (₹)
Equity share capital (₹ 10)	4,00,000
Reserve and surplus	1,00,000
8% Debentures	3,00,000
Total	8,00,000

Current equity dividend is 14%. Tax rate is 50%. Compute the weighted average cost of capital.

Solution:

1. Cost of equity capital:

$$k_e = \frac{D_1}{P_0} + g$$

Substituting the values,

$$k_e = \frac{1.4}{10} + 0 = 0.14 = 14\%$$

2. Cost of debentures:

$$k_d = \frac{I}{B_0}(1-t)$$

Substituting the values,

$$k_d = 0.08(1-0.5) = 0.04 = 4\%$$

Computation of weighted average cost of capital

Particulars	Amount (₹)	W	k	WACC
Equity shares	4,00,000	0.5	14%	7.0%
Reserves and surplus	1,00,000	0.125	14%	1.75%
8% Debentures	3,00,000	0.375	4%	1.5%
Total	8,00,000			10.25%

Problem 8. Rama Ltd. is planning to raise ₹ 2 crore by the issue of 12% preference shares of ₹ 100 each at 12% discount. The underwriting expenses are expected to be 2%. Find out the cost of preference share capital in each of the following cases:

(i) If the preference shares are irredeemable.

(ii) If preference shares are redeemable at the end of 10th year at 15% premium. Use short cut method.

Solution:

(i) We know that:

$$k_p = \frac{D}{P_0}$$

Substituting the values,

$$k_p = \frac{12}{86} = 0.1395 = 13.95\%$$

(ii) We know that:

$$k_p = \frac{D + \dfrac{(RV - P_0)}{n}}{\dfrac{(RV + P_0)}{2}}$$

Substituting the values,

$$k_p = \frac{12 + \dfrac{(115 - 86)}{10}}{\dfrac{(115 + 86)}{2}}$$

$$k_p = 0.1682 = 16.82\%.$$

Problem 9. Assuming that firm pays tax at 50%, compute the weighted average cost of capital from the following:

5000 equity shares of ₹ 100 each	₹ 5,00,000
10% preference shares	₹ 2,00,000
10% debentures	₹ 3,00,000

The current market price of the share is ₹ 110. The company is expected to declare a dividend of ₹ 10 at the end of current year, with an expected growth rate of 9%. Use book value weights.

Solution: Computation of weighted cost of capital

Particulars	Amount (₹)	W	k	WACC
Equity shares	5,00,000	0.5	18.09%	9.045%
10% Pref. shares	2,00,000	0.2	10%	2%
10% Debentures	3,00,000	0.3	5%	1.5%
Total	10,00,000			12.545%

Thus, the weighted cost of capital is 12.545%.

Notes: 1. Cost of equity capital:

$$k_e = \frac{D_1}{P_0} + g$$

$$k_e = \frac{10}{110} + 0.09 = 0.1809 = 18.09\%$$

2. Cost of preference shares:

$$k_p = \frac{D}{P_0}$$

$$k_p = \frac{10}{100} = 0.10 = 10\%$$

3. Cost of debentures:

$$k_d = \frac{I}{B_0}(1-t)$$

$$k_d = \frac{10}{100}(1-0.5) = 0.05 = 5\%.$$

Problem 10. Calculate the cost of capital in each of the following cases:

(i) A company issues 10% irredeemable preference shares at ₹ 90 each (face value = ₹ 100).

(ii) The current market price of a share is ₹ 95 and the expected dividend at the end of the current year is ₹ 4.5 with a growth rate of 8 percent.

(iii) A company issues ₹ 10,00,000 10 percent debentures of ₹ 100 each at 10 percent discount. The debentures are redeemable after the expiry of fixed period of 7 years. The company is in 35 percent tax bracket.

Solution:

(i) We know that:

$$k_p = \frac{D}{P_0}$$

Substituting the values,

$$k_p = \frac{10}{90} = 0.1111 = 11.11\%$$

(ii) Cost of equity capital:

$$k_e = \frac{D_1}{P_0} + g$$

$$k_e = \frac{4.5}{95} + 0.08 = 0.1274 = 12.74\%$$

(iii) We know that cost of debt:

$$k_d = \frac{I(1-t) + \dfrac{(RV - B_0)}{n}}{\dfrac{(RV + B_0)}{2}}$$

Substituting the values, we get:

$$k_d = \frac{10(1-0.35) + \dfrac{(100-90)}{7}}{\dfrac{(100+90)}{2}}$$

$$k_d = \frac{6.5 + 1.43}{95} = 0.0835 = 8.35\%.$$

Problem 11. A company has the following capital structure:

50,000 Equity shares	₹ 5,00,000
10% Preference shares	₹ 2,00,000
10% Debentures	₹ 3,00,000
Total	₹ 10,00,000

The equity share of the company is currently selling at ₹ 20. It is expected that the company shall pay a dividend of ₹ 3 per share with growth rate of 5% p.a. forever. The tax rate applicable is 30%. Preference shares and debentures are traded at par. Compute Weighted Average Cost of Capital on the existing capital structure. *(D.U., B.Com. 2015, N.C.)*

Solution: Computation of weighted cost of capital

Particulars	**Amount (₹)**	**W**	**k**	**WACC**
Equity shares	5,00,000	0.5	20%	10%
10% Pref. shares	2,00,000	0.2	10%	2%
10% Debentures	3,00,000	0.3	7%	2.1%
Total	10,00,000			14.1%

Thus, the weighted cost of capital is 14.1%.

Notes: 1. Cost of equity capital:

$$k_e = \frac{D_1}{P_0} + g$$

$$k_e = \frac{3}{20} + 0.05 = 0.20 = 20\%$$

2. Cost of preference shares:

$$k_p = \frac{D}{P_0}$$

$$k_p = \frac{10}{100} = 0.10 = 10\%$$

3. Cost of debentures:

$$k_d = \frac{I}{B_0}(1 - t)$$

$$k_d = \frac{10}{100}(1 - 0.3) = 0.07 = 7\%.$$

Problem 12. A Ltd. has issued 30,000 irredeemable 12% debentures of ₹ 100 each. The company's taxation rate is 35%. Calculate the cost of debt (before tax as well as after tax) in each of the following cases:

(i) When the debentures are issued at par.
(ii) When debentures are issued at 10% discount.
(iii) When the debentures are issued at a premium of 8%.

Solution: Computation of cost of capital

Particulars	**At par**	**10% discount**	**8% premium**
Annual interest	12	12	12
Issue price	100	90	108
Before tax cost of capital	12%	13.33%	11.11%
After tax cost of capital	7.8%	8.66%	7.22%

Problem 13. The following information is available from the balance sheet of a company:

Equity share capital (10,000 shares of ₹ 100 each)	₹ 10,00,000
10% Debentures	₹ 5,00,000
15% Term loan	₹ 5,00,000
Total	₹ 20,00,000

Determine the weighted average cost of capital of the company. The company had been paying a dividend of ₹ 20 per share ($g = 0$). Income tax rate is 50%.

Solution: Computation of weighted cost of capital

Particulars	**Amount (₹)**	**W**	**k**	**WACC**
Equity shares	10,00,000	0.5	20%	10.00%
10% Debentures	5,00,000	0.25	5%	1.25%
15% Term loan	5,00,000	0.25	7.5%	1.875%
Total	20,00,000			13.125%

Thus, the weighted cost of capital is 13.125%.

Notes: 1. Cost of equity capital:

$$k_e = \frac{D_1}{P_0} + g$$

$$k_e = \frac{20}{100} + 0 = 0.2 = 20\%$$

2. Cost of debentures:

$$k_d = \frac{I}{B_0}(1-t)$$

$$k_d = \frac{10}{100}(1-0.5) = 0.05 = 5.0\%$$

3. Cost of Term-Loan

$$k_d = \frac{I}{B_0}(1-t)$$

$$k_d = \frac{15}{100}(1-0.5) = 0.075 = 7.5\%.$$

THEORETICAL QUESTIONS

1. What is cost of capital? How is it important in financial decision-making? *(D.U., B.Com. 2011)*
2. Define the cost of capital. Distinguish between 'Explicit' and 'Implicit' cost of capital. *(D.U., B.Com. 2016)*
3. Differentiate between specific cost of capital and overall cost of capital. Also specify out of these two which cost is used while taking capital budgeting decision and why? *(D.U., B.Com. 2013)*
4. Explain the behaviour of cost of debt, cost of equity capital and overall cost of capital under the traditional approach to capital structure. *(D.U., B.Com. 2009, Corres.)*
5. Comment:
   (i) "New equity is costlier than the retained earnings."
   (ii) "Debt is a cheaper source of finance than equity."
6. "As there is no explicit cost of retained earnings, these funds are free of cost." Comment.

PRACTICAL PROBLEMS

1. K Ltd. is planning to raise ₹ 1 crore by the issue of 12% preference shares of ₹ 1,000 each at 10% discount. The underwriting expenses are expected to be 2%. Find out the cost of preference share capital in each of the following cases:
   (i) If the preference shares are irredeemable.
   (ii) If preference shares are redeemable at the end of 10th year at 15% premium. Use short-cut method. *(D.U., B. Com. 2009, Corres.)*

   [**Ans.** (i) 13.64%; (ii) 14.48%]
2. Kamani Ltd. is planning to raise ₹ 100 crore by the issue of 13% debentures of ₹ 100 each at 10% discount. The underwriting expenses are expected to be 4%. Find out the cost of debentures in each of the following cases:
   (i) If debentures are irredeemable.
   (ii) If debentures are redeemable at the end of 10th year at 15% premium. Use short-cut method.

Assume tax rate is 35%. (*D.U., B.Com. 2010, Corres.*)

[**Ans.** (i) 9.83%; (ii) 11.29%]

3. S.B. International Ltd. has the following capital structure:

Particulars	Book value (₹)	Market value (₹)
Equity capital (25,000 shares of ₹ 10 each)	2,50,000	4,50,000
13% Preference capital (500 shares of ₹ 100 each)	50,000	45,000
Reserves and surplus	1,50,000	–
14% Debentures (1500 debentures of ₹ 100 each)	1,50,000	1,45,000

The expected dividend per share is ₹ 1.40 and dividend per share is expected to grow at a rate of 8% forever. Preference shares and debentures are redeemable at par after 5 years and 6 years respectively. Tax rate for company is 50%.

Compute the weighted average cost of capital for the existing capital structure using market value as weights. (*D.U., B.Com. 2011, Corres.*)

[**Ans.** 13.98%]

4. Assuming that firm pays tax at 50%, compute the weighted average cost of capital from the following:

5000 Equity shares of ₹ 100 each	₹ 5,00,000
10% Preference shares	₹ 1,00,000
12% Debentures	₹ 4,00,000

The current market price of the share is ₹ 120. The company is expected to declare a dividend of ₹ 12 at the end of current year, with an expected growth rate of 8%. Use book value weights. (*D.U., B.Com. 2012, Corres.*)

[**Ans.** 12.4%]

5. Star company has the following capital structure:

Equity share capital	₹ 80,00,000
10% Preferential shares	₹ 20,00,000
14% Debentures	₹ 60,00,000
Total	₹ 1,60,00,000

The shares of the company sell for ₹ 25. It is expected that the company will pay a dividend of ₹ 2 per share which will grow at 7% forever. Assume the tax rate of 50%.

Compute a weighted average cost of capital on existing capital structure.

(*D.U., B.Com. 2013, Corres.*)

[**Ans.** 11.375%]

6. Calculate the cost of capital in each of the following cases:
   (i) A company issues 10% irredeemable preference shares at ₹ 95 each (face value = ₹ 100).
   (ii) The current market price of a share is ₹ 90 and the expected dividend at the end of the current year is ₹ 4.5 with a growth rate of 8 percent.
   (iii) A company issues ₹ 10,00,000 12 percent debentures of ₹ 100 each at 10 percent discount. The debentures are redeemable after the expiry of fixed period of 7 years. The company is in 35 percent tax bracket. *(D.U., B.Com. 2014, Corres.)*

   [**Ans.** (i) 10.52%; (ii) 13%; (iii) 9.72%]

7. A company has the following capital structure:

40,000 Equity shares	₹ 8,00,000
10% Preference shares	₹ 6,00,000
10% Debentures	₹ 2,00,000
Total	₹ 16,00,000

   The equity share of the company is currently selling at ₹ 25. It is expected that the company shall pay a dividend of ₹ 2 per share with growth rate of 5% p.a. forever. The tax rate applicable is 30%. Preference shares and debentures are traded at par. Compute Weighted Average Cost of Capital on the existing capital structure.

   (D.U., B.Com. 2015, N.C.)

   [**Ans.** 11.125%]

8. Calculate the after tax cost of capital in each of the following cases, given that the tax rate applicable to the company is 40%:
   (i) 15% Preference share sold at par value of ₹ 100.
   (ii) An irredeemable debenture of par value of ₹ 1,000 sold at a coupon rate of 15%.
   (iii) An 8%, ten-year debenture of face value of ₹ 1,000 sold at ₹ 950, redeemable at 10% premium.
   (iv) An equity share with a market price of ₹ 110 with expected dividend of ₹ 11 and a growth rate of 10%. The par value of equity share is ₹ 100.

   (D.U., B.Com. 2015, Corres.)

   [**Ans.** (i) 15%; (ii) 9%; (iii) 6.15%; (iv) 20%]

9. A Ltd. has issued 30,000 irredeemable 12% debentures of ₹ 100 each. The company's taxation rate is 35%. Calculate the cost of debt (before tax as well as after tax) in each of the following cases:
   (i) When the debt issued at par.
   (ii) When the debt is issued at a premium of 8%. *(D.U., B.Com. 2016, N.C.)*

   [**Ans.** (i) 12%, 7.8%; (ii) 11.11%, 7.22%]

10. The following information is available from the balance sheet of a company:

Equity share capital (16,000 Shares of ₹ 100 each)	₹ 16,00,000
10% Debentures	₹ 16,00,000
15% Term loan	₹ 48,00,000
Total	₹ 80,00,000

Determine the weighted average cost of capital of the company. The company had been paying a dividend of ₹ 20 per share ($g = 0$). Income tax rate is 50%.

(D.U., B.Com. 2016, Corres.)

[**Ans.** 9.50%]

Financing Decisions: Leverage

6

Chapter Outline

6.1 Introduction
6.2 Operating Leverage
6.3 Financial Leverage
6.4 Combined Leverage
6.5 Importance of Leverage Analysis
6.6 Difference Between Business Risk and Financial Risk
6.7 Difference Between Operating Leverage and Financial Leverage
6.8 EBIT-EPS Analysis
6.9 Indifference Level of EBIT
6.10 Financial Break Even Point

6.1 Introduction

In physics, leverage implies magnification of small force by use of a lever. Literary, leverage implies that a given percentage change in one variable leads to a more than proportionate change in the other related variable. In business, leverage refers to the use of fixed costs in an attempt to increase profitability. The operating leverage is due to fixed operating costs associated with the production of goods or services. In operating leverage, a given percentage change in sales leads to a more than proportionate change in operating profit (EBIT). The financial leverage is due to the existence of fixed financial costs—in particular, interest on debt. In financial leverage, a given percentage change in operating profit (EBIT) leads to a more than proportionate change in earnings per share.

The degree of operating leverage indicates the business risk involved, while financial leverage is concerned with financial risk in a firm. Others things held constant, the higher a firm's operating leverage, the higher its business risk. Higher financial leverage increases expected EPS, but it also increases financial risk. This chapter deals with operating leverage, financial leverage, combined leverage in a firm and the issues related to them.

6.2 Operating Leverage

The operating leverage is created by a firm through using fixed operating costs in the production. Operating leverage comes into operation when changes in sales bring more than proportionate change in operating profit (EBIT).

According to Solomon Ezra, "Operating leverage is the tendency of the operating profit to vary disproportionately with sales."

According to John Hampton, "Operating leverage exists when changes in revenue produce greater changes in EBIT."

Table 6.1 shows working of operating leverage in case of three firms having varying operating cost structure. In next year, when sales revenue increase by 100%, the operating profits of the three firms increase by varying percentages, i.e. by 700% in case of firm A, 200% in firm B and by 533% in firm C. This happens because of different operating leverages of the firms. The ratio of contribution to EBIT in a firm indicates its operating leverage. And the contribution depends of presence of fixed costs in the operating cost structure of a firm.

Table 6.1: Effect of operating leverage

Initial sales			
	Company A	**Company B**	**Company C**
Sales (₹)	10,000	15,000	20,000
Operating Costs:			
Fixed cost (FC)	6,000	3,000	13,000
Variable cost (VC)	3,000	9,000	4,000
Operating profit (EBIT) (₹)	1,000	3,000	3,000
Operating Ratios			
FC/Total cost	0.67	0.25	0.76
FC/Sales	0.60	0.20	0.65
Degree of operating leverage (DOL)	7.00	2.00	5.33
Sales after 100% increase in next year			
Sales (₹)	20,000	30,000	40,000
Operating Costs:			
Fixed cost (FC)	6,000	3,000	13,000
Variable cost (VC)	6,000	18,000	8,000
Operating profit (EBIT) (₹)	8,000	9,000	19,000
Percent change in EBIT	700%	200%	533%

The operating leverage in a firm is calculated by using following formula:

$$\text{Degree of operating leverage (DOL)} = \frac{\text{Percentage change in operating profit}}{\text{Percentage change in sales}}$$

$$\text{DOL} = \frac{\text{Contribution}}{\text{EBIT}}$$

$$\text{DOL} = \frac{\text{Sales} - \text{Variable cost}}{\text{Sales} - \text{Variable cost} - \text{fixed cost}}$$

$$\text{DOL} = \frac{\text{Fixed cost} + \text{EBIT}}{\text{EBIT}} = 1 + \frac{\text{Fixed cost}}{\text{EBIT}}$$

Thus, operating leverage in a firm depends on the following factors:

(i) Fixed costs

(ii) EBIT.

Higher the degree of operating leverage in a firm, higher will be the increase in operating profit for a given change in volume of sales.

In fact, there will be no operating leverage if there are no fixed operating costs. Operating leverage creates 'operating risk' or 'business risk' in a firm. Business risk is the firm's inability to meet the fixed operating costs. Higher the fixed operating costs in relation to operating profits, higher is the degree of operating leverage and higher will be the business/operating risk for the firm.

The operating leverage is based on the theory of cost volume profit analysis. The presence of fixed costs in total costs gives birth to operating leverage. However, it would be an error to assume that the firm with largest absolute or relative amount of fixed assets automatically leads to highest degree of operating leverage.

Significance of operating leverage. The knowledge of operating leverage is very useful in deciding sales policy or capital structure of a firm. With the help of operating leverage the manager would know in advance the impact of potential change in sales on the operating profit. Firms may take decision to make some changes in its sales policy or cost structure on the basis of prior knowledge of operating leverage. Usually, firms do not like to operate under the conditions of a high degree of operating leverage. If a firm operates under a high degree of operating leverage, a small drop in sales may cause operating loss.

Highly automated firms bear a heavy fixed cost and operate under condition of high degree of operating leverage. A small change in sales in such firms may cause huge change in operating revenue.

Applications of operating leverage. The operating leverage can be used to meet the following purposes:

1. **Selection of investment projects:** The advance knowledge of operating leverage helps in selection of investment projects. If other conditions remain same, the investment project with lower degree of operating leverage should be selected.
2. **Selection of capital structure:** The capital structure of a firm shows the mix of debt and equity. If the operating leverage of a firm is high, the firm should use low amount of debt in its capital so that in case of loss the burden of fixed interest for the debt could be avoided.
3. **Assessment of operating or business risk:** The degree of operating leverage indicates the degree of operating or business risk involved in a firm. This helps a firm in preparing its long-term business/profit policy.
4. **Selection of sales policy:** The operating leverage helps in advance in determining the impact of change in volume of sales on operating profit of a firm. Having the prior knowledge of such impact, a firm can easily decide its sales policy.

Example 1. From the following information, calculate the operating leverage:

Particulars	₹ (in lakhs)
Sales	8,000
EBIT	1,950
Variable cost is 70% of sales.	

Solution: We know that: Contribution = sales – variable costs

Hence, contribution = 8,000 – 70% of 8,000 = 2,400

We know that:

$$\text{DOL} = \frac{\text{Contribution}}{\text{EBIT}}$$

Substituting the values,

$$\text{DOL} = \frac{2{,}400}{1{,}950} = 1.23.$$

6.3 Financial Leverage

Financial leverage is created by use of fixed charge securities in the capitalisation of a firm. Financial leverage is defined as the firm's ability to use fixed financial expenses in such a way that any increase in operating profit (EBIT) has magnifying impact on the net profit (EPS).

According to Hampton, "Financial leverage exists whenever a firm has debt or other sources of funds that carry fixed charges."

In the words of Gitman, "The ability of a firm to use fixed financial charges to magnify the effects of changes in EBIT on the firm's earnings per share is financial leverage."

The following example given in Table 6.2 will help in explaining the concept of financial leverage. The three companies A, B and C have different capital mix in the total capitalisation of ₹ 5 lakh. Each company earns operating profit ₹ 1,00,000. Their EPS are different owning to different proportion of fixed charge securities in the capitalisation. In the next year, operating profit (EBIT) increases by 100% in case of all the three companies. The EPS increases by 100% in case of company A, while it increases by 140% and 125% respectively in case of companies B and C. This happens due to different degrees of financial leverage in these companies caused by varying proportion of fixed charge securities (debt and preferential shares) in their total capital. Company A has no fixed charge securities in its capital, hence % change in EPS is equal to % change in Operating profit. Company B has ₹ 2,00,000 preferential share capital and its EPS increased by 140%. Company C has ₹ 2,00,000 debt and its EPS increases by 125%. This shows that the presence of fixed charge securities in capital structure of a firm has magnifying impact on its EPS.

Table 6.2: Effect of financial leverage

Capital structure			
	Company A	Company B	Company C
Equity share capital (₹ 10 each share)	5,00,000	3,00,000	3,00,000

10% Preference share capital	–	2,00,000	–
10% Debentures	–	–	2,00,000
Initial EBIT			
EBIT	1,00,000	1,00,000	1,00,000
Less: Interest	–	–	20,000
Earnings before tax	1,00,000	1,00,000	80,000
Less: Tax @ 30%	30,000	30,000	24,000
Earnings after tax	70,000	70,000	56,000
Preference stock dividend	–	20,000	–
Earnings available for equity capital	70,000	50,000	56,000
Earnings per share (EPS)	1.40	1.67	1.87
Degree of financial leverage (DFL)	1.00	1.40	1.25
EBIT increase by 100% in next year			
EBIT	2,00,000	2,00,000	2,00,000
Less: Interest	–	–	20,000
Earnings before tax	2,00,000	2,00,000	1,80,000
Less: Tax @ 30%	60,000	60,000	54,000
Earnings after tax	1,40,000	1,40,000	1,26,000
Preference stock dividend	–	20,000	–
Earnings available for equity capital	1,40,000	1,20,000	1,26,000
Earnings per share (EPS)	2.80	4.00	4.20
Percent change in EPS	100%	140%	125%

The following formulae are used to calculate degree of financial leverage of a firm:

$$\text{Degree of financial leverage (DFL)} = \frac{\text{Percentage change in earnings per share (EPS)}}{\text{Percentage change in operating profit (EBIT)}}$$

$$\text{Degree of financial leverage (DFL)} = \frac{\text{EBIT}}{\text{EBIT} - \left(\text{Interest charge} + \dfrac{\text{Preference dividend}}{(1 - \text{Tax rate})}\right)}$$

Financial leverage indicates the financial risk involved in the operation of a firm. Financial risk is the risk of a firm's inability to meet the fixed financial obligations. Higher the proportion of debt in the capitalisation of a firm, the higher will be the degree of financial leverage and the higher financial risk. There is more probability that a firm fails to discharge its financial obligations.

The financial leverage is said to be favourable or positive, when the firm earns more on its investment than what it pays to fixed charge securities in the form of preferential dividend or interest. The surplus after payment of fixed financial charges belong to equity owners. If the firm earns a return on investment less than the rate at which it pays interest to debt holders, then it negative or unfavourable leverage. In such a situation, firm pays the interest on debt from the profit belonging to the shareholders. In other words, there exists no financial leverage.

If degree of financial leverage is less than 1, there exists no financial leverage. In case the degree of financial leverage is equal to 1, the return on investment is equal to rate of interest payable to debt holders. If degree of financial leverage is more than 1, there exists financial leverage. In this case, return on investment is greater than rate of interest payable to debt holders.

If financial leverage exists in firm, when degree of financial leverage is greater than 1, it is called trading on equity. This implies that the firm's rate return on investment is greater than the rate of interest payable to debt holders. In this situation, an increase in operating profit of the firm leads to more than proportionate increase in earnings per share.

Importance of financial leverage. Financial leverage signifies the use of debt and preferential share capital for magnifying the profit available to the equity shareholders. A business firm may increase the profit for equity shareholders by increasing the EBIT through the raising of funds from fixed cost sources e.g. debentures, loans and preferential share capital.

The degree of financial leverage helps us to understand how earning per share would change with respect to change in the operating profit. Debt is relatively cheaper source of funds than equity and preferential share capital. The use of debt reduces the overall or weighted average cost of capital of a firm. The reduced overall cost of capital contributes to increased valuation of the firm. This is the basic purpose of financial management.

The degree of financial leverage indicates the financial risk involved in a firm. The knowledge of financial leverage helps in judiciously designing the capital structure of a firm in such a way to reduce the overall cost. The understanding of financial leverage also helps in the capital budgeting of a project.

Applications of financial leverage. The degree of financial leverage in a firm depends on its capital structure. The understanding of financial leverage helps the management of a firm to decide about any change in use fixed cost securities in the total capital of the firm.

The financial leverage is said to be favourable or positive, when the firm earns more on its investment than what it pays to fixed charge securities in the form of preferential dividend or interest. If the firm earns a return on investment less than the rate at which it pays interest to debt holders, then it negative or unfavourable leverage. In such a situation, firm pays the interest on debt from the profit belonging to the shareholders. In other words, there exists no financial leverage.

If degree of financial leverage is less than 1, there exists no financial leverage. In case the degree of financial leverage is equal to 1, the return on investment is equal to rate interest payable to debt holders. If degree of financial leverage is more than 1, there exists financial leverage. In this case, return on investment is greater than rate of interest payable to debt holders.

If financial leverage exists in firm, when degree of financial leverage is greater than 1, it is called trading on equity. This implies that the firm's rate return on investment is greater than the rate of interest payable to debt holders. In this situation, an increase in operating profit of the firm leads to more than proportionate increase in earnings per share.

If rate of return on investment is equal to the cost of debt, then the firm should not use leverage. In such a situation, more use of debt capital will increase the financial risk instead of the EPS.

Example 2. From the following information, calculate different types of leverages:

Particulars	₹ (in lakhs)
Sales	10000
EBIT	3950
EBT	2950
Tax rate	30%

Solution: We know that: Interest = EBIT – EBT

Thus, Interest = 3,950 – 2,950= 1,000

We know that:

$$\text{Degree of financial leverage (DFL)} = \frac{\text{EBIT}}{\text{EBIT} - \left(\text{Interest charge} + \dfrac{\text{Preference dividend}}{(1 - \text{Tax rate})}\right)}$$

Substituting the values,

$$\text{Degree of financial leverage (DFL)} = \frac{3{,}950}{3{,}950 - 1{,}000} = 1.34$$

6.4 Combined Leverage

The operating leverage shows the effect of change in sales on the operating profit of a firm. Similarly, financial leverage shows the effect of change in operating profit on earnings per share of a firm. The combination of operating and financial leverages would give total or combined leverage which will explain the combined effect of both the leverages. The combined leverage shows the change in EPS in response to change in sales of a firm.

The combined leverage is calculated by applying the following formula:

$$\text{Degree of combined leverage} = \text{DOL} \times \text{DFL} = \frac{\text{Percentage change in EPS}}{\text{Percentage change in sales}}$$

$$\text{DCL} = \frac{\text{Contribution}}{\text{EBT}}$$

The operating leverage indicates the business risk in a firm. While, financial leverage indicates financial risk in a firm. The combined leverage of a firm shows the total risk involved in a firm.

- If degree of combined leverage is 1, then there is no combined risk in the business of a firm.
- The combined risk is involved in a firm, if degree of combined leverage is more than 1. In this case, a percentage change in sales would cause more than proportionate percentage change in EPS in a firm.
- The firm having higher combined leverage is more risky than a firm having lower leverage.

The combined leverage is helpful in measuring the total risk involved in a firm. The combined leverage is useful in evaluating the projects in context of risk involved in a firm.

Example 3. From the following information, calculate the combined leverage:

Particulars	₹ (in lakhs)
Sales	10,000
EBIT	3,950
PBT	2,950
Tax rate	30%

Variable cost is 60% of sales.

Solution: We know that: Contribution = sales – variable costs

Hence, contribution = 10,000 – 60% of 10,000 = 4,000

We know that:

$$\text{DOL} = \frac{\text{Contribution}}{\text{EBIT}}$$

Substituting the values,

$$\text{DOL} = \frac{4,000}{3,950} = 1.0$$

We know that: Interest = EBIT – EBT

Thus, Interest = 3,950 – 2,950 = 1,000

We know that:

$$\text{Degree of financial leverage (DFL)} = \frac{\text{EBIT}}{\text{EBIT} - \left(\text{Interest charge} + \dfrac{\text{Preference dividend}}{(1 - \text{Tax rate})}\right)}$$

Substituting the values,

$$\text{Degree of financial leverage} = \frac{3,950}{3,950 - 1,000} = 1.34$$

We know that:

$$\text{Degree of combined leverage} = \text{DOL} \times \text{DFL}$$

Substituting the values,

$$\text{Degree of combined leverage} = 1.01 \times 1.34$$

$$\text{Degree of combined leverage} = 1.35.$$

6.5 Importance of Leverage Analysis

With the understanding of leverage, a finance manager can increase earnings per share and dividend per share to equity shareholders as well as market value of the firm. When the rate of return on investment is more than cost of debt capital, it gives more rate of return on equity capital. This in turn maximise shareholders' wealth, which is the basic objective of financial management. The leverage can help increasing both the EPS and EBT. The significance of leverage can be judged from the following points:

1. Leverage is an important technique in deciding the optimum capital structure of a firm. With the help of this technique, it easy to determine the ratio of various securities comprising the capital structure of a firm at which the average cost of capital is minimum. If financial leverage is present in a firm, it is possible to increase EPS by increasing the EBIT in a firm.
2. Leverage is also very helpful in taking a capital budgeting decision. If contribution in a firm is not able to meet the fixed operating costs, then business will suffer loss. In other words, the degree of operating leverage must be greater than 1 to make the project operationally profitable.
3. Leverage is most important in assessing the risk involved in a firm. Operating leverage measures the business risk of a firm. Financial leverage measures the financial risk in a firm. The combined leverage measures the total risk involved in a firm.

Though the above mentioned properties make the leverage analysis very important, there certain limitations of leverage analysis. In leverage analysis, it is assumed that cost of capital always remains constant. But, after a certain limit, the cost of financing generally starts increasing.

The use of more debt capital increases the risk level in a firm which results into reduction in the value of shares. Thus, in leverage analysis, explicit cost of debt capital is considered, while its implicit costs is ignored. Leverage principle assumes that the required additional debt capital should be raised till the expected rate of return on investment is higher than cost of debt capital.

6.6 Difference Between Business Risk and Financial Risk

The technique of leverage is widely used in analysing the risk involved in a business firm. The difference between business risk and financial risk is explained below:

S. No.	Business Risk	Financial Risk
1	Business risk is the risk measured by a firm's inability to meet the fixed operating costs.	Financial risk is the risk measured by a firm's inability to meet fixed financial costs.
2	Presence of fixed operating costs in the manufacturing costs causes the business risk.	Presence of fixed financial costs in capitalisation causes the financial risk.
3	Business risk is measured by degree of operating leverage of a firm.	Financial leverage is measured by degree of financial leverage.
4	Higher the degree of operating leverage, higher is the business risk in a firm.	Higher the degree of financial leverage, higher is the financial risk in a firm.
5	Business risk arises due to capital budgeting decision of a firm.	Financial risk arises due to capital structure decision of a firm.
6	Business risk cannot be completely eliminated.	Financial risk can be completely eliminated by using all equity capital.
7	It affects the EBIT of a firm.	It affects the EPS of a firm.

6.7 Difference Between Operating Leverage and Financial Leverage

The difference between operating leverage and financial leverage is summarised below:

S. No.	Operating leverage	Financial leverage
1	Operating leverage measures the business risk of a firm.	Financial leverage measures the financial risk of a firm.
2	Operating leverage is caused by presence of fixed manufacturing costs.	Financial leverage is caused by presence of fixed charge securities.
3	Operating leverage measures percentage change in EBIT caused percentage change in sales.	Financial leverage measures percentage change in EPS caused by percentage change in EBIT.
4	Operating leverage should be used when contribution is greater than fixed operating costs.	Financial leverage should be used when return on investment is greater than the cost of debt capital.
5	Operating leverage is favourable when degree of operating leverage is greater than 1.	Financial leverage is favourable when degree of financial leverage is greater than 1.
6	Since operating leverage relates EBIT to sales, it is called first stage leverage.	Since financial leverage relates EPS to EBIT, it is called second stage leverage.
7	It is measured by following formula: $\text{DOL} = \dfrac{\text{Percentage change in EBIT}}{\text{Percentage change in sales}}$	It is measured by following formula: $\text{DFL} = \dfrac{\text{Percentage change in EPS}}{\text{Percentage change in EBIT}}$

6.8 EBIT-EPS Analysis

The EBIT-EPS analysis is carried out to assess the impact of different financial proposals on the value (EPS) of the company. Since the basic aim of financial management is to maximise the wealth of shareholders, the EBIT-EPS analysis is crucial in maximising the wealth of the company. The financial proposal having the highest EPS is considered for the execution. The different financial proposals may be the use of: only equity, combination of equity and debt, combination of equity and preferential capital, or any combination of equity, debt and preferential capital. EBIT-EPS analysis shows the impact of financial leverage on the EPS of the company under different financial proposals. The example given below explains the concept of EBIT-EPS analysis.

Example 4. Tulip Limited is planning to set up an industrial plant costing ₹ 40,00,000. It is expected the plant will yield an EBIT of ₹ 8,00,000 per annum. The company has following financial proposals to meet the cost of the plant:

(i) To finance the project by issuing 4,00,000 equity shares of ₹ 10 each,

(ii) To finance the project by issuing 3,00,000 equity shares of ₹ 10 each and 1,00,000 10% preferential shares of ₹ 10 each,

(iii) To finance the project by issuing 3,00,000 equity shares of ₹ 10 each and raising ₹ 10,00,000 by way of debt at 10%, or

on: We know that, Contribution = sales – variable cost

us, contribution = 8,000 – 70% of 8,000 = ₹ 2,400

erest = EBIT – PBT = 1,950 – 950 = ₹ 1,000

We know that the degree of operating leverage

$$DOL = \frac{Contribution}{EBIT}$$

Substituting the values,

$$DOL = \frac{2,400}{1,950} = 1.23$$

We know that the degree of financial leverage:

$$\text{Degree of financial leverage (DFL)} = \frac{EBIT}{EBIT - \left(\text{Interest charge} + \dfrac{\text{Preference dividend}}{(1 - \text{Tax rate})}\right)}$$

Substituting the values,

$$\text{Degree of financial leverage} = \frac{1,950}{1,950 - 1,000} = 2.06$$

We know that degree of combined leverage:

$$DCL = \frac{Contribution}{EBT}$$

Substituting the values,

$$DCL = \frac{2400}{950} = 2.52$$

2: Given below are the data of two companies:

Particulars	R Ltd.	S Ltd.
Sales (₹)	40,00,000	35,00,000
Variable cost	30% of sales	30% of sales
Fixed cost	2,50,000	3,00,000
Interest	14,00,000	1,50,000

ate degree of Operating Leverage and degree of Financial Leverage.

(D.U., B.Com. 2009)

Computation of EBT

Particulars	R Ltd.	S Ltd.
Sales (₹)	40,00,000	35,00,000
Less: Variable cost	12,00,000	10,50,000

(iv) To finance the project by issuing 2,00,000 equity shares of ₹ 10 each, 1,00,000 10% preferential shares of ₹ 10 each and raising ₹ 10,00,000 by way of debt at 10%.

If the company is in 40% tax bracket, which financial proposal is best?

Solution: Computation of EPS under different financial proposals:

	Proposal I	Proposal II	Proposal III	Proposal IV
EBIT	8,00,000	8,00,000	8,00,000	8,00,000
Less: Interest	–	–	1,00,000	1,00,000
EBT	8,00,000	8,00,000	7,00,000	7,00,000
Less: Tax	3,20,000	3,20,000	2,80,000	2,80,000
EAT	4,80,000	4,80,000	4,20,000	4,20,000
Less: Pref. dividend	–	1,00,000	–	1,00,000
Profit on equity	4,80,000	3,80,000	4,20,000	3,20,000
No. of equity shares	4,00,000	3,00,000	3,00,000	2,00,000
EPS	1.20	1.27	1.40	1.60

The maximum EPS is provided by proposal IV. Thus proposal IV should be selected.

6.9 Indifference Level of EBIT

Indifference level of EBIT is the EBIT at which the EPS is same for different financial proposals. Beyond the indifference level of EBIT, the financial leverage starts providing the benefits in respect to EPS. Below the indifference level of EBIT, it is better to not to use debt financing. Above the indifference level of EBIT, the use of debt in financing the project will be more beneficial.

The following formula is used in finding the indifference level of EBIT:

$$\frac{[(EBIT^{*} - I_1)(1-t) - PD_1]}{N_1} = \frac{[(EBIT^{*} - I_2)(1-t) - PD_2]}{N_2}$$

Where, EBIT* = Indifference level of EBIT

I_1 = Interest payment on proposal I

I_2 = Interest payment on proposal II

t = Tax rate

PD_1 = Preference dividend under proposal I

PD_2 = Preference dividend under proposal II

N_1 = No. of equity shares in proposal I

N_2 = No. of equity shares in proposal II

The following example will clear the concept of indifference level of EBIT.

Example 5. Prem Limited is planning to raise ₹ 10,00,000 for its project for which the following financial proposals are available:

Particulars	Equity (₹ 10 each)	10% Debt	10% Pref. shares
Proposal A	60%	40%	–
Proposal B	40%	30%	30%

Annual expected EBIT of the company is ₹ 3,00,000. The company pays tax @ 40%. Find the indifference level of EBIT and EPS for each proposal.

Solution: We know that:

$$\frac{[(\text{EBIT}^* - I_1)(1-t) - PD_1]}{N_1} = \frac{[(\text{EBIT}^* - I_2)(1-t) - PD_2]}{N_2}$$

Proposal A, interest charge = 10% of ₹ 4,00,000 = ₹ 40,000

Proposal B, interest charge = 10% of ₹ 3,00,000 = ₹ 30,000 and preferential dividend = ₹ 30,000

Substituting the values,

$$\frac{[(\text{EBIT}^* - 40{,}000)(1-0.4) - 0]}{60{,}000} = \frac{[(\text{EBIT}^* - 30{,}000)(1-0.4) - 30{,}000]}{40{,}000}$$

$$2[0.6\ \text{EBIT}^* - 24{,}000] = 3[0.6\ \text{EBIT}^* - 18{,}000 - 30{,}000]$$

$$1.2\ \text{EBIT}^* - 48{,}000 = 1.8\ \text{EBIT}^* - 1{,}44{,}000$$

$$0.6\ \text{EBIT}^* = 96{,}000$$

$$\text{EBIT}^* = ₹\ 1{,}60{,}000$$

Thus, indifference level of EBIT is ₹ 1,60,000. At this level of EBIT, the EPS of both proposals is ₹ 1.20.

Calculation of EPS

Particulars	Proposal A	Proposal B
EBIT	3,00,000	3,00,000
Less: Interest	40,000	30,000
EBT	2,60,000	2,70,000
Less: Tax	1,04,000	1,08,000
EAT	1,56,000	1,62,000
Less: Pref. dividend	–	30,000
Profit on equity	1,56,000	1,32,000
No. of equity shares	60,000	40,000
EPS	2.60	4.40

6.10 Financial Break Even Point

The level of EBIT at which EPS of a company is equal to zero is called financial break-even point of the company. Higher the financial break-even point, higher the degree of financial risk involved in a company. The following formula is used in calculation of financial break-even point:

$$\text{Financial break even EBIT} = \text{Interest amount} + \frac{\text{Preferenceividen}}{(1 - \text{Tax rate})}$$

The financial break even EBIT is just sufficient to cover the fixed financial given below explains the concept of financial break-even level of EBIT.

Example 6. The capital structures of company A and company B are giver

Particulars	Equity (₹ 10 each)	10% Debt	10
Company A	60%	40%	
Company B	40%	30%	

Each company has total capital of ₹ 10,00,000. The companies pay financial break-even point of EBIT.

Solution: We know that:

$$\text{Financial break even EBIT} = \text{Interest amount} + \frac{\text{Preference divid}}{(1 - \text{Tax rate})}$$

For company A:

Interest amount = 10% of 4,00,000 = ₹ 40,000 and preference divi

Thus,

$$\text{Financial break even EBIT} = 40{,}000 + \frac{0}{(1 - 0.40)}$$

$$\text{Financial break even EBIT} = 40{,}000$$

For company B:

Interest amount = 10% of 3,00,000 = ₹ 30,000 and preference di

Thus,

$$\text{Financial break even EBIT} = 30{,}000 + \frac{30{,}000}{(1 - 0.40)}$$

$$\text{Financial break even EBIT} = ₹\ 80{,}000.$$

SOLVED PROBLEMS

Problem 1. From the following information, calculate different type

Particulars	₹ (in lakhs)
Sales	8,000
EBIT	1,950
PBT	950
Tax rate	40%

Variable cost is 70% of sales.

Contribution	28,00,000	24,50,000
Less: Fixed cost	2,50,000	3,00,000
EBIT	25,50,000	21,50,000
Less: Interest	14,00,000	1,50,000
EBT	11,50,000	20,00,000

(A) R Ltd.

(i) We know that the degree of operating leverage:

$$\text{DOL} = \frac{\text{Contribution}}{\text{EBIT}}$$

Substituting the values,

$$\text{DOL} = \frac{28,00,000}{25,50,000} = 1.10$$

(ii) We know that the degree of financial leverage:

$$\text{Degree of financial leverage (DFL)} = \frac{\text{EBIT}}{\text{EBIT} - \left(\text{Interest charge} + \dfrac{\text{Preference dividend}}{(1 - \text{Tax rate})}\right)}$$

Substituting the values,

$$\text{Degree of financial leverage} = \frac{25,50,000}{25,50,000 - 14,00,000} = 2.22$$

(B) S. Ltd.

(i) We know that the degree of operating leverage

$$\text{DOL} = \frac{\text{Contribution}}{\text{EBIT}}$$

Substituting the values,

$$\text{DOL} = \frac{24,50,000}{21,50,000} = 1.14$$

(ii) We know that the degree of financial leverage:

$$\text{Degree of financial leverage (DFL)} = \frac{\text{EBIT}}{\text{EBIT} - \left(\text{Interest charge} + \dfrac{\text{Preference dividend}}{(1 - \text{Tax rate})}\right)}$$

Substituting the values,

$$\text{Degree of financial leverage} = \frac{21,50,000}{21,50,000 - 1,50,000} = 1.08$$

Problem 3. A firm has sales of ₹ 15,00,000, variable cost of ₹ 8,40,000 and fixed cost of ₹ 1,20,000. It has a debt of ₹ 9,00,000 at 9% and equity of ₹ 11,00,000.

(i) What is the firm's ROI (Return on investment)?

(ii) What are the operating and financial leverages of the firm?

(iii) If the sales drop to ₹ 9,00,000, what will be the new EBIT? Verify.

(D.U., B.Com. 2011)

Solution: Computation of EBT

Particulars	Amount (₹)	Amount (₹)
Sales (₹)	15,00,000	9,00,000
Less: Variable cost	8,40,000	5,04,000
Contribution	6,60,000	3,96,000
Less: Fixed cost	1,20,000	1,20,000
EBIT	5,40,000	2,76,000
Less: Interest	81,000	
EBT	4,59,000	

(i) Return on investment = (EBIT ÷ Total capital employed) × 100

= (5,40,000 ÷ 20,00,000) × 100 = 27%

(ii) We know that the degree of operating leverage:

$$\text{DOL} = \frac{\text{Contribution}}{\text{EBIT}}$$

Substituting the values,

$$\text{DOL} = \frac{6,60,000}{5,40,000} = 1.22$$

(iii) We know that the degree of financial leverage:

$$\text{Degree of financial leverage (DFL)} = \frac{\text{EBIT}}{\text{EBIT} - \left(\text{Interest charge} + \dfrac{\text{Preference dividend}}{(1 - \text{Tax rate})}\right)}$$

Substituting the values,

$$\text{Degree of financial leverage} = \frac{5,40,000}{5,40,000 - 81,000} = 1.18$$

(iv) If sales drops to ₹ 9,00,000, the new EBIT can be calculated by following formula:

$$\text{Degree of operating leverage (DOL)} = \frac{\text{Percentage change in operating profit}}{\text{Percentage change in sales}}$$

Decrease in sales = [(15,00,000 – 9,00,000) ÷ 15,00,000] × 100 = 40%

Substituting the values,

$$1.22 = \frac{\text{Percentage change in operating profit}}{-40\%}$$

Percentage change in operating profit = –48.8%

New EBIT = EBIT – 48.8% of EBIT = ₹ 2,76,480

The new EBIT has been calculated in the above table. The difference is due to rounding off.

Problem 4. Calculate Operating and Financial Leverage from the following data of ABC Ltd.:

Earnings Before Interest and Taxes (EBIT)	₹ 20,00,000
Profit After Tax (PAT)	₹ 9,00,000
Operating Fixed Cost	₹ 15,00,000
Tax Rate	40%

If the company wants to increase its PAT by 40%, what should be the percentage rise in EBIT?

(D.U., B.Com. 2012)

Solution: We know that, EBT – (1 – t) EBT = EAT

Substituting the values,

EBT – 0.4 EBT = 9,00,000

EBT = ₹ 15,00,000

Contribution = EBIT + Fixed cost = 20,00,000 + 15,00,000 = 35,00,000

Interest = EBIT – EBT = 20,00,000 – 15,00,000 = ₹ 5,00,000

(i) We know that the degree of operating leverage:

$$\text{DOL} = \frac{\text{Contribution}}{\text{EBIT}}$$

Substituting the values,

$$\text{DOL} = \frac{35,00,000}{20,00,000} = 1.75$$

(ii) We know that the degree of financial leverage:

$$\text{Degree of financial leverage (DFL)} = \frac{\text{EBIT}}{\text{EBIT} - \left(\text{Interest charge} + \dfrac{\text{Preference dividend}}{(1 - \text{Tax rate})}\right)}$$

Substituting the values,

$$\text{Degree of financial leverage} = \frac{20,00,000}{20,00,000 - 5,00,000} = 1.33$$

As per the financial leverage 1% increase in EBIT increases 1.33% of EPS (profit after tax). Thus, to increase the profit after tax by 40%, the EBIT should increase by 40% (1 ÷ 1.33) or 30.08%.

Problem 5. A firm has sales of ₹ 10 lacs and fixed costs of ₹ 1.5 lacs. Contribution margin is 30%. It has 10% debt of ₹ 8 lacs. Find out operating and financial leverage. Also find out that if firm wants to double its EBIT, how much % increase in sales is needed? Verify the results.

(D.U., B. Com. 2013)

Solution: Computation of EBIT

Particulars	Amount (₹)
Sales	10,00,000
Less: Variable cost	7,00,000
Contribution	3,00,000
Less: Fixed costs	1,50,000
EBIT	1,50,000
Less: Interest	80,000
EBT	70,000

(i) We know that the degree of operating leverage:

$$\text{DOL} = \frac{\text{Contribution}}{\text{EBIT}}$$

Substituting the values,

$$\text{DOL} = \frac{3,00,000}{15,00,000} = 2.00$$

(ii) We know that the degree of financial leverage:

$$\text{Degree of financial leverage (DFL)} = \frac{\text{EBIT}}{\text{EBIT} - \left(\text{Interest charge} + \dfrac{\text{Preference dividend}}{(1 - \text{Tax rate})}\right)}$$

Substituting the values,

$$\text{Degree of financial leverage} = \frac{1,50,000}{1,50,000 - 80,000} = 2.14$$

The degree of operating leverage is 2. It means 50% increase in sales will cause 100% increase in EBIT. Thus, ₹ 5,00,000 increase in sales will double the EBIT i.e., ₹ 3,00,000. The proof is given below:

Particulars	Amount (₹)
Sales	15,00,000
Less: Variable cost	10,50,000
Contribution	4,50,000
Less: Fixed costs	1,50,000
EBIT	3,00,000

Problem 6. From the following information, calculate EBIT, Sales, Variable cost and fixed cost:

Variable cost as % of sales	50%
Interest	₹ 20,000
Degree of operating leverage	3
Degree of financial leverage	2
Tax rate	55%

(D.U., B.Com. 2015)

Solution: We know that:

$$\text{Degree of financial leverage (DFL)} = \frac{\text{EBIT}}{\text{EBIT} - \left(\text{Interest charge} + \dfrac{\text{Preference dividend}}{(1 - \text{Tax rate})}\right)}$$

Substituting the values,

$$2 = \frac{\text{EBIT}}{\text{EBIT} - 20{,}000}$$

Thus, EBIT = ₹ 40,000

We know that the degree of operating leverage:

$$\text{DOL} = \frac{\text{Contribution}}{\text{EBIT}}$$

Substituting the values,

$$3 = \frac{\text{Contribution}}{40{,}000}$$

Thus, Contribution = ₹ 1,20,000

Computation of sales, fixed costs

Particulars	**Amount (₹)**
Sales	2,40,000
Less: Variable cost	1,20,000
Contribution	1,20,000
Less: Fixed costs	80,000
EBIT	40,000
Less: Interest	20,000
EBT	20,000
Less: Tax	11,000
EAT	9,000

Problem 7: Given below are the data of two companies:

Particulars	A Ltd.	B Ltd.
Sales (₹)	50,00,000	30,00,000
Variable cost	30% of sales	30% of sales
Fixed cost	4,50,000	3,00,000
Interest	15,00,000	1,00,000

Calculate degree of Operating Leverage and degree of Financial Leverage.

Solution: Computation of EBT

Particulars	A Ltd.	B Ltd.
Sales (₹)	50,00,000	30,00,000
Less: Variable cost	15,00,000	9,00,000
Contribution	35,00,000	21,00,000
Less: Fixed cost	4,50,000	3,00,000
EBIT	30,50,000	18.00,000
Less: Interest	15,00,000	1,00,000
EBT	15,50,000	17,00,000

(A) A Ltd.

(i) We know that the degree of operating leverage

$$\text{DOL} = \frac{\text{Contribution}}{\text{EBIT}}$$

Substituting the values,

$$\text{DOL} = \frac{35,00,000}{30,50,000} = 1.15$$

(ii) We know that the degree of financial leverage:

$$\text{Degree of financial leverage (DFL)} = \frac{\text{EBIT}}{\text{EBIT} - \left(\text{Interest charge} + \frac{\text{Preference dividend}}{(1 - \text{Tax rate})}\right)}$$

Substituting the values,

$$\text{Degree of financial leverage} = \frac{30,50,000}{30,50,000 - 15,00,000} = 1.97$$

(B) B Ltd.

(i) We know that the degree of operating leverage

$$\text{DOL} = \frac{\text{Contribution}}{\text{EBIT}}$$

Substituting the values,

$$DOL = \frac{21,00,000}{18,00,000} = 1.17$$

(ii) We know that the degree of financial leverage:

$$\text{Degree of financial leverage (DFL)} = \frac{\text{EBIT}}{\text{EBIT} - \left(\text{Interest charge} + \frac{\text{Preference dividend}}{(1 - \text{Tax rate})}\right)}$$

Substituting the values,

$$\text{Degree of financial leverage} = \frac{18,00,000}{18,00,000 - 1,00,000} = 1.06$$

Problem 8. A firm has sales of ₹ 25,00,000, variable cost of ₹ 15,40,000 and fixed cost of ₹ 3,20,000. It has a debt of ₹ 12,00,000 at 10% and equity of ₹ 13,00,000.

(i) What is the firm's ROI (Return on investment)?

(ii) What are the operating and financial leverages of the firm?

(iii) If the sales drop to ₹ 15,00,000, what will be the new EBIT? Verify.

Solution: Computation of EBT

Particulars	Amount (₹)	Amount (₹)
Sales (₹)	25,00,000	15,00,000
Less: Variable cost	15,40,000	9,24,000
Contribution	9,60,000	5,76,000
Less: Fixed cost	3,20,000	3,20,000
EBIT	6,40,000	2,56,000
Less: Interest	1,20,000	
EBT	5,20,000	

(i) Return on investment = (EBIT ÷ Total capital employed) × 100
= (6,40,000 ÷ 25,00,000) × 100 = 25.6%

(ii) We know that the degree of operating leverage:

$$DOL = \frac{\text{Contribution}}{\text{EBIT}}$$

Substituting the values,

$$DOL = \frac{9,60,000}{6,40,000} = 1.50$$

(iii) We know that the degree of financial leverage:

$$\text{Degree of financial leverage (DFL)} = \frac{\text{EBIT}}{\text{EBIT} - \left(\text{Interest charge} + \dfrac{\text{Preference dividend}}{(1 - \text{Tax rate})}\right)}$$

Substituting the values,

$$\text{Degree of financial leverage} = \frac{6,40,000}{6,40,000 - 1,20,000} = 1.23$$

(iv) If sales drops to ₹ 15,00,000, the new EBIT can be calculated by following formula:

$$\text{Degree of operating leverage (DOL)} = \frac{\text{Percentage change in operating profit}}{\text{Percentage change in sales}}$$

Decrease in sales = [(25,00,000 – 15,00,000) ÷ 25,00,000] × 100 = 40%
Substituting the values,

$$1.50 = \frac{\text{Percentage change in operating profit}}{-40\%}$$

Percentage change in operating profit = –60%

New EBIT = EBIT – 60% of EBIT = ₹ 2,56,000

The new EBIT has been calculated in the above table.

Problem 9. Calculate Operating and Financial Leverage from the following data of Varun Ltd.:

Earnings Before Interest and Taxes (EBIT)	₹ 25,00,000
Profit After Tax (PAT)	₹ 10,50,000
Operating Fixed Cost	₹ 16,00,000
Tax Rate	30%

If the company wants to increase its PAT by 30%, what should be the percentage rise in EBIT?

Solution: We know that, EBT – (1 – t) EBT = EAT

Substituting the values,

EBT – 0.3EBT = 10,50,000

EBT = ₹ 15,00,000

Contribution = EBIT + Fixed cost = 25,00,000 + 16,00,000 = 41,00,000

Interest = EBIT – EBT = 25,00,000 – 15,00,000 = ₹ 10,00,000

(i) We know that the degree of operating leverage:

$$\text{DOL} = \frac{\text{Contribution}}{\text{EBIT}}$$

Substituting the values,

$$\text{DOL} = \frac{41,00,000}{25,00,000} = 1.64$$

(ii) We know that the degree of financial leverage:

$$\text{Degree of financial leverage (DFL)} = \frac{\text{EBIT}}{\text{EBIT} - \left(\text{Interest charge} + \dfrac{\text{Preference dividend}}{(1 - \text{Tax rate})}\right)}$$

Substituting the values,

$$\text{Degree of financial leverage} = \frac{25{,}00{,}000}{25{,}00{,}000 - 10{,}00{,}000} = 1.67$$

As per the financial leverage 1% increase in EBIT increases 1.67% of EPS (profit after tax). Thus, to increase the profit after tax by 30%, the EBIT should increase by 30% (1 ÷ 1.67) or 17.96%.

Problem 10. From the following information, calculate EBIT, Sales, Variable cost and fixed cost:

Variable cost as % of sales	60%
Interest	₹ 40,000
Degree of operating leverage	3
Degree of financial leverage	2
Tax rate	50%

Solution: We know that:

$$\text{Degree of financial leverage (DFL)} = \frac{\text{EBIT}}{\text{EBIT} - \left(\text{Interest charge} + \dfrac{\text{Preference dividend}}{(1 - \text{Tax rate})}\right)}$$

Substituting the values,

$$2 = \frac{\text{EBIT}}{\text{EBIT} - 40{,}000}$$

Thus, EBIT = ₹ 80,000

We know that the degree of operating leverage:

$$\text{DOL} = \frac{\text{Contribution}}{\text{EBIT}}$$

Substituting the values,

$$3 = \frac{\text{Contribution}}{80{,}000}$$

Thus, Contribution = ₹ 2,40,000

Computation of sales, fixed costs

Particulars	Amount (₹)
Sales	6,00,000
Less: Variable cost	3,60,000
Contribution	2,40,000
Less: Fixed costs	1,60,000
EBIT	80,000
Less: Interest	40,000
EBT	40,000
Less: Tax	20,000
EAT	20,000

Sales = contribution ÷ 0.4 = 2,40,000 ÷ 0.4 = ₹ 6,00,000.

Problem 11. Sumit Ltd. is selling its product at ₹ 5 per unit. The variable cost of manufacturing has been estimated at ₹ 3 per unit. While the fixed cost at present sales level of 1,00,000 units comes to ₹ 1,00,000. The company has issued 10% debentures of ₹ 1,00,000. Find out the operating, financial and combined leverage for the firm. Also find out percentage increase in sales if the company wants to double its EPS.

Solution: Computation of EBIT

Particulars	Amount (₹)
Sales	5,00,000
Less: Variable cost	3,00,000
Contribution	2,00,000
Less: Fixed cost	1,00,000
EBIT	1,00,000
Less: Interest on debentures	10,000
EBT	90,000

(i) We know that the degree of operating leverage

$$\text{DOL} = \frac{\text{Contribution}}{\text{EBIT}}$$

Substituting the values,

$$\text{DOL} = \frac{2,00,000}{1,00,000} = 2.00$$

(ii) We know that the degree of financial leverage:

$$\text{Degree of financial leverage (DFL)} = \frac{\text{EBIT}}{\text{EBIT} - \left(\text{Interest charge} + \frac{\text{Preference dividend}}{(1 - \text{Tax rate})}\right)}$$

Substituting the values,

$$\text{Degree of financial leverage} = \frac{1{,}00{,}000}{1{,}00{,}000 - 10{,}000} = 1.11$$

(iii) We know that degree of combined leverage:

$$\text{DOL} = \frac{\text{Contribution}}{\text{EBT}}$$

Substituting the values,

$$\text{DCL} = \frac{2{,}00{,}000}{90{,}000} = 2.22$$

Combined leverage shows that 1% change in sales will lead to 2.22% change in EPS. So, if company wants to double its EPS then % change in sales:

$$(200 - 100)\ \% \div 2.22 = 45.04\%.$$

Problem 12. The following data of XYZ Ltd. are given below:

Sales	₹ 20,00,000
Variable cost	₹ 12,00,000
Fixed cost	₹ 4,00,000
Interest	₹ 2,00,000

Calculate degree of operating leverage and degree of financial leverage. By what percentage will EBIT increase if there is a 10% increase in sales?

Solution: Computation of EBIT

Particulars	**Amount (₹)**
Sales	20,00,000
Less: Variable cost	12,00,000
Contribution	8,00,000
Less: Fixed cost	4,00,000
EBIT	4,00,000
Less: Interest on debentures	2,00,000
EBT	2,00,000

(i) We know that the degree of operating leverage

$$\text{DOL} = \frac{\text{Contribution}}{\text{EBIT}}$$

Substituting the values,

$$DOL = \frac{8,00,000}{4,00,000} = 2.00$$

(ii) We know that the degree of financial leverage:

$$\text{Degree of financial leverage (DFL)} = \frac{\text{EBIT}}{\text{EBIT} - \left(\text{Interest charge} + \frac{\text{Preference dividend}}{(1 - \text{Tax rate})}\right)}$$

Substituting the values,

$$\text{Degree of financial leverage} = \frac{4,00,000}{4,00,000 - 2,00,000} = 2.00$$

Operating leverage shows that 1% change in sales will lead to 2.0% change in EBIT. So, if there is 10% increase in sales, the EBIT will increase by 20%.

Problem 13. Using the data given below, find out EBIT and EAT of the companies X and Y.

	X	Y
V.C. as % of sales	60%	50%
Interest expenses	2,00,000	3,00,000
DOL	3	4
DFL	2	3
Income Tax Rate	50%	50%

Solution: (i) Company X:

We know that:

$$\text{Degree of financial leverage (DFL)} = \frac{\text{EBIT}}{\text{EBIT} - \left(\text{Interest charge} + \frac{\text{Preference dividend}}{(1 - \text{Tax rate})}\right)}$$

Substituting the values,

$$2 = \frac{\text{EBIT}}{\text{EBIT} - 2,00,000}$$

Thus, EBIT = ₹ 4,00,000

We know that the degree of operating leverage:

$$DOL = \frac{\text{Contribution}}{\text{EBIT}}$$

Substituting the values,

$$3 = \frac{\text{Contribution}}{4,00,000}$$

Thus, Contribution = ₹ 12,00,000

Computation of sales, fixed costs

Particulars	Amount (₹)
Sales	30,00,000
Less: Variable cost	18,00,000
Contribution	12,00,000
Less: Fixed costs	8,00,000
EBIT	4,00,000
Less: Interest	2,00,000
EBT	2,00,000
Less: Tax	1,00,000
EAT	1,00,000

Sales = contribution ÷ 0.4 = 12,00,000 ÷ 0.4 = ₹ 30,00,000

(ii) Company Y:

We know that:

$$\text{Degree of financial leverage (DFL)} = \frac{\text{EBIT}}{\text{EBIT} - \left(\text{Interest charge} + \dfrac{\text{Preference dividend}}{(1 - \text{Tax rate})}\right)}$$

Substituting the values,

$$3 = \frac{\text{EBIT}}{\text{EBIT} - 3{,}00{,}000}$$

Thus, EBIT = ₹ 4,50,000

We know that the degree of operating leverage:

$$\text{DOL} = \frac{\text{Contribution}}{\text{EBIT}}$$

Substituting the values,

$$4 = \frac{\text{Contribution}}{4{,}50{,}000}$$

Thus, Contribution = ₹ 18,00,000

Computation of sales, fixed costs

Particulars	Amount (₹)
Sales	36,00,000
Less: Variable cost	18,00,000
Contribution	18,00,000

Less: Fixed costs	13,50,000
EBIT	4,50,000
Less: Interest	3,00,000
EBT	1,50,000
Less: Tax	75,000
EAT	75,000

Sales = contribution ÷ 0.5 = 18,00,000 ÷ 0.5 = ₹ 36,00,000.

Problem 14. Calculate the Degree of Operating Leverage (DOL) and Degree of Financial Leverage (DFL) for the following firms and interpret the results:

Particulars	Firm A	Firm B	Firm C
Output (units)	9,000	2,500	15,000
Selling price (p.u.)	6	5	2
Variable cost (p.u.)	2	2	1
Fixed cost	10,000	4,000	6,000
Interest on borrowed funds	8,000	2,000	–

Solution: Computation of EBT

Particulars (₹)	A	B	C
Sales	54,000	12,500	30,000
Less: Variable cost	18,000	5,000	15,000
Contribution	36,000	7,500	15,000
Less: Fixed costs	10,000	4,000	6,000
EBIT	26,000	3,500	9,000
Less: Interest	8,000	2,000	–
EBT	18,000	1,500	–

We know that the degree of operating leverage:

$$\text{DOL} = \frac{\text{Contribution}}{\text{EBIT}}$$

Substituting the values,

$$\text{DOL (A)} = \frac{36{,}000}{26{,}000} = 1.38$$

$$\text{DOL (B)} = \frac{7{,}500}{3{,}500} = 2.14$$

$$\text{DOL (C)} = \frac{15{,}000}{9{,}000} = 1.67$$

We know that:

$$\text{Degree of financial leverage (DFL)} = \frac{\text{EBIT}}{\text{EBIT} - \left(\text{Interest charge} + \dfrac{\text{Preference dividend}}{(1 - \text{Tax rate})}\right)}$$

Substituting the values,

$$\text{DFL (A)} = \frac{26{,}000}{26{,}000 - 8{,}000} = 1.44$$

$$\text{DFL (B)} = \frac{3{,}500}{3{,}500 - 2{,}000} = 2.33$$

$$\text{DFL (C)} = \frac{9{,}000}{9{,}000} = 1.00$$

Problem 15. From the following information for firm P and firm Q, calculate EPS, degree of operating leverage and degree of financial leverage:

Particulars	Firm P	Firm Q
Sales (in units)	10,000	20,000
Selling price per unit	₹ 15	₹ 15
Variable cost per unit	₹ 10	₹ 12
Fixed cost	₹ 30,000	₹ 30,000
Interest	₹ 15,000	₹ 20,000
Tax	50%	50%
Number of equity shares	2,500	5,000

Solution: Computation of EBT

Particulars (₹)	P	Q
Sales	1,50,000	3,00,000
Less: Variable cost	1,00,000	2,40,000
Contribution	50,000	60,000
Less: Fixed costs	30,000	30,000
EBIT	20,000	30,000
Less: Interest	15,000	20,000
EBT	5,000	10,000
Less: tax	2,500	5,000
EAT	2,500	5,000
EPS	1.00	1.00

We know that the degree of operating leverage:

$$\text{DOL} = \frac{\text{Contribution}}{\text{EBIT}}$$

Substituting the values,

$$\text{DOL (P)} = \frac{5{,}000}{20{,}000} = 2.50$$

$$\text{DOL (Q)} = \frac{60{,}000}{30{,}000} = 2.00$$

We know that:

$$\text{Degree of financial leverage (DFL)} = \frac{\text{EBIT}}{\text{EBIT} - \left(\text{Interest charge} + \dfrac{\text{Preference dividend}}{(1 - \text{Tax rate})}\right)}$$

Substituting the values,

$$\text{DFL (P)} = \frac{20{,}000}{20{,}000 - 15{,}000} = 4.0$$

$$\text{DFL (Q)} = \frac{30{,}000}{30{,}000 - 20{,}000} = 3.0$$

Problem 16. Using the data given below, prepare income statement of X Ltd.:

V.C. as % of sales	60%
Interest expenses	₹ 50,000
DOL	2
DFL	3
Income tax rate	40%

Solution: We know that:

$$\text{Degree of financial leverage (DFL)} = \frac{\text{EBIT}}{\text{EBIT} - \left(\text{Interest charge} + \dfrac{\text{Preference dividend}}{(1 - \text{Tax rate})}\right)}$$

Substituting the values,

$$3 = \frac{\text{EBIT}}{\text{EBIT} - 50{,}000}$$

Thus, EBIT = ₹ 75,000

We know that the degree of operating leverage:

$$\text{DOL} = \frac{\text{Contribution}}{\text{EBIT}}$$

Substituting the values,

$$3 = \frac{\text{Contribution}}{75,000}$$

Thus, Contribution = ₹ 2,25,000

Computation of sales, fixed costs

Particulars	Amount (₹)
Sales	5,62,500
Less: Variable cost	3,37,500
Contribution	2,25,000
Less: Fixed costs	1,50,000
EBIT	75,000
Less: Interest	50,000
EBT	25,000
Less: Tax	12,500
EAT	12,500

Sales = Contribution ÷ 0.4 = 2,25,000 ÷ 0.4 = ₹ 5,62,500.

Problem 17. The following data are available for XYZ Ltd.

Particulars	Amount (₹)
Sales	4,00,000
Less: Variable cost	1,20,000
Contribution	2,80,000
Less: Fixed cost	2,00,000
EBIT	80,000
Less: Interest	10,000
Profit before tax	70,000

(i) Calculate the degree of operating leverage. What will be the percentage increase in EBIT if sales increase by 20%? Verify your result.

(ii) Calculate the degree of financial leverage. What will be the percentage increase in taxable income if EBIT increases by 10%? Verify your result.

Solution: (i) We know that the degree of operating leverage:

$$\text{DOL} = \frac{\text{Contribution}}{\text{EBIT}}$$

Substituting the values,

$$\text{DOL} = \frac{2{,}80{,}000}{80{,}000} = 3.5$$

Degree of operating leverage indicates that 1% increase in sales will increase the EBIT by 3.5%. Thus, 20% increase in sales will increase EBIT by 70%. The proof is given below:

Particulars	Amount (₹)
Sales	4,80,000
Less: Variable cost	1,44,000
Contribution	3,36,000
Less: Fixed cost	2,00,000
EBIT	1,36,000
Less: Interest	10,000
Profit before tax	1,26,000

The change in EBIT = [(1,36,000 – 80,000) ÷ 80,000] × 100 = 70%.

(ii) We know that:

$$\text{Degree of financial leverage (DFL)} = \frac{\text{EBIT}}{\text{EBIT} - \left(\text{Interest charge} + \dfrac{\text{Preference dividend}}{(1 - \text{Tax rate})}\right)}$$

Substituting the values,

$$\text{DFL} = \frac{80{,}000}{80{,}000 - 10{,}000} = 1.14$$

Degree of financial leverage indicates that 1% increase in EBIT will increase taxable income by 1.14%. Thus, 10% increase in EBIT will increase taxable income by 11.4%.

The proof is given below:

Particulars	Amount (₹)
Sales	—
Less: Variable cost	—
Contribution	—
Less: Fixed cost	—
EBIT	88,000
Less: Interest	10,000
Profit before tax	78,000

The change in taxable income = [(78,000 – 70,000) ÷ 70,000] × 100 = 11.4%.

Problem 18. A firm has sales of ₹ 6,00,000 and fixed costs of ₹ 1,00,000. Contribution margin is 30%. It has 10% debt of ₹ 3,00,000. Find out operating and financial leverage. Also, find out if the firm wants to double its EBIT, how much % increase in sales is needed? Verify the results.

Solution: Computation of EBIT

Particulars	Amount (₹)
Sales	6,00,000
Less: Variable cost	4,20,000
Contribution	1,80,000
Less: Fixed costs	1,00,000
EBIT	80,000
Less: Interest	30,000
EBT	50,000

(i) We know that the degree of operating leverage:

$$\text{DOL} = \frac{\text{Contribution}}{\text{EBIT}}$$

Substituting the values,

$$\text{DOL} = \frac{1{,}80{,}000}{80{,}000} = 2.25$$

(ii) We know that the degree of financial leverage:

$$\text{Degree of financial leverage (DFL)} = \frac{\text{EBIT}}{\text{EBIT} - \left(\text{Interest charge} + \dfrac{\text{Preference dividend}}{(1 - \text{Tax rate})}\right)}$$

Substituting the values,

$$\text{Degree of financial leverage} = \frac{80{,}000}{80{,}000 - 30{,}000} = 1.6$$

The degree of operating leverage is 2.25. It means (100 ÷ 2.25) = 44.44% increase in sales will cause 100% increase in EBIT. Thus, ₹ 2,66,667 increase in sales will double the EBIT i.e., ₹ 1,60,000. The proof is given below:

Particulars	Amount (₹)
Sales	8,66,667
Less: Variable cost	6,06,667
Contribution	2,60,000
Less: Fixed costs	1,00,000
EBIT	1,60,000

Problem 19. The following data are available for Sun Ltd.

Particulars	Amount (₹)
Sales	8,00,000
Less: Variable cost	2,40,000
Contribution	5,60,000
Less: Fixed cost	4,00,000
EBIT	1,60,000
Less: Interest	20,000
Profit before tax	1,40,000

(i) Calculate the degree of operating leverage. What will be the percentage increase in EBIT if sales increase by 10%? Verify your result.

(ii) Calculate the degree of financial leverage. What will be the percentage increase in taxable income if EBIT increases by 10%. Verify your result.

Solution: (i) We know that the degree of operating leverage:

$$\text{DOL} = \frac{\text{Contribution}}{\text{EBIT}}$$

Substituting the values,

$$\text{DOL} = \frac{5{,}60{,}000}{1{,}60{,}000} = 3.5$$

Degree of operating leverage indicates that 1% increase in sales will increase the EBIT by 3.5%. Thus, 20% increase in sales will increase EBIT by 70%. The proof is given below:

Particulars	Amount (₹)
Sales	9,60,000
Less: Variable cost	2,88,000
Contribution	6,72,000
Less: Fixed cost	4,00,000
EBIT	2,72,000
Less: Interest	20,000
Profit before tax	2,52,000

The change in EBIT = [(2,72,000 – 1,60,000) ÷ 1,60,000] × 100 = 70%.

(ii) We know that:

$$\text{Degree of financial leverage (DFL)} = \frac{\text{EBIT}}{\text{EBIT} - \left(\text{Interest charge} + \dfrac{\text{Preference dividend}}{(1 - \text{Tax rate})}\right)}$$

Substituting the values,

$$DFL = \frac{1,60,000}{1,60,000 - 20,000} = 1.14$$

Degree of financial leverage indicates that 1% increase in EBIT will increase taxable income by 1.14%. Thus, 10% increase in EBIT will increase taxable income by 11.4%.

The proof is given below:

Particulars	Amount (₹)
Sales	—
Less: Variable cost	—
Contribution	—
Less: Fixed cost	—
EBIT	1,76,000
Less: Interest	20,000
Profit before tax	1,56,000

The change in taxable income = [(1,56,000 – 1,40,000) ÷ 1,40,000] × 100 = 11.4%.

Problem 20. A firm has sales of ₹ 15,00,000, variable cost of ₹ 10,00,000 and fixed cost of ₹ 3,00,000 inclusive of interest of ₹ 1,00,000.

(i) Calculate its operating, financial and combined leverages.

(ii) If the firm decides to double its EPS, how much of a rise in the sales would be needed on a percentage basis.

Solution: Contribution = Sales – Variable cost

Thus, contribution = 15,00,000 – 10,00,000 = ₹ 5,00,000

EBIT = 5,00,000 – 2,00,000 = 3,00,000

(i) We know that the degree of operating leverage:

$$DOL = \frac{\text{Contribution}}{\text{EBIT}}$$

Substituting the values,

$$DOL = \frac{5,00,000}{3,00,000} = 1.67$$

(ii) We know that the degree of financial leverage:

$$\text{Degree of financial leverage (DFL)} = \frac{\text{EBIT}}{\text{EBIT} - \left(\text{Interest charge} + \dfrac{\text{Preference dividend}}{(1 - \text{Tax rate})}\right)}$$

Substituting the values,

$$\text{Degree of financial leverage} = \frac{3,00,000}{3,00,000 - 1,00,000} = 1.50$$

(iii) We know that degree of combined leverage:

$$DCL = \frac{\text{Contribution}}{\text{EBT}}$$

Substituting the values,

$$DCL = \frac{5,00,000}{2,00,000} = 2.50$$

(iv) Degree of combined leverage indicates that 1% increase in sales will increase EPS by 2.5%. Thus, 40% (100 ÷ 2.5) increase in sales will increase EPS by 100% and will double it.

THEORETICAL QUESTIONS

1. Define "Leverage". What are the different types of leverages? Explain them. *(D.U., B.Com. 2016)*
2. Distinguish between operating leverage and financial leverage. How the two leverages can be measured? *(D.U., B.Com. 2010)*
3. "Financial leverage is a double-edged sword". Comment.
4. What is EBIT-EPS analysis? How is it different from leverage analysis?
5. What is financial Break Even Point?
6. What is indifferent level of EBIT?

PRACTICAL PROBLEMS

1. A firm has sales of ₹ 20,00,000, variable cost of ₹ 14,00,000 and fixed cost of ₹ 3,00,000 inclusive of interest of ₹ 1,00,000.
   (i) Calculate its operating, financial and combined liverages.
   (ii) If the firm decides to double its EPS, how much of a rise in the sales would be needed on a percentage basis. *(D.U., B.Com. 2009, Corres.)*
   [**Ans.** (i) DOL = 2.00, DFL = 1.50, DCL = 3.00; (ii) 33.3%]
2. Suri Ltd. is selling its product at ₹ 2 per unit. The variable cost of manufacturing has been estimated at 75%. While the fixed cost at present sales level of 1,00,000 units comes to ₹ 25,000. The company has issued 10% debentures of ₹ 26,000. Find out the operating, financial and combined leverages for the firm. Also find out percentage increase in sales if the company wants to double its EPS. *(D.U., B.Com. 2010, Corres.)*
   [**Ans.** (i) DOL = 2.00, DFL = 1.12, DCL = 2.24; (ii) 44.64%]
3. The following data of XYZ Ltd. is given below:

Sales	₹ 80,00,000
Variable cost	₹ 50,00,000
Fixed cost	₹ 12,00,000
Interest	₹ 6,00,000

Calculate degree of operating leverage and degree of financial leverage. By what percentage will EBIT increase if there is a 10% increase in sales?

(D.U., B.Com. 2012, Corres.)

[**Ans.** (i) DOL = 1.67, DFL = 1.50; (ii) 16.7%]

4. Using the data given below, find out EBIT and EAT of the companies X and Y.

	X	Y
V.C. as % of sales	50%	60%
Interest expenses	20,000	6,000
DOL	3	5
DFL	2	3
Income Tax Rate	55%	55%

(D.U., B.Com. 2013, Corres.)

[**Ans.** X: EBIT = 40,000, EAT = 9,000; Y: EBIT = 9,000, EAT = 1,350]

5. Calculate the Degree of Operating Leverage (DOL) and Degree of Financial Leverage (DFL) for the following firms and interpret the results:

Particulars	Firm A	Firm B	Firm C
Output (units)	6,000	1,500	10,000
Selling price (₹ p.u.)	6	5	1
Variable cost (₹ p.u.)	2	1.5	0.5
Fixed cost (₹)	8,000	2,000	4,000
Interest on borrowed funds (₹)	5,000	3,000	–

(D.U., B.Com. 2014, Corres.)

[**Ans.** DOL: A = 1.33, B =1.62, C = 5.00; DFL: A = 1.45 , B = 13.0, C = 1.00]

6. From the following information for firm P and firm S, calculate EPS, degree of operating leverage and degree of financial leverage:

Particulars	Firm P	Firm S
Sales (in units)	20,000	40,000
Selling price per unit	₹ 15	₹ 30
Variable cost per unit	₹ 10	₹ 25
Fixed cost	₹ 30,000	₹ 60,000
Interest	₹ 15,000	₹ 40,000

Tax	40%	40%
Number of equity shares	5,000	12,000

(*D.U., B.Com. 2015, N.C.*)

[**Ans.** DOL: P = 1.43, S =1.43; DFL: P = 1.27, S = 1.40; EPS: P = 6.60, S = 5.00]

7. Using the data given below, prepare income statement of X Ltd.:

V.C. as % of sales 70%
Interest expenses ₹ 5,000
DOL 1.5
DFL 2
Income tax rate 40% (*D.U., B.Com. 2015, Corres.*)

[**Ans.** EAT = ₹ 3,000]

8. The following data are available for XYZ Ltd.

Particulars	Amount (₹)
Sales	2,00,000
Less: Variable cost	60,000
Contribution	1,40,000
Less: Fixed cost	1,00,000
EBIT	40,000
Less: Interest	5,000
Profit before tax	35,000

(i) Calculate the degree of operating leverage. What will be the percentage increase in EBIT if sales increase by 10%? Verify your result.

(ii) Calculate the degree of financial leverage. What will be the percentage increase in taxable income if EBIT increases by 6%? Verify your result.

(*D.U., B.Com. 2016, N.C.*)

[**Ans.** (i) 3.5, 35%; (ii) 1.14, 6.84%]

9. A firm has sales of ₹ 12,00,000 and fixed costs of ₹ 2,00,000. Contribution margin is 30%. It has 10% debt of ₹ 6,00,000. Find out operating and financial leverages. Also, find out if the firm wants to double its EBIT, how much % increase in sales is needed? Verify the results. (*D.U., B.Com. 2016, Corres.*)

[**Ans.** DOL= 2.25; DFL = 1.6, 44.4%]

10. The following data are available for Avon Ltd.

Particulars	Amount (₹)
Sales	4,00,000
Less: Variable cost	1,20,000
Contribution	2,80,000

Less: Fixed cost	2,00,000
EBIT	80,000
Less: Interest	10,000
Profit before tax	70,000

(i) Calculate the degree of operating leverage. What will be the percentage increase in EBIT if sales increase by 10%? Verify your result.

(ii) Calculate the degree of financial leverage. What will be the percentage increase in taxable income if EBIT increases by 6%. Verify your result.

[**Ans.** (i) 3.5, 35%; (ii) 1.14, 6.84%]

Capital Structure: Valuation of Firm

7

Chapter Outline

7.1 Introduction
7.2 Assumptions regarding the capital structure theories
7.3 Net income approach
7.4 Net operating income approach
7.5 Modigliani-Miller approach
7.6 Traditional approach
7.7 Difference between net income approach and net operating income approach
7.8 Factors affecting the capital structure
7.9 Features of an appropriate capital structure

7.1 Introduction

The capital structure of a firm is made of different sources of long-term funds used to finance its investment in long-term productive assets. The proportion of different sources of funds in the capitalisation of a firm creates the financial leverage. Whether financial leverage affects the value of a firm or not is a controversial issue.

According to Gerstenberg, "The type of securities to be issued and the proportionate amount that make up the capitalisation is known as capital structure."

The value of a firm is calculated by applying the following formula:

$$\text{Value of a firm} = \frac{\text{Earnings before interest and tax (EBIP)}}{\text{Overall cost of capital } (k_o)}$$

The relationship between capital structure (leverage), cost of capital, and the value of a firm has been one of the most debated area of financial management.

The following approaches are generally used in examining the relationship between the capital structure and value of a firm.

(i) Net income approach
(ii) Net operating income approach
(iii) Modigliani-Miller approach
(iv) Traditional approach

7.2 Assumptions Regarding the Capital Structure Theories

To assess the relationship between the value of a firm and capital structure under different approaches the following assumptions are made:

1. There are only two sources of capital, namely, debt and equity.
2. There are no corporate taxes.
3. Entire earnings are distributed as dividend to shareholders, i.e., dividend pay-out ratio is 100%.
4. The operating profits of the company are given and are not expected to grow.
5. All investors have the same subjective probability distribution of the expected future earnings before interest and tax for given firm.
6. The total assets of the firm are given and these are not expected to change over a period of time.
7. The firm has a perpetual life.
8. Business risk is constant over time and is independent of its capital structure and financial risk.

7.3 Net Income Approach

According to net income approach, promoted by Durand, there exists a relationship between the value of the firm and its cost of capital. The value of firm is dependent on the capital structure of the firm. The change in capital structure results into change in the value of a firm through change in the overall cost of capital.

The value of a firm is calculated as given below:

$$\text{Value of firm} = \text{Value of equity} + \text{Value of debt}$$

The overall cost of capital is as given below:

$$\text{Value of firm} = \frac{\text{EBIT}}{\text{Overall cost of capital}}$$

Value of equity is calculated by applying the following formula:

$$\text{Value of equity} = \frac{\text{Income after interest}}{\text{Equity capitalisation rate}}$$

In net income approach, market value of equity is calculated on net income and equity capitalisation rate basis.

The value of the firm is given by:

$$V = \frac{\text{EBIT}}{k_e} + D\left(1 - \frac{k_d}{k_e}\right)$$

Where, EBIT: Earnings before interest and tax

D: value of debt

k_e: cost of equity

k_d: cost of debt

The net income approach states that the increase in the proportion of debt in the capital structure of the firm leads to decline in the overall cost of capital because debt is cheapest source of finance. The decline in overall cost of capital in turn increases the value of cost.

The relationship between leverage and cost of capital in net income approach is presented in figure 1.

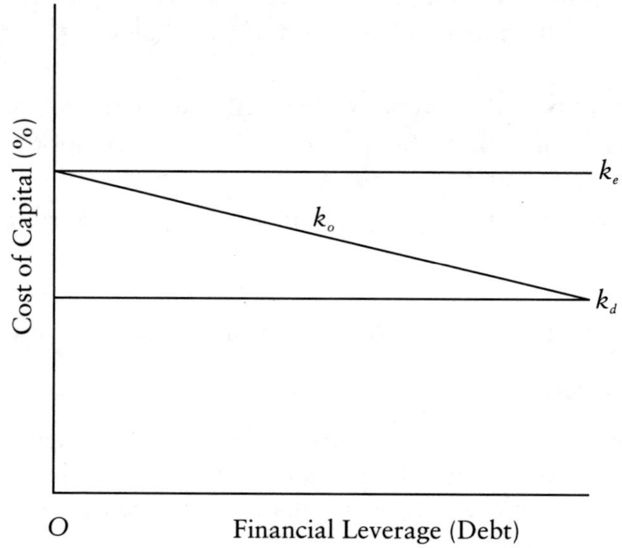

Fig. 1: Net Income Approach

This approach is based on the following assumptions:

1. The cost of debt is cheaper than cost of equity.
2. There are no corporate taxes.
3. The increase in proportion of debt in the capital structure does not change the risk perception of the shareholders. Cost of equity capital remains constant.

According to this approach, with the judicious use of the debt and equity, a firm can achieve an optimal capital structure where the overall cost of capital is minimum resulting in the maximisation of value of the firm.

Net income is capitalised to find the value of equity capital. The value of debt is added to it to find the value of firm. Suppose a firm has an annual EBIT of ₹ 1,50,000. The firm has 10% debentures amounting to ₹ 5,00,000. Equity capitalisation rate is 12%. The overall cost of capital and the value of firm is calculated as per net income approach as given below:

Calculation of value of firm

Particulars	Amount
EBIT	1,50,000
Less: Interest on debentures	50,000
EBT	1,00,000

k_e	12%
Value of equity (E)[1]	8,33,333
Value of debt	5,00,000
Value of firm	13,33,333
Overall cost of capital[2]	11.25%

Workings:

1. $$E = \frac{1,00,000}{0.12} = 8,33,333$$

2. $$k_o = \frac{1,50,000}{13,33,333} = 0.1125 = 11.25\%$$

Example 1. A company is expecting an annual EBIT of ₹ 1,00,000. The company has ₹ 5,00,000 in 8% debentures. The equity capitalisation rate is 12.5%. It was decided to issue 8% debentures amounting ₹ 1,00,000 and utilise the proceeds thereof to buy back and cancel the equity of same amount. Compute the value of firm in both cases according to NI approach.

Solution:

Statement of value of firm

Particulars	Before (₹)	After (₹)
EBIT	1,00,000	1,00,000
Less: Interest on debentures	40,000	48,000
Net profit	60,000	52,000
Market value of equity at 12.5% (E)	4,80,000[1]	4,16,000[2]
Market value of debt (D)	5,00,000	6,00,000
Total value of firm	**9,80,000**	**10,16,000**
Overall cost of capital	10.2%[3]	9.8%[4]

WACC = cost of equity × equity weight + cost of debt × debt weight

1. $$E = \frac{60,000}{0.125} = 4,80,000$$

2. $$E = \frac{52,000}{0.125} = 4,16,000$$

3. $$k_o = 12.5\% \times \frac{4,80,000}{9,80,000} + 8\% \times \frac{5,00,000}{9,80,000} = 10.2\%$$

4. $$k_o = 12.5\% \times \frac{4,16,000}{10,16,000} + 8\% \times \frac{6,00,000}{10,16,000} = 9.8\%$$

7.4 Net Operating Income Approach

The net operating approach was also developed by Durand. This approach is in just contrast to net income approach. According to this approach, there is no relationship between capital structure and the value of the firm. The overall cost of capital of a firm and its value remains constant irrespective of proportion of debt in the capitalisation of the firm.

In net operating income, market value of firm (equity + debt) is capitalised on net operating income basis (EBIT).

$$\text{Value of firm} = \frac{\text{EBIT}}{\text{Overall cost of capital}}$$

$$k_e = k_o + (k_o - k_d)\frac{D}{E}$$

Where, E: value of equity

D: value of debt

k_e: cost of equity

k_d: cost of debt

The relationship between financial leverage and cost of capital as per net operating income approach is presented in figure 2.

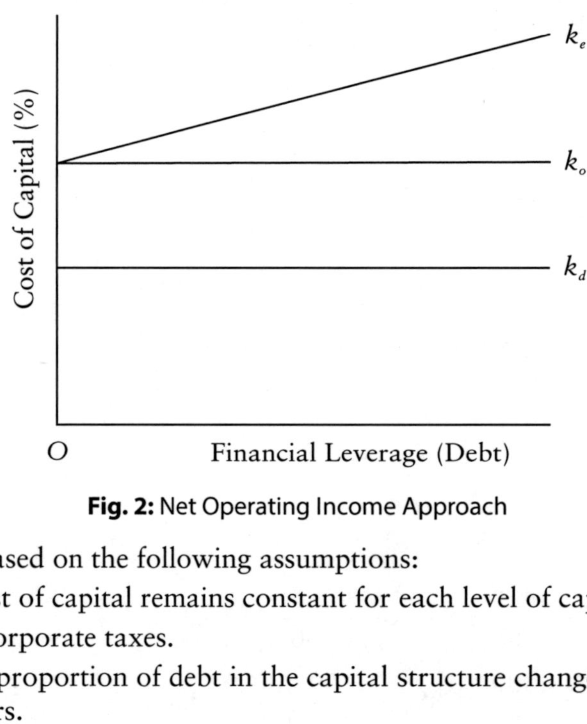

Fig. 2: Net Operating Income Approach

This approach is based on the following assumptions:

1. The overall cost of capital remains constant for each level of capital structure.
2. There are no corporate taxes.
3. The change in proportion of debt in the capital structure changes the risk perception of the shareholders.
4. The investors capitalise the total earnings of the firm to find the value of the firm as whole.

5. The value of equity is residual value calculated by deducting the value of debt from the total value of the firm.
6. Cost of debt remains constant.

This approach is based on the perception that as proportion of debt increases in the total capital of a firm, its interest burden increases, which enhances the financial risk in the firm. This increase in financial risk increases the risk perception of shareholders towards the firm. Consequently, the investors expect more return from the firm. This leads to increase in the cost of equity capital of the firm.

According to this approach, every capital structure is optimum capital structure. Therefore, there is nothing like optimum capital structure. The change in the capital structure of a firm cannot change the value of the firm. Whatever be the proportion of debt in the capital of a firm, its market value remains unchanged.

Suppose a firm has an annual EBIT of ₹ 2,00,000. The firm has 10% debentures amounting to ₹ 5,00,000. Overall capitalisation rate is 12.5%. The cost of equity capital and the value of firm is calculated as per net operating income approach as given below:

Calculation of value of firm

Particulars	Amount
EBIT	2,00,000
Overall capitalisation rate	12.5%
Value of firm	16,00,000
Less: Value of debt	5,00,000
Market value of equity (*E*)	11,00,000
Earnings available for shareholders[1]	1,50,000
Equity capitalisation rate[2]	13.64%

Workings:

1. Earnings for shareholders = 2,00,000 – 50,000 = 1,50,000
2. $k_e = \dfrac{1,50,000}{11,00,000} = 0.1364 = 13.64\%$

Example 2. A company has EBIT of ₹ 1,00,000. The company has 8% debentures amounting ₹ 4,00,000. The overall capitalisation rate is 10%. The company is planning to 8% debentures amounting ₹ 1,00,000 and utilising the proceeds to buy back and cancel the equity shares. Compute the value of firm in both cases according to NOI approach.

Statement showing value of firm

Particulars	Before (₹)	After (₹)
EBIT	1,00,000	1,00,000
Overall capitalisation rate (k_o)	10%	10%
Market value of firm	10,00,000	10,00,000

Value of debt (D)	4,00,000	5,00,000
Value of equity (E)	6,00,000	5,00,000
Interest on debentures	32,000	40,000
Net profit	68,000	60,000
Equity capitalisation rate	11.33%	12.0%
Overall capitalisation rate	10.0%[1]	10.0%[2]

WACC = cost of equity × equity weight + cost of debt × debt weight

1. $k_o = 11.33\% \times \dfrac{6,00,000}{10,00,000} + 8\% \times \dfrac{4,00,000}{10,00,000} = 10.0\%$

2. $k_o = 12.0\% \times \dfrac{5,00,000}{10,00,000} + 8\% \times \dfrac{5,00,000}{10,00,000} = 10.0\%$

The cost of equity (k_e) can be calculated as given below:

$$k_e = \frac{EBT}{E} = \frac{68,000}{6,00,000} = 0.1133$$

$$k_e = \frac{60,000}{5,00,000} = 0.12.$$

7.5 Modigliani-Miller Approach

Modigliani and Miller make a challenging attack on the traditional approach by offering behavioural justification for having the firm's overall capitalisation rate constant throughout the entire range of financial leverage possibilities. The MM approach is similar to the net operating income approach in its conclusions. But, the justification for constant overall cost of capital is different from that of net operating income approach. The MM approach offers that investors have the ability to substitute personal leverage for corporate financial leverage. The arbitrage process makes the value of a firm independent of its capital structure.

Modigliani and Miller approach says that capital structure of a firm is irrelevant to its value. Whatever be the capital structure of a firm, its value will remain same. The approach says that the total risk for all security holders of a firm is not altered by changes in the firm's capital structure. Hence, the total value of the firm must remain constant, regardless of the firm's capital structure.

The MM approach is based on the following assumptions:

1. There are no corporate taxes.
2. The dividend pay-out ratio is 100%.
3. There are perfect capital markets. It implies that:
   - The investors are free to buy and sell securities.
   - The investors can borrow in the market on the same terms on which the firm can borrow.

- There are no transaction costs.
- The investors are well informed and they behave rationally.

4. All firms categorised in specific risk class will have same level of business risk.
5. All investors have the same expectations of the firm's operating profits and accordingly evaluate the firm.

Arbitrage process: If two assets are essentially same, the process of buying the cheaper and selling the expensive in the market is called arbitrage. Therefore, two firms alike in every aspect except for capital structure must have the same value. Otherwise, there is the possibility of arbitrage, which will cause the two firms to sell in the market at the same total value. The following illustration will explain how arbitrage causes the two firms similar in every respect except capital structure to have the same total value.

Let there be two firms, namely, X and Y identical in every respect except the capital structure. Firm X is unleveraged, while firm Y is leveraged. The following information is related the two firms.

Particulars	Firm X	Firm Y
EBIT	₹ 1,00,000	₹ 1,00,000
12% Debenture	–	₹ 3,00,000
Equity capitalisation rate	15%	16%

The valuation of two firms is assumed as given below:

Calculation of values of firms

Particulars	Firm X	Firm Y
EBIT	1,00,000	1,00,000
Less: Interest on debentures	–	36,000
EBT	1,00,000	64,000
k_e	15%	16%
Value of equity	6,66,667	4,00,000
Value of debt	–	3,00,000
Value of firm	6,66,667	7,00,000
WACC (k_o)	15.00%	14.28%

WACC (X) = 1,00,000 ÷ 6,66,667 = 0.15 = 15%

WACC (Y) = 1,00,000 ÷ 7,00,000 = 0.1428 = 14.28%

The leveraged firm Y is over-valued. The MM approach uphold that this situation cannot continue because arbitrage will drive the total values of the firms same. So, investors will sell off shares in this company and invest in company X, till the valuations of both the companies come in equilibrium. Eventually, the share price of two firms will come to same level in the market.

A rational investor having 10% share in firm Y would be interested in the exercise as described below:

1. He sells 10% stock in firm Y at ₹ 40,000.
2. He borrows ₹ 30,000 at 12% interest. This amount of personal debt is equal to 10% debt of firm Y, the same percentage as of ownership in firm Y. Now, he has total capital available for investment equal to ₹ 70,000 (₹ 30,000 + ₹ 40,000).
3. He buys 10% shares in firm X at ₹ 66,667.

Before the sale of shares in firm Y, the investor was getting a dividend of ₹ 6,400. The income by dividend from firm Y will be as given below:

Particulars	Firm X	Firm Y
Dividend (10% of profit)	10,000	6,400
Less: Interest on loan	3,600	–
Net income	6,400	6,400

Thus, the income of investor is same after switching over to firm X. However, the investor now has a capital surplus of ₹ 3,333 (₹ 70,000 – ₹ 66,667).

The important element in this process is the presence of rational investors in the market who are willing to substitute personal or homemade leverage for corporate financial leverage. The arbitrage process explained above maintains that a firm cannot change its total value or its weighted average cost of capital by using financial leverage or having a different capital structure.

Limitations of MM approach: The MM approach, which says that value of a firm is independent of its capital structure has the following limitations:

1. **Unrealistic arbitrage process:** The underlying assumptions for arbitrage process include that markets are perfect and investors are rational. But, in reality, markets are not perfect and investors are not rational.
2. **Substitution of corporate leverage with the personal leverage:** The MM approach assumes that the investor substitutes corporate leverage with personal leverage. But, in fact, personal leverage is not perfect substitute for corporate leverage. A lender generally lends to a firm at a lower rate relative to the individual borrower, since the more risk is involved in case of an individual borrower as compared to corporate borrower.
3. **Absence of transaction cost:** The MM approach assumes that there are no transaction costs. But, in fact, when investor sells or purchases securities, he incurs some expenses in the exercise. The net amount received by an investor on selling the stocks of levered firm would be less than the amount as assumed in the arbitrage process. Similarly, an investor purchasing stocks in unleveraged firm has to pay more than the amount as assumed in the arbitrage process. This would reduce the investible amount in the exercise. Eventually, the friction caused by transaction costs may cause less than full adjustment in the value of a firm subject to change in the capital structure.
4. **Institutional restrictions:** The MM approach assumes that it very easy to switch from one firm to another firm for investors. But, there some institutional investors who does not indulge in frequent selling and buying of stocks of companies. This creates a limitation to the MM approach.

5. **No corporate tax:** In original MM approach, it is assumed that there are no corporate taxes. The interest paid on debt is tax deductible, while dividend on stocks is taxable. This would help in maintaining the higher value of stocks of levered company as compared to the unlevered company.

   However, another theory was developed later on to incorporate the taxes in the MM approach.

Example 3. There are two companies L Ltd. and U Ltd. Both the companies are identical in all respects except that L Ltd. has a debt of ₹ 3,00,000 raised at the interest rate of 10%. Both the companies have earnings of ₹ 75,000. Further, L Ltd. is having equity capitalisation rate of 20% whereas U Ltd. has equity capitalisation rate of 15%. Illustrate using MM approach that how an investor X holding 10% shares of L Ltd. will be better off by switching over to U Ltd.

Solution: Calculation of values of firms

Particulars	L Ltd.	U Ltd.
EBIT	75,000	75,000
Less: Interest on debentures	30,000	–
EBT	45,000	75,000
k_e	20%	15%
Value of equity	2,25,000	5,00,000
Value of debt	3,00,000	–
Value of company	5,25,000	5,00,000
WACC (k_o)	14.29%	15%

WACC (L) = 75,000 ÷ 5,25,000 = 0.1429 = 14.29%

WACC (U) = 75,000 ÷ 5,00,000 = 0.15 = 15%

The leveraged company L is over-valued. So, investors will sell off shares in this company and invest in company U, till the valuations of both the companies comes in equilibrium.

The company L Ltd. distributes ₹ 45,000 among shareholders, while company U distributes ₹ 75, 000 among the shareholders. The investor will be well off under MM approach, by selling the shares in L Ltd. and purchasing shares of U Ltd. through the arbitrage process.

By selling 10% shares in L Ltd., investor will get ₹ 22,500. Now, if he takes 10% loan of ₹ 30,000 (10% of ₹ 3,00,000) and purchases 10% shares of U Ltd. for ₹ 50,000, he will have a surplus capital fund of ₹ 2,500 (52,500 – 50,000). The profit by dividend will be as given below:

Particulars	L Ltd.	U Ltd.
Dividend (10% of profit)	4,500	7,500
Less: Interest on loan	–	3,000
Net profit	4,500	4,500

Thus, by switching over from L Ltd. to U Ltd., the investor is better off, not in terms of income, but in terms of having surplus capital fund of ₹ 2,500, which he can invest somewhere else.

7.6 Traditional Approach

The Traditional approach is a combination of net income approach and net operating income approach. This approach is also known as intermediate approach.

According to the traditional approach, there is an optimal capital structure and the management can increase the total value of the firm through judicious use of financial leverage. This approach assumes that the firm can initially lower its cost of capital and increase total value by employing more fixed charge debt. Although investor raises required rate of return on equity in response to increased risk perception caused by increased proportion of debt in capitalisation, the increase in cost of equity capital does not entirely offset the benefit of using cheaper debt funds.

Figure 3 shows how cost of equity capital and overall cost of a firm responds to varying degrees of financial leverage.

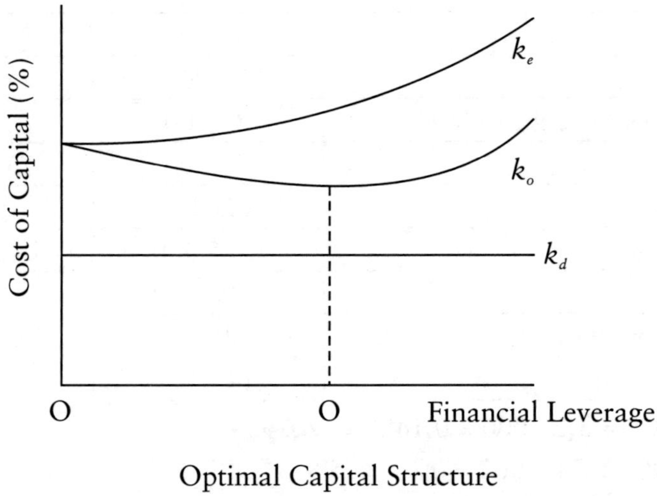

Fig. 3: Traditional Approach

The response of capitalisation costs to financial leverage can be divided into three phases. The cost of debt remains constant in all the three phases. The equity capitalisation cost is assumed to rise at an increasing rate with financial leverage. In first phase, the overall cost of capital declines with financial leverage because the rise in cost of equity does not entirely off set the benefit incurred by using the cheaper fixed cost debt. The second phase contains the only point at which the benefits of using cheaper debt are entirely offset by rise in the cost of equity. At this point the overall cost of capital is minimum. The optimum capital structure is at this point. After this point, the third phase starts. The overall cost of capital begins to rise because the rise in cost of equity is more the benefits of cheaper debt.

At the optimum structure, the firm's overall cost of capital (weighted average cost of capital) is lowest and its value is highest. Thus, the traditional approach to capital structure implies that (1) the cost of capital is dependent on the capital structure of the firm and (2) there is an optimal capital structure.

Example 4. A company's current operating income is ₹ 2 lakh. The firm has ₹ 5 lakh of 10% debt outstanding. Its cost of equity capital is estimated to be 12%.

(i) Determine current value of the firm and overall cost of capital, using traditional approach.

(ii) The firm is considering increasing its leverage by raising an additional ₹ 5 lakhs debt and using the proceeds to retire the amount of equity. As a result of increased financial risk, k_d is likely to go up to 12% and k_e to 15%. Would you recommend the plan?

Solution: Calculation of value and overall cost of capital of firm

Particulars	Debt ₹ 5 lakhs	Debt ₹ 10 lakhs
EBIT	2,00,000	2,00,000
Less: Interest on debentures	50,000	1,20,000
EBT	1,50,000	80,000
Cost of equity	0.12	0.15
Value of equity	12,50,000	5,33,333
Cost of debt	0.10	0.12
Value of debt	5,00,000	10,00,000
Total value of firm	**17,50,000**	**15,33,333**
Overall cost of capital (k_o)	11.42%[1]	13.04%[2]

WACC = cost of equity × equity weight + cost of debt × debt weight

1. $k_o = 12\% \times \frac{12,50,000}{17,50,000} + 10\% \times \frac{5,00,000}{17,50,000} = 11.42\%$

2. $k_o = 15\% \times \frac{5,33,333}{15,33,333} + 12\% \times \frac{10,00,000}{15,33,333} = 13.04\%$

The company should not take the plan as value of firm is declining and cost of capital is increasing.

7.7 Difference between Net Income Approach and Net Operating Income Approach

The net income approach and net operating income approach are contrary to each other. The main differences between net income approach and net operating income approach are given below:

S. No.	Net income approach	Net operating income approach
1	The net income approach says that the value of a firm depends on its capital structure.	The net operating income says that the value of a firm is independent of its capital structure.
2	Cost of equity capitalisation remains constant.	Cost of equity capitalisation is dependent on financial leverage.
3	Financial leverage decreases the cost of capital and increases the value of firm.	Financial leverage does not change cost of capital and the value of firm.

4	The optimum capital structure can be achieved by having higher financial leverage.	The optimum capital structure can be achieved by having right mix of debt and equity capital.
5	Overall cost of capita is reduced by increasing the proportion of debt in capital structure because debt is cheapest source of funds.	Overall cost of capital remains constant as debt proportion increases in the capital structure, because cost of equity capital increases.
6	Equity shareholders are supposed to be inactive to any change in the degree of financial leverage.	Equity shareholders are supposed to active to any change in the degree of financial leverage.

7.8 Factors Affecting the Capital Structure

The main factors affecting the capital structure of a firm are mentioned below:

1. **Profitability:** The basic objective of financial management of a firm is to maximise shareholders' wealth. The management should select such a capital structure that maximises EPS for a given EBIT. If operating profits are higher, debt capital can be used in larger proportion, as chances of default on interest on debt are small. The additional profits are incurred to equity shareholders because of use of other forms of funds, viz., preferential capital and debentures. This type of capital structure provides "trading on equity".
2. **Cost of capital:** Each source of capital has its specific cost. Debt requires interest payments and share capital holders are paid dividends. The relative advantage incurred in employing different sources in the project in reducing the overall cost of capital will help in deciding the capital structure of a firm. The cost of debt is generally lower than the cost of equity.
3. **Nature of business of firm:** The nature of business of a firm is a decisive factor in the capital structure. If the firm operates in a perfect competitive market, there are chances of suffering loss. In such a case, the firm should use debt in small proportion so that in case of loss in a year, the burden of interest payment could not affect the business of firm adversely.
4. **Cash flows:** The operating profit should not only cover the interest payments, it should also be sufficient to meet routine obligations and expenditures. The irregular cash flow may cause the requirement of borrowing. Thus, the capital structure should be such that the sufficient cash flows are available and borrowed funds are not required to meet daily requirements.
5. **Control of firm:** If control of the firm has to be in few hands, then low proportion of capital should be raised by issue of equity capital and a larger portion of capital should be raised through issue of debt. The existing firm should raise new capital by issuing debt if it does not want to dilute the control of the firm.
6. **Capital market conditions:** The capital structure of a firm is affected by the prevailing market conditions at the time of raising the funds. When the securities market bears an optimistic outlook, the issue of equity shares and preference shares might get a better

response from investors. If a pessimistic outlook is prevailing in securities market, then raising of funds by issuing debentures might get better response from investors, because of the certainty of the fixed interest rate.

7. **Legal requirements:** While raising the funds, the company management has to follow certain legal requirements. For example, banking companies are required to issue only equity shares to raise funds as per the provisions of the Banking Companies Regulation Act.
8. **Tax benefits:** The payment of interest on debt reduces the tax liability of firm and increases its after tax profits. Thus, payment of interest on debt acts as a tax shield for the firm. While, company pays tax on profit before payment of dividend to shareholders and shareholders are not required to pay tax. Therefore, in framing capital structure, the firm should take into consideration the tax shields available.
9. **Growth prospects:** The growth prospects of a firm also influence its capital structure. Firms with fair growth prospects can use debt in larger proportion and can increase additional benefits for shareholders. Such firms should use debt with lower maturity so that funds can be raised at lower interest rate. If firms are facing financial problems, the lower debt ratio should be employed to avoid situation of financial bankruptcy.
10. **Floatation and other costs:** Floatation and other costs incurred in raising funds from different sources should be considered while deciding capital structure of a firm. It is better to use retained earnings if the costs in raising the funds from external sources are high.

7.9 Features of an Appropriate Capital Structure

The appropriate capital structure is designed in such a way that the balance is made between return, risk and control of the firm. The following are main features of an appropriate capital structure:

1. **Financial leverage:** The appropriate capital structure should maximise the return on stocks. The return can be maximised by having the proper mix of debt and equity capital in the capital structure of the firm. The debt is cheapest source of funds. Thus, by increasing the proportion of debt in the capital of the firm, return on stocks can be increased. However, the use of debt in capitalisation will depend on expected profits of the firm. Financial risk factor is involved the use of debt in the total capital of a firm. If profits are low, lower proportion of debt should be used so that interest burden on the firm does not pose a threat to the existence of the firm. If profits are high, higher level of debt can be used to maximise the earnings on shares. This will serve the objective of finance manager i.e., to maximise the wealth of shareholders.
2. **Financial risk:** The capital structure of a firm should provide maximum return to equity shareholders at the minimum financial risk. As the degree of financial leverage increases, the financial risk increases in a firm. Financial risk increases in tandem to increased use of debt in the capital structure of the firm. A firm can use debt in larger proportion in the capital structure of a firm, if level of expected profits is high. Otherwise, debt should be used in small proportion in the capital of a firm. An appropriate capital structure should strike a balance between financial risk and return.

3. **Ownership control:** If management wants to keep the control of firm in few hands, then larger proportion of the capital should be raised by debt capital. The increasing proportion of debt will not dilute the control of the firm. The appropriate capital structure should maintain proper mix of debt and equity capital so that management of the firm can function in the democratic way.
4. **Flexibility in raising funds:** The capital structure of a firm should be flexible. It should have some financial slack. The capital structure should provide a room for expansion or starting of new projects by raising debt and equity capital when need arises. An appropriate capital structure of a firm should have the scope for raising funds as need arises.

Thus, an appropriate capital structure should be such as to maximise the returns on stock at the minimum level of financial risk. Further, there should be scope for expansion of business by raising the capital as when required. The capital structure of a firm should not pose risk to ownership control.

SOLVED PROBLEMS

Problem 1. Companies U and L are in every aspect except that U is unlevered and L has 20 lakhs of 8% debt. EBIT of both firms is ₹ 6 lakhs and tax rate is 35%. Equity capitalisation rate for U is 10%.

Calculate the value of each firm using M-M approach and cost of equity for L Ltd.

(D.U., B.Com. 2016)

Solution: We know that:

$$\text{Value of firm} = \frac{\text{EBIT } (1 - t)}{\text{cost of capital}}$$

Thus, the value of company U is:

$$V_U = \frac{6{,}00{,}000(1-0.35)}{0.1} = ₹\,39{,}00{,}000$$

We know that:

$$V_L = V_U + D.t$$

Substituting the values,

$$V_L = 39{,}00{,}000 + 20{,}00{,}000 \times 0.35 = ₹\,46{,}00{,}000$$

Calculation of cost of equity for company L

Particulars	Amount (₹)
Value of company	46,00,000
Value of debt	20,00,000
Value of equity	26,00,000
EBIT	6,00,000

Less: Interest on debentures	1,60,000
EBT	4,40,000
Less: Tax	1,54,000
EAT	2,86,000
Cost of equity	11%

Cost of equity = 2,86,000 ÷ 26,00,000 = 0.11 = 11%.

Problem 2. There are two companies A Ltd. and B Ltd. which are identical in all respects except in terms of their capital structure as can be observed from the details given below:

Particulars	A Ltd.	B Ltd.
EBIT	1,00,000	1,00,000
12% debentures	5,00,000	–
k_e	20%	16%

Calculate the values of the two firms and illustrate using MM Approach how an investor holding 10 percent shares of A Ltd. will be benefited by switching over his investment from A Ltd. to B Ltd. *(D.U., B.Com. 2011)*

Solution: Calculation of values of firm

Particulars	A Ltd.	B Ltd.
EBIT	1,00,000	1,00,000
Less: Interest on debentures	60,000	–
EBT	40,000	1,00,000
k_e	20%	16%
Value of equity	2,00,000	6,25,000
Value of debt	5,00,000	–
Value of company	7,00,000	6,25,000
WACC	14.29%	16%

WACC (A) = 1,00,000 ÷ 7,00,000 = 0.1429 = 14.29%

WACC (B) = 1,00,000 ÷ 6,25,000 = 0.16 = 16%.

Problem 3. Rohtas Ltd. provides the following information:

EBIT	₹ 6,00,000
Interest on 8% debentures	₹ 2,00,000
Tax rate	Nil
Cost of equity	12.5%

Calculate the overall cost of capital and value of Rohtas Ltd. using NI approach. *(D.U., B.Com. 2012)*

Solution: Calculation of value of firm

Particulars	Rohtas Ltd.
EBIT	6,00,000
Less: Interest on debentures	2,00,000
EBT	4,00,000
k_e	12.5%
Value of equity	32,00,000
Value of debt	25,00,000
Value of company	57,00,000
WACC	10.53%

WACC = 6,00,000 ÷ 57,00,000 = 0.1053 = 10.53%.

Problem 4. L Ltd. and H Ltd. belong to the same risk class where equity capitalisation rate of 12% is considered appropriate. Both firms expect an operating profit of ₹ 5,00,000. L Ltd. has raised ₹ 20,00,000 and H Ltd. ₹ 40,00,000 by way of 9% debt. Find out the value and overall cost of capital of both the firms assuming that Net Income approach applies. Which firm has more value and why? *(D.U., B.Com. 2013)*

Solution: Calculation of values of firm

Particulars	L Ltd.	H Ltd.
EBIT	5,00,000	5,00,000
Less: Interest on debentures	1,80,000	3,60,000
EBT	3,20,000	1,40,000
k_e	12%	12%
Value of equity (E)	26,66,667	11,66,667
Value of debt (D)	20,00,000	40,00,000
Value of company (E + D)	46,66,667	51,66,667
WACC	10.71%	9.68%

WACC (L) = 5,00,000 ÷ 46,66,667 = 0.1071 = 10.71%

WACC (H) = 5,00,000 ÷ 51,66,667 = 0.0968 = 9.68%

Company has more value and its cost of capital is less.

Problem 5. There are two companies X Ltd. and Y Ltd. Both the companies have earnings of 25% of the total assets worth ₹ 20,00,000. Further, X Ltd. has debt of ₹ 10,00,000 borrowed at the rate of 12%. Both the companies are subject to 50% tax rate and have capitalisation rate of 15%. Calculate the value of both the firms using NI and NOI approach. *(D.U., B.Com. 2015)*

Solution: Statement of value using NI approach

Particulars	X Ltd.	Y Ltd.
EBIT	5,00,000	5,00,000
Less: Interest on debenture	1,20,000	–
EBT	3,80,000	5,00,000
Less: Tax	1,90,000	2,50,000
EAT	1,90,000	2,50,000
Value of equity	12,66,667	16,66,667
Value of debt	10,00,000	0
Total Value	22,66,667	16,66,667

Statement using NOI approach

Particulars	X Ltd.	Y Ltd.
EBIT	5,00,000	5,00,000
Capitalisation rate	15%	15%
Market value of the firm	33,33,333	33,33,333
Value of debt (D)	10,00,000	–
Value of equity (E)	23,33,333	33,33,333
Interest on debentures	1,20,000	–
EBT	3,80,000	5,00,000
Tax	1,90,000	2,50,000
Net profit	1,90,000	2,50,000
Equity capitalisation rate	8.14%	7.5%

Problem 6. From the following selected data determine the average cost of capital and value of Yes Ltd. as per net income approach:

Net operating income	₹ 2,50,000
Interest on income	₹ 1,00,000
Cost of equity	0.15
Cost of debt	0.10

The company further raises ₹ 5,00,000 from debt carrying 10% interest and uses this money to repurchase its equity and hence increases debt-equity ratio. What happens to value of the firm assuming net operating income approach applies and there are no taxes? Why?

Solution: Calculation of value and average cost of capital of firm

Particulars	Before (₹)	After (₹)
EBIT	2,50,000	2,50,000
Less: Interest on debentures	1,00,000	1,50,000

EBT	1,50,000	1,00,000
Cost of equity	0.15	0.20
Value of equity	10,00,000	5,00,000
Cost of debt	0.10	0.10
Value of debt	10,00,000	15,00,000
Total Value of firm	20,00,000	20,00,000
Overall cost of capital	12.5%[1]	12.5%[2]

WACC = cost of equity × equity weight + cost of debt × debt weight

1. $k_o = 15\% \times \frac{10,00,000}{20,00,000} + 10\% \times \frac{10,00,000}{20,00,000} = 12.5\%$
2. $k_o = 20\% \times \frac{5,00,000}{20,00,000} + 10\% \times \frac{15,00,000}{20,00,000} = 12.5\%$

Problem 7. A company's current operating income is ₹ 2 lakh. The firm has ₹ 5 lakh of 10% debt outstanding. Its cost of equity capital is estimated to be 15%.

1. Determine current value of the firm and overall cost of capital, using traditional approach.
2. The firm is considering increasing its leverage by raising an additional ₹ 3 lakhs debt and using the proceeds to retire the amount of equity. As a result of increased financial risk, k_i is likely to go up to 12% and k_c to 18%. Would you recommend the plan?

Solution: Calculation of value and overall cost of capital of firm

Particulars	Before (₹)	After (₹)
EBIT	2,00,000	2,00,000
Less: Interest on debentures	50,000	96,000
EBT	1,50,000	1,04,000
Cost of equity	0.15	0.18
Value of equity	10,00,000	5,77,777
Cost of debt	0.10	0.12
Value of debt	5,00,000	8,00,000
Total value of firm	15,00,000	13,77,777
Overall cost of capital	13.33%[1]	14.52%[2]

WACC = cost of equity × equity weight + cost of debt × debt weight

1. $k_o = 15\% \times \frac{10,00,000}{15,00,000} + 10\% \times \frac{5,00,000}{15,00,000} = 13.33\%$
2. $k_o = 18\% \times \frac{5,77,777}{13,77,777} + 12\% \times \frac{8,00,000}{13,77,777} = 14.52\%$

The company should not take the plan as value of firm is declining and cost of capital is increasing.

Problem 8. Given the financial data of two companies X Ltd. and Y Ltd., calculate the values of the two companies using NI approach:

Particulars	X Ltd.	Y Ltd.
EBIT	₹ 2,50,000	₹ 2,50,000
Debt	₹ 5,00,000	–
Rate of debt	10%	–
Equity capitalisation rate	15%	15%
Corporate tax	40%	40%

Assuming both the companies are homogenous in all respects except leverage.

Solution: Calculation of values of companies

Particulars	X Ltd.	Y Ltd.
EBIT	2,50,000	2,50,000
Less: Interest on debentures	50,000	–
EBT	2,00,000	2,50,000
Less: Tax	80,000	1,00,000
EAT	1,20,000	1,50,000
k_e	15%	15%
Value of equity	8,00,000	10,00,000
Value of debt	5,00,000	–
Value of company	13,00,000	10,00,000
WACC (k_o)	19.23%[1]	25.0%[2]

1. $k_o = \dfrac{2,50,000}{13,00,000} \times 100 = 19.23\%$

2. $k_o = \dfrac{2,50,000}{10,00,000} \times 100 = 25.0\%$

Problem 9. There are two firms which are identical in all respects except in terms of their capital structure as can be observed from the details given below:

Particulars	R Ltd.	S Ltd.
EBIT (₹)	1,50,000	1,50,000
Debt (₹)	4,00,000	0
Rate	15%	–
k_e	20%	18%

Calculate the values of two firms and illustrate using MM approach how an investor holding 10% shares of R Ltd. will be benefited by switching over his investment from R Ltd. to S Ltd.

Solution: Calculation of values of firm

Particulars	R Ltd.	S Ltd.
EBIT	1,50,000	1,50,000
Less: Interest on debentures	60,000	–
EBT	90,000	1,50,000
k_e	20%	18%
Value of equity	4,50,000	8,33,333
Value of debt	4,00,000	–
Value of company	8,50,000	8,33,333
WACC (k_o)	17.65%	18%

WACC (R) = 1,50,000 ÷ 8,50,000 = 0.1765 = 17.65%

WACC (S) = 1,50,000 ÷ 8,33,333 = 0.18 = 18%.

The company R Ltd. distributes ₹ 90,000 among shareholders, while company S distributes ₹ 1,50,000 among the shareholders. The investor will be well off under MM approach, by selling the shares in R Ltd. and purchasing shares of S Ltd. through the arbitrage process.

By selling 10% shares in R Ltd., investor will get ₹ 45,000. Now, if he takes 15% loan of ₹ 40,000 (10% of ₹ 4,00,000) and purchases 10% shares of S Ltd. for ₹ 83,333, he will have a surplus capital fund of ₹ 1,667 (85,000 – 83,333). The profit by dividend will be as given below:

Particulars	R Ltd.	S Ltd.
Dividend (10% of profit)	9,000	15,000
Less: Interest on loan	–	6,000
Net profit	9,000	9,000

Thus, by switching over from R Ltd. to S Ltd., the investor is better off, not in terms of income, but in terms of having surplus capital fund of ₹ 1,667, which he can invest somewhere else.

Problem 10. The market values and earnings of A Ltd. and B Ltd. are summarised below:

Particulars	A Ltd.	B Ltd.
Equity	₹ 1,20,000	₹ 60,000
Debt	–	₹ 50,000
Total value	₹ 1,20,000	₹ 1,10,000
Earnings	₹ 18,000	₹ 18,000
Less: Interest	–	₹ 4,000
Net profit	₹ 18,000	₹ 14,000
k_e	15%	20%
k_d	–	8%

Show how an investor holding 10% equity of A Ltd. can be benefited by employing an arbitrage process.

Solution: Calculation of values of firms

Particulars	A Ltd.	B Ltd.
EBIT	18,000	18,000
Less: Interest on debentures	–	4,000
EBT	18,000	14,000
k_e	15%	20%
Value of equity	1,20,000	70,000
Value of debt	–	50,000
Value of company	1,20,000	1,20,000
WACC (k_o)	15.0%	15.0%

WACC (A) = 18,000 ÷ 1,20,000 = 0.15 = 15%

WACC (B) = 18,000 ÷ 1,20,000 = 0.15 = 15%

The company A Ltd. distributes ₹ 18,000 among shareholders, while company B distributes ₹ 14,000 among the shareholders. The investor will be well off under MM approach, by selling the shares in A Ltd. and purchasing shares and debt of B Ltd. through the arbitrage process.

By selling 10% shares in A Ltd., investor will get ₹ 12,000. Now, if he invests ₹ 11,000 in company B, he will get 10% shares and debt of company B. He will earn the same amount ₹ 1,800 but he will have surplus fund of ₹ 1,000.

Thus, by switching over from A Ltd. to B Ltd., the investor is better off in terms of surplus fund of ₹ 1,000.

Problem 11. Consider a firm Z Ltd. having the following details:

EBIT = ₹ 50,000

Debt borrowed at the rate of 10% = ₹ 2,50,000

Overall capitalisation rate (k_o) = 12.5%

Using Net Operating Income approach find the value of the firm when:

(i) Debt is increased by ₹ 1,00,000

(ii) Decreased by ₹ 1,00,00

Solution: Statement showing values of firm

Particulars	Debt ₹ 2,50,000	Debt ₹ 3,50,000	Debt ₹ 1,50,000
EBIT	50,000	50,000	50,000
Overall capitalisation rate (k_o)	10%	10%	10%
Market value of firm	5,00,000	5,00,000	5,00,000
Value of debt (D)	2,50,000	3,50,000	1,50,000

Value of equity (E)	2,50,000	1,50,000	3,50,000
Interest on debentures	25,000	35,000	15,000
Net profit	25,000	15,000	35,000
Equity capitalisation rate	10.0%	10.0%	10.0%
Overall capitalisation rate (k_o)	10.0%[1]	10.0%[2]	10.0%[3]

WACC = cost of equity × equity weight + cost of debt × debt weight

1. $k_o = 10\% \times \frac{2,50,000}{5,00,000} + 10\% \times \frac{2,50,000}{5,00,000} = 10.0\%$
2. $k_o = 10\% \times \frac{1,50,000}{5,00,000} + 10\% \times \frac{3,50,000}{5,00,000} = 10.0\%$
3. $k_o = 10\% \times \frac{3,50,000}{5,00,000} + 10\% \times \frac{1,50,000}{5,00,000} = 10.0\%$

Problem 12. There are two companies L Ltd. and U Ltd. Both the companies are identical in all respects except that L Ltd. has a debt of ₹ 3,00,000 raised at the interest rate of 10%. Both the companies have earnings of ₹ 75,000. Further, L Ltd. is having equity capitalisation rate of 20% whereas U Ltd. has equity capitalisation rate of 15%. Illustrate using MM approach that how an investor X holding 10% shares of L Ltd. will be better off by switching over to U Ltd.

Solution: Calculation of values of firms

Particulars	L Ltd.	U Ltd.
EBIT	75,000	75,000
Less: Interest on debentures	30,000	–
EBT	45,000	75,000
k_e	20%	15%
Value of equity	2,25,000	5,00,000
Value of debt	3,00,000	–
Value of company	5,25,000	5,00,000
WACC (k_o)	14.29%	15%

WACC (L) = 75,000 ÷ 5,25,000 = 0.1429 = 14.29%

WACC (U) = 75,000 ÷ 5,00,000 = 0.15 = 15%

The company L Ltd. distributes ₹ 45,000 among shareholders, while company U distributes ₹ 75, 000 among the shareholders. The investor will be well off under MM approach, by selling the shares in L Ltd. and purchasing shares of U Ltd. through the arbitrage process.

By selling 10% shares in L Ltd., investor will get ₹ 22,500. Now, if he takes 10% loan of ₹ 30,000 (10% of ₹ 3,00,000) and purchases 10% shares of U Ltd. for ₹ 50,000, he will have a surplus capital fund of ₹ 2,500 (52,500 – 50,000). The profit by dividend will be as given below:

Particulars	L Ltd.	U Ltd.
Dividend (10% of profit)	4,500	7,500
Less: Interest on loan	–	3,000
Net profit	4,500	4,500

Thus, by switching over from L Ltd. to U Ltd., the investor is better off, not in terms of income, but in terms of having surplus capital fund of ₹ 2,500, which he can invest somewhere else.

Problem 13. A Ltd. has employed 15 percent debt of ₹ 2,00,000 in its capital structure. The net operating income of the firm is ₹ 2,00,000 and it has an equity capitalisation rate of 17 percent. Assuming that there is no tax, find out the value of the firm under net income approach.

Solution: Calculation of value of firm

Particulars	A Ltd.
EBIT	2,00,000
Less: Interest on debentures	30,000
EBT	1,70,000
k_e	17%
Value of equity	10,00,000
Value of debt	2,00,000
Value of company	12,00,000
WACC	16.67%

WACC = 2,00,000 ÷ 12,00,000 = 0.1667 = 16.67%.

Problem 14. The following details are available for a firm as per traditional approach:

Net operation income	₹ 4,00,000
Total investment	₹ 25,00,000
Capitalisation rate	
If the firm has no debt	10%
If the firm uses ₹ 10,00,000 debt	11%
If the firm uses ₹ 12,00,000 debt	12%

The interest rate on ₹ 10,00,000 debt is 8% and that on ₹ 12,00,000 debt is 10%. Calculate for each of the above cases:

(i) Value of shares

(ii) Market value of the firm

(iii) Overall/Weighted average cost of capital.

Solution: Calculation of value and overall cost of capital of firm

Particulars	No Debt	Debt ₹ 10 lakhs	Debt ₹ 12 lakhs
EBIT	4,00,000	4,00,000	4,00,000
Less: Interest on debentures	–	80,000	1,20,000
EBT	4,00,000	3,20,000	2,80,000
Cost of equity	0.10	0.11	0.12
Value of equity	40,00,000	29,09,090	23,33,333
Cost of debt	–	0.08	0.10
Value of debt	–	10,00,000	12,00,000
Total Value of firm	40,00,000	39,09,090	35,33,333
Overall cost of capital (k_o)	10%[1]	10.23%[2]	11.32%[3]

1. $k_o = \dfrac{4,00,000}{40,00,000} \times 100 = 10.0\%$

2. $k_o = \dfrac{4,00,000}{39,09,090} \times 100 = 10.23\%$

3. $k_o = \dfrac{4,00,000}{35,33,333} \times 100 = 11.32\%.$

Problem 15. The following information is given to you for firm A and firm B:

Firm	EBIT (₹)	Interest (₹)	k_e (%)
A	7,50,000	1,20,000	12
B	10,50,000	1,50,000	15

The interest rate on debt is 12%. Calculate:

(i) Total market value of both the firms and

(ii) Overall/Weighted average cost of capital of both the firms.

Solution: Calculation of value and overall cost of capital of firm

Particulars	Firm A	Firm B
EBIT	7,50,000	10,50,000
Less: Interest on debentures	1,20,000	1,50,000
EBT	6,30,000	9,00,000
Cost of equity	0.12	0.15
Value of equity	52,50,000	60,00,000
Cost of debt	0.12	0.12
Value of debt	10,00,000	12,50,000
Total value of firm	62,50,000	72,50,000
Overall cost of capital (k_o)	12%[1]	14.48%[2]

1. $k_o = \frac{7,50,000}{62,50,000} \times 100 = 12.0\%$

2. $k_o = \frac{10,50,000}{72,50,000} \times 100 = 14.48\%$

Problem 16. A and B are two firms, identical in all respects, except that firm A has 10% ₹ 20,00,000 debentures. The earnings before interest and taxes of both the firms are ₹ 5,00,000. The equity capitalisation rate of firm A is 20% and that of firm B is 15%. Calculate:

(i) Total value of each firm

(ii) The overall cost of capital of each firm

Solution: Calculation of values of firms

Particulars	A Ltd.	B Ltd.
EBIT	5,00,000	5,00,000
Less: Interest on debentures	2,00,000	–
EBT	3,00,000	5,00,000
k_e	20%	15%
Value of equity	15,00,000	33,33,333
Value of debt	20,00,000	–
Value of company	35,00,000	33,33,333
WACC (k_o)	14.29%	15%

WACC (A) = 5,00,000 ÷ 35,00,000 = 0.1429 = 14.29%

WACC (B) = 5,00,000 ÷ 33,33,333 = 0.15 = 15%

Problem 17. A company expects an operating income of ₹ 10 lakhs. It has 10% ₹ 30,00,000 debentures outstanding. The overall cost of capital is 12.5%.

(i) What will be total value of the firm and equity capitalisation rate as per Net Operating Income approach?

(ii) How will the firm's value and k_e change if the amount of debt is raised to ₹ 40,00,000 (Net Operating Income Approach)?

Comment on your findings.

Solution: Statement of values using NOI approach

Particulars	Before	After
EBIT	10,00,000	10,00,000
Capitalisation rate	12.5%	12.5%
Market value of the firm	80,00,000	80,00,000
Value of debt (D)	30,00,000	40,00,000
Value of equity (E)	50,00,000	40,00,000

Interest on debentures	3,00,000	4,00,000
EBT	7,00,000	6,00,000
Equity capitalisation rate (k_e)	14.0%[1]	15%[2]

1. $k_e = \frac{7,00,000}{50,00,000} \times 100 = 14.0\%$
2. $k_e = \frac{6,00,000}{40,00,000} \times 100 = 15.0\%$

Thus, the increase in leverage raises the cost of equity.

Problem 18. Companies U and L are same in every aspect except that U is unlevered and L has 10 lakhs of 10% debt. EBIT of both firms is ₹ 5 lakhs and tax rate is 30%. Equity capitalisation rate for U is 10%.

Calculate the value of each firm using MM approach and cost of equity for L Ltd.

Solution: We know that:

$$\text{Value of firm} = \frac{\text{EBIT}(1-t)}{\text{Cost of capital}}$$

Thus, the value of company U is:

$$V_U = \frac{5,00,000(1-0.3)}{0.1} = ₹35,00,000$$

We know that:

$$V_L = V_U + D.t$$

Substituting the values,

$$V_L = 35,00,000 + 10,00,000 \times 0.30 = ₹\ 38,00,000$$

Calculation of cost of equity for company L

Particulars	Amount (₹)
Value of company	38,00,000
Value of debt	10,00,000
Value of equity	28,00,000
EBIT	5,00,000
Less: Interest on debentures	1,00,000
EBT	4,00,000
Less: Tax	1,20,000
EAT	2,80,000
Cost of equity	10%

Cost of equity = 2,80,000 ÷ 28,00,000 = 0.10 = 10%.

Problem 19. There are two companies A Ltd. and B Ltd. which are identical in all respects except in terms of their capital structure as can be observed from the details given below:

Particulars	A Ltd.	B Ltd.
EBIT	50,000	50,000
12% debentures	3,00,000	–
k_e	14%	12.5%

Calculate the values of the two firms and illustrate using MM approach how an investor holding 10 percent shares of A Ltd. will be benefited by switching over his investment from A Ltd. to B Ltd.

Solution: Calculation of values of firms

Particulars	A Ltd.	B Ltd.
EBIT	50,000	50,000
Less: Interest on debentures	36,000	–
EBT	14,000	50,000
k_e	14%	12.5%
Value of equity	1,00,000	4,00,000
Value of debt	3,00,000	–
Value of company	4,00,000	4,00,000
WACC	12.5%	12.5%

WACC (A) = 50,000 ÷ 4,00,000 = 0.125 = 12.5%

WACC (B) = 50,000 ÷ 4,00,000 = 0.125 = 12.5%

The company A Ltd. distributes ₹ 14,000 among shareholders, while company B distributes ₹ 50, 000 among the shareholders. The investor will be well off under MM approach, by selling the shares in A Ltd. and purchasing shares of B Ltd. through the arbitrage process.

By selling 10% shares in A Ltd., investor will get ₹ 10,000. Now, he takes 12% loan of ₹ 30,000 (10% of ₹ 3,00,000) and purchases 10% shares of B Ltd. for ₹ 40,000. The profit by dividend will be as given below:

Particulars	L Ltd.	U Ltd.
Dividend (10% of profit)	1,400	5,000
Less: Interest on loan	–	3,600
Net profit	1,400	1,400

Thus, by switching over from L Ltd. to U Ltd., the investor is not better off.

Problem 20. Milap Ltd. provides the following information:

EBIT	₹ 9,00,000
Interest on 8% debentures	₹ 3,00,000

Tax rate	Nil
Cost of equity	15%

Calculate the overall cost of capital and value of Milap Ltd. using NI approach.

Solution: Calculation of value of firm

Particulars	A Ltd.
EBIT	9,00,000
Less: Interest on debentures	3,00,000
EBT	6,00,000
k_e	15%
Value of equity	40,00,000
Value of debt	37,50,000
Value of company	77,50,000
WACC	11.61%

WACC = 9,00,000 ÷ 77,50,000 = 0.1053 = 11.61%.

THEORETICAL QUESTIONS

1. The 'Modigliani-Miller' model is the behavioural justification of the NOI approach to the capital structure theory. Explain. *(D.U., B.Com. 2012)*
2. Distinguish between Net Income Approach and Net Operating Income Approach of Capital Structure. *(D.U., B.Com. 2016)*
3. Give a critical appraisal of the Modigliani-Miller Approach to the theory of capital structure. *(D.U., B.Com. 2009)*
4. Under the traditional approach to the capital structure, what happens to the cost of debt and cost of equity when leverage increases? Also describe the behaviour of overall cost of capital under traditional approach. *(D.U., B.Com. 2010)*
5. Briefly discuss three important factors affecting capital structure. *(D.U., B.Com. 2013)*
6. Explain and illustrate "Net Operative Income" approach to capital structure.
7. Write short notes on:
   (i) Arbitrage process
   (ii) Traditional theory of capital structure.
8. What are the assumptions and implications of net income approach to capital structure? *(D.U., B.Com. 2009, Corres.)*
9. Explain and illustrate the concept of home made leverage and arbitrage process under MM approach to capital structure. *(D.U., B.Com. 2013)*

PRACTICAL PROBLEMS

1. From the following selected data determine the average cost of capital and value of Vardhaman Ltd. as per net operating income approach:

Net operating income	₹ 25,00,000
Interest on income	₹ 10,00,000
Cost of equity	0.15
Cost of debt	0.10

The company further raises ₹ 50,00,000 from debt carrying 10% interest and uses this money to repurchase its equity and hence increases debt-equity ratio. What happens to value of the firm assuming net operating income approach applies and there are no taxes? Why? *(D.U., B.Com. 2009, Corres.)*

[**Ans.** 12.5%, ₹ 2,00,00,000; no change in value and overall cost of capital]

2. A company's current operating income is ₹ 4 lakh. The firm has ₹ 10 lakh of 10% debt outstanding. Its cost of equity capital is estimated to be 15%.
   (i) Determine current value of the firm and overall cost of capital, using traditional approach.
   (ii) The firm is considering increasing its leverage by raising an additional ₹ 6 lakhs debt and using the proceeds to retire the amount of equity. As a result of increased financial risk, k_d is likely to go up to 12% and k_e to 18%. Would you recommend the plan? *(D.U., B.Com. 2010, Corres.)*

[**Ans.** (i) ₹ 30,00,000, 13.33%; (ii) ₹ 27,55,555, 14.52%, No]

3. Given the financial data of two companies X Ltd. and Y Ltd., calculate the values of the two companies using NI Approach:

Particulars	X Ltd.	Y Ltd.
EBIT	₹ 1,50,000	₹ 1,50,000
Debt	₹ 3,50,000	–
Rate of debt	8%	–
Equity capitalisation rate	12%	12%
Corporate tax	40%	–

Assuming both the companies are homogenous in all respects except leverage. *(D.U., B.Com. 2011, Corres.)*

[**Ans.** X: ₹ 9,60,000; Y: ₹ 7,50,000]

4. There are two firms which are identical in all respects except in terms of their capital structure as can be observed from the details given below:

Particulars	R Ltd.	S Ltd.
EBIT (₹)	1,50,000	1,50,000
Debt (₹)	6,00,000	0
Rate	15%	–
k_e	22%	18%

Calculate the values of two firms and illustrate using MM approach how an investor holding 10% shares of R Ltd. will be benefited by switching over his investment from R Ltd. to S Ltd. *(D.U., B.Com. 2011, Corres.)*

[**Ans.** R: ₹ 8,72,727, S: ₹ 8,33,333; capital fund of ₹ 3940]

5. The market values and earnings of U Ltd. and L Ltd. are summarised below:

Particulars	U Ltd.	L Ltd.
Equity	₹ 60,000	₹ 30,000
Debt	–	₹ 25,000
Total Value	₹ 60,000	₹ 55,000
Earnings	₹ 9,000	₹ 9,000
Less: interest	–	₹ 2,000
Net profit	₹ 9,000	₹ 7,000
k_e	15%	23.3%
k_d	–	8%
k_o	15%	16.4%

Show how an investor holding 10% equity of U Ltd. can be benefited by employing an arbitrage process. *(D.U., B.Com. 2012, Corres.)*

[**Ans.** capital fund surplus ₹ 500]

6. Consider a firm X Ltd. having the following details:

EBIT = ₹ 1,00,000

Debt borrowed at the rate of 10% = ₹ 5,00,000

Overall capitalisation rate (k_o) = 12.5%

Using Net Operating Income approach find the value of the firm when:

(i) Debt is increased by ₹ 2,00,000

(ii) Decreased by ₹ 2,00,000

Also calculate cost of equity in each case. *(D.U., B.Com. 2012, Corres.)*

[**Ans.** (i) ₹ 8,00,000; (ii) ₹ 8,00,000]

7. There are two companies L Ltd. and U Ltd. Both the companies are identical in all respects except that L Ltd. has a debt of ₹ 30,00,000 raised at the interest rate of 10%. Both the companies have earnings of ₹ 7,50,000. Further, L Ltd. is having equity capitalisation rate of 20% whereas U Ltd. has equity capitalisation rate of 15%. Illustrate using MM

approach that how an investor X holding 10% shares of L Ltd. will be better off by switching over to U Ltd. *(D.U., B.Com. 2013, Corres.)*

[**Ans.** Income same, capital fund surplus ₹ 25,000]

8. X Ltd. has employed 15 percent debt of ₹ 12,00,000 in its capital structure. The net operating income of the firm is ₹ 5,00,000 and it has an equity capitalisation rate of 16 percent. Assuming that there is no tax, find out the value of the firm under net income approach. *(D.U., B.Com. 2014, Corres.)*

   [**Ans.** ₹ 32,00,000]

9. The following details are available for a firm as per traditional approach:

Net operation income	₹ 3,50,000
Total Investment	₹ 15,00,000
Capitalisation rate	
If the firm has no debt	10%
If the firm uses ₹ 8,00,000 debt	11%
If the firm uses ₹ 10,00,000 debt	13%

   The interest rate on ₹ 8,00,000 debt is 6% and that on ₹ 10,00,000 debt is 8%. Calculate for each of the above cases:

   (i) Value of shares

   (ii) Market value of the firm

   (iii) Overall/Weighted average cost of capital. *(D.U., B.Com. 2015, N.C.)*

   [**Ans.** (i) ₹ 35,00,000, 27,45,455, 20,76,923; (ii) ₹ 35,00,000, 35,45,455, 30,76,923; (iii) 10%, 9.87%, 11.38%]

10. The following information is given to you for firm A and firm B:

Firm	EBIT (₹)	Interest (₹)	k_e (%)
A	7,50,000	1,20,000	12
B	10,50,000	1,50,000	18

   The interest rate on debt is 12%. Calculate:

   (i) Total market value of both the firms and

   (ii) Overall/Weighted average cost of capital of both the firms.

   (D.U., B.Com. 2015, Corres.)

   [**Ans.** (i) ₹ 52,00,000, 62,50,000; (ii) 14.42%, 16.8%]

11. A and B are two firms, identical in all respects, except that firm A has 10% ₹ 25,00,000 debentures. The earnings before interest and taxes of both the firms are ₹ 5,00,000. The equity capitalisation rate of firm A is 20% and that of firm B is 12.5%. Calculate:

   (i) Total value of each firm

   (ii) The overall cost of capital of each firm. *(D.U., B.Com. 2016, N.C.)*

   [**Ans.** (i) ₹ 25,00,000, 45,00,000; (ii) 20%, 11.11%]

12. A company expects an operating income of ₹ 5 lakhs. It has 10% ₹ 18,00,000 debentures outstanding. The overall cost of capital is 12.5%.
    (i) What will be total value of the firm and equity capitalisation rate as per Net Operating Income approach?
    (ii) How will the firm's value and k_e change if the amount of debt is raised to ₹ 25,00,000 (Net Operating Income Approach)?

    Comment on your findings. *(D.U., B.Com. 2016, Corres.)*

    [**Ans.** (i) ₹ 40,00,000, 14.55%; (ii) 40,000, 16.67%]

Dividend Policy

8

Chapter Outline

8.1 Introduction
8.2 Factors Influencing the Dividend Decision
8.3 Significance of Dividend Decision
8.4 Types of Dividend Policies
8.5 Forms of Dividends
8.6 Significance of Stable Dividend Policy

8.1 Introduction

After investment and financing decisions, the dividend decision is another important decision. The term dividend refers to that portion of profit which is distributed among the shareholders. The part of profit which is not distributed is known as retained earnings. The dividend decision is an important decision which influences the investment decisions of the firm. Each firm has to develop its dividend policy. The dividend-payout ratio indicates the percentage of a firm's earnings that is paid out to shareholders in cash. The dividend-payout ratio determines the amount of earnings that can be retained in the firm. The main aspect of the dividend policy of a firm is to determine the appropriate allocation of profits between dividend payments and additions to the firm's retained earnings. It is important for the management of a firm to strike a proper balance distribution of dividend and retained earnings. It will help in accomplishing the objective of maximising the shareholders' wealth.

8.2 Factors Influencing the Dividend Decision

When a firm decides its dividend policy, it considers a numbers of matters. In addition to consideration of these matters, other factors also influence the dividend policy of a firm. The important factors affecting the dividend policy of a firm given below:

1. **Funding needs of the firm:** A firm should consider the financial needs for expansion of business or financial needs for increased working capital before making the dividend decision. If the firm distributes all profits as dividend to shareholders, it may face difficulties in expanding the business by taking new profitable projects. The no retention of profits may also hamper the smooth functioning of business of the firm, in case there

arises requirement for increased working capital. Thus, before declaring the dividend the management of the firm should consider the future financial requirements.

2. **Legal restrictions:** Before the declaration of dividend, the management of the firm has to abide by the various legal requirements. There are various provisions regarding the declaration of dividend in the Companies Act, which are to be followed at the time of declaration of dividend. These legal restrictions play a role in establishing the dividend policy of a firm.
3. **Liquidity:** Since dividends represent out flow of cash, the strong cash position and liquidity are a precondition in declaring the dividend. The profitability of a firm is different from its liquidity. Stronger the liquidity position of a firm, higher is its ability to pay the cash dividends. The firms having a strong liquidity position may able to pay dividends despite having low profits.
4. **Ownership control:** The dividend policy of a firm is influenced by ownership motive. If the firm is not interested in the dilution of control, it will have to have low pay-outs in its dividend policy. In such a case, the firm can use retained earnings for future expansion or working requirements without raising the additional equity capital. On the other hand, if a firm pays high dividends without retaining much profit, it will have to go the capital markets to finance its expansion plans. Then, raising of new equity capital will increase the number of shareholders and the control of the firm will get diluted. Thus, the ownership motive of the firm will influence its dividend policy.
5. **Ability to borrow:** If a firm has the ability to borrow on comparatively short notice, it may be financially more flexible. The larger and more established a firm, more is the reputation of the firm and the better is its access to the capital market. The greater the ability of the firm to borrow, the greater its financial flexibility and greater its ability to pay a cash dividend. With easy access to the capital markets, the management can easily pay cash dividends. Such firms can adopt the stable dividend policy. The firms can maintain a low retention ratio. Thus, the ability of a firm to borrow easily from market is decisive factor in deciding the dividend policy of a firm.
6. **Nature of earnings:** If the earnings of a firm are stable, it is easy to predict future earnings of the firm. Such firms can pay higher dividends and can maintain low profit retention ratio. On the other hand, if a firm has fluctuating earnings, it difficult to predict its future earnings. Such a firm has to maintain high profit retention ratio. The payout ratio of such firms will be low. Thus, stability in earnings plays a role in constructing the dividend policy of a firm.
7. **Past dividend declarations:** Generally, companies maintain consistency in dividend payments. If an existing company recommends a significantly increased dividend, it causes speculation in the shares of company. The significant deviation in dividend rate of a company is averse to investors' expectations. Hence, while constructing the dividend policy of a firm, consistency in dividend rate should be maintained.
8. **Shareholders' expectations:** When investors invest their funds in the shares of a firm, they make certain expectations about dividend payments. Now, if the firm overlook their expectation in declaring dividend rate, it may face two problems. First, if there is sudden downfall in dividend rate, investors will switch to another firm paying higher dividends.

This will cause a decline in market price of shares and the value of the firm will decline. This will defeat the very purpose of the firm i.e., maximisation of shareholders' wealth. Second, unstable dividend policy of the firm may damage the reputation of the firm in the market. If this happens, the firm may face difficulties in raising the funds from the market in future. Thus, while constructing the dividend policy a firm cannot ignore the expectations of investors regarding the dividend rate.

9. **State of capital markets:** The access of a firm to capital market and the state of capital market have an important bearing on decision of dividend rate taken by board of the firm. If the firm has easy access to capital market, it can take a decision to pay high dividends. Otherwise, not having an easy access to capital market, the firm have to construct conservative dividend policy.

   The state of capital market also influence the dividend rate declared by a firm. In case the market condition is good, the firm may declare a high dividend rate. On the other hand, if market conditions are not good, the firm should adopt a conservative dividend policy by retaining the profits for future use.

10. **General economic environment:** The dividend policy of a firm has to be constructed according to the economic policies of government. Sometimes, government fixes the limit of dividend rate to be declared by a firm.

    The prevailing economic condition also influence the dividend rate decided by a firm. If the rate of inflation is high in country, the firm should declare high rate of dividends. On the other hand, if the prevailing rate of inflation is low, then a low rate of dividend can be recommended.

11. **Taxation policies:** The corporate taxation policy of government affects the rate dividends of firms. The high rate of corporate taxation, reduces the residual profits after tax available to shareholders. As a result, the rate of dividend is affected.

    The direct tax rates also influence the rate of dividend. If income tax rate are high, shareholders would insist the board of directors to pay dividend in kind and not in cash. They may prefer stock dividend and capital gains.

    Thus, the rate of dividend and type of dividend are influenced by the taxation policies of the government.

8.3 Significance of Dividend Decision

The dividend policy of a firm has the effect of dividing its net earnings into two parts, namely, retained earnings and dividends. If dividend decision is treated as financing decision, net earnings of the firm may be treated as a source of long-term finance. In this case, the dividends are paid when the firm does not have any profitable project for investment. But, this approach is contrary to the expectations of the shareholders. Thus, dividend decision is an important decision and has bearing on the firm's functioning and existence, and on the parties concerned with the firm. The following reasons emphasise the importance of dividend decision in a firm:

1. **Retained earnings as source of finance:** Dividend decision determines profit retention ratio. Though the firm may raise finance by external equity, the retained earnings are preferred as source of funding due to several reasons. First, retained earnings do not involve any

floatation costs. Second, if the ability of the firm to borrow or finance from market is not strong, the retained earnings may be used in such situation. Third, if market sentiments are weak, the retained earnings can be used in financing the profitable projects. Fourth, if the need arises, the retained earnings may be utilised for increased working capital. Thus, parting the profits of a firm in retained earnings and dividend is an important decision.

2. **Uncertainty:** The shareholders are not indifferent between dividends and retained earnings. Since future is uncertain, the shareholders may prefer near dividends to future dividends and capital gains. The investors who are old aged and more risk averse and need current income would prefer regular dividend payments. Dividend payments eliminate ambiguity about future. The non-payment of dividends may result in creation of value for firm and investor may be benefited by capital gains. But, capital gains are realised in future and future is not certain. Thus, investors would prefer current dividend payments over future payments of dividends and capital gains. Hence, dividend decision is an important decision from point of view of investors.
3. **Distribution of excess cash:** If the firms do not have profitable projects to invest in and have excess cash, then distribution of dividends is a better option. The shareholders who receive cash dividends can make invest in good return giving projects. Thus, shareholders would be better off and the idle cash of the firm is utilised in productive ways. This indeed is required to fulfil the objective of the firm of maximising the shareholders' wealth. In case firm does not pay dividend, it will be able to maintain idle cash which will dishearten shareholders and will bring down the market value of the firm.
4. **Information signalling:** The dividend decisions convey important information about the firm. The investors take investment decisions not only on the basis of book values, they also observe the dividend payment patterns of the firms concerned. The market value of the firm is also determined by dividend payment history of the firm. The dividend payment patterns of the firms help the market analysts in valuing the firms. Hence, dividend decisions are helpful in valuing a firm in the market and provide valuable information to prospective investors in the firms.

The above discussion highlights the importance of dividend decisions. The decisions affect the firm itself along with shareholders, third parties dealing with the firm. A proper dividend decision helps in smooth functioning of firm, maintaining the value of firm and providing valuable information to the parties dealing with the firm. Therefore, finance managers carefully and meticulously deal with the framing of dividend decision.

8.4 Types of Dividend Policies

The dividend policies of the firms can be broadly categorise in three categories: (i) Residual dividend policy, (ii) stable dividend policy and (iii) flexible dividend policy.

1. **Residual dividend policy:** In this policy, if the firm has earnings left after financing all acceptable opportunities, these earnings would then be distributed to shareholders in the form of cash dividends. If not, then there would be no dividends. If the number of acceptable investment opportunities involves more amount than the retained earnings, then the firm would finance the excess needs with a combination of new equity capital and debt.

The payout ratio will fluctuate from year to year in consonance with fluctuations in the amount of acceptable investment opportunities available to the firm.

The percentage of earnings to be paid out as dividends will fluctuate from period to period depending on fluctuations in the amount of acceptable investment opportunities available to the firm. If the firm has no profitable investment opportunities available, then dividend payout ratio will be 100%.

The residual dividend policy implies that dividends are irrelevant. Financing the investment opportunity through the retained earnings is given priority over dividend payouts. For example, a company has equity capital of ₹ 100,00,000 comprising 10,00,000 shares. If earnings of the company after payment of interest and tax are ₹ 28,00,000 and the company has investment opportunity of ₹ 20,00,000, then the company would pay ₹ 0.80 per share as dividend.

2. **Stable dividend policy:** In stable dividend policy, the payment of dividend remains constant for a long period. The payment of dividend can be constant on two bases. First, the amount of dividend will remain constant from year to year. For example, a firm decides to pay dividends at rate of ₹ 2 per share for the coming 5 years, it is a stable dividend in amount policy. Second, the company may fix percentage of profit to be distributed as dividend for a number of years. For example, if a company decides that 50% of profit after interest and tax would be paid to equity shareholders as dividend, it is a stable percentage dividend policy.

   Stable dividend policy is possible if the earnings of the company do not fluctuate much.

3. **Flexible dividend policy:** This policy is the combination of above-mentioned two policies. In flexible dividend policy, some extra dividend is paid in years of super normal profits in addition to a constant dividend payment. For example, a company has a dividend policy of paying dividend of ₹ 2 per share per year plus 50% of super normal profits. The company has 1,00,000 shares of ₹ 10 each and its normal profits are ₹ 30,00,000. Now, if the company earns after tax profits of ₹ 40,00,000 in a year, it will pay ₹ 3 per share as dividend. In this amount, ₹ 2 are from constant dividend and ₹ 1 per share from super normal profits (₹ 40,00,000 – ₹ 30,00,000 divided by 10,00,000 shares).

   This dividend policy is more practical as compared to the first two dividend policies. It ensures more dividend payouts to shareholders in periods of super normal profits.

8.5 Forms of Dividends

There three forms to pay dividends to shareholders as given below:

(i) Cash, (ii) Bonus shares or stock dividends and (iii) Buyback of shares.

Companies generally pay dividend in cash.

1. **Cash dividends:** The common form of dividend payments to shareholders in a company is cash dividends. The decision on cash dividends depends on cash position of the company. The company should prepare cash budget for the coming period before the declaration of cash dividend. If the company follows a stable dividend cash policy, the preparation of cash budget becomes a necessity. Investors general prefer cash dividends as most of them are interested in current and regular income.

The cash dividend payments reduces the balances in the cash account and reserve account of the company. It affects net worth and the value of the company. The market price of shares of the dividend paying company generally decline in consonance with the amount of dividend paid.

2. **Bonus shares:** Bonus shares are shares issued to the existing shareholders without seeking any payment from them. These shares are issued by converting the profits of the company into share capital. Hence, it is called capitalisation of profits of company. Since bonus shares are issued proportionately to existing shareholders, there is no dilution in the ownership of the company. The issue of bonus is merely an accounting transfer from reserves and surplus to paid up capital.

   Advantages of issuing bonus shares: The issue of bonus shares is advantageous to both the shareholders and the company.

   The **shareholders** have following advantages on issue of bonus shares:

   (i) **Tax benefits:** The cash dividend received by shareholders from the company is taxable in the hand of investor itself. But, the receipt of bonus shares by the stockholders is not taxable as income. Further, shareholders can sell issued bonus shares as per their need and pay capital gain taxes, which are normally less than income tax on cash dividends.

   (ii) **Indication of higher profits:** The board of directors normally declares bonus shares when they expect higher earnings in future. The higher earnings offset the increase in additional capital. The shareholders usually interpret the issuance of bonus shares as indication of higher profitability of the company.

   (iii) **Appreciation in the market value:** The issue of bonus shares changes the market perception about the company and leads to more sale purchase transactions in the shares. As a result, this may lead to an appreciation in the market value of shares of the company.

   (iv) **Possibility of increase in future dividend:** In cases, where companies are paying dividends on fixed amount basis, the issuance of bonus shares will result in increase in future dividends.

   The **company** issuing bonus shares has following advantages:

   (i) **Conservation of cash resources:** The issuance of bonus shares retains the cash balance of the company. This cash can be invested in profitable opportunities. Such an exercise will result in increasing the profitability of the company.

   (ii) **Increased marketability of shares:** The number of shares of the company will increase in the capital market on issue of bonus shares. The shareholders, who need the cash, will start selling the shares. On the other hand, investors viewing the prospects of the company bright will start purchasing the shares of the company. Consequently, the issue of bonus share will increase the marketability of shares of the company.

   (iii) **Maintenance of investors' confidence in financial distress:** The bonus share can be issued in financial distress. This act on part of management will maintain confidence of shareholders in the company intact.

3. **Buyback of shares:** Buyback of shares means repurchasing of its own shares by a company. The buyback of shares results in payments of dividends by company because shares are repurchased at a higher price in comparison of current market price. The Companies Act, 1999 permits companies in India to buyback their own shares. A number of companies, like—India Nippon Electricals Limited, Reliance Industries Limited, Ashok Leyland Limited, Tata Consultancy Services etc. offered to buyback their equity shares.

   There are two methods which a company in India can apply to buyback its equity shares. First, a company can buy its shares in open market through an authorised agent. Second, a company can make a tender offer specifying the purchase price of share, the total amount of purchase and the time period within which share will be bought back.

   There may be several reasons for buying back of its own shares by a company. First, the company may like to return surplus cash, which it cannot put into any profitable investment, to the shareholders. Second, the company may like to use surplus cash to buyback shares rather than pay large dividends, which it cannot maintain in coming periods. Third, the company may buyback shares to reduce the availability of shares in the market and hence, to protect itself against hostile takeovers. Fourth, the company may buyback shares to achieve the target capital structure. There may be several other reasons for buyback of shares by the company.

   The advantages of buy back of shares are given below:

   (i) If a company has more equity capital in its capital structure, then it can achieve the targeted capital structure by buying back the shares.

   (ii) The shareholders of the company will get benefited as the share are bought back by the company at higher price than the current market price.

   (iii) Since the operating efficiency of the company remains unchanged, the earnings per share (EPS) of the company will increase.

   (iv) The control of the company will get consolidated. The buyback of shares by the company will reduce the number of its shareholders.

   (v) The buyback of shares will provide tax benefit to shareholders selling the shares. The dividend is taxable in the hand of shareholders.

   (vi) The company may protect itself from hostile takeovers by reducing the number of shares in the market through buyback of its shares.

   In brief, buyback of shares is a financial tool to restructure the capital of the company when warranted. It is beneficial to both, the shareholders and the company.

8.6 Significance of Stable Dividend Policy

Investors prefer stable dividend policy of the company and will be willing to pay premium on shares of a company having stable dividend policy. The stable dividend policy is also in interest of the company itself, as it enhances the reputation of the company in the market. The stable dividend policy of a company is significant for the following reasons:

1. **Resolves investors' uncertainty:** The investors do not like unstable dividend policy of the company. Stable dividend policy of the company boost the confidence of shareholders and they make in mind that the company will also pay dividend in non-profit period.

In case of abnormal profits, the amount of dividend is increased by the company. Thus, stable dividend policy of the company removes uncertainty of payments in the mind of shareholders.

2. **Investors' desire for current income:** Investors, usually, prefer current income over the capital gains. Dividends are like wages and salaries for many investors, like—old age and retired persons, women investors. This class of investors needs the regular income to meet their living expenses. The stable dividend policy provides regular and upward moving income to the investors. Unstable dividend policy creates uncertainty about dividend payments. The investors believe that current income is better than future income because future is uncertain.
3. **Institutional investors' requirement:** The institutional investors also invest in shares of the companies. Various government bodies prepare list of companies/securities in which institutional investors, like—pension funds, insurance companies, banks and other institutional investors may invest. The recommendatory list is prepared on certain criteria including uninterrupted pattern of dividends.
4. In India, financial institutions, like—IDBI, LIC, IFCI and certain other financial institutions, invest in corporate securities. These institutional investors generally invest in shares of companies that use to pay regular dividends. Thus, the stable dividend policy of a company is a pre-requirement for investment by institutional investors in its securities.
5. **Raising additional finances:** The stable dividend policy is advantageous to the company in raising further funds from the market. The investors preferably invest in securities of a company paying regular dividends. The stable dividend policy also enhance the reputation of the company in the market and market may have more confidence in the company. These factors help in raising additional finances when the company requires these for investment in profitable opportunities.
6. **Informational contents:** The stable dividend policy of a company generally conveys the view of management that the future of the company is better. A company not performing well cannot sustain the stable dividend payments. Thus, stable dividend policy signals the informational contents about the performance of the company. If a company is making loss or earning lower profits and paying stable dividends for a number of years, then there is something wrong in the function of the firm. The market evaluate the companies on the basis of informational contents of the companies. Stable dividend policy signals positive contents about the company.

THEORETICAL QUESTIONS

1. Enumerate the factors which have a bearing on the dividend policy of a company. *(D.U., B.Com. 2009)*
2. Explain briefly the factors which influence the dividend policy of a firm. What are the advantages of a stable dividend policy? *(D.U., B.Com. 2010)*
3. What do you mean by stability of dividends? Why do firms follow a policy of stable dividends? *(D.U., B.Com. 2011)*

4. Briefly discuss the different types of dividend policy from the point of view of stability. Which policy is generally followed in the corporate world and why?
(*D.U., B.Com. 2013*)
5. What is stable dividend policy? Explain its significance. (*D.U., B.Com. 2015*)
6. "The contention that dividends have an impact on the share prices has been characterised as the bird-in-hand argument." Explain the essentials of this argument.

Dividend and Valuation of Firm

9

Chapter Outline

9.1 Introduction
9.2 Concept
9.3 Significance
9.4 Dividend and Valuation of Firm
9.5 Walter Model
9.6 Gordon Model
9.7 Modigliani-Miller Hypothesis

9.1 Introduction

When companies earn profits, there are three possibilities of use of profits. The profits can be reinvested in operating assets, can be used to retire debt or can be distributed to shareholders as dividends. When decision is taken to distribute dividends, three important issues arise:

1. How much of profits should be distributed as dividends?
2. Should the dividends be in form of cash, bonus share or buyback of shares?
3. How stable should the dividend policy be?

After the above-mentioned issues are settled, the next question is: are dividends relevant? In other words, does dividend distribution affect the share price or the value of the firm? In this chapter, we will deal with this issue.

9.2 Concept

As far as the effect of dividend distribution on the valuation of a firm is concerned, there are two school of thoughts. According to one school of thought the payment of dividends affects the value of the firm. In other words, the distribution of dividends is relevant. This school of thought is supported by Walter Model and Gordon Model. The other school of thought says that distribution of dividends is irrelevant. It says that there is no relation between dividend distribution and the value of the firm.

In this chapter, we shall discuss the both schools of thoughts.

9.3 Significance

The basic objective of the firm is to maximise the shareholders' wealth. Hence, indeed, it becomes significant to study the relationship between dividend payments and the valuation of the firm. Apart from valuation of firm point, it is reality that investors, class apart, intend to get dividends from the firm. Investors are of view that future is uncertain. Hence, they prefer current income over capital gains.

The distribution of dividends gives informational signal to the parties dealing with the firm. The pattern of dividend distribution shows future prospects of the firm. Market analysts make their opinion about the firm after analysing the profits and dividend payment patters of the firms. Public agencies also categorise the corporate securities on the basis of dividend payments.

The distribution of dividends helps in raising additional finances for the firm to invest in growth opportunities. If the shareholders are getting regular and stable dividends, the reputation of the firm will be built in the market. The confidence of shareholders will enhance in the firm. These factors may help in raising additional finances for the firm.

In addition to payment of dividends, the issue of retained earnings of a firm is also important. The optimum dividend policy should maintain a balance between distribution of profits and the growth of the firm.

Thus, apart from valuation point, the distribution of dividends is significant on the counts as mentioned above. Whether the distribution of dividends has any link with the value of firm, it is discussed in next part.

9.4 Dividend and Valuation of Firm

Whether dividend payments affect the value of a firm still remains a controversial issue. But, it is significant to know the relationship between dividend payments and the valuation of the firm. The main objective of finance manager is to maximise the shareholders' wealth. Hence, the knowledge of relationship between dividend payments and the valuation of firm will help in accomplishing the objective.

The main models explaining the relationship between dividend payments and the value of a firm are mentioned below:

(i) Walter's Model

(ii) Gordon's Model

(iii) Miller-Modigliani Theory of Dividend.

These models have been explained below:

9.5 Walter Model

J.E. Walter argues that dividend policy of a firm affects its value. He says that the choice of dividend policies almost always affect the value of firm. He argues that in the long run, share prices reflect only the present value of expected dividends. According to this model, the payment of dividends may have negative or positive effect on the valuation of firm depending on the cost of capital and rate of return of the firm.

The Walter's model is based on the following assumptions:

1. The firm finances all investment opportunities through retained earnings. It does not issue new equity capital. It does not use debt capital. The only cost of capital is cost of equity.
2. The cost of capital of the firm and its rate of return remain constant.
3. The values of earning per share (EPS) and dividend per share are assumed to remain constant.
4. All earnings are either distributed as dividends or reinvested internally immediately.
5. Firm has infinite life.

The following formula is used to determine the market price per share:

$$P = \frac{D}{k_e} + \frac{\left(\frac{r}{k_e}\right)(E-D)}{k_e}$$

Where, P = Market price per share

D = Dividend per share

k_e = Cost of capital or capitalisation rate

r = Rate of return

E = Earnings per share

The market price of share is made up of two components, as shown in the above formula. First, the present value of infinite stream of constant dividends. Second, the present value of the infinite stream of capital gains arising from internal growth.

Explanation of Walter's model: According to Walter's model, a firm should adopt its dividend policy on the basis of cost of capital (k_e) and firm's rate of return (r). The optimal dividend rate is one that maximises the share price of the firm and its market value. On the basis of k_e and r, the firms can be classified into three categories and then suitable dividend policy is adopted to maximise the value of the firm.

(a) **Growth firm:** The firms where $k_e < r$. Such firms have ample investment opportunities yielding a return higher than the cost of equity capital. Thus, if retained earnings of the firm are reinvested, these will yield more return than cost of equity. The optimal payout ratio in such firms should be zero. Hence, all profits should be retained by the firm. This would maximise the value of firms.

(b) **Declining firm:** The firms where $k_e > r$. Such firms do not have good opportunities to invest their earnings in profitable projects. Thus, if retained earnings of the firm are reinvested, these will yield less return than the cost of equity. The optimal payout ratio in such firms is 100%. Thus, all profits of the firm should be distributed as dividends. This would maximise shareholders' wealth.

(c) **Normal firm:** The firms where $k_e = r$. These firms are normal and their rate of return is equal to cost of capital. The dividend payments are irrelevant in these firms because they will not affect the value of the firms. There is no optimal dividend payout ratio of the firm.

In nutshell, the payment of dividends is a financing decision in Walter's model. Thus, payment of cash dividends is passive residual according to Walter's approach.

ed on the following assumptions:

nces all investment opportunities th

pital. It does not

Limitations o

lationship betwe

ing limitations:

1. The model assumes that only retained earnings are used to finance the investment opportunities of the firm. Further, there is no debt in the capital of the firm.
2. It assumes that the cost of capital, k_e and rate of return, r of the firm remain constant. This is not realistic, as firm invests more the risk perception of investors will change.
3. It fails to suggest the dividend policy when the cost of capital is equal to the rate of return of the firm.

Example 1. Earnings per share of Shiva Ltd. is ₹ 10. The face value of its equity share is ₹ 100. Its rate of return on investment is 20%. Capitalisation rate for its risk class is 15%. Using Walter's dividend model, find out:

(i) The optimum payout ratio

(ii) The market price per share if the payout ratio is zero

(iii) The market price at a payout of 50%.

Solution: We know, that the price per share is:

$$P = \frac{D}{k_e} + \frac{\left(\frac{r}{k_e}\right)(E-D)}{k_e}$$

Here, E = ₹ 10, $r = 20\%$, $k_e = 16\%$

(i) Since $r > k_e$, optimum payout ratio is 0%

(ii) When dividend payout ratio is 0, $D = 0$

$$P = \frac{0}{0.16} + \frac{\left(\frac{0.2}{0.16}\right)(10-0)}{0.16}$$

P = ₹ 78.13

(iii) When payout ratio is 50%, D ₹ 5

$$P = \frac{5}{0.16} + \frac{\left(\frac{0.20}{0.16}\right)(10-5)}{0.16}$$

$P = 31.25 + 39.06 =$ ₹ 70.31.

9.6 Gordon Model

Gordon argues that investors do have a preference for current dividends and there is a direct relationship between the dividend policy and the market value of the shares.

The model assumes that investors are risk averse and they will willing to pay premium on certain and current income whereas to put discount on uncertain and future income. The basic premise of Gordon's model is "a bird in hand is better than two in bush".

The model is bas

1. The firm fina … through retained earnings. It does n… new equity ca… use debt capital. The only cost of capital is cost of equity.
2. The cost of capital (k_e) of the firm and its rate of return (r) remain constant.
3. The firm has infinite life and its stream of earnings are perpetual.
4. The dividend retention ratio (b) is constant and growth rate of earnings (g) is calculated as multiplication of dividend retention ratio (b) and return on investment (r).
5. The cost of capital (k_e) is greater than the growth rate of earnings (g).
6. Corporate taxes do not exist.

According to the model, the market price of the share is equal to the present value of an infinite stream of dividends received by the shareholder. When there is constant growth rate in earnings, the price share is:

$$P_0 = \frac{D_1}{k_e - g}$$

Where, P_0 = Market price per share
D_1 = Dividend at the end of year 1
g = Growth rate of earnings
k_e = Cost of capital.

Substituting $E(1 - b)$ for D_1 and br for g, the following formula can be used to determine the market price of share:

$$P_0 = \frac{E(1-b)}{k_e - br}$$

Where, P_0 = Market price per share
b = Retention ratio
k_e = Cost of capital
r = Rate of return
E = Expected earnings per share
$br = g$ = growth of the firm.

Explanation of the model: The optimal dividend policy of the firm is decided on the basis of its type according to Gordon model as explained below:

(a) **Growth firm:** The firms where $k_e < r$. Such firms have ample investment opportunities yielding a return higher than the cost of equity capital. Thus, if retained earnings of the firm are reinvested, these will yield more return than cost of equity. Hence, the firm should distribute as less dividends as possible. This will maximise shareholders' wealth. The optimal payout ratio in such firms is the lowest possible. If the payout ratio is zero price cannot be determined according to Gordon model.

(b) **Declining firm:** The firms where $k_e > r$. Such firms do not have good opportunities to invest their earnings in profitable projects. Thus, if retained earnings of the firm are reinvested, these will yield less return than the cost of equity. The optimal payout ratio in such firms is 100%. Thus, all profits of the firm should be distributed as dividends. This would maximise shareholders' wealth.

(c) **Normal firm:** The firms where $k_e = r$. These firms are normal and their rate of return is equal to cost of capital. The dividend payments are irrelevant in these firms because they will not affect the value of the firms. There is no optimal dividend payout ratio of the firm.

The model shows that there exists a relationship between payout ratio, cost of capital (k_e), rate of return (r) and the market value of shares.

The Gordon's model gives similar conclusions regarding the relationship between the dividend policy and the valuation of the firm to that of Walter's model. The similarity in conclusions is due to the resemblance of assumptions that both the models assume.

Limitations of the model: The Gordon's model of dividend has limitations due to its unrealistic assumptions as explained below:

1. The model assumes that only retained earnings are used to finance the investment opportunities of the firm. Further, there is no debt in the capital of the firm.
2. It assumes that the cost of capital, k_e and rate of return, r of the firm remain constant. This is not realistic, as firm invests more the risk perception of investors will change.
3. It fails to work when there is zero dividend payout ratio in a firm.

Example 2. Rama Ltd. is currently having 1,00,000 equity shares of the face value of ₹ 10 each. It is expected that company will have year-end net profit of ₹ 6,00,000. Due to recessionary conditions, the company expects 10% return on its investment in future. The equity capitalisation rate is 11%. Find out the market price per share according to Gordon Model under different payout ratios of 40%, 60% and 80%.

Solution: We know that the market price per share is:

$$P_0 = \frac{E(1-b)}{k_e - br}$$

$$E = ₹\ 6{,}00{,}000 \div 1{,}00{,}000 = ₹\ 6$$

$$r = 10\%,\ k_e = 11\%$$

Substituting the values,

(i) When payout ratio is 40%:

$$P_0 = \frac{6(1-0.6)}{0.11 - 0.6 \times 0.1}$$

$$P_0 = \frac{2.4}{0.11 - 0.06}$$

$$P_0 = ₹\ 48$$

(ii) When payout ratio is 60%:

$$P_0 = \frac{6(1-0.4)}{0.11 - 0.4 \times 0.1}$$

$$P_0 = \frac{3.6}{0.11 - 0.04}$$

$$P_0 = ₹\ 51.4$$

(iii) When payout ratio is 80%:

$$P_0 = \frac{6(1 - 0.2)}{0.11 - 0.2 \times 0.1}$$

$$P_0 = \frac{4.8}{0.11 - 0.02}$$

$$P_0 = ₹\ 53.3$$

9.7 Modigliani-Miller Hypothesis

The hypothesis says that dividend payments are irrelevant to valuation of firm. The value of firm depends on its earning potentiality and investment policy and not on the pattern of income distribution. Thus, the dividend decision, dividing the earnings into dividends and retained earnings, is of no significance in the valuation of the firm.

MM Hypothesis says that whatever increase in shareholders wealth results from dividend payments, will be exactly offset by the decline in the market price of the shares because of external financing and, hence, there will be no change in the total wealth of the shareholders.

Assumptions of the model: The MM Hypothesis is based on the following assumptions:

1. The capital markets are perfect. Perfect capital markets implies that (i) investors behave rationally, (ii) information is freely available to all, (iii) transaction and floatation costs do not exists and (iv) no investor is large enough to influence the share price in the market.
2. There are either no taxes or there are no differences in the tax rates applicable to dividends and capital gains.
3. The investment policy of the firm is fixed.
4. There is certainty about future dividends and share prices. Investors are able to forecast future prices and dividends precisely.

Explanation of the model: The crux of MM Hypothesis on dividend is the arbitration process. The MM Hypothesis says that when a firm pays dividend the funds which have been earned by the firm during the period gets eroded. The firm may fall short of funds to finance its investment opportunities. In order to finance its investment opportunities, the firm would raise new equity capital which will result in increase in the number of shares of the firm in the capital market. As a result, the share price of the firm would decline. Finally, the value of the firm would remain same even after payment of dividends.

The share price at present is the discounted value of cash inflows received by the investor in the form of dividends and selling price at the end of year.

$$P_0 = \frac{(D_1 + P_1)}{(1 + k_e)}$$

The market price of share (P_1) at the end of the period can be calculated by employing the following formula:

$$P_1 = P_0(1 + k_e) - D_1$$

Where, P_0 = Market price per share at the beginning of the period

P_1 = Market price per share at the end of the period

D_1 = Dividend to be received at the end of the period

k_e = cost of equity capital

The number of shares (m) issued at the end of the period to finance the investment opportunities can be calculated by the following formula:

$$m = \frac{I - (X - nD_1)}{P_1}$$

Where, I = Investment expenditure

m = Number of new shares to be issued at the end of the period

D_1 = Dividend to be received at the end of the period

X = Total net profit during the year

P_1 = Market price per share at the end of the period

n = Number of shares outstanding

The value of the firm will be:

$$V = n.P_1 + I - (X - nD_1)$$

The value of the firm remains constant whether dividends are paid or not. The example 3 will clear the working of the hypothesis.

Limitations of the model: The MM Hypothesis is criticised for its unrealistic assumptions as explained below:

1. The assumption of perfect capital is unrealistic.
2. Generally, capital gains are taxed at lower rates as compared to dividend income.
3. The assumption of absence of transaction costs and floatation costs is unrealistic.
4. The hypothesis assumes that there is no uncertainty. This assumption is unrealistic.
5. The hypothesis assumes investors are rational and are well informed.

Example 3. Lakshmi Ltd. currently has 10 lakh equity shares outstanding. Current market price per share is ₹ 10. The net income for the current year is ₹ 20,00,000 and investment budget is also of ₹ 20,00,000. Cost of equity is 10%. The company is contemplating declaration of dividend @ ₹ 1 per share. Assuming MM Approach:

(i) Calculate market price per share if dividend is declared and if dividend is not declared.

(ii) How many new equity shares are to be issued under both options?

(iii) Show that the total market value of shares remains unaffected by the dividend decision.

Solution: We know that the market price of share (P_1) at the end of the period can be calculated by employing the following formula:

$$P_1 = P_0 (1 + k_e) - D_1$$

Here, P_0 = ₹ 10, $k_e = 0.10$, and D_1 = ₹ 1

Substituting the values,

(i) When dividend is paid:

$$P_1 = 10(1 + 0.10) - 1$$

$$P_1 = ₹\ 10$$

(ii) When dividend is not paid:

$$P_1 = 10(1 + 0.1) - 0$$

$$P_1 = ₹\ 11$$

(iii) Number of shares, when dividend is declared:

$$m = \frac{I - (X - nD_1)}{P_1}$$

Substituting the values,

$$m = \frac{20,00,000 - (20,00,000 - 10,00,000)}{10}$$

$$m = 1,00,000 \text{ shares}$$

(iv) Number of shares, when dividend is not declared:

$$m = \frac{I - (X - nD_1)}{P_1}$$

Substituting the values,

$$m = \frac{20,00,000 - (20,00,000 - 0)}{11}$$

$$m = 0$$

(v) Value of firm when dividend is declared:

$$V = (10,00,000 + 1,00,000) \times 10 = ₹\ 110,00,000$$

(vi) Value of firm when dividend is not declared:

$$V = (10,00,000) \times 11 = ₹\ 110,00,000$$

Thus, payment of dividends does not affect the value of the company.

SOLVED PROBLEMS

Problem 1. ABC Ltd. is currently having 1,00,000 equity shares of the face value of ₹ 10 each. It is expected that company will have year-end net profit of ₹ 5,00,000. Due to recessionary conditions, the company expects 10% return on its investment in future. The equity capitalisation rate is 12%. Find out the market price per share according to Gordon Model under different payout ratios of 40%, 60% and 80%. *(D.U., B.Com. 2016)*

Solution: We know that the market price per share is:

$$P_0 = \frac{E(1 - b)}{k_e - br}$$

$E = ₹\ 5{,}00{,}000 \div 1{,}00{,}000 = ₹\ 5$

$r = 10\%,\ k_e = 12\%$

Substituting the values,

(i) When payout ratio is 40%:

$$P_0 = \frac{5(1-0.6)}{0.12-0.6\times0.1}$$

$$P_0 = \frac{2}{0.12-0.06}$$

$$P_0 = ₹\ 33.33$$

(ii) When payout ratio is 60%:

$$P_0 = \frac{5(1-0.4)}{0.12-0.4\times0.1}$$

$$P_0 = \frac{3}{0.12-0.04}$$

$$P_0 = ₹\ 37.5$$

(iii) When payout ratio is 80%:

$$P_0 = \frac{5(1-0.2)}{0.12-0.2\times0.1}$$

$$P_0 = \frac{4}{0.12-0.02}$$

$$P_0 = ₹\ 40.0.$$

Problem 2. Earnings per share of ABC Ltd. are ₹ 10. The face value of its equity share is ₹ 100. Its rate of return on investment is 20%. Capitalisation rate for its risk class is 15%. Using Walter's dividend model, find out:

(i) The optimum payout ratio.
(ii) The market price per share if the payout ratio is zero.
(iii) The market price at a payout of 60%. *(D.U., B.Com. 2016)*

Solution: We know that the price per share is:

$$P = \frac{D}{k_e} + \frac{\left(\frac{r}{k_e}\right)(E-D)}{k_e}$$

Here, $E = ₹\ 10,\ r = 20\%,\ k_e = 15\%$

(i) Since $r > k_e$, optimum payout ratio is 0%

(ii) When dividend payout ratio is 0, $D = 0$

$$P = \frac{0}{0.15} + \frac{\left(\frac{0.2}{0.15}\right)(10-0)}{0.15}$$

$P = ₹\ 88.89$

(iii) When payout ratio is 60%, D ₹ 6.

$$P = \frac{6}{0.15} + \frac{\left(\frac{0.20}{0.15}\right)(10-6)}{0.15}$$

$$P = 40 + \frac{5.33}{0.15}$$

$P = 40 + 35.33 = ₹\ 75.33.$

Problem 3. Use Walter's Model to determine the value of the firm in the following cases:

(a) 100% retention

(b) 50% retention

(c) No retention

The firm has 10 lakh equity shares of ₹ 10 each. Cost of capital is 10%, and Rate of return on investment is 15%. The earnings per share are ₹ 5. *(D.U., B.Com. 2009)*

Solution: We know that the price per share is:

$$P = \frac{D}{k_e} + \frac{\left(\frac{r}{k_e}\right)(E-D)}{k_e}$$

Here, $E = ₹\ 5, r = 15\%, k_e = 10\%$

(i) When 100% retention, dividend payout ratio is 0, and $D = 0$.

$$P = \frac{0}{0.10} + \frac{\left(\frac{0.15}{0.10}\right)(5-0)}{0.10}$$

$P = ₹\ 75$

(ii) When 50% retention, payout ratio is 50%, D ₹ 2.5.

$$P = \frac{2.5}{0.10} + \frac{\left(\frac{0.15}{0.10}\right)(5-2.5)}{0.10}$$

$P = 25 + 37.5$

$P = ₹\ 62.5$

(iii) When no retention, pay-out ratio is 100% and dividend is ₹ 5.

$$P = \frac{5}{0.10} + \frac{\left(\frac{0.15}{0.10}\right)(5-5)}{0.10}$$

$$P = 50 + 0$$

$$P = ₹\ 50.$$

Problem 4. Following information is available about a company: cost of capital = 10%, rate of return on investment = 15% and earnings per share = ₹ 5.

The company has 10,00,000 equity shares of ₹ 10 each. Use Walter's model to determine the value of the firm in three cases:

(a) 100 percent retention,

(b) 50 percent retention and

(c) No retention. *(D.U., B.Com. 2010)*

Solution: We know that the price per share is:

$$P = \frac{D}{k_e} + \frac{\left(\frac{r}{k_e}\right)(E-D)}{k_e}$$

Here, $E = ₹\ 5, r = 15\%, k_e = 10\%$

(i) When 100% retention, dividend payout ratio is 0, and $D = 0$.

$$P = \frac{0}{0.10} + \frac{\left(\frac{0.15}{0.10}\right)(5-0)}{0.10}$$

$$P = ₹\ 75$$

Value of the firm = Price per share × number of shares

= ₹ 75 × 10,00,000 = ₹ 7,50,00,000

(ii) When 50% retention, payout ratio is 50%, D ₹ 2.5.

$$P = \frac{2.5}{0.10} + \frac{\left(\frac{0.15}{0.10}\right)(5-2.5)}{0.10}$$

$$P = 25 + 37.5$$

$$P = ₹\ 62.5$$

Value of the firm = Price per share × number of shares

= ₹ 62.5 × 10,00,000 = ₹ 6,25,00,000

(iii) When no retention, payout ratio is 100% and dividend is ₹ 5.

$$P = \frac{2.5}{0.10} + \frac{\left(\frac{0.15}{0.10}\right)(5-5)}{0.10}$$

$P = 50 + 0$

$P = ₹\ 50$

Value of the firm = Price per share × number of shares

= ₹ 50 × 10,00,000 = ₹ 5,00,00,000.

Problem 5. The following information is available in respect of X Ltd.:

(i) EPS = ₹ 10

(ii) Rate of return = 20%

(iii) And required rate of return of equity investment (k_e) = 16%.

Find out the market price of the share under Gordon model if the firm follows a payout of (i) 50 percent or (ii) 25 percent. *(D.U., B.Com. 2010)*

Solution: We know that the market price per share is:

$$P_0 = \frac{E(1-b)}{k_e - br}$$

Here, $E = ₹\ 10, r = 20\%, k_e = 16\%$

Substituting the values,

(i) When payout ratio is 50%:

$$P_0 = \frac{10(1-0.5)}{0.16 - 0.5 \times 0.2}$$

$$P_0 = \frac{5}{0.16 - 0.1}$$

$$P_0 = ₹\ 83.33$$

(ii) When payout ratio is 25%:

$$P_0 = \frac{10(1-0.75)}{0.16 - 0.75 \times 0.2}$$

$$P_0 = \frac{2.5}{0.16 - 0.15}$$

$$P_0 = ₹\ 250.$$

Problem 6. The earnings per share of the face value of ₹ 100 of A Ltd. is ₹ 20. It has a rate of return of 25%. Capitalisation rate of its risk class is 12.5%. If Walter's model is used:

(a) What would be the optimum payout ratio?

(b) What should be the market price per share if the payout ratio is zero?

(D.U., B.Com. 2011)

Solution: We know that the price per share is:

$$P = \frac{D}{k_e} + \frac{\left(\frac{r}{k_e}\right)(E - D)}{k_e}$$

Here, $E = ₹\ 20,\ r = 25\%,\ k_e = 12.5\%$

(i) Since $r > k_e$, optimum payout ratio is 0%.

(ii) When dividend payout ratio is 0, $D = 0$.

$$P = \frac{0}{0.125} + \frac{\left(\frac{0.25}{0.125}\right)(20-0)}{0.125}$$

$$P = ₹\ 320.$$

Problem 7. Paras Ltd. has recently issued 10,00,000 equity shares of ₹ 10 each. It forecasts the year end EPS of ₹ 1. The cost of equity is 10%. The management is contemplating to declaration of equity dividend @ 50% but the Finance Manager proposes to retain profits and not declare any dividend. Using MM model, compute the end of the year share price if (i) Dividend is paid, and (ii) dividend is not paid. *(D.U., B.Com. 2012)*

Solution: We know that:

The market price of share (P_1) at the end of the period can be calculated by employing the following formula:

$$P_1 = P_0(1 + k_e) - D_1$$

Here, $P_0 = ₹\ 10,\ k_e = 0.10$, and $D_1 = ₹\ 1$

Substituting the values,

(i) When dividend is paid:

$$P_1 = 10(1 + 0.1) - 0.5$$

$$P_1 = ₹\ 10.5$$

(ii) When dividend is not paid:

$$P_1 = 10(1 + 0.1) - 0$$

$$P_1 = ₹\ 11.$$

Problem 8. A company has a total equity capital of ₹ 50,00,000 comprising equity share of ₹ 10 each. It earns a return of 12% on its investments of ₹ 50,00,000. The appropriate discount rate for the firm is 10%. Using Gordon's model, compute the share price of the company if the company has a policy of declaring 50% dividend.

What would be your answer if the company earns a return of 8% on its investments? *(D.U., B.Com. 2012)*

Solution: We know that the market price per share is:

$$P_0 = \frac{E(1-b)}{k_e - br}$$

Here, $E = ₹\ 1.2,\ r = 12\%,\ k_e = 10\%$

Substituting the values,

(i) When payout ratio is 50% and rate of return is 12%:

$$P_0 = \frac{1.2(1-0.5)}{0.10-0.5\times0.12}$$

$$P_0 = \frac{0.6}{0.10-0.06}$$

P_0 = ₹ 15

(ii) When payout ratio is 50% and rate of return is 8%:

Then, E = ₹ 0.8, $r = 8\%$, $k_e = 10\%$

$$P_0 = \frac{0.8(1-0.5)}{0.10-0.5\times0.08}$$

$$P_0 = \frac{0.4}{0.10-0.04}$$

P_0 = ₹ 6.67.

Problem 9. A company has total investment of ₹ 10,00,000 and 1,00,000 outstanding shares of face value of ₹ 10 each. It earns a rate of return of 11% on its investment and has a policy of paying 60% of its earnings as dividend. Compute share price? Is it optimum dividend policy as per Walter policy? What is the optimum policy and why? Assume that the required rate of return is 12%. Show the working. *(D.U., B.Com. 2013)*

Solution: We know that the price per share is:

$$P = \frac{D}{k_e} + \frac{\left(\frac{r}{k_e}\right)(E-D)}{k_e}$$

Here, E = ₹ 1.1, $r = 11\%$, $k_e = 12\%$ and D = ₹ 0.

Substituting the values,

$$P = \frac{0.66}{0.12} + \frac{\left(\frac{0.11}{0.12}\right)(1.1-0.66)}{0.12}$$

$P = 5.5 + 3.36$

P = ₹ 8.86

According to Walter model, if $r < k_e$ the payout should be 100% and the firm should not retain any profit.

This is not an optimum policy as per Walter's model. The optimum policy will be 100% payout.

Problem 10. The shares of a company are currently selling at ₹ 53 per share in the stock market. The company paid dividend at the rate of ₹ 3 per share last year. The estimated growth rate of dividend is 6%. The required rate of return is 12%.

Determine the estimated market price of the equity share if the growth rate of dividend turns out to be as:

(i) Estimated,
(ii) Rises to 8%,
(iii) Falls to 4%. (*D.U., B.Com. 2013*)

Solution: The price of share is calculated as given below:

$$P_0 = \frac{D_1}{k_e - g}$$

In this case, D_0 = ₹ 3, $k_e = 0.12$

(i) D_1 = ₹ 3.18, then:

$$P_0 = \frac{3.18}{0.12 - 0.06}$$

P = ₹ 53

(ii) D_1 = ₹ 3.24, then:

$$P_0 = \frac{3.24}{0.12 - 0.08}$$

P = ₹ 81

(iii) D_1 = ₹ 3.12, then:

$$P_0 = \frac{3.12}{0.12 - 0.04}$$

P = ₹ 39.

Problem 11. The earnings of a company are ₹ 10 per share. The capitalisation rate applicable to the company is 10%. If the company's return on investment is 15%, what is the optimum payout ratio using Walter's formula? What is the share price at that payout? What will be the share price at a payout of 20%, 50% and 80%, using the Walter's formula? (*D.U., B.Com. 2015*)

Solution: We know that the price per share is:

$$P = \frac{D}{k_e} + \frac{\left(\frac{r}{k_e}\right)(E - D)}{k_e}$$

Here, E = ₹ 10, $r = 15\%$, $k_e = 10\%$

(i) Since $r > k_e$, optimum payout ratio is 0%.

(ii) When 100% retention, dividend payout ratio is 0, and $D = 0$.

$$P = \frac{0}{0.10} + \frac{\left(\frac{0.15}{0.10}\right)(10 - 0)}{0.10}$$

P = ₹ 150

(iii) When 80% retention, dividend payout ratio is 20%, and $D = 2$.

$$P = \frac{2}{0.10} + \frac{\left(\frac{0.15}{0.10}\right)(10-2)}{0.10}$$

$$P = ₹\,140$$

(iv) When 50% retention, payout ratio is 50%, $D = ₹\,5$.

$$P = \frac{5}{0.10} + \frac{\left(\frac{0.15}{0.10}\right)(10-5)}{0.10}$$

$$P = 50 + 75$$

$$P = ₹\,125$$

(v) When no retention, payout ratio is 80% and dividend is ₹ 8.

$$P = \frac{8}{0.10} + \frac{\left(\frac{0.15}{0.10}\right)(10-8)}{0.10}$$

$$P = 80 + 30$$

$$P = ₹\,110.$$

Problem 12. ABC Ltd. has a capital of ₹ 20,00,000 in equity shares of ₹ 100 each. The current market price of these shares is ₹ 120 each. The company proposes to declare a dividend of ₹ 10 per share at the end of current financial year. The capitalisation rate for the company's risk is 10%. Based on Modigliani-Miller approach, calculate the market price per share of the company if:

(i) Dividend is declared.

(ii) Dividend is not declared. *(D.U., B.Com. 2015)*

Solution: We know that:

The market price of share (P_1) at the end of the period can be calculated by employing the following formula:

$$P_1 = P_0\,(1 + k_e) - D_1$$

Here, $P_0 = ₹\,120$, $k_e = 0.10$, and $D_1 = ₹\,10$

Substituting the values,

(i) When dividend is paid:

$$P_1 = 120(1 + 0.1) - 10$$

$$P_1 = ₹\,122$$

(ii) When dividend is not paid:

$$P_1 = 120(1 + 0.1) - 0$$

$$P_1 = ₹\,132.$$

Problem 13. Rama Ltd. currently has 1 lakh equity shares outstanding current market price per share is ₹ 10. The net income for the current year is ₹ 3 lakh and investment budget is ₹ 6 lakh.

Cost of equity is 10%. The company is contemplating declaration of dividends @ ₹ 1 per share. Assuming MM approach:

(i) Calculate market price per share if dividend is declared and if dividend is not declared.

(ii) How many equity shares are to be issued under both the options?

Solution: We know that:

The market price of share (P_1) at the end of the period can be calculated by employing the following formula:

$$P_1 = P_0(1 + k_e) - D_1$$

Here, P_0 = ₹ 10, $k_e = 0.10$, and D_1 = ₹ 1

Substituting the values,

(i) When dividend is paid:

$$P_1 = 10(1 + 0.1) - 1$$

$$P_1 = ₹\ 10$$

(ii) When dividend is not paid:

$$P_1 = 10(1 + 0.1) - 0$$

$$P_1 = ₹\ 11$$

(iii) Number of shares, when dividend is declared:

$$m = \frac{I - (X - nD_1)}{P_1}$$

Substituting the values,

$$m = \frac{6,00,000 - (3,00,000 - 1,00,000)}{10}$$

$$m = 40,000$$

(iv) Number of shares, when dividend is not declared:

$$m = \frac{I - (X - nD_1)}{P_1}$$

Substituting the values,

$$m = \frac{6,00,000 - (3,00,000 - 0)}{11}$$

$$m = 27,273.$$

Problem 14. Krishna Ltd. currently has 100 lakh equity shares outstanding. Current market price per share is ₹ 10. The net income for the current year is ₹ 2 crore and investment budget is also of ₹ 2 crore. Cost of equity is 12%. The company is contemplating declaration of dividend @ ₹ 1 per share. Assuming MM Approach:

(i) Calculate market price per share if dividend is declared and if dividend is not declared.

(ii) How many new equity shares are to be issued under both options?

(iii) Show that the total market value of shares remains unaffected by the dividend decision.

Solution: We know that:

The market price of share (P_1) at the end of the period can be calculated by employing the following formula:

$$P_1 = P_0 (1 + k_e) - D_1$$

Here, P_0 = ₹ 10, $k_e = 0.12$, and D_1 = ₹ 1

Substituting the values,

(i) When dividend is paid:

$$P_1 = 10(1 + 0.12) - 1$$

$$P_1 = ₹\ 10.2$$

(ii) When dividend is not paid:

$$P_1 = 10(1 + 0.1) - 0$$

$$P_1 = ₹\ 11.2$$

(iii) Number of shares, when dividend is declared:

$$m = \frac{I - (X - nD_1)}{P_1}$$

Substituting the values,

$$m = \frac{2{,}00{,}00{,}000 - (2{,}00{,}00{,}000 - 1{,}00{,}00{,}000)}{10.2}$$

$$m = 9{,}80{,}392$$

(iv) Number of shares, when dividend is not declared:

$$m = \frac{I - (X - nD_1)}{P_1}$$

Substituting the values,

$$m = \frac{2{,}00{,}00{,}000 - (2{,}00{,}00{,}000 - 0)}{11.2}$$

$$m = 0$$

(v) Value of firm when dividend is declared:

$$V = (1{,}00{,}00{,}000 + 9{,}80{,}392) \times 10.2 = ₹\ 11{,}19{,}99{,}999$$

(vi) Value of firm when dividend is not declared:

$$V = 1{,}00{,}00{,}000 \times 11.2 = ₹\ 11{,}20{,}00{,}000.$$

Problem 15. The earnings per share of a company are ₹ 8. It has rate of return of 12% and capitalisation rate of risk class is 10%. If the Walter's model is used:

(i) What should be the optimum payout ratio of the firm?

(ii) What would be the price of the share at this payout ratio?

(iii) How shall the price of the share be affected if a different payout ratio was employed?

Solution: We know that the price per share is:

$$P = \frac{D}{k_e} + \frac{\left(\frac{r}{k_e}\right)(E - D)}{k_e}$$

Here, $E = ₹\ 8,\ r = 12\%,\ k_e = 10\%$

(i) Since $r > k_e$, optimum payout ratio is 0%.

(ii) When 100% retention, dividend payout ratio is 0, and $D = 0$.

$$P = \frac{0}{0.10} + \frac{\left(\frac{0.12}{0.10}\right)(8 - 0)}{0.10}$$

$$P = ₹\ 96$$

(iii) When 75% retention, dividend payout ratio is 25%, and $D = 2$.

$$P = \frac{2}{0.10} + \frac{\left(\frac{0.12}{0.10}\right)(8 - 2)}{0.10}$$

$$P = ₹\ 92.$$

Problem 16. The following information is available about a company:

$k_e = 10\%$

EPS = ₹ 20

Assume the rate of return on investments as 12%. Calculate the market price of shares using Walter's model when dividend payout ratio is:

(i) 25%

(ii) 50%

(iii) 75%

Find out the optimum dividend policy for the above company.

Solution: We know that the price per share is:

$$P = \frac{D}{k_e} + \frac{\left(\frac{r}{k_e}\right)(E - D)}{k_e}$$

Here, $E = ₹\ 20,\ r = 12\%,\ k_e = 10\%$

(i) When 75% retention, dividend payout ratio is 25%, and $D = 5$.

$$P = \frac{5}{0.10} + \frac{\left(\frac{0.12}{0.10}\right)(20 - 5)}{0.10}$$

$$P = ₹\ 230$$

(ii) When 50% retention, payout ratio is 50%, D = ₹ 10.

$$P = \frac{10}{0.10} + \frac{\left(\frac{0.12}{0.10}\right)(20-10)}{0.10}$$

$$P = 100 + 120$$

$$P = ₹\ 220$$

(iii) When 25% retention, payout ratio is 75% and dividend is ₹ 15.

$$P = \frac{15}{0.10} + \frac{\left(\frac{0.12}{0.10}\right)(20-15)}{0.10}$$

$$P = 150 + 60$$

$$P = ₹\ 210.$$

Problem 17. ABC Ltd. has a capital of ₹ 10,00,000 in equity shares of ₹ 100 each. The current market price of these shares is ₹ 140 each. The company proposes to declare a dividend of ₹ 8 per share at the end of current financial year. The capitalisation rate for the risk class to which the company belongs is 12 percent.

Based on Modigliani-Miller approach, calculate the market price per share of the company if:

(i) The dividend is not declared and

(ii) The dividend is declared.

Solution: We know that:

The market price of share (P_1) at the end of the period can be calculated by employing the following formula:

$$P_1 = P_0(1 + k_e) - D_1$$

Here, P_0 = ₹ 140, $k_e = 0.12$, and D_1 = ₹ 8

Substituting the values,

(i) When dividend is paid:

$$P_1 = 140(1 + 0.12) - 8$$

$$P_1 = ₹\ 148.8$$

(ii) When dividend is not paid:

$$P_1 = 140(1 + 0.12) - 0$$

$$P_1 = ₹\ 156.8.$$

Problem 18. X Ltd. earns ₹ 8 per share, having capitalisation rate of 12 percent and has a return on investment at 15 percent. According to Walter's model, what should be the price per share at 30 percent dividend payout ratio? Is this optimum payout ratio as per Walter's model?

Solution: We know that the price per share is:

$$P = \frac{D}{k_e} + \frac{\left(\frac{r}{k_e}\right)(E-D)}{k_e}$$

Assume the rate of return on investments as 10%. Calculate the market price of shares using Walter's model when dividend payout ratio is:

(i) 25%

(ii) 50%

(iii) 75%.

Find out the optimum dividend policy for the above company.

(D.U., B.Com. 2013, Corres.)

[Ans. (i) ₹ 100; (ii) ₹ 111; (iii) ₹ 122]

ABC Ltd. has a capital of ₹ 10,00,000 in equity shares of ₹ 100 each. The current market price of these shares is ₹ 150 each. The company proposes to declare a dividend of ₹ 8 per share at the end of current financial year. The capitalisation rate for the risk class to which the company belongs is 12 percent.

Based on Modigliani-Miller approach, calculate the market price per share of the company if:

(i) The dividend is not declared and

(ii) The dividend is declared. *(D.U., B.Com. 2014, Corres.)*

[Ans. (i) ₹ 160; (ii) ₹ 168]

X Ltd. earns ₹ 6 per share, having capitalisation rate of 10 percent and has a return on investment at 20 percent. According to Walter's model, what should be the price per share at 30 percent dividend payout ratio? Is this optimum payout ratio as per Walter's model? *(D.U., B.Com. 2014, Corres.)*

[Ans. ₹ 102; No, optimum payout is 0%]

The following information is available in respect of a company:

EPS	₹ 10
Rate of return	20%
Required rate of return on equity	16%

Find out the market price of shares under Gordon's model if the firm follows a dividend payout of:

(i) 25%

(ii) 50%

(iii) 75% *(D.U., B.Com. 2015, N.C.)*

[Ans. (i) ₹ 250; (ii) ₹ 83.3; (iii) ₹ 68.2]

A company has a capital of ₹ 10,00,000 in equity shares of ₹ 100 each. The shares are currently quoted at par. The company proposes to declare a dividend of ₹ 10 per share at the end of current financial year. The capitalisation rate for the risk to which company belongs is 12%. What will be the market price of the new share at the end of the year, if:

(i) A dividend is not declared;

(ii) A dividend is declared;

Here, $E = ₹\ 8, r = 15\%, k_e = 12\%$

(i) When 70% retention, dividend pay-out ratio is 30%, and $D = 2.4$.

$$P = \frac{2.4}{0.12} + \frac{\left(\frac{0.15}{0.12}\right)(8-2.4)}{0.12}$$

$$P = 20 + 58.33$$

$$P = ₹\ 78.33$$

(ii) No. this is not optimum payout ratio because r is greater than cost of capital. The optimum payout ratio is 0%.

Problem 19. The following information is available in respect of a company:

EPS	₹ 10
Rate of return	15%
Required rate of return on equity	12%

Find out the market price of shares under Gordon's model if the firm follows a dividend payout of:

(i) 25%

(ii) 50%

(iii) 75%

We know that the price per share is:

$$P = \frac{D}{k_e} + \frac{\left(\frac{r}{k_e}\right)(E-D)}{k_e}$$

Here, $E = ₹\ 10, r = 15\%, k_e = 12\%$

(i) When 75% retention, dividend payout ratio is 25%, and $D = 2.5$.

$$P = \frac{2.5}{0.12} + \frac{\left(\frac{0.15}{0.12}\right)(10-2.5)}{0.12}$$

$$P = 20.83 + 78.13$$

$$P = ₹\ 98.96$$

(ii) When 50% retention, payout ratio is 50%, $D = ₹\ 5$.

$$P = \frac{5}{0.12} + \frac{\left(\frac{0.15}{0.12}\right)(10-5)}{0.12}$$

$$P = 41.67 + 52.08$$

$$P = ₹\ 93.75$$

(iii) When 25% retention, payout ratio is 75% and dividend is ₹ 7.5.

$$P = \frac{7.5}{0.12} + \frac{\left(\frac{0.15}{0.12}\right)(10 - 7.5)}{0.12}$$

$$P = 62.5 + 26.04$$

$$P = ₹\ 88.54.$$

Problem 20. A company has a capital of ₹ 10,00,000 in equity shares of ₹ 100 each. The shares are currently quoted at par. The company proposes to declare a dividend of ₹ 8 per share at the end of current financial year. The capitalisation rate for the risk to which company belongs is 10%. What will be the market price of the new share at the end of the year, if:

(i) A dividend is not declared;

(ii) A dividend is declared;

(iii) Assuming that the company pays the dividend and has net profits of ₹ 5,00,000 and makes new investments of ₹ 10,00,000 during the period.

How many new shares must be issued? Use MM model.

Solution: We know that:

The market price of share (P_1) at the end of the period can be calculated by employing the following formula:

$$P_1 = P_0(1 + k_e) - D_1$$

Here, $P_0 = ₹\ 100$, $k_e = 0.10$, and $D_1 = ₹\ 8$

Substituting the values,

(i) When dividend is paid:

$$P_1 = 100(1 + 0.1) - 8$$

$$P_1 = ₹\ 102$$

(ii) When dividend is not paid:

$$P_1 = 100(1 + 0.1) - 0$$

$$P_1 = ₹\ 110$$

(iii) Number of shares, when dividend is paid:

$$m = \frac{I - (X - nD_1)}{P_1}$$

Substituting the values,

$$m = \frac{10,00,000 - (5,00,000 - 80,000)}{102}$$

$$m = 5686.$$

THEORETICAL QUESTIONS

1. Write a note on Gordon's approach to relevance of dividend decis
2. Explain the Modigliani-Miller hypothesis of dividend irrelevance.
3. Explain Walter's dividend model. What are its shortcomings?
4. Explain Gordon's model of dividend. What are its assumption? firm is affected by its dividend policy as per this model?
5. What is informational contents of dividend payment? How does i

PRACTICAL PROBLEMS

1. Ghajini Ltd. currently has 10 lakh equity shares outstanding cur share is ₹ 100. The net income for the current year is ₹ 3 crore and ₹ 4 crore. Cost of equity is 10%. The company is contemplating de @ ₹ 5 per share. Assuming MM approach:

   (i) Calculate market price per share if dividend is declared and if di

   (ii) How many equity shares are to be issued under both the optic

   (D.U., B

   [**Ans.** (i) 105, 110; (ii) 1,42,857, 90,910]

2. Rammayya Ltd., currently has 100 lakh equity shares outstanding. per share is ₹ 15. The net income for the current year is ₹ 2 crore a is also of ₹ 2 crore. Cost of equity is 12%. The company is contem dividend @ ₹ 1 per share. Assuming MM Approach:

   (i) Calculate market price per share if dividend is declared and if di

   (ii) How many new equity shares are to be issued under both opti

   (iii) Show that the total market value of shares remains unaffected by

   (D.U., B

   [**Ans.** (i) ₹ 15.80, ₹ 16.80; (ii) 6,32,911, 0; (iii) ₹ 15 crore, ₹ 15 cr

3. The earnings per share of a company are ₹ 20. It has rate of capitalisation rate of risk class is 12.5%. if the Walter's model is u

   (i) What should be the optimum payout ratio of the firm?

   (ii) What would be the price of the share at this payout ratio?

   (iii) How shall the price of the share be affected if a different payou

   (D.U., B

   [**Ans.** (i) 0%; (ii) ₹ 192; (iii) ₹ 184]

4. The following information is available about a company:

   $k_e = 15\%$ EPS = ₹ 20

(iii) Assuming that the company pays the dividend and has net profits of ₹ 5,00,000 and makes new investments of ₹ 10,00,000 during the period.

How many new shares must be issued? Use MM model. *(D.U., B.Com. 2015, N.C.)*

[**Ans.** (i) ₹ 112; (ii) ₹ 102; (iii) ₹ 102, 5883 shares]

9. M Ltd. belongs to a risk class for which the appropriate capitalisation rate is 16%. It currently has ₹ 4,00,000 shares selling at ₹ 10 each. The company is planning to declare a dividend of ₹ 1.20 at the end of the current financial year. The company expects a net income of ₹ 10,00,000 and has a proposal for making new investments of ₹ 20 lakhs. What will be price of the share at the end of the year and how many new shares must be issued? Apply MM Approach. *(D.U., B.Com. 2015, Corres.)*

   [**Ans.** ₹ 10.40, 1,42,308 shares]

10. There are two firms A and B. The equity capitalisation rate of both the firms is 10%. Rate of return on investments is 15% for firm A and 10% for firm B. The earnings per share of each firm is ₹ 5. Both the firms have 10,000 equity shares. Apply Walter's model and:

    (i) Calculate the price of the share and value of each firm for a retention ratio of (a) 50% and (b) no retention.

    (ii) What would be the optimum dividend pay-out ratio of each firm?

    (iii) State the relationship between dividend pay-out ratio and share price for each firm. *(D.U., B.Com. 2015, Corres.)*

    [**Ans.** (i) (a) ₹ 62.5, ₹ 50; (b) ₹ 50, ₹ 50; (ii) 0% pay-out, no optimum pay-out ratio]

11. The following information is provided to you for a company:

Earnings of the company:	₹ 5,00,000
Dividend paid:	₹ 3,00,000
Number of shares outstanding:	1,00,000
Price earnings ratio:	8
Rate of return on investment:	15%

    (i) What is the price per share and the market value of the company at present?

    (ii) Using Walter's model, are you satisfied with the current dividend policy of the firm?

    (iii) If not, what should be the optimal dividend payout ratio? *(D.U., B.Com. 2016, N.C.)*

    [**Ans.** (i) ₹ 43.2; (ii) no; (iii) payout ratio should be zero]

12. A company currently has outstanding 25,000 equity shares selling at ₹ 100 each. The company proposes to declare a dividend of ₹ 5 per share at the end of the current financial year. The capitalisation rate for the risk class to which the company belongs is 10%. The company expects to have a net income of ₹ 2.5 lakhs and it has a proposal for making an investment of ₹ 5 lakhs.

    What will be the market price of the share at the end of the year, if:

    (a) A dividend is not declared

    (b) A dividend is declared

(c) How many new shares must be issued in case of (a) and (b) above?

(d) Determine the value of the firm in case of both (a) and (b) above. Use the MM model. *(D.U., B.Com. 2016, N.C.)*

[**Ans.** (a) ₹ 110; (b) ₹ 105; (c) 2277, 3571; (d) ₹ 25,00,000, ₹ 25,00,000]

13. The following information is available in respect of two firms *P* and *Q*:

r = 14% and 12% respectively for firm *P* and *Q*,

k_e = 14%

Earnings per share = ₹ 20 (for both firms)

Determine the value of the share of each firm according to Walter's model for a dividend payment ratio of:

(i) 20%, (ii) 30%, (iii) 40%. *(D.U., B.Com. 2016, Corres.)*

[**Ans.** (i) ₹ 142.9, ₹ 126.5; (ii) ₹ 142.9, ₹ 128.6; (iii) ₹ 142.9, ₹ 130.6]

14. XYZ Ltd. has 10,00,000 equity shares outstanding. The ruling market price per share is ₹ 150. The Board of Directors of the company contemplates declaring ₹ 8 per share as dividend at the end of current year. The rate of capitalisation of the risk-class to which the company belongs is 12%.

(i) Based on Modigliani-Miller Approach, calculate the market price per share of the company when the contemplated dividend is (a) declared, and (b) not declared.

(ii) How many new shares are to be issued by the company at the end of the year on the assumption that the Net Income for the year is ₹ 2 crore? Investment budget is ₹ 4 crore and (a) the above dividend are distributed and (b) they are not distributed.

(iii) Show that the total market value of the shares at the end of the accounting year will remain the same whether dividends are distributed or not distributed. Also, find out the current market value of the firm. *(D.U., B. Com. 2016, Corres.)*

[**Ans.** (i) ₹ 160, ₹ 160; (ii) 1,75,000, 1,19,048; (iii) ₹ 18,80,00,000, ₹ 18,80,00,000]

15. The earnings of a company are ₹ 10 per share. The capitalisation rate applicable to the company is 10%. If the company's return on investment is 20%, what is the optimum payout ratio using Walter's formula? What is the share price at that payout? What will be the share price at a payout of 20%, 50% and 80%, using the Walter's formula? *(D.U., B.Com. 2015)*

[**Ans.** (i) 0; (ii) ₹ 200; (iii) ₹ 180, ₹ 150, ₹ 120]

Working Capital Management 10

Chapter Outline

10.1 Introduction
10.2 Concepts of Working Capital
10.3 Need for Working Capital
10.4 Types of Working Capital
10.5 Determinants of Working Capital
10.6 Financing of Working Capital
10.7 Operating Cycle and Cash Cycle
10.8 Estimation of Working Capital

10.1 Introduction

Working capital is needed to meet day-to-day requirements of production and operation in a firm. Gross working capital of a firm refers to its total investment in current assets. The current assets are the assets which can be converted into cash within an accounting year. The current assets includes cash, marketable securities, receivables and inventory. Net working capital is the difference between current assets and current liabilities. Current liabilities refers the debts of the firm that have to be repaid within a year. Current liabilities include accounts payables, bank overdrafts, outstanding expenses etc.

The working capital management refers to the administration of the firm's current assets, namely—cash, marketable securities, receivables and inventory—and the financing needed to support the current assets. The current assets in a firm should be managed efficiently to maintain the liquidity.

10.2 Concepts of Working Capital

Working capital is needed in a firm to meet its day-to-day requirements. The day-to-day requirements of the firm are assessed after adjusting the amount of current liabilities. There are two concepts of working capital.

(i) **Gross working capital:** Gross working capital means the firm's total investment in current assets. The current assets are the assets which can be converted into cash within an accounting year. The current assets includes cash, marketable securities, receivables and inventory.

(ii) **Networking capital:** The networking capital is equal to the difference between current assets and current liabilities. Current liabilities refers to the debts of the firm that have to be repaid within a year. Current liabilities include accounts payables, bank overdrafts, outstanding expenses etc. Thus, the networking capital means that portion of current assets which is financed with the long-term debt.

The both concepts are equally important in management of operations of a firm.

10.3 Need for Working Capital

After set up of the project, working capital is required for day-to-day business of the firm. Working capital is required for the period starting from the purchase of raw material to collection of cash from debtors. The period is called operating cycle of the firm. Longer the operating cycle, higher is the amount of working capital required. For example, in a firm 2 months are needed to convert the raw material into finished goods, 15 days are required to sale the finished goods and 15 days are required to collect the cash from debtors. Hence, the operating cycle of firm is three months. Then, the working capital is required for three months and after three months the cash collected will be used in the next operating cycle i.e., three months.

Since the objective of the firm is to maximise shareholders' wealth, the smooth and full capacity operation of the firm becomes imperative to accomplish the objective. Thus, maintenance of optimal level of working capital is essential for smooth production operation in the firm. Deficiency of working capital in a firm will result in irregular production of goods and it will results in lower profits or loss to the firm. Excess of working capital will result in increased burden in form of increased interest on working capital, which will lead to a decline in profits of the firm. Thus, the maintenance of appropriate level of working capital in a firm is vital for smooth production and maximisation of shareholders' wealth. A firm has to assess its requirement of working capital by taking into consideration the credit policy, purchase policy, stock turnover rate, operating cycle and the rate of inflation.

10.4 Types of Working Capital

The operating cycle in a firm causes the need for working capital. Production of goods is continuous process in the firm. Thus, current assets are required continuously in a firm. But, the amount of current assets needed may vary on certain occasions. On the basis of necessity, the working capital can be of two types:

(i) **Permanent working capital:** Permanent working capital is the minimum level of working capital continuously required in a firm in order to maintain its operational activities. Each firm have to maintain this minimum level of working capital irrespective of its operation level. The permanent working capital required in firm will increase with the expansion of its business. Permanent working capital is generally financed through long-term sources of finance.

(ii) **Fluctuating working capital:** The additional working capital required above the minimum level of working capital in order to meet the requirement arising out of fluctuations in sales. The demand for temporary or variable working capital may arise due to change in seasonal demand of products of the firm. Temporary working capital is generally financed by short-term funds.

10.5 Determinants of Working Capital

The requirement of working capital in a firm depends on a number of factors as explained below:

1. **Nature and size of business:** The requirement of working capital depends on the size of the firm and its business. Large firms require more working capital as compared to small firms. Trading, labour oriented and financial firms require a large amount of money to be invested in working capital and small investment in fixed assets. On the other hand, manufacturing and capital intensive industries require more investment in fixed assets and less in working capital.
2. **Economic cycle:** When there is prosperity in the economy, sales will increase and the firm will need additional working capital. There may arise need of business expansion in a firm during the prosperity period, hence more working capital may be required to maintain the operational activities of the firm smoothly. On the other hand, when economy is in depression, the business activities shall have downward swing. Hence, sales of the firms will decline and the firms will need less working capital.
3. **Seasonal operations:** The sales of goods in a firm may be affected by a season. For example, the sale of products of a woollen garments manufacturing will down in summer season and up in winter season. When sales of products in firm are up, more working capital will be required to maintain higher production of products and their inventory. On the other hand, when sales are down, the firm would require less working capital.
4. **Operating cycle:** The operating cycle refers the time period between acquisition of raw material and the collection of cash from debtors. The longer is the operating cycle in a firm, the larger is the amount of working capital needed. The simple reason is the funds will be tied for a longer period of time.
5. **Credit policy of the firm:** The credit policy of a firm affects the amount of working capital required in a firm. The credit policy of a firm will decide the time period of realisation of cash from customers whom goods have been sold on credit basis and the discount allowed to them. If the time period of cash realisation is longer, higher will be the amount of working capital required by the firm. The working capital requirement of a firm selling its product on cash basis will be lower than that of the firm selling products on credit basis.
6. **Credit availability from suppliers:** The working capital requirement of a firm will decline, if the supplier(s) of raw material allow(s) it the purchases on credit basis. Suppliers' credit finances the firm's inventories and reduces its cash conversion cycle. If credit is not allowed by suppliers, the firm will borrow funds from the bank and the working capital amount will increase.
7. **Technology and manufacturing policy:** The production cycle of a firm affects its working capital requirements. The manufacturing cycle or the inventory cycle refers the time period between the purchase of raw material and the production of finished goods. Longer the manufacturing cycle in a firm, larger will be the amount of working capital required.

   The technology used by a firm affects its manufacturing cycle. The more efficient technology will reduce the manufacturing cycle of a firm. With a reduced manufacturing cycle, the firm will have shorter cash conversion cycle. This will help in reducing the working capital requirement the firm.

8. **Inflation:** When deciding the working capital requirements, a firm should also make adjustment for price rise during the operating cycle. If rate of inflation is high, the firm will need more funds to purchase the supplies, which will increase the working capital requirements of the firm.
9. **Dividend policy:** The dividend policy of the firm also affects the working capital requirements. A firm having conservative dividend policy will have more cash left with it after the payment of dividends. The firm with more cash in hand will need less working capital. On the other hand, firm adopting liberal dividend policy will be left with less cash after the payment of dividends to shareholders. The firm with less cash in hand will require more working capital.

10.6 Financing of Working Capital

A firm can use three types of financing to meet the working capital requirements as mentioned below:

1. **Long-term financing:** Long-term financing is generally used by a firm to finance the permanent working capital requirements. The equity share capital, preference share capital, long-term debts from financial institutions, retained earnings are the sources of long-term finance of working capital. The cost of long-term finance is generally higher than short-term finance.
2. **Short-term financing:** The short-term financing is preferably used by a firm to finance the flexible working capital requirements. The short-term finance is obtained for a period less than one year. The sources of short-term finance are working capital funds from banks, commercial paper, public deposits, discounting of receivables, etc.
3. **Spontaneous financing:** Spontaneous financing means the automatic sources of short-term funds arising during the normal course of business. These sources are not specifically taken by the firm. The sources of spontaneous are credit from suppliers, outstanding expenses.

A firm can use any of the three approaches in devising the technique (a mix of long-term finance and short-term finance) to finance its current assets as explained below. There is risk and cost/profit trade-off in all the three approaches.

1. **Hedging approach:** In hedging (maturity matching) approach, each asset is offset with a financing instrument of approximately same maturity. All fixed assets and permanent current assets would be financed with long-term debt or equity, while short-term or seasonal variations in current assets would be financed with short-term debt.

   The net working capital in this case will be equal to permanent current assets only. This will happen because current assets are matched with current liabilities. This approach has minimum cost of networking capital, but it is a risky approach.
2. **Conservative approach:** In conservative approach, all the permanent current assets and some part of variable current assets would be financed with long-term finance, i.e., long-term debt or equity. In case the firm does not need variable current assets for some periods, the interest on the fund tied up for financing the variable current assets will be

borne by the firm. Thus, the cost of financing of current assets will increase if the firm adopts this approach. However, the firm will have minimum risk of having the shortage of funds for current assets. In all the three approaches, this approach is least risky, but will incur maximum cost.

3. **Aggressive approach:** In aggressive approach, the firm finances its all the current assets and some part of fixed assets as well with short-term finance. Since the cost of short-term finance is less than long-term finance, this approach costs minimum to the firm. But, the firm would incur maximum risk if this approach is implemented. There is negative margin of safety in this approach.

There is trade-off between risk and profitability in all the three approaches. If we compare the three approaches of mixing the long-term and short-term finances explained above to finance the assets of a firm, it is found that the matching approach has moderate risk and cost. The aggressive approach costs least to a firm, but it is most risky. On the other hand, the conservative approach is least risky, but it costs maximum to a firm.

10.7 Operating Cycle and Cash Cycle

The gross operating cycle of a firm refers the period starting from the purchase of raw material to collection of sales proceeds. The net operating or cash cycle is calculated by making an adjustment for creditors/payables deferral period in the gross operating cycle. The cash cycle is calculated by subtracting creditors deferred period from the gross operating cycle. There are three important periods, which are used in calculating gross operating period and cash cycle/net operating cycle as mentioned below:

(i) **Inventory conversion period:** Inventory conversion period is the average time taken to convert the raw material in finished goods and sell them. It is the sum of raw material conversion period, work-in-progress conversion period and finished goods conversion period.

The raw material conversion period is the average time taken to convert raw material into work-in-progress. The work-in-progress conversion period is the average time taken to convert work-in-progress into finished goods. The finished goods conversion period is the average time taken to sell the finished goods.

(ii) **Debtors conversion period:** The debtors conversion period is the average time taken to convert credit sales into cash.

(iii) **Creditors deferred period:** The creditors deferred period is the average time taken by the firm in paying its suppliers of raw material.

Gross operating cycle = Inventory conversion period + debtors conversion period

Net operating/cash cycle = Gross operating cycle – Creditors deferred period

The format of calculation of operating cycle of a firm is given below:

Calculation of operating cycle in days

1. Inventory conversion period	Days
(i) Raw material	–
(ii) Work-in-progress	–

(iii) Finished goods	–
2. Debtors conversion period	–
Gross operating cycle (1 + 2)	–
3. Payment deferred period	–
Net operating cycle (1 + 2 – 3)	–

Calculation of components of operating cycle:

1. Raw material coversion period = $\frac{\text{Average raw material}}{\text{Total purchase}} \times 365$ days
2. Work-in-progress conversion period = $\frac{\text{Average work-in-progress}}{\text{Total cost of production}} \times 365$ days
3. Finished goods conversion period = $\frac{\text{Average debtors}}{\text{Total cost of goods sold}} \times 365$ days
4. Debtors conversion period = $\frac{\text{Average debtors}}{\text{Total sales}} \times 365$ days
5. Creditors deferred period = $\frac{\text{Average creditors}}{\text{Total purchase}} \times 365$ days

The following examples will clear the concept of calculation of operating cycle.

Example 1. From the following information, compute the operating cycle of a firm:

Period covered: 365 days

Average of total debtors outstanding: ₹ 4,80,000

Raw material consumption: ₹ 44,00,000

Total production cost: ₹ 1,00,00,000

Total cost of sales: ₹ 1,05,00,000

Sales for the year: ₹ 1,60,00,000

Value of average stock maintained:

Raw material: ₹ 3,20,000

Work-in-progress: ₹ 3,50,000

Finished goods: ₹ 2,60,000

The average period of credit allowed by suppliers is 16 days.

Solution: Calculation of operating cycle in days

Inventory conversion period	**Days**
Raw material[1]	27
Work-in-progress[2]	13
Finished goods[3]	9

Debtors conversion period[4]	11
Gross operating cycle (1 + 2)	60
Payment deferred period	16
Net operating cycle (1 + 2 – 3)	44

Notes: 1. Raw material = (3,20,000 ÷ 44,00,000) × 365 = 27 days
2. Work-in-progress = (3,50,000 ÷ 100,00,000) × 365 = 13 days
3. Finished goods = (2,60,000 ÷ 105,00,000) × 365 = 9 days
4. Debtor conversion = (4,80,000 ÷ 160,00,000) × 365 = 11 days

Example 2. Mohan Ltd. has provided the following information:

Sales	₹ 1,50,00,000
Cost of sales	₹ 95,00,000
Raw material consumed	₹ 40,00,000
Cost of production	₹ 85,00,000

Value of average stock maintained:

Raw material ₹ 3,00,000
Work-in-progress ₹ 3,20,000
Finished goods ₹ 2,50,000

The average period of credit allowed by suppliers is 15 days and all sales are made on cash basis. You are required to compute operating cycle in days.

Solution: Calculation of operating cycle in days

Inventory conversion period	**Days**
Raw material[1]	27
Work-in-progress[2]	14
Finished goods[3]	10
Debtors conversion period	0
Gross operating cycle (1 + 2)	51
Payment deferred period	15
Net operating cycle (1 + 2 – 3)	36

Notes: 1. Raw material = (3,00,000 ÷ 40,00,000) × 365 = 27 days
2. Work-in-progress = (3,20,000 ÷ 85,00,000) × 365 = 14 days
3. Finished goods = (2,50,000 ÷ 95,00,000) × 365 = 10 days

10.8 Estimation of Working Capital

Since smooth and efficient operation of the firm depends on working capital, it becomes significant to assess the working capital requirement accurately. The managers of the firm should also consider a safety margin to meet any contingencies in the day-to-day operation of the firm. Working capital requirements of a firm can be estimated on the basis of:

(i) Operating cycle concept
(ii) Ratio of sales
(iii) Ratio of fixed investment.

When working capital requirements of a firm is assessed on operating cycle basis; the requirements for cash, raw material, work-in-progress, finished goods, and credit sales are summed up. To find the networking capital requirements, the amount of credit allowed to the firm by its suppliers of raw material, labour, etc. is deducted from the working capital requirements.

Depreciation is a non-cash expense and funds are not tied up in depreciation. Hence, depreciation is neither included in the calculation of working capital nor in the valuation of finished goods.

To ascertain the working capital requirement, the firm should also include a safety margin to meet the contingencies faced by it. The quantum of contingencies depends on the nature of the firm.

Generally, 100% cost of raw material is included in semi-finished work in a firm, while 50% of cost of labour and overheads each is included.

The format to ascertain the working capital requirements of a firm is given below:

Statement of working capital

	Current assets	**Amount**
1.	Raw material inventory (for – months)	–
2.	Work-in-progress (for – months)	–
3.	Stock of finished goods (for – months)	–
4.	Sundry debtors or receivables (for – months)	–
5.	Advance payments	–
6.	Cash (for day-to-day expenses)	–
	Gross working capital (A)	–
	Current liabilities: Deferred payments	
1.	Creditors for raw material (for – months)	–
2.	Deferred wages (for – months)	–
3.	Deferred overheads (for – months)	–
	Total deferred payments (B)	–
	Networking capital (A – B)	–
	Add: Safety margin (Contingencies)	–
	Networking capital requirement	–

The examples given below shall clear the concept of ascertainment of working capital of a firm.

Example 3. Compute the working capital requirements of Mohan Ltd. from the following details:

Budgeted sales	50,000 units per annum
Raw material cost per unit	₹ 6
Direct labour per unit	₹ 6
Overhead per unit	₹ 1
Total Cost	₹ 13
Profit per unit	₹ 2
Selling price per unit	₹ 15

Additional information:

(i) Debtors are allowed 8 weeks credit

(ii) Suppliers provide 5 weeks credit

(iii) Raw material will be carried in stock for 4 weeks and finished goods for 2 weeks

(iv) Factory process will take on an average 3 weeks.

Assume labour and overhead expenses to accrue evenly throughout the production cycle.

Solution: Statement of working capital

Current assets	Amount (₹)
Raw material inventory[1]	23,077
Work in progress[2]	27,404
Stock of finished goods[3]	25,000
Sundry debtors[4]	1,00,000
Gross working capital (A)	1,75,481
Current liabilities: Deferred payments	
Creditors[5]	28,846
Total deferred payments (B)	28,846
Networking capital (A – B)	1,46,635

Working notes:

1. Stock of raw material = 50,000 × 6 × (4 ÷ 52) = 23,077
2. Raw material = 50,000 × 6 × (3 ÷ 52) = 17,308
   Direct labour = 50% of [50,000 × 6 × (3 ÷ 52)] = 8,654
   Overheads = 50% of [50,000 × 1 × (3 ÷ 52)] = 1,442
   17,308 + 8,654 + 1,442 = 27,404
3. Finished goods stock = 50,000 × 13 × (2 ÷ 52) = 25,000
4. Debtors = 50,000 × 13 × (8 ÷ 52) = 1,00,000
5. Creditors = 50,000 × 6 × (5 ÷ 52) = 28,846

Example 4. Compute the working capital requirement from the following details:

Budgeted Sales	**30,000 units per annum**
Raw material cost per unit	₹ 8
Direct labour cost per unit	₹ 6
Overheads per unit	₹ 2
Total Cost per unit	₹ 16
Profit per unit	₹ 2
Selling price per unit	₹ 18

Additional information:

(i) Debtors are allowed 7 weeks credit
(ii) Suppliers provide 4 weeks credit
(iii) Raw material will be carried in stock for 4 weeks and finished goods for 2 weeks
(iv) Factoring processing will take on an average 4 weeks.

Assume labour and overhead expenses to accrue evenly throughout the production cycle.

Solution: Statement of working capital

	Current assets	**Amount**
1.	Raw material inventory[1]	18,462
2.	Work-in-progress[2]	27,693
3.	Stock of finished goods[3]	18,462
4.	Debtors[4]	64,615
	Gross working capital (A)	1,29,232
	Current liabilities: Deferred payments	
1.	Creditors for raw material[5]	18,462
	Total deferred payments (B)	18,462
	Networking capital (A – B)	1,10,770

Working notes:

1. Stock of raw material = 30,000 × 8 × (4 ÷ 52) = 18,462
2. Raw material = 30,000 × 8 × (4 ÷ 52) = 18,462
   Direct labour = 50% of [30,000 × 6 × (4 ÷ 52)] = 6,923
   Overheads = 50% of [30,000 × 2 × (4 ÷ 52)] = 2,308
   18,462 + 6,923 + 2,308 = 27,693
3. Finished goods stock = 30,000 × 16 × (2 ÷ 52) = 18,462
4. Debtors = 30,000 × 16 × (7 ÷ 52) = 64,615
5. Creditors = 30,000 × 8 × (4 ÷ 52) = 18,462

SOLVED PROBLEMS

Problem 1. Compute the working capital requirements from the following details:

Budgeted sales	30,000 units per annum
Raw material cost per unit	₹ 8
Direct labour per unit	₹ 8
Overhead per unit	₹ 2
Total Cost	₹ 18
Profit per unit	₹ 2
Selling price per unit	₹ 20

Additional information:

(i) Debtors are allowed 8 weeks credit

(ii) Suppliers provide 5 weeks credit

(iii) Raw material will be carried in stock for 4 weeks and finished goods for 2 weeks

(iv) Factory process will take on an average 3 weeks.

Assume labour and overhead expenses to accrue evenly throughout the production cycle.

(D.U., B.Com. 2016)

Solution: Statement of working capital

Current assets	Amount (₹)
Raw material inventory[1]	18,462
Work-in-progress[2]	22,500
Stock of finished goods[3]	20,769
Sundry debtors[4]	83,077
Gross working capital (A)	1,44,808
Current liabilities: Deferred payments	
Creditors[5]	23,077
Total deferred payments (B)	23,077
Networking capital (A – B)	1,21,731

Working notes:

1. Stock of raw material = 30,000 × 8 × (4 ÷ 52) = 18,462
2. Raw material = 30,000 × 8 × (3 ÷ 52) = 13,846
   Direct labour = 50% of [30,000 × 8 × (3 ÷ 52)] = 6,823
   Overheads = 50% of [30,000 × 2 × (3 ÷ 52)] = 1,731
   13,846 + 6,823 + 1,731 = 22,500
3. Finished goods stock = 30,000 × 18 × (2 ÷ 52) = 20,769

4. Debtors = 30,000 × 18 × (8 ÷ 52) = 83,077
5. Creditors = 30,000 × 8 × (5 ÷ 52) = 23,077

Problem 2. Suresh Ltd. has provided the following information:

Sales	₹ 1,60,00,000
Cost of sales	₹ 1,05,00,000
Raw material consumed	₹ 44,00,000
Cost of production	₹ 1,00,00,000

Value of average stock maintained:

Raw material	₹ 320,000
Work-in-progress	₹ 350,000
Finished goods	₹ 260,000

The average period of credit allowed by suppliers is 15 days and all sales are made on cash basis. You are required to compute operating cycle in days. *(D.U., B.Com. 2012)*

Solution: Calculation of operating cycle in days

Inventory conversion period	**Days**
Raw material[1]	27
Work-in-progress[2]	13
Finished goods[3]	9
Debtors conversion period	0
Gross operating cycle (1 + 2)	49
Payment deferred period	15
Net operating cycle (1 + 2 – 3)	34

Notes: 1. Raw material = (3,20,000 ÷ 44,00,000) × 365 = 27 days
2. Work-in-progress = (3,50,000 ÷ 1,00,00,000) × 365 = 13 days
3. Finished goods = (2,60,000 ÷ 1,05,00,000) × 365 = 9 days

Problem 3. A firm is projecting sales of 50,000 units next year. Sales price will be ₹ 20 per unit. Raw material cost, labour cost and overhead cost are estimated to be 25%, 20% and 30% respectively. Raw material remains in stock on an average for 2 weeks, work-in-progress for one week and finished goods for three week. Debtors are allowed 1 month credit while suppliers give 6 week credit. 25% of sales are on cash basis. 10% margin is kept for contingencies. Prepare a statement showing funds to be arranged for working and capital requirements.

(D.U., B.Com. 2013)

Solution: The estimated cost per unit of production:

Raw material (25% of ₹ 20)	₹ 5
Labour (20% of ₹ 20)	₹ 4
Overhead (30% of ₹ 20)	₹ 6

Statement of working capital

	Current assets	Amount
1.	Raw material inventory[1]	9,615
2.	Work-in-progress[2]	9,616
3.	Stock of finished goods[3]	43,269
4.	Debtors[4]	43,269
	Gross working capital (A)	1,05,769
	Current liabilities: Deferred payments	
1.	Creditors for raw material[5]	28,846
	Total deferred payments (B)	28,846
	Networking capital (A – B)	76,923
	Contingencies	
1.	10% contingencies	7,692
	Total contingencies (C)	7,692
	Working capital requirement (A – B + C)	84,615

Working notes:

1. Stock of raw material = 50,000 × 5 × (2 ÷ 52) = 9,615
2. Raw material = 50,000 × 5 × (1 ÷ 52) = 4,808
   Direct labour = 50% of [50,000 × 4 × (1 ÷ 52)] = 1,923
   Overheads = 50% of [50,000 × 6 × (1 ÷ 52)] = 2,885
   4,808 + 1,923 + 2,885 = 9,616
3. Finished goods stock = 50,000 × 15 × (3 ÷ 52) = 43,269
4. Debtors = 75% of [50,000 × 15 × (4 ÷ 52)] = 43,269
5. Creditors = 50,000 × 5 × (6 ÷ 52) = 28,846.

Problem 4. Compute the working capital requirement from the following details:

Budgeted Sales	40,000 units per annum
Raw material cost per unit	₹ 9
Direct labour cost per unit	₹ 7
Overheads per unit	₹ 3
Total cost per unit	₹ 19
Profit per unit	₹ 1
Selling price per unit	₹ 20

Additional information:

1. Debtors are allowed 7 weeks credit.

2. Suppliers provide 4 weeks credit.
3. Raw material will be carried in stock for 4 weeks and finished goods for 2 weeks.
4. Factoring processing will take on an average 4 weeks.

Assume labour and overhead expenses to accrue evenly throughout the production cycle.

(D.U., B.Com. 2015)

Solution: Statement of working capital

	Current assets	Amount
1.	Raw material inventory[1]	27,692
2.	Work in progress[2]	43,076
3.	Stock of finished goods[3]	29,231
4.	Debtors[4]	1,02,308
	Gross working capital (A)	2,02,307
	Current liabilities: Deferred payments	
1.	Creditors for raw material[5]	27,692
	Total deferred payments (B)	27,692
	Net working capital (A – B)	1,74,615

Working notes:

1. Stock of raw material = 40,000 × 9 × (4 ÷ 52) = 27,692
2. Raw material = 40,000 × 9 × (4 ÷ 52) = 27,692
   Direct labour = 50% of [40,000 × 7 × (4 ÷ 52)] = 10,769
   Overheads = 50% of [40,000 × 3 × (4 ÷ 52)] = 4,615
   27,692 + 10,769 + 4,615 = 43,076
3. Finished goods stock = 40,000 × 19 × (2 ÷ 52) = 29,231
4. Debtors = 40,000 × 19 × (7 ÷ 52) = 1,02,308
5. Creditors = 40,000 × 9 × (4 ÷ 52) = 27,692.

Problem 5. From the following information, compute the operating cycle in days:

Period covered	365 days
Average period of credit allowed by suppliers	15 days
Average of total debtors outstanding	₹ 4,00,000
Raw material consumption	₹ 45,00,000
Total Production cost	₹ 110,00,000
Total Cost of sales	₹ 115,00,000
Sales for the year	₹ 200,00,000

Value of average stock maintained	
Raw materials	₹ 3,00,000
Work-in-progress	₹ 3,80,000
Finished goods	₹ 2,80,000

Solution: Calculation of operating cycle in days

Inventory conversion period	Days
Raw material[1]	24
Work in progress[2]	13
Finished goods[3]	9
Debtors conversion period[4]	7
Gross operating cycle (1 + 2)	53
Payment deferred period	15
Net operating cycle (1 + 2 – 3)	38

Notes: 1. Raw material = (3,00,000 ÷ 45,00,000) × 365 = 24 days
2. Work-in-progress = (3,80,000 ÷ 1,10,00,000) × 365 = 13 days
3. Finished goods = (2,80,000 ÷ 1,15,00,000) × 365 = 9 days
4. Debtor conversion = (4,00,000 ÷ 2,00,00,000) × 365 = 7 days

Problem 6. Prepare an estimate of networking capital requirements of XYZ Ltd. from the data given below:

Cost per unit	
Raw material	₹ 50
Direct labour	₹ 30
Overheads	₹ 20
Total	₹ 100

The following additional information is given:

Selling price: ₹ 250

Level of activity: 52,000 units per annum

Raw materials in stock: average 4 weeks

Work-in-progress (assuming 100% completion of materials and 50% for labour and overhead): average 2 weeks

Finished goods in stock: average 4 weeks

Credit allowed by suppliers: average 4 weeks

Credit allowed to debtors: average 8 weeks

Cash at bank is expected to be ₹ 30,000.

Assume production is sustained during 52 weeks of the year.

Solution: Statement of working capital

Current assets	Amount (₹)
Raw material inventory[1]	2,00,000
Work-in-progress[2]	1,50,000
Stock of finished goods[3]	4,00,000
Debtors[4]	8,00,000
Cash	30,000
Gross working capital (A)	15,80,000
Current liabilities: Deferred payments	
Creditors[5]	2,00,000
Total deferred payments (B)	2,00,000
Net working capital (A – B)	13,80,000

Working notes:

1. Stock of raw material = 52,000 × 50 × (4 ÷ 52) = 2,00,000
2. Raw material = 52,000 × 50 × (2 ÷ 52) = 1,00,000
   Direct labour = 50% of [52,000 × 30 × (2 ÷ 52)] = 30,000
   Overheads = 50% of [52,000 × 20 × (2 ÷ 52)] = 20,000
   1,00,000 + 30,000 + 20,000 = 1,50,000
3. Finished goods stock = 52,000 × 100 × (4 ÷ 52) = 4,00,000
4. Debtors = 52,000 × 100 × (8 ÷ 52) = 8,00,000
5. Creditors = 52,000 × 50 × (4 ÷ 52) = 2,00,000.

Problem 7. From the following data, compute the duration of the operating cycle:

Stock	Amount
Raw material	₹ 25,000
Work-in-progress	₹ 15,000
Finished goods	₹ 25,000
Purchases	₹ 1,00,000
Cost of goods sold	₹ 1,40,000
Sales	₹ 1,80,000
Debtors	₹ 40,000
Creditors	₹ 20,000

Assume 360 days in a year.

Solution: Calculation of operating cycle in days

Inventory conversion period	Days
Raw material[1]	90
Work-in-progress[2]	39
Finished goods[3]	64
Debtors conversion period[4]	80
Gross operating cycle (1 + 2)	259
Payment deferred period[5]	72
Net operating cycle (1 + 2 – 3)	201

Notes: 1. Raw material = (25,000 ÷ 1,00,000) × 360 = 90 days
2. Work-in-progress = (15,000 ÷ 1,40,000) × 360 = 39 days
3. Finished goods = (25,000 ÷ 1,40,000) × 360 = 64 days
4. Debtors conversion = (40,000 ÷ 1,80,000) × 360 = 80 days
5. Creditors conversion = (20,000 ÷ 1,00,000) × 360 = 72 days.

Problem 8. Prepare an estimate of networking capital requirements of X Ltd. from the following data:

Estimated cost per unit (₹)	
Raw material	100
Direct labour	40
Overheads	60
Total	200

The following is the additional information:

Selling price: ₹ 250 p.u.

Output: 52,000 p.a.

Raw material in stock: average 4 weeks

Work-in-progress (assume 100% stage of completion of material and 50% for labour and overhead): average 2 weeks

Finished goods in stock: average 4 weeks

Credit allowed to debtors: average 8 weeks

Credit allowed by suppliers: average 8 weeks

Cash at bank expected to be ₹ 50,000.

Assume production is sustained during 52 weeks of the year.

Solution: Statement of working capital

Current assets	**Amount (₹)**
Raw material inventory[1]	4,00,000
Work-in-progress[2]	3,00,000
Stock of finished goods[3]	2,00,000
Debtors[4]	16,00,000
Cash	50,000
Gross working capital (A)	25,50,000
Current liabilities: Deferred payments	
Creditors[5]	8,00,000
Total deferred payments (B)	8,00,000
Networking capital (A – B)	17,50,000

Working notes:

1. Stock of raw material = 52,000 × 100 × (4 ÷ 52) = 4,00,000
2. Raw material = 52,000 × 100 × (2 ÷ 52) = 2,00,000
   Direct labour = 50% of [52,000 × 40 × (2 ÷ 52)] = 40,000
   Overheads = 50% of [52,000 × 60 × (2 ÷ 52)] = 60,000
   2,00,000 + 40,000 + 60,000 = 3,00,000
3. Finished goods stock = 52,000 × 200 × (4 ÷ 52) = 2,00,000
4. Debtors = 52,000 × 200 × (8 ÷ 52) = 16,00,000
5. Creditors = 52,000 × 100 × (8 ÷ 52) = 8,00,000.

Problem 9. Following information is collected from the records of ABC Manufacturing Ltd. for the year 2016:

Cost of goods sold	₹ 4,00,000
Cost of production	₹ 2,50,000
Raw material consumed during the year	₹ 3,00,000
Average finished goods	₹ 20,000
Average work-in-progress	₹ 15,000
Average raw material	₹ 25,000
Debtors collection period	40 days
Creditor payment period	30 days

Find out the Operating Cycle. How many operating cycles does the firm have in a year (360 days)?

Solution: Calculation of operating cycle in days

Inventory conversion period	Days
Raw material[1]	30
Work-in-progress[2]	22
Finished goods[3]	18
Debtors conversion period	40
Gross operating cycle (1 + 2)	110
Payment deferred period	30
Net operating cycle (1 + 2 – 3)	80

Number of operating cycles in a year = 360 ÷ 80 = 4.5 cycles.

Notes: 1. Raw material = (25,000 ÷ 3,00,000) × 360 = 30 days

2. Work-in-progress = (15,000 ÷ 2,50,000) × 360 = 22 days

3. Finished goods = (20,000 ÷ 4,00,000) × 360 = 18 days.

Problem 10. A firm is projecting sales of 10,000 units next year. Sale price will be ₹ 20 per unit. Raw material cost, labour cost and overhead cost are estimated to be ₹ 5, ₹ 4 and ₹ 6 respectively. Raw materials remain in stock on an average for 2 weeks, work-in-progress for 1 week and finished goods for 3 weeks. Debtors are allowed 4 weeks credit while suppliers give 6 weeks credit. 25% sales are on cash basis. 10% margin is kept for contingencies. Prepare a statement showing funds to be arranged for working capital requirement on cost basis. Assume 52 weeks in a year.

Solution: Statement of working capital

	Current assets	Amount (₹)
1.	Raw material inventory[1]	1,923
2.	Work-in-progress[2]	1,924
3.	Stock of finished goods[3]	8,654
4.	Debtors[4]	8,654
	Gross working capital (A)	21,155
	Current liabilities: Deferred payments	
1.	Creditors for raw material[5]	5,769
	Total Deferred payments (B)	5,769
	Networking capital (A – B)	15,386
	Contingencies	
1.	10% contingencies	1,539
	Total Contingencies (C)	1,539
	Working capital requirement (A – B + C)	16,925

Working notes:

1. Stock of raw material = 10,000 × 5 × (2 ÷ 52) = 1,923
2. Raw material = 10,000 × 5 × (1 ÷ 52) = 962
   Direct labour = 50% of [10,000 × 4 × (1 ÷ 52)] = 385
   Overheads = 50% of [10,000 × 6 × (1 ÷ 52)] = 577
   962 + 385 + 577 = 1,924
3. Finished goods stock = 10,000 × 15 × (3 ÷ 52) = 8,654
4. Debtors = 75% of [10,000 × 15 × (4 ÷ 52)] = 8,654
5. Creditors = 10,000 × 5 × (6 ÷ 52) = 5,769.

THEORETICAL QUESTIONS

1. Write short note on Operating cycle method of working capital. *(D.U., B.Com. 2016)*
2. What is the importance of working capital management for a manufacturing firm? Describe the factors that affect working capital requirements of a company. *(D.U., B.Com. 2010)*
3. What is management of working capital? How is it different from capital budgeting? State briefly the repercussions if a firm has (i) Paucity of working capital and (ii) Excess of working capital. *(D.U., B.Com. 2011)*
4. 'Excessive working capital' as well as 'Paucity of working capital' is not desirable for a business firm. Explain. *(D.U., B.Com. 2012)*
5. What are the different approaches to financing of working capital requirements? Explain.
6. Differentiate between permanent and temporary working capital.
7. Explain how working capital management policies affect the profitability and liquidity of a firm?

PRACTICAL PROBLEMS

1. From the following information, compute the operating cycle in days:

Period covered	365 days
Average period of credit allowed by suppliers	18 days
Average of total debtors outstanding	₹ 4,90,000
Raw material consumption	₹ 45,00,000
Total Production cost	₹ 110,00,000
Total Cost of sales	₹ 115,00,000
Sales for the year	₹ 200,00,000

Value of average stock maintained	
Raw materials	₹ 3,50,000
Work-in-progress	₹ 3,80,000
Finished goods	₹ 2,70,000

(D.U., B.Com. 2011, Corres.)

[**Ans.** 41 days]

2. Prepare an estimate of networking capital requirements of XYZ Ltd. from the data given below:

Raw material	₹ 50
Direct labour	₹ 20
Overheads	₹ 10
Total	₹ 110

The following additional information is given:

Selling price: ₹ 240
Level of activity: 52,000 units per annum
Raw materials in stock: average 4 weeks
Work-in-progress (assuming 100% completion of materials and 50% for labour and overhead): average 2 weeks
Finished goods in stock: average 4 weeks
Credit allowed by suppliers: average 4 weeks
Credit allowed to debtors: average 8 weeks
Cash at bank is expected to be ₹ 20,000.

Assume production is sustained during 52 weeks of the year.

(D.U., B.Com. 2012, Corres.)

[**Ans.** ₹ 15,00,000]

3. From the following data, compute the duration of the operating cycle:

Stock	Amount
Raw material	₹ 25,000
Work-in-progress	₹ 16,000
Finished goods	₹ 24,000
Purchases	₹ 1,00,000
Cost of goods sold	₹ 1,50,000
Sales	₹ 1,75,000

Debtors	₹ 40,000
Creditors	₹ 20,000

Assume 360 days in a year. *(D.U., B.Com. 2013, Corres.)*

[**Ans.** 196 days]

4. Prepare an estimate of networking capital requirements of X Ltd. from the following data:

Estimated cost per unit (₹)	
Raw material	200
Direct labour	75
Overheads	125
Total	400

The following is the additional information:

Selling price: ₹ 500 p.u.

Output: ₹ 52,000 p.a.

Raw material in stock: average 4 weeks

Work-in-progress (assume 100% stage of completion of material and 50% for labour and overhead): average 2 weeks

Finished goods in stock: average 4 weeks

Credit allowed to debtors: average 8 weeks

Cash at bank expected to be ₹ 25,000.

Assume production is sustained during 52 weeks of the year.

(D.U., B.Com. 2014, Corres.)

[**Ans.** 46,25,000]

5. Following information is collected from the records of ABC Manufacturing Ltd. for the year 2014:

Cost of goods sold	₹ 8,00,000
Cost of production	₹ 5,00,000
Raw material consumed during the year	₹ 6,00,000
Average finished goods	₹ 40,000
Average work-in-progress	₹ 30,000
Average raw material	₹ 50,000
Debtors collection period	45 days
Creditor payment period	30 days

Find out the Operating Cycle. How many operating cycles does the firm have in a year (360 days)? *(D.U., B.Com. 2016, Corres.)*

[**Ans.** 85 days, 4.24 cycles]

6. A firm is projecting sales of 50,000 units next year. Sale price will be ₹ 20 per unit. Raw material cost, labour cost and overhead cost are estimated to be ₹ 5, ₹ 4 and ₹ 6 respectively. Raw materials remain in stock on an average for 2 weeks, work-in-progress for 1 week and finished goods for 3 weeks. Debtors are allowed 4 weeks credit while suppliers give 6 weeks credit. 25% sales are on cash basis. 10% margin is kept for contingencies. Prepare a statement showing funds to be arranged for working capital requirement on cost basis. Assume 52 weeks in a year. *(D.U., B.Com. 2015, Corres.)*

   [**Ans.** Networking capital = ₹ 84,615]

7. Compute the working capital requirements from the following details:

Budgeted sales	**50,000 units per annum**
Raw material cost per unit	₹ 8
Direct labour per unit	₹ 8
Overhead per unit	₹ 2
Total cost	₹ 18
Profit per unit	₹ 2
Selling price per unit	₹ 20

   Additional information:

   (i) Debtors are allowed 8 weeks credit
   (ii) Suppliers provide 5 weeks credit
   (iii) Raw material will be carried in stock for 4 weeks and finished goods for 2 weeks
   (iv) Factory process will take on an average 3 weeks.

   Assume labour and overhead expenses to accrue evenly throughout the production cycle.

   [**Ans.** ₹ 2,02,882]

8. Suresh Ltd. has provided the following information:

Sales	₹ 16,000
Cost of sales	₹ 10,500
Raw material consumed	₹ 4,400
Cost of production	₹ 10,000

   Value of average stock maintained:

   Raw material ₹ 320
   Work-in-progress ₹ 350
   Finished goods ₹ 260

   The average period of credit allowed by suppliers is 15 days and all sales are made on cash basis. You are required to compute operating cycle in days.

   [**Ans.** 34 days]

9. A firm is projecting sales of 1,00,000 units next year. Sales price will be ₹ 20 per unit. Raw material cost, labour cost and overhead cost are estimated to be 25%, 20% and 30%

respectively. Raw material remains in stock on an average for 2 weeks, work-in-progress for one week and finished goods for three week. Debtors are allowed one 1 month credit while suppliers give 6-week credit. 25% of sales are on cash basis. 10% margin is kept for contingencies. Prepare a statement showing funds to be arranged for working capital requirements.

[**Ans.** ₹ 1,69,230]

10. Compute the working capital requirement from the following details:

Budgeted Sales	**40,000 units per annum**
Raw material cost per unit	₹ 18
Direct labour cost per unit	₹ 14
Overheads per unit	₹ 6
Total cost per unit	₹ 38
Profit per unit	₹ 3
Selling price per unit	₹ 41

Additional information:

(i) Debtors are allowed 7 weeks credit

(ii) Suppliers provide 4 weeks credit

(iii) Raw material will be carried in stock for 4 weeks and finished goods for 2 weeks

(iv) Factoring processing will take on an average 4 weeks.

Assume labour and overhead expenses to accrue evenly throughout the production cycle.

[**Ans.** ₹ 3,49,230]

Cash Management

11

Chapter Outline

11.1 Introduction
11.2 Motives of Holding Cash
11.3 Objectives of Cash Management
11.4 Factors Determining Cash Holdings in a Firm
11.5 Cash Budget
11.6 Efficiency in Cash Management

11.1 Introduction

After the overall level of current assets is determined, the next question is: how much should be cash-in-hand in the firm? The basic objective of cash management is to minimise the cash balance and meet cash requirements as and when they arise. In ordinary meaning cash implies to ready money or its equivalent. For cash management objective, the term cash is used in broader sense. As such, it covers cash, cash equivalent and those assets which can be immediately converted into cash.

A finance manager has to manage the cash flows (inflows as well as outflows) arising out of the operations of the firm. The finance manager is required to forecast the cash inflows from sales and outflows of expenses and costs. The finance manager is also required to identify the sources for the procurement of required cash on short-term basis and identify the investments where excess cash can be invested for a short period.

The maintenance of proper level of cash is very significant in a firm. The insufficiency of cash at any stage of operations of the firm may fail it in discharging its obligations or may compel it to sell-off other assets immediately to raise the required cash. Similarly, the excess of cash in the firm may result in uneconomic investments. Since the objective of the firm is to maximise its value, the maintenance of proper level of cash balance in the firm is important.

11.2 Motives of Holding Cash

J.M. Keynes suggested three motives for individuals to hold cash. These three categories of motives are also applicable in case of firms to hold cash balance. The motives are explained below:

1. **Transaction motive:** The transaction motive requires a firm to hold cash to conduct its business operations without interruption. A firm may need cash basically to make payments

for purchases, wages, operating expenses, financial charges, like interest obligations, dividends, taxes etc. A firm receives cash from sales of products, return on investments etc. If receipts and payments in a firm are not perfectly synchronised, there will be need to hold the cash. To meet the transactions, the firm may keep cash or invest in marketable securities. To reduce the holding of cash, the firm should synchronise the inflows and outflows of cash to the extent possible. If the cash outflows and inflows arising out of transactions in a firm are perfectly synchronised, there would be no need to hold the cash balance to meet the transactions.

2. **Precautionary motive:** A firm also needs to hold cash to meet any unforeseen contingencies in future. It would be judicious to hold cash balance to meet the unknown and contingent needs, for which forecasting is not easy. The precautionary balance may be kept in cash and marketable securities. The role of marketable securities is vital in maintaining precautionary balance because holding the cash balance will not earn anything. The other factor important in deciding the precautionary cash balance is the ability of the firm to borrow from the market at short notice.

   Incidents, like workers' strike, fire, lockouts, non-payments by customers, accidents would create loss to the firm and the hard cash is needed in such situation to overcome the interruption in the operation of business. The firm should maintain sufficient cash balance to meet such financial difficulties. The funds for such precautionary motive should be invested in high-liquid and low-risk marketable securities.

3. **Speculative motive:** A firm may hold cash for investing in profit-making opportunities as and when they occur. For example, availability of raw material at very low prices, purchasing of securities when interest is expected to fall. In such situations, firms may use their speculative cash holdings and can earn profits.

   The basic objective of speculative cash holdings is to capitalise an opportunity by making an unexpected profit. The firms may use speculative cash holdings when the markets are in their highs or lows. The firms using speculation strategy should assess the results accurately and precisely so as to avoid any loss in the course of speculation.

The main motive of holding cash in firm is to make transactions. This is a basic requirement in every firm. The holding of cash balances as precaution is a necessity in every firm to meet the cash requirements caused by unforeseen events. The holding of cash for speculative purpose is not a necessity in firms to conduct the operations. It is the choice of individual firms whether to hold the cash balance for speculation or not.

Cash management involves the efficient collection, disbursement, and temporary investment of cash in marketable short-term securities when it is required. The treasury department of a firm is responsible for its cash management. The cash budget is prepared for cash management in a firm.

11.3 Objectives of Cash Management

The basic objective of cash management in a firm is to minimise the cash balance and meet cash requirements as and when they arise. The objectives of cash management are explained below:

1. **To meet the cash disbursement needs:** The finance manager of firm should ensure that when a payment need arises, there is sufficient cash balance to meet the requirement.

In this exercise, the finance manager has to do future planning of cash inflows and outflows. If the need arises, the manager should ensure that the short-term borrowings may be arranged as and when required.

Since the shortage of cash may interrupt the operational activities of the firm, the cash management should be given due significant. If the operations of the firm are interrupted or become irregular, it will bring down the profits of the firm. Finally, the objective of the firm to maximise the wealth of shareholders will remain unaccomplished. Thus, the finance manager of the firm has to maintain sufficient cash balance to meet the disbursement needs as and when arise.

2. **To minimise funds committed to cash balances:** If a firm maintains excess funds with it, it will cost to the firm and the profits of the firm will come down. Because the idle cash has its opportunity cost, the manager has to tie the minimum funds to the cash balance. The cash balance which remains idle with the firm earns nothing. If investment is made in marketable short-term securities, the rate of interest is low on it. On the other hand, if the idle cash is invested in the project, it would earn much higher as compared to investment in short-term marketable securities.

   Thus, minimum funds should be tied to cash balance in firm, as such it would increase the profits and maximise the shareholders' wealth. While considering the minimum level of cash balance, it should be ensured that the operations of the firm are not interrupted due to shortage of funds.

The above explanation of objectives clears that both the objectives are contradictory. The firm has to maintain the optimal cash balance with it. In the other words, there is neither excess nor shortage of funds tied with the cash balance of the firm. The finance manager has to achieve a trade-off between liquidity and profitability while deciding the optimal cash level in the firm.

11.4 Factors Determining Cash Holdings in a Firm

There are a number of factors affecting the cash holdings in a firm. The finance manager should take into consideration these factors while deciding the optimal cash level with the firm. The factors affecting the cash holdings of a firm are mentioned below:

1. **Cash cycle:** The gross operating cycle of a firm refers the period starting from the purchase of raw material to collection of sales proceeds. The net operating or cash cycle is calculated by making an adjustment for creditors/payables deferral period in the gross operating cycle. The cash cycle is calculated by subtracting creditors deferred period from the gross operating cycle.

   The level of cash holdings in a firm is affected by the duration of cash cycle. Longer the cash cycle of the firm, higher the level of cash holdings in it.

2. **Synchronisation of cash flows:** A firm may need cash basically to make payments for purchases, wages, operating expenses, financial charges, like interest obligations, dividends, taxes etc. A firm receives cash from sales of products, return on investments etc. If receipts and payments in a firm are not perfectly synchronised, there will be need to hold the cash.

   The degree of synchronisation in receipts and payments of cash in a firm will determine its level of cash holdings. The higher is the level of synchronisation in a firm, lower is the holdings of cash. The finance manager can achieve synchronisation by preparing the cash budget for the firm. The cash budget will show the time periods when there is excess or shortage of cash in the firm. On the basis of this, the manager can decide the optimal level of cash holdings to be maintained in the firm.

3. **Cost of excess cash balance:** The minimum level of cash holdings is affected by the cost of holding excess cash balance. The excess cash with the firm has its opportunity cost. On the excess cash holdings interest is lost or the profit which could otherwise have been earned on the investment somewhere else or in the firm itself is lost.

   The higher is the opportunity cost, lower is the holding of cash balance in the firm. In other words, if the opportunity cost of idle cash is higher, the firm would try not maintain cash balance above the minimum level of cash required.

4. **Ability to borrow funds at short notice:** The level of cash holdings in a firm is affected by its ability to borrow at short notice in the market. If the firm has ability to borrow at the short notice, it can meet the excess cash requirements as and when arise by financing from the market. The firm in such situation will maintain cash holdings as low as possible.

   The cost of procurement of funds from the market also affects the level of minimum cash holdings in a firm.

5. **Uncertainty level:** The level of uncertainty in inflows and outflows of funds in a firm determine the level of minimum cash holdings in a firm. In a firm, which has volatile inflows and outflows of finds, the level of cash holdings will be higher.

   The nature of business is associated with the uncertainty level in inflows and outflows of funds in a firm and affects the minimum level of cash holdings.

There are certain other factors, like dividend policy, payment of salary, bonus etc., also affect the level of cash holdings in a firm.

11.5 Cash Budget

The cash budget is a statement of estimated cash receipts and cash payments in a firm for each period of the budget period. It shows the surplus or shortage of cash in the firm in the budget period. Budget may be prepared on daily, weekly, monthly or yearly basis, as required. It provides the basis for financial planning for smooth day-to-day operations of the firm. On the basis of it, the finance manager can decide the short-term borrowing needs of the firm. It helps the finance manager in determining the optimum level of cash holdings in a firm.

The following information is required for preparation of a cash budget:

1. Estimation of cash receipts
2. Estimation of cash payments
3. Time lag on account of credit transactions
4. Time lag in revenue and expenditure items.

Advantage of preparing cash budget: Cash budget is very useful in estimating net cash flows of the firm and making arrangement for surplus or deficit of cash as required so that the operations of the firm are run smoothly. The main advantages of preparing the cash budget are given below:

1. It helps in synchronising cash inflows and outflows so that minimum cash holdings are required in the firm.
2. It ensures the availability of sufficient cash as and when required by the firm.
3. It shows the periods when there is expected surplus or deficiency of cash so that timely measures can be undertaken to prevent it by the management.
4. The cash budget ensures that all payments and receipts take place in time.
5. Since the cash position is known, the firm can take investment opportunities if permitted by cash position as shown by cash budget.
6. Cash budget helps the management in preparing a suitable dividend policy.

Preparation of cash budget: There are two methods to prepare cash budget (short-term cash forecasting) as given below:

1. The receipts and payments method
2. The adjusted net income method.

The adjusted net income method is generally used for longer duration forecasts ranging from few months to a year. On the other hand, receipts and payments method is preferred to forecast for short periods, such as a week or month.

The following steps are taken in preparing cash budget according to receipts and payments method:

1. The first step in the preparation of cash budget is to decide the period for which cash budget is to be prepared.
2. The opening cash balance is first considered.
3. All the estimated cash receipts are added to opening cash balance. The cash receipts may be divided into two categories, i.e., revenue receipts and capital receipts. Capital receipts are, like—receipts on sale of fixed assets, cash received on issue of securities: debentures, equity shares etc. Revenue receipts are from sale of goods and services; receipts of dividends, interest, brokerage, commission etc.
4. From the total of cash receipts and opening balance, all expected cash payments are subtracted to find the closing balance. Cash payments can be divided into two categories, i.e., capital payments and revenue payments. Capital payments are like, redemption of preference shares, repayment of loan, purchase of fixed assets etc. Revenue payments are like, payments for purchase of raw materials, payments for wages and overheads, payment of interest and dividends, tax payments etc.

A proforma of a cash budget prepared under the receipts and payments method is given below:

Cash Budget
(Period: Jan. – June)

Particulars	Jan.	Feb.	March	April	May	June
A: Opening balance	–	–	–	–	–	–
B: Cash inflows						
(i) Cash sales	–	–	–	–	–	–

(ii) Collection from debtors	–	–	–	–	–	–
(iii) Collection for B/R	–	–	–	–	–	–
(iv) Loan from banks	–	–	–	–	–	–
(v) Interest on investments	–	–	–	–	–	–
(vi) Sale of fixed assets	–	–	–	–	–	–
(vii) Issue of shares	–	–	–	–	–	–
(viii) Issue of debentures	–	–	–	–	–	–
Total receipts	–	–	–	–	–	–
C: Cash outflows						
(i) Cash purchases	–	–	–	–	–	–
(ii) Payment to suppliers	–	–	–	–	–	–
(iii) B/P payments	–	–	–	–	–	–
(iv) Payment of expenses	–	–	–	–	–	–
(v) Payment of dividends	–	–	–	–	–	–
(vi) Interest on loans	–	–	–	–	–	–
(vii) Payment of loans	–	–	–	–	–	–
(viii) Purchase of fixed assets	–	–	–	–	–	–
Total Payments	–	–	–	–	–	–
Balance (A + B – C)	–	–	–	–	–	–

The closing balance in cash budget shows the shortage or excess of cash in the firm for a particular period. The examples given below shall clear the process of preparation of cash budget.

Example 1. The income and expenditure forecasts of a firm for the months of March to July, 2017 are given below:

Month	Sales (₹)	Purchases (₹)	Wages (₹)	Office and selling expenses (₹)
March	20,000	8,000	3,000	7,000
April	24,000	10,000	5,000	8,000
May	26,000	14,000	5,000	5,000
June	30,000	15,000	7,000	6,000
July	34,000	18,000	9,000	7,000

Prepare a cash budget for three months starting on 1st May, 2017 keeping in view the following information:

(i) Cash balance on 1st May, 2017 is ₹ 10,000

(ii) Advance tax instalment of ₹ 6,000 each are payable in March and June, 2016

(iii) Period of credit allowed to customers is one month and that allowed by suppliers is two months

(iv) Lag in payment of wages is one month

(v) Lag in payment of Office and Selling Expenses is half month.

Solution: Cash budget (May – July 2017)

Particulars	May	June	July
Opening balance	10,000	14,500	14,000
Receipts			
Collection from debtors	24,000	26,000	30,000
Total	34,000	40,500	44,000
Payments			
Payment to creditors	8,000	10,000	14,000
Wages	5,000	5,000	7,000
Office and selling expenses	6,500	5,500	6,500
Advance tax	–	6,000	–
Total	19,500	26,500	27,500
Closing balance	14,500	14,000	16,500

Example 2. Prepare the cash budget for July-December from the following information:

(i) The estimated sales, expenses etc. (in Lakh of rupees) are as follows:

Particulars	June	July	Aug.	Sept.	Oct.	Nov.	Dec.
Sales	70	80	80	100	100	120	130
Purchases	30	40	40	44	44	50	60
Wages	14	18	18	20	30	30	30
Misc. exp.	5	6	6	6	7	7	7
Interest received	2	–	–	2	–	–	2
Sales of shares	–	–	20	–	–	–	–

(ii) 20 percent of the sales are on cash and the balance on credit.

(iii) 2 percent debts are uncontrollable; 50 percent of the total accounts receivable are collected in the month of sales and the rest during the next months.

(iv) The time lag in payment of Misc. exp. and purchases is one month. Wages and salaries are paid fortnightly with a time lag of 15 days.

Solution: Calculation of collection from debtors (in lakhs of Rupees)

Particulars	June	July	Aug.	Sept.	Oct.	Nov.	Dec.
Credit sales	56.0	64.0	64.0	80.0	80.0	96.0	104.0
Collection same month (50%)	28.0	32.0	32.0	40.0	40.0	48.0	52.0

Collection Next month (48%)	–	26.88	30.72	30.72	38.4	38.4	46.08
Total Collection		58.88	62.72	70.72	78.4	86.4	98.08

Cash budget (in lakhs of Rupees)

Particulars	July	Aug.	Sept.	Oct.	Nov.	Dec.
Receipts						
Cash sales	16.00	16.00	20.00	20.00	24.00	26.00
Debtors	58.88	62.72	70.72	78.40	86.40	98.08
Interest	–	–	2.00	–	–	2.00
Sale of shares	–	20	–	–	–	–
Total receipts	74.88	98.72	92.72	98.40	110.4	126.08
Payments						
Creditors	30.00	40.00	40.00	44.00	44.00	50.00
Wages and salary	16.00	18.00	19.00	25.00	30.00	30.00
Misc. Exp.	5.00	6.00	6.00	6.00	7.00	7.00
Total Payments	51.00	64.00	65.00	75.00	81.00	87.00
Increase in cash balance	23.88	34.72	27.72	23.40	29.04	39.08

11.6 Efficiency in Cash Management

After the preparation of cash budget, the finance manager has to control inflows and outflows of cash in the firm so that actual cash flows do not deviate much from the estimated cash flows. This task can be achieved by maintaining efficiency in the cash management system. The efficiency in the cash management system can be achieved by applying the following two approaches:

1. Speedy cash collections
2. Controlling cash disbursements.

Speedy cash collections: A firm can reduce its cash holding requirements by speeding up the collection of cash from customers and hence reducing the cash cycle. The following techniques are generally used by the finance manager to speed up the collection of cash in the firm:

(i) **Early payment by customers:** A firm can adopt a number of measures to ensure early collection of cash. The invoice processing time and order processing time can be reduced. The firm may offer discount to its customers for making spot cash payments. The firm can develop a system of speedy recovery of cash on receivables even by offering a little discount. These measures can help in reducing the cash cycle of the firm.

(ii) **Concentration banking:** A decentralised cash collection procedure is known concentration banking. In concentration banking, a firm uses an operation system by establishing a number of collection centres spread over its large business area, instead of a single cash collection centre at head office. The collection centres are required to collect cheques from customers and deposit these in their local bank accounts. The system will reduce the mailing time taken by customers and processing time taken by the head office.

(iii) **Lock-box system:** In a lock-box system, a firm instructs its customers to mail their remittances to the boxes hired by it at different post offices. The firm's local bank is given the authority to pick up the remittances directly from the local-box. The bank collects the mail several times in a day and deposit the cheques in the firm's account. The bank prepares the statement of cheques picked up and the amount collected.

The system reduces the time taken in collection of cash in the firm. The cost involved in lock-box system of cash collection is also low. Thus, lock-box cash collection system is beneficial to the firm.

(iv) **Collection float:** The float means the time span involved in the mailing of cheque by the customer and the realisation of cash by the bank. The float may be of two types, namely, collection float and disbursement float.

The collection float causes the difference between book balance and bank balance of the firm. Larger is the collection float of the firm, longer is the time taken realising the cash by bank. The finance manager should reduce the collection float by taking the necessary steps.

Controlling cash disbursements: The following techniques can be applied by the finance manager to make cash disbursement slow in the firm:

(i) **Centralised disbursements:** In centralised disbursement payments are made through head office. The firms not having large network and business may adopt this strategy. Such arrangement would enable the firm to delay the payments and conserve the cash.

The delay in disbursement of cash will result in increase in the availability of cash holdings in the firm. However, there is risk of down fall in the credibility of the firm in the market. Thus, the finance manager should consider the relevant factors in deciding about the centralised disbursement system. If the size of the firm is large and its business is spread over a large area, the firm should not adopt the centralised disbursement system.

(ii) **Disbursement float:** The disbursement float is a technique to maximise cash holdings in a firm. The disbursement float is the time span between the submission of cheque by the firm and the realisation of cash by the bank of supplier. The larger disbursement float maximise the cash holdings in the firm.

(iii) **Avoidance of early payments:** The firm should make payments only when they are due, but it should avoid interest and penalty. The payments made before due date carry the opportunity cost and increase the cash cycle of the firm. The firm should make purchases on credit to the fullest possible terms after weighing the benefits of this.

The firm should make cash payments on the last day of credit period and avoid the cash discount offered for early payments. But, if the cash discount for early payments is significant, the firm should make early payments.

But, the time has changed now and electronic fund transfer has become an important tool for transfer of cash between firms and the parties dealing with them. This has almost eliminated float in cash transfers from and to firms. The system of electronic fund transfer has made some of techniques of efficient cash management mentioned above ineffective, like—lock-box system of cash collection, early collection of cash on sale etc. However, the proper application of above mentioned techniques can maximise the cash holdings in a firm. The sufficient cash holdings in firms ensures uninterrupted operation of their business.

SOLVED PROBLEM

Problem 1. Summarised below are the income and expenditure forecasts for the months of March to July 2016:

Months	Sales (₹)	Purchases (₹)	Wages (₹)	Office and selling expenses (₹)
March	40,000	26,000	5,000	7,000
April	34,000	34,000	7,000	8,000
May	56,000	42,000	8,000	10,000
June	60,000	30,000	9,000	12,000
July	54,000	35,000	10,000	12,000

Prepare a cash budget for three months starting on 1st May, 2016 keeping in view the following information:

(i) Cash balance on 1st May, 2016 is ₹ 20,000.

(ii) Advance tax instalment of ₹ 10,000 each are payable in March and June, 2016.

(iii) Period of credit allowed to customers is one month and that allowed by suppliers is two months.

(iv) Lag in payment of wages is one month.

(v) Lag in payment of Office and Selling Expenses is half month.

Solution: Cash budget (May – July 2016)

Particulars	May	June	July
Opening balance	20,000	12,000	5,000
Receipts			
Collection from debtors	34,000	56,000	60,000
Total	54,000	68,000	65,000
Payments			
Payment to creditors	26,000	34,000	42,000
Wages	7,000	8,000	9,000
Office and selling expenses	9,000	11,000	12,000
Advance tax	–	10,000	–
Total	42,000	63,000	63,000
Closing balance	12,000	5,000	2,000

Problem 2. Prepare the cash budget for July-December from the following information:

(i) The estimated sales, expenses, etc. are as follows:

Particulars	June	July	Aug.	Sept.	Oct.	Nov.	Dec.
Sales	35	40	40	50	50	60	65
Purchases	14	16	17	20	20	25	28
Wages	12	14	14	18	18	20	22
Misc. exp.	5	6	6	6	7	7	7
Interest received	2	–	–	2	–	–	2
Sales of shares	–	–	20	–	–	–	–

(ii) 20 percent of the sales are on cash and the balance on credit.

(iii) 2 percent debts are uncontrollable; 50 percent of the total accounts receivable are collected in the month of sales and the rest during the next months.

(iv) The time lag in payment of Misc. exps. and purchases is one month. Wages and salaries are paid fortnightly with a time lag of 15 days.

Solution: Calculation of collection from debtors (in lakhs of Rupees)

Particulars	June	July	Aug.	Sept.	Oct.	Nov.	Dec.
Credit sales	28.00	32.00	32.00	40.00	40.00	48.00	52.00
Collection same month (50%)	14.00	16.00	16.00	20.00	20.00	24.00	26.00
Collection Next month (48%)	–	13.44	15.36	15.36	19.20	19.20	23.04
Total Collection		29.44	31.36	35.36	39.20	43.20	40.04

Cash budget (in lakhs of Rupees)

Particulars	July	Aug.	Sept.	Oct.	Nov.	Dec.
Receipts						
Cash sales	8.00	8.00	10.00	10.00	12.00	13.00
Debtors	29.44	31.36	35.36	39.20	43.20	49.04
Interest	–	–	2.00	–	–	2.00
Sale of shares	–	20	–	–	–	–
Total Receipts	37.44	59.36	47.36	49.20	55.20	64.04
Payments						
Creditors	14.00	16.00	17.00	20.00	20.00	25.00
Wages and salary	13.00	14.00	16.00	18.00	19.00	21.00
Misc. Exps.	5.00	6.00	6.00	6.00	7.00	7.00
Total Payments	32.00	36.00	39.00	44.00	46.00	53.00
Increase in cash balance	5.44	23.36	8.36	5.20	9.20	11.04

Problem 3. From the following information prepare a Cash Budget for three months, April-June:

Month	Sales	Materials	Wages	Overheads
Jan.	60,000	40,000	10,000	4,000
Feb.	50,000	44,000	12,000	6,000
March	62,000	50,000	13,000	7,000
April	70,000	60,000	14,000	8,000
May	80,000	64,000	15,000	10,000
June	84,000	70,000	17,000	12,000

Expected cash balance on 1st April is ₹ 20,000. Other information:

(i) Material and overheads are to be paid during the month following the month of supply.
(ii) Wages are to be paid during the month in which they are incurred.
(iii) Half of the sales are paid when due and other half to be paid during next month.
(iv) 5% commission to be paid within the month following the actual sales.
(v) Preference dividend of ₹ 40,000 is to be paid on 1st May.
(vi) Share call money for ₹ 30,000 is due on 1st April and 1st June.
(vii) Machinery of ₹ 5,000 is purchased in April and payment is made on 1st June.

Solution: Cash budget

Particulars	April	May	June
Opening balance	20,000	41,500	–10,500
Receipts			
Collection from debtors	35,000	40,000	42,000
	31,000	35,000	40,000
Share call money	30,000	–	30,000
Total	1,16,000	1,16,500	1,01,500
Payments			
Materials	50,000	60,000	64,000
Overheads	7,000	8,000	10,000
Wages	14,000	15,000	17,000
Sales commission	3,500	4,000	4,200
Preference dividend	–	40,000	–
Machinery	–	–	5,000
Total	74,500	1,27,000	1,00,400
Closing balance	41,500	–10,500	1,100

Problem 4. Summarised below are the income and expenditure forecasts for the months of March to July, 2016:

Months	Sales (₹)	Purchases (₹)	Wages (₹)	Office and selling expenses (₹)
March	20,000	10,000	2,000	2,000
April	24,000	14,000	3,000	3,000
May	26,000	16,000	4,000	4,000
June	30,000	20,000	5,000	5,000
July	34,000	24,000	6,000	7,000

Prepare a cash budget for three months starting on 1st May, 2016 keeping in view the following information:

(i) Cash balance on 1st May, 2016 is ₹ 1,000.

(ii) Advance tax instalment of ₹ 2,000 each are payable in March and June, 2016.

(iii) Period of credit allowed to customers is one month and that allowed by suppliers is two months.

(iv) Lag in payment of wages is one month.

(v) Lag in payment of Office and Selling Expenses is half month.

Solution: Cash budget (May – July 2016)

Particulars	May	June	July
Opening balance	1,000	8,500	10,000
Receipts			
Collection from debtors	24,000	26,000	30,000
Total	25,000	34,500	40,000
Payments			
Payment to creditors	10,000	14,000	16,000
Wages	3,000	4,000	5,000
Office and selling expenses	3,500	4,500	6,000
Advance tax	–	2,000	–
Total	16,500	24,500	27,000
Closing balance	8,500	10,000	13,000

Problem 5. From the following information prepare a Cash Budget for three months, April-June:

Month	Sales	Materials	Wages	Overheads
Jan.	20,000	15,000	2,000	1,000
Feb.	18,000	16,000	3,000	2,000
March	24,000	17,000	4,000	3,000

April	26,000	20,000	5,000	2,000
May	28,000	22,000	6,000	4,000
June	30,000	25,000	7,000	6,000

Expected cash balance on 1st April is ₹ 20,000. Other information:

(i) Material and overheads are to be paid during the month following the month of supply.

(ii) Wages are to be paid during the month in which they are incurred.

(iii) Half of the sales are paid when due and other half to be paid during next month.

(iv) 5% commission to paid within the month following the actual sales.

(v) Preference dividend of ₹ 10,000 is to be paid on 1st May.

(vi) Share call money for ₹ 10,000 is due on 1st April and 1st June.

(vii) Machinery of ₹ 10,000 is purchased in April and payment is made on 1st June.

Solution: Cash budget

Particulars	April	May	June
Opening balance	20,000	28,800	16,500
Receipts			
Collection from debtors for same month	13,000	14,000	15,000
Collection from debtors for last month	12,000	13,000	14,000
Share call money	10,000	–	10,000
Total	55,000	55,800	55,500
Payments			
Materials	17,000	20,000	22,000
Overheads	3,000	2,000	4,000
Wages	5,000	6,000	7,000
Sales commission	1,200	1,300	1,400
Preference dividend	–	10,000	–
Machinery	–	–	10,000
Total	26,200	39,300	44,400
Closing balance	28,800	16,500	11,100

THEORETICAL QUESTIONS

1. Write short notes on:

   (a) Concentration Banking *(D.U., B.Com. 2009)*

   (b) Cash budget *(D.U., B.Com. 2011)*

(c) Motives for holding cash in a business firm *(D.U., B.Com. 2012)*

(d) Float management *(D.U., B.Com. 2013)*

2. What are the factors affecting the cash needs of a firm?
3. What are the objectives of cash management?
4. Explain the importance of cash management.

PRACTICAL PROBLEMS

1. Summarised below are the income and expenditure forecasts for the months of March to July, 2014:

Months	Sales (₹)	Purchases (₹)	Wages (₹)	Office and selling expenses (₹)
March	40,000	16,000	5,000	7,000
April	30,000	24,000	6,000	8,000
May	66,000	32,000	8,000	10,000
June	50,000	30,000	6,500	12,800
July	54,000	35,000	7,000	12,000

Prepare a cash budget for three months starting on 1st May, 2014 keeping in view the following information:

(i) Cash balance on 1st May, 2014 is ₹ 10,000.

(ii) Advance tax instalment of ₹ 5,000 each are payable in March and June, 2014.

(iii) Period of credit allowed to customers is one month and that allowed by suppliers is two months.

(iv) Lag in payment of wages is one month.

(v) Lag in payment of Office and Selling Expenses is half month.

(D.U., B.Com. 2016, N.C.)

[**Ans.** Closing balances, May: ₹ 13,000, June: ₹ 31,000, July: 30,100]

2. Prepare the cash budget for July-December from the following information:

(i) The estimated sales, expenses, etc. (in lakh Rupees) are as follows:

Particulars	June	July	Aug.	Sept.	Oct.	Nov.	Dec.
Sales	30	40	50	60	70	80	90
Purchases	14	16	18	24	30	36	40
Wages	12	14	14	18	18	20	22
Misc. exp.	4	6	7	6	7	8	7
Interest received	2	–	–	2	–	–	2
Sales of shares	–	–	30	–	–	–	–

(ii) 20 percent of the sales are on cash and the balance on credit.

(iii) 3 percent debts are uncontrollable; 50 percent of the total accounts receivable are collected in the month of sales and the rest during the next months.

(iv) The time lag in payment of Misc. exps. and purchases is one month. Wages and salaries are paid fortnightly with a time lag of 15 days.

[**Ans.** Increase in cash: ₹ 4.28, 39.04, 15.80, 17.04, 18.32, 19.08]

3. From the following information prepare a Cash Budget for three months, April-June:

Month	Sales	Materials	Wages	Overheads
Jan.	7,000	4,000	1,000	1,000
Feb.	5,000	4,000	1,000	1,000
March	7,000	5,000	1,200	1,200
April	8,000	5,200	1,400	1,600
May	9,000	5,400	1,600	2,000
June	10,000	6,000	2,000	2,200

Expected cash balance on 1st April is ₹ 5,000. Other information:

(i) Material and overheads are to be paid during the month following the month of supply.

(ii) Wages are to be paid during the month in which they are incurred.

(iii) Half of the sales are paid when due and other half to be paid during next month.

(iv) 5% commission to be paid within the month following the actual sales.

(v) Preference dividend of ₹ 4,000 is to be paid on 1st May.

(vi) Share call money for ₹ 3,000 is due on 1st April and 1st June.

(vii) Machinery of ₹ 2,000 is purchased in April and payment is made on 1st June.

[**Ans.** Cash balance: April: ₹ 7,500, May: ₹ 7,150, June: ₹ 7,750]

4. Summarised below are the income and expenditure forecasts for the months of March to July, 2016:

Months	Sales (₹)	Purchases (₹)	Wages (₹)	Office and selling expenses (₹)
March	20,000	13,000	3,000	3,000
April	17,000	17,000	4,000	4,000
May	28,000	21,000	4,000	5,000
June	30,000	15,000	5,000	6,000
July	27,000	18,000	5,000	6,000

Prepare a cash budget for three months starting on 1st May, 2016 keeping in view the following information:

(i) Cash balance on 1st May, 2016 is ₹ 10,000.

(ii) Advance tax instalment of ₹ 5,000 each are payable in March and June, 2016.
(iii) Period of credit allowed to customers is one month and that allowed by suppliers is two months.
(iv) Lag in payment of wages is one month.
(v) Lag in payment of Office and Selling Expenses is half month.

[**Ans.** Cash balance May: ₹ 5,500, June: ₹ 2,000, July: ₹ 0]

5. From the following information prepare a Cash Budget for three months, April-June:

Month	Sales	Materials	Wages	Overheads
Jan.	6,000	4,000	1,000	1,000
Feb.	5,000	4,000	1,000	1,000
March	6,000	5,000	1,000	1,000
April	7,000	6,000	1,000	2,000
May	8,000	6,000	1,500	2,000
June	8,000	7,000	1,500	2,000

Expected cash balance on 1st April is ₹ 2,000. Other information:

(i) Material and overheads are to be paid during the month following the month of supply.
(ii) Wages are to be paid during the month in which they are incurred.
(iii) Half of the sales are paid when due and other half to be paid during next month.
(iv) 5% commission to paid within the month following the actual sales.
(v) Preference dividend of ₹ 2,000 is to be paid on 1st May.
(vi) Share call money for ₹ 3,000 is due on 1st April and 1st June.
(vii) Machinery of ₹ 5,000 is purchased in April and payment is made on 1st June.

[**Ans.** Cash balance April: ₹ 4,200, May: ₹ –150, June: ₹ –4,050]

Receivables Management

12

Chapter Outline

12.1 Introduction
12.2 Objectives of Receivables Management
12.3 Costs and Benefits of Receivables Management
12.4 Elements of Receivables Management
12.5 Credit Control
12.6 Evaluation of Credit Policies

12.1 Introduction

The sale of goods on credit and the deferment of payment by customers create receivables in a firm. The receivables include both accounts receivable and bills receivables. The customers who purchased the goods and services from the firm on credit basis and have not paid the amount till the end of accounting period are known as debtors or accounts receivables. The bills (or promissory notes) drawn by the seller and accepted by the customer in exchange of credit sales are known as bills receivables.

According to Hampton, "The receivables are asset accounts, representing amount owed to the firm as a result of the sale of goods or services in the ordinary course of business."

The receivables are part of current assets of the firm. The credit policy of the firm decides the amount of receivables in the firm. The amount of receivables in the firm affects its requirements for the working capital. Thus, the credit policy and management of receivables in the firm becomes significant. The finance manager of the firm should analyse costs and benefits associated with the receivables when deciding the investment in receivables.

12.2 Objectives of Receivables Management

The receivables management is also known as credit management. The objective of receivables management is to promote sales and profits of the firm up to the level where the return on investment in further receivables becomes less than cost of additional investment in receivables. The objective of receivables management should be helpful in achieving the firm's goal of maximising shareholders' wealth. Thus, the finance manager has to decide the optimal credit policy of the firm which gives maximum return on investment in receivables.

To achieve this objective, the finance manager has:

1. to decide the optimal sale of goods and services,
2. to control the cost of receivable, cost of collections, bad debts and other administrative expenses.

12.3 Costs and Benefits of Receivables Management

The finance manager shall have to evaluate the costs and benefits associated with receivables while designing the credit policy of the firm. The liberal credit policy may result in increased sales of goods and services and higher profits, but at the same time the increased bad debts. On the other hand, stringent credit policy may restrict the growth in sales, but it will also reduce the amount of bad debts in the firm. The costs and benefits associated with credit sales and accounts receivables are explained below:

(A) Costs of receivables: A firm may face the following costs in extending credit on sales to its customers:

(i) ***Opportunity costs*:** There is a time lag between sale of goods and services to customers and collection of cash from the customers, when firm sells goods and services on credit basis. Eventually, the firm needs funds for the gap period between sales and collection of cash. These funds have opportunity cost because the funds could have been invested somewhere else and have earned return there. The finance manager has to compare the opportunity costs of the funds with the benefits on credit sales while designing credit policy of the firm.

(ii) ***Administration costs*:** When a firm sells goods and services to its customers on credit basis, it maintains records of credit customers. The officials of the firm collect information on the credit worthiness of the customers. The internal processing is required before the approval. The firm incurs expenses on collecting the cash from debtors. These costs could have been avoided had the firm sold goods and services to the customers on cash basis.

(iii) ***Delinquency costs*:** When a customer fails to make payments within stipulated time, the firm starts required process to recover the dues. The firm bears the cost of funds blocked for the extended time taken in the recovery. The firm incurs costs in sending reminders to the debtors. If the need arises, the firm may hire legal services for the recovery of receivables. These costs shall not incur in case of cash sales.

(iv) ***Bad debts*:** Bad debts occurs when the firm fails to recover the dues from customers after making the required efforts. The firm has to bear the cost of bad debts. More liberal is the credit policy of the firm, higher is the amount of bad debts. The finance manager should establish a proper system to assess the credit worthiness of customers and their past payment history.

(B) Benefits of receivables: The credit policy of a firm does not result in increasing cost only, rather it brings some benefits to the firm. A firm may be benefited on the following fronts while extending credit to its customers:

(i) ***Increased sales*:** The credit policy of the firm facilitates the customers to purchase the goods and services who would otherwise may not intend or able to make purchases. The sales of goods and services on credit basis along with cash sales increases the sales of products of the firm. Despite these facts, the finance manager should be prudent while deciding the credit policy of the firm. The optimal level of credit sales in the firm should be determined.

(ii) ***Increased profit***: The increased sales of goods and services results in increased profit of the firm. The profit is increased by higher profit margin on credit sales of goods and services and increased volume of sales of goods and services. But, at the same time, the risk of bad debts also increases.

(iii) ***Expansion of the firm***: The credit sales increase the profit and sales volume of products of the firm. The firm expects further increase in sales and invest part of profits in the expansion of the firm.

(iv) ***Increased competitiveness***: The rival firms selling their products on credit basis may take up the some market share of the firm not selling its product on credit basis. Hence, to remain in the market and to increase the competitiveness, the firm becomes bound to sell its products on credit basis along with cash sales. The sales on credit basis will increase the customer base of the firm. The credit sales enhance the association of customers with the firm and it helps in retaining the loyal customers with the firm.

12.4 Elements of Receivables Management

The level of accounts receivables in a firm depends on prevailing economic conditions, product pricing, product quality and the credit policy of the firm. The finance manager can vary the amount of receivables through credit policy keeping in mind the trade-off between profitability and risk.

The credit policy of the firm defines the parameters and principles that govern the extension of credit to its customers. A firm may adopt liberal or stringent credit policy. Lowering credit standards may stimulate the demand resulting in higher sales and profits. But, this would lead to higher level of accounts receivables, greater risk of bad debt losses and low liquidity in the firm. On the other hand, stringent credit policy may result in increased liquidity and lower bad debts, but also in lower sales and profits.

The finance manager has to determine the credit policy keeping in mind the following elements:

1. **Credit standards:** A firm before providing credit to its customers sets the norms relating to customer's capacity to pay, customer's desire to pay, customer's financial position, assets for pledge, prevailing economic conditions etc. These norms of the firm are called its credit standards. Customers willing to avail the credit facility shall submit with the firm the documents and proofs of information provided by them to the firm relating to the norms/credit standards applicable.

   Experts prescribe five Cs i.e., Character, Capacity, Capital, Collateral and Condition should be considered in formulating credit standards. The character represents the willingness of the customer to make the payments. Capacity means the ability of the customer to pay. Capital shows whether the customer would have necessary funds at the time of payment becoming due. Collateral means the assets to be pledged by the customer with the firm. Condition represents the prevailing economic conditions which may affect the customer's ability to pay. A firm can prepare scales for these parameters and can put the customers into applicable categories on the basis of defined scales.

2. **Credit analysis:** The process of credit analysis starts on receiving the relevant information on norms/credit standards from the customers. The credit analysis is an internal and time consuming process of the firm. The firm may outsource the credit analysis work to an agency in the field if the size of credit and sales demands so. The firm may categorise the customers using the information according their credit worthiness and default risk based on five C's. The firm can put a customer in any of the following three categories on the basis of his credit worthiness:

   (i) *Good accounts*: The financially strong customers
   (ii) *Marginal accounts*: The customers with moderate financial health
   (iii) *Bad accounts*: The financially weak customers.

   The firm can easily approve the credit to customers with financially strong position. The customers with financially weak position are outrightly rejected. The firm further analyse the information about the customers with moderate financial health. If the firm is willing to expand its sales, it can expand credit to moderate financial health customers. But, this may increase bad debts of the firm. The firm should extend credit to marginal accounts up to the level where incremental return equals incremental cost.

   The credit analysis plays important role in deciding the level of accounts receivables in a firm. The manager has to work out profitability and bad risk trade-off while deciding on extending credit to customers with moderate financial health. The customers with week financial position must not be extended credit by the firm. The firm should maintain balance between liquidity and sale while deciding the optimal level of credit sales.

3. **Credit terms:** The credit terms refers to the period for which credit is allowed and the size of the cash discount available for making early payments. A firm can vary the level of account receivables through the credit terms in addition to the credit standards.

   Credit period: Credit term of a firm stipulates the length of time over which credit is extended to a customer and the discount, if any, given for early payments. For example, a firm's credit term may be expressed as "3/10, net 30". The term "3/10" says that if the payments are made within 10 days of the invoice date, a 3 percent discount is given to the customer. The term "net 30" means that the full payment is due by the 30th day from the invoice date, if the discount is not availed by the customer.

   If the credit period is longer, the sales volume may go up. However, higher will be the amount of accounts receivables in the firm and higher will be the opportunity cost of accounts receivables.

   Cash discount period and cash discount: Cash discount is generally offered to the customers to induce them to make early payments. Cash discount period refers to the specific period of time when the cash discount can be availed. Cash discount period is shorter than the credit period. In the above example, the term "3/10" says that if the payments are made within 10 days of the invoice date. Thus, here cash discount period is 10 days.

   Cash discount is the amount available as an advantage to the customers who pay the due amount within cash discount period. The amount of advantage is reduced from the total credit amount. The customer pays net amount to the firm within the cash discount period. In the above example, the term "3/10" says that a 3 percent cash discount is given to the customer, if the payments are made within the cash discount period.

4. **Cash collection policy:** A firm has to formulate its cash collection policy so that the customers repay the credit on time. The cash collection policy of the firm lays down the procedures to be followed in order to collect the cash from customers. The main aim of cash collection policy is minimise the bad debts.

   The cash collection procedures of the firm should be clear. The collection procedures for recovery of dues remaining after the expiry of credit period and delinquent account should also be formulated in clear terms at the time designing of cash collection policy.

   The firm may adopt various types of collection efforts i.e., letters, reminders, electronic conversations, personal contacts, involvement of collection agencies etc. The firm should use legal action against customers as last resort to collect dues. The legal action involves cost and can spoil the relationship with customers. The images of both the firm and the customer get tarnished if legal action is followed.

   The swift cash collection of receivables increases the turnover of working capital in a firm. The credit standards and terms of a firm affects the speed of collection of cash from receivables. If the firm adopts stringent credit standards, the collection efforts will be less. On the other hand, in case of liberal credit standards more efforts are needed in cash collections on receivables.

12.5 Credit Control

After formulation of the credit policy, next important task for finance manager is to control the credit. The firm has to assess how its credit policy is working in managing the receivables. Merely formulating the credit standards and terms is not sufficient for a firm, equally important is their implementation to control the receivables. To accomplish this aim, the finance manager has to work on two ways as explained below:

1. **Collection of receivables:** To control the credit, the timely recovery of receivables is important. Thus, the firm must develop a policy to deal with the customers who fails to repay or delaying the repayments. The collection policy should lay down clear cut collection procedures. The responsibility for collection and the follow up should be clearly defined. The responsibility of receivables collection may be entrusted to a separate department or accounts department; or to sales department.

   A well-defined and stringent collection procedure helps in timely collection of receivables. After expiry of cash collection period, the firm should promptly prepare the list of defaulters. First of all, the firm should send reminders to the customers who have failed in making the repayment. The personal contact through agents may be next option for the firm. Even after this exercise the customer fails to repay, the legal action may be followed. Though, the legal action cannot do anything with the ability of customer to repay, it can provide the legal relief.

   Thus to control the credit in the firm, the finance manager must make prompt and strict efforts to recover the credit from customers.

2. **Monitoring of receivables:** In addition to timely recovery of receivables, the firm can control the level of credit in it. There are a number of methods to measure the level of

credit in a firm. There should be continuous and regular monitoring of the level of credit in the firm. The important techniques to monitoring the credit level in a firm are explained below:

(a) ***Ratio analysis:*** The important ratios to monitor the receivables in a firm are given below:

1. **Debtors' turnover ratio:** This ratio measures the numbers of times the average investment in receivables turns over to generate the particular credit sales. It is calculated by dividing the number of days in a year by average collection period.

$$\text{Debtors' turnover} = \frac{360}{\text{Average collection period}}$$

Higher debtors/receivables' turnover ratio means the good level of receivables in the firm. The firm can improve the debtors' turnover ratio by reducing the average collection period, which in turn can be reduced by stringent credit standards and collection procedure.

2. **Average collection period:** Average collection period is another technique used for analysis and control of credit in a firm. It is the period during which credit sales are collected on an average. Average collection period is calculated by dividing the average accounts receivables by daily credit sales.

$$\text{Average collection period} = \frac{\text{Average accounts receivable}}{\text{Daily credit sales}}$$

And,

$$\text{Average accounts receivables} = \frac{\text{Opening balance} + \text{Closing balance}}{2}$$

Average collection period is different from the credit period. Average collection period can be longer or shorter; or equal to credit period. If average collection period is longer than the credit period, the credit management is not good. This indicates that not all customers are paying on time. There is scope to control the receivables. On the other hand, if average collection period is shorter than the credit period, it indicates that credit is under control and receivables management is good. It implies that the customers are paying before the due date.

If the average collection period is equal to the credit period, then the customers are paying on time and receivables management is good. In other words, credit is under control in the firm.

3. **Average investment in receivables:** Average investment in accounts receivables can also be used to assess the level of receivables in a firm and to control the credit. It is calculated by dividing the total cost of sales by debtors' turnover.

$$\text{Average investment in accounts receivables} = \frac{\text{Total cost of sales}}{\text{Debtors' turnover}}$$

$$\text{Investment in receivables} = \frac{\text{Variable cost} + \text{Fixed cost}}{360} \times \text{Credit period}$$

High the level of average investment in accounts receivables indicates poor management of receivables. Credit can be controlled by improving the cash collections. If the investment in receivables is more than the target fixed by management, then there is need to control the credit in the firm.

(b) *Ageing schedule*: In this techniques, a schedule of debtors is prepared. They are classified according to their time span. The cumulative percentage is then calculated. The percentage of amount which is due or overdue can be known from the schedule. The time span of cumulative percentage can be compared with some benchmark to know whether the collection of receivables is good or bad. For example, the ageing schedule of a firm as on 1st January, 2017 is as given below:

Time span (days)	Receivables (₹)	% of total	Cumulative %
0 – 30	10,00,000	50	50
31 – 45	5,00,000	25	75
46 – 60	3,00,000	15	90
61 – 75	1,50,000	7.5	97.5
More than 75	50,000	2.5	100

The finance manager can compare the above schedule of receivables with the benchmark. If the receivables are overdue as per the benchmark, the corrective steps are needed to control the credit in the firm.

12.6 Evaluation of Credit Policies

A firm can apply a liberal credit policy or tight credit policy; or optimal credit policy. Each type of credit policy has its costs and benefits to be bore by the firm implementing the policy. The firm should adopt the optimal credit policy. In optimal policy, the return on receivables after adjusting the opportunity cost is maximum. In case of liberal credit policy, the firm can increase its sales, at the cost of bad debts and low liquidity. On the other hand, by adopting the tight credit policy, the firm can reduce the bad debts and increase the liquidity, but at the cost of decreased sales. The cost and benefits associated with liberal and tight credit policies are discussed below:

A. Liberal Credit Policy

The costs and benefits of liberal credit policy are given below:

1. **Benefits:** The benefits of liberal credit policy are given below:
   (i) The liberal credit policy of a firm extends the credit to the customers for longer duration and at easier credit terms. Thus, it makes the customers able to purchase the goods and services which they were otherwise unable to purchase. Hence, the sales are increased by using liberal credit policy.
   (ii) Since the liberal credit policy leads to increased sales of goods and services, the profits of the firm also get increased.
   (iii) The credit is extended for longer period in liberal credit policy which results in lower initial costs in the collection of payments of receivables.

2. **Costs:** The costs associated with liberal credit policy are given below:
   (i) The credit in liberal credit policy is extended for longer period and on easier terms to the customers. This would lead to more investment in accounts receivables. Attendant to this, the opportunity cost of capital will be higher.
   (ii) Since the credit is extended for longer period on easier terms, the amount of potential bad debts will be higher. This would reduce the liquidity in the firm. Thus, the firm has to bear the cost of low liquidity if liberal credit policy is adopted.
   (iii) Because the credit period is longer and credit terms are easy, the subsequent cost of collection of payments will be higher.

B. Tight Credit Policy

The costs and benefits of tight credit policy are given below:

1. **Benefits:** The benefits of tight credit policy are given below:
   (i) The credit in tight credit policy is extended for shorter period and on stringent terms to the customers. This would lead to less investment in accounts receivables. Attendant to this, the opportunity cost of capital will be lower.
   (ii) Since the credit is extended for shorter period and on stringent terms, the amount of potential bad debts will be low. This would increase the liquidity in the firm. Thus, the firm will get the benefit of high liquidity if tight credit policy is adopted.
   (iii) The credit is extended for shorter period in tight credit policy which results in lower subsequent costs in the collection of payments of receivables. The liquidity in the firm will be high.
2. **Costs:** The costs of tight credit policy are given below:
   (i) The tight credit policy of a firm extends the credit to the customers for shorter duration and at stringent credit terms. Thus, it makes the customers unable to purchase the goods and services which they were otherwise able to purchase with the credit facility. Hence, the sales are decreased if the liberal credit policy is adopted.
   (ii) Since the tight credit policy leads to decreased sales of goods and services, the profits of the firm also decline.
   (iii) Because the credit period is shorter and the credit terms are stringent, the initial cost of collection of payments will be higher.

Both the liberal as well as tight credit policies have their costs and benefits for the firm. Thus, a firm should adopt an optimal credit policy, which is neither liberal nor tight, to maximise the profit on investment in receivables. Since the objective of the firm is to maximise the shareholders' wealth, it should implement the optimal credit policy. This will help in achieving the objective of the firm.

Example 1. The following projections are made regarding the operation of a firm:

Sales	10,000 units
Selling price per unit	₹ 4.0
Variable cost per unit	₹ 2.50
Total cost per unit	₹ 3.5
Credit period allowed	One month

The firm intends to increase the credit period for its customers from one month to two months. It is expected that the sale will increase by 10% due to such change. The desired rate of return on investment is 25%. Evaluate the proposed change in the credit policy.

Solution: Evaluation of credit policy

Particulars	Present	Proposed	Incremental
Sales (in units)	10,000	11,000	1,000
Sales (₹)	40,000	44,000	4,000
Credit period	1 month	2 months	–
Variable cost (₹)	25,000	27,500	2,500
Fixed cost (₹)	10,000	10,000	0
Total Cost	35,000	37,500	2,500
Contribution (₹)[1]	15,000	16,500	1,500
Average debtors at cost (₹)[2]	2,917	6,250	3,333

We know that:

$$\text{Incremental return} = \frac{\text{Increased contribution}}{\text{Extra fund employed}} \times 100$$

Substituting the values,

$$\text{Incremental return} = \frac{1{,}500}{3{,}333} \times 100$$

$$\text{Incremental return} = 45.0\%$$

Since the incremental return is more than the desired return, the proposal is profitable. Hence, it should be accepted.

Working notes:

1. Contribution = Total cost – Variable cost
2. Average debtors at cost = 35,000 ÷ 12 = ₹ 2,917

   Average debtors at cost = 37,500 ÷ 6 = ₹ 6,250.

Example 2. A company is planning to change its credit policy. The change in policy would increase the sale from ₹ 10,00,000 to ₹ 11,00,000. The fixed cost would remain ₹ 1,00,000. The bad debt would increase from 1% to 2%. The account receivable turnover ratio would decrease from 10 to 8. The PV ratio of company is 25%. Evaluate the proposal, if the required rate of return of company is 25%.

Solution: Cost of investment in account receivables

Particulars	Present	Proposed
Cost of sales	8,50,000	9,25,000
Account receivable turnover ratio	10	8

Investment in account receivables	85,000	1,15,625
Cost of investment in accounts receivables (@25%)	21,250	28,906

Cost of sales = variable cost + fixed cost

$$\text{Average investment in account receivable} = \frac{\text{Total cost of sales}}{\text{Debtor turnover}}$$

Change in income of the company

Particulars	Present	Proposed	Change
Sales	10,00,000	11,00,000	1,00,000
Less: Variable cost	7,50,000	8,25,000	75,000
Less: Fixed cost	1,00,000	1,00,000	0
Less: Bad debts	10,000	22,000	12,000
Less: Cost of investment in A/R	21,250	28,906	7,656
Income	1,18,750	1,24,094	5,344

Since the proposed change in credit policy is increasing income of the company, the proposal should be accepted.

Example 3. A company sells 1,000 units @ ₹ 200 per unit in a year. The variable cost is ₹ 130 per unit and fixed cost is ₹ 50,000 per annum. The company is planning to increase the credit period to 2 months from the current period of credit of 1 month. The change in credit policy will result in 10% increase in sales and bad debts will increase from 1% to 2%. The company's required rate of return is 20%. Evaluate the proposal.

Solution: Evaluation of credit policy

Particulars	Present	Proposed
Credit period	1 month	2 months
Sales (in units)	1,000	1,100
Sales (₹)	2,00,000	2,20,000
Less: Variable cost (₹)	1,30,000	1,43,000
Less: Fixed cost (₹)	50,000	50,000
Gross profit	20,000	27,000
Less: Cost of receivable (20%)	3,000[1]	6,433[2]
Less: Bad debts	2,000	2,200
Net profit (₹)	15,000	18,367

Since the net profit is increasing by ₹ 3,267, the proposal to change the credit policy should be accepted.

Working notes:

$$\text{Investment in receivables} = \frac{\text{Variable cost + Fixed cost}}{12} \times \text{Credit period}$$

1. 20% of (1,30,000 + 50,000) ÷ 12 = 3,000
2. 20% of (1,43,000 + 50,000) ÷ 6 = 6,433.

Example 4. The following projections are made regarding the operation of a firm:

Sales	10,000 units
Selling price per unit	₹ 4.0
Variable cost per unit	₹ 2.50
Total cost per unit	₹ 3.5
Credit period allowed	One month

The firm intends to increase the credit period for its customers from one month to two months. It is expected that the sale will increase by 10% due to such change. The desired rate of return on investment is 25%. Evaluate the proposed change in the credit policy.

Solution: Evaluation of credit policy

Particulars	Present	Proposed	Incremental
Sales (in units)	10,000	11,000	1,000
Sales (₹)	40,000	44,000	4,000
Credit period	1 month	2 months	–
Variable cost (₹)	25,000	27,500	2,500
Fixed cost (₹)	10,000	10,000	0
Total Cost	35,000	37,500	2,500
Contribution (₹)[1]	15,000	16,500	1,500
Average debtors at cost (₹)[2]	2,917	6,250	3,333

We know that:

$$\text{Incremental return} = \frac{\text{Increased contribution}}{\text{Extra fund employed}} \times 100$$

Substituting the values,

$$\text{Incremental return} = \frac{1,500}{3,333} \times 100$$

$$\text{Incremental return} = 45.0\%$$

Since the incremental return is more than the desired return, the proposal is profitable. Hence, it should be accepted.

Working notes:

1. Contribution = Total cost – Variable cost
2. Average debtors at cost = 35,000 ÷ 12 = ₹ 2917

   Average debtors at cost = 37,500 ÷ 6 = ₹ 6,250.

Example 5. A company sells 1,000 units @ ₹ 200 per unit in a year. The variable cost is ₹ 130 per unit and fixed cost is ₹ 50,000 per annum. The company is planning to increase the credit period to 2 months from the current period of credit of 1 month. The change in credit policy will result in 10% increase in sales and bad debts will increase from 1% to 2%. The company's required rate of return is 20%. Evaluate the proposal.

Solution: Evaluation of credit policy

Particulars	Present	Proposed
Credit period	1 month	2 months
Sales (in units)	1,000	1,100
Sales (₹)	2,00,000	2,20,000
Less: Variable cost (₹)	1,30,000	1,43,000
Less: Fixed cost (₹)	50,000	50,000
Gross profit	20,000	27,000
Less: Cost of receivable (20%)	3,000	6,433
Less: Bad debts	2,000	4,400
Net profit (₹)	15,000	16,167

$$\text{Investment in receivables} = \frac{\text{Variable cost + Fixed cost}}{12} \times \text{Credit period}$$

Since the net profit is increasing by ₹ 1,167, the proposal to change the credit policy should be accepted.

SOLVED PROBLEMS

Problem 1. A company sells 10,000 units @ ₹ 40 per unit in a year. The variable cost is ₹ 30 per unit and fixed cost is ₹ 50,000 per annum. The company is planning to increase the credit period to 2 months from the current period of credit of 1 month. The change in credit policy will result in 10% increase in sales and bad debts will increase from 1% to 2%. The company's required rate of return is 25%. Evaluate the proposal.

Solution: Evaluation of credit policy

Particulars	Present	Proposed
Credit period	1 month	2 months
Sales (in units)	10,000	11,000

Sales (₹)	4,00,000	4,40,000
Less: Variable cost (₹)	3,00,000	3,30,000
Less: Fixed cost (₹)	50,000	50,000
Gross profit	50,000	60,000
Less: Cost of receivable (25%)	7,292	15,833
Less: Bad debts	4,000	8,800
Net profit (₹)	38,708	35,367

$$\text{Investment in receivables} = \frac{\text{Variable cost + Fixed cost}}{12} \times \text{Credit period}$$

Since the net profit is decreasing by ₹ 3,341, the proposal to change the credit policy should not be accepted.

Problem 2. The following projections are made regarding the operation of a firm:

Sales	1,00,000 units
Selling price per unit	₹ 5.0
Variable cost per unit	₹ 3.50
Total cost per unit	₹ 4.5
Credit period allowed	One month

The firm intends to increase the credit period for its customers from one month to two months. It is expected that the sale will increase by 12% due to such change. The desired rate of return on investment is 30%. Evaluate the proposed change in the credit policy.

Solution: Evaluation of credit policy

Particulars	Present	Proposed	Incremental
Sales (in units)	1,00,000	1,12,000	12,000
Sales (₹)	5,00,000	5,60,000	60,000
Credit period	1 month	2 months	–
Variable cost (₹)	3,50,000	3,92,000	42,000
Fixed cost (₹)	1,00,000	1,00,000	0
Total Cost	4,50,000	4,92,000	42,000
Contribution (₹)[1]	1,50,000	1,68,000	18,000
Average debtors at cost (₹)[2]	37,500	82,000	44,500

We know that:

$$\text{Incremental return} = \frac{\text{Increased contribution}}{\text{Extra fund employed}} \times 100$$

Substituting the values,

$$\text{Incremental return} = \frac{18{,}000}{44{,}500} \times 100$$

$$\text{Incremental return} = 40.05\%.$$

Since the incremental return is more than the desired return, the proposal is profitable. Hence, it should be accepted.

Working notes:

1. Contribution = Total cost – Variable cost
2. Average debtors at cost = 4,50,000 ÷ 12 = ₹ 37,500

   Average debtors at cost = 4,92,000 ÷ 6 = ₹ 82,000.

Problem 3. A company sells 5,000 units @ ₹ 100 per unit in a year. The variable cost is ₹ 70 per unit and fixed cost is ₹ 1,00,000 per annum. The company is planning to increase the credit period to 2 months from the current period of credit of 1 month. The change in credit policy will result in 10% increase in sales and bad debts will increase from 1% to 2%. The company's required rate of return is 25%. Evaluate the proposal.

Solution: Evaluation of credit policy

Particulars	Present	Proposed
Credit period	1 month	2 months
Sales (in units)	5,000	5,500
Sales (₹)	5,00,000	5,50,000
Less: Variable cost (₹)	3,50,000	3,85,000
Less: Fixed cost (₹)	1,00,000	1,00,000
Gross profit	50,000	65,000
Less: Cost of receivables (25%)	9,375	20,208
Less: Bad debts	5,000	11,000
Net profit (₹)	35,625	33,792

Since the net profit is decreasing by ₹ 1,833, the proposal to change the credit policy should not be accepted.

$$\text{Investment in receivables} = \frac{\text{Variable cost + Fixed cost}}{12} \times \text{Credit period}$$

Problem 4. The following projections are made regarding the operation of a firm:

Sales	1,00,000 units
Selling price per unit	₹ 6.00
Variable cost per unit	₹ 4.20
Total Cost per unit	₹ 5.00
Credit period allowed	One month

The firm intends to increase the credit period for its customers from one month to two months. It is expected that the sale will increase by 10% due to such change. The desired rate of return on investment is 25%. Evaluate the proposed change in the credit policy.

Solution: Evaluation of credit policy

Particulars	Present	Proposed
Credit period	1 month	2 months
Sales (in units)	1,00,000	1,10,000
Sales (₹)	6,00,000	6,60,000
Less: Variable cost (₹)	4,20,000	4,62,000
Less: Fixed cost (₹)	80,000	80,000
Gross profit	1,00,000	1,18,000
Less: Cost of receivables	10,417	22,583
Net profit	89,583	95,417

$$\text{Investment in receivables} = \frac{\text{Variable cost} + \text{Fixed cost}}{12} \times \text{Credit period}$$

Working notes:

1. Gross profit = Sales – Variable cost – Fixed cost
2. Average debtors at cost = 5,00,000 ÷ 12 = ₹ 41,667
   Average debtors at cost = 5,42,000 ÷ 6 = ₹ 90,333.

Problem 5. A company is planning to change its credit policy. The change in policy would increase the sale from ₹ 5,00,000 to ₹ 6,00,000. The fixed cost would remain ₹ 60,000. The bad debt would increase from 1% to 3%. The account receivable turnover ratio would decrease from 10 to 8. The PV ratio of company is 30%. Evaluate the proposal, if the required rate of return of company is 20%.

Solution: Cost of investment in account receivables

Particulars	Present	Proposed
Cost of sales	4,10,000	4,80,000
Account receivable turnover ratio	10	8
Investment in account receivables	41,000	60,000
Cost of investment in accounts receivables (@20%)	8,200	12,000

Cost of sales = variable cost + fixed cost

$$\text{Average investment in account receivable} = \frac{\text{Total cost of sales}}{\text{Debtor turnover}}$$

PV ratio is 30%. Thus, variable cost is 70%.

Change in income of the company

Particulars	Present	Proposed	Change
Sales	5,00,000	6,00,000	1,00,000
Less: Variable cost	3,50,000	4,20,000	70,000
Less: Fixed cost	60,000	60,000	0
Less: Bad debts	5,000	18,000	13,000
Less: Cost of investment in A/R	8,200	12,000	3,800
Income	76,800	90,000	13,200

Since the proposed change in credit policy is increasing income of the company, the proposal should be accepted.

THEORETICAL QUESTIONS

1. Write a note on valuation of credit policy. *(D.U., B.Com. 2016)*
2. Define Receivable Management. Briefly discuss its objectives. *(D.U., B.Com. 2009)*
3. What are credit terms? State the significance of the term "3/10 net 45"?
4. What do you mean by liberal credit policy? What are the costs and benefits associated with a liberal credit policy? *(D.U., B.Com. 2012)*
5. What are the costs and benefits associated with receivables?
6. What is credit policy? What are the elements of a credit policy?
7. Describe the evaluation of credit policies.

PRACTICAL PROBLEMS

1. The following projections are made regarding the operation of a firm:

Sales	50,000 units
Selling price per unit	₹ 5.00
Variable cost per unit	₹ 3.50
Total Cost per unit	₹ 4.00
Credit period allowed	One month

The firm intends to increase the credit period for its customers from one month to two months. It is expected that the sale will increase by 10% due to such change. The desired rate of return on investment is 20%. Evaluate the proposed change in the credit policy.

[**Ans.** Return 38.3%, the proposal should be accepted]

2. A company is planning to change its credit policy. The change in policy would increase the sale from ₹ 1,00,000 to ₹ 1,10,000. The fixed cost would remain ₹ 10,000. The bad debt would increase from 1% to 2%. The account receivable turnover ratio would decrease

from 10 to 8. The PV ratio of company is 25%. Evaluate the proposal, if the required rate of return of company is 25%.

[**Ans.** Income increases by ₹ 534, proposal should be accepted]

3. A company sells 10,000 units @ ₹ 20 per unit in a year. The variable cost is ₹ 13 per unit and fixed cost is ₹ 50,000 per annum. The company is planning to increase the credit period to 2 months from the current period of credit of 1 month. The change in credit policy will result in 10% increase in sales and bad debts will increase from 1% to 2%. The company's required rate of return is 20%. Evaluate the proposal.

   [**Ans.** Profit increases by ₹ 1,167, proposal should be accepted]

4. The following projections are made regarding the operation of a firm:

Sales	**10,000 units**
Selling price per unit	₹ 40
Variable cost per unit	₹ 25
Total Cost per unit	₹ 35
Credit period allowed	One month

   The firm intends to increase the credit period for its customers from one month to two months. It is expected that the sale will increase by 10% due to such change. The desired rate of return on investment is 25%. Evaluate the proposed change in the credit policy.

   [**Ans.** Return is 45%, proposal should be accepted]

5. A company sells 2,000 units @ ₹ 20 per unit in a year. The variable cost is ₹ 14 per unit and fixed cost is ₹ 5,000 per annum. The company is planning to increase the credit period to 2 months from the current period of credit of 1 month. The change in credit policy will result in 10% increase in sales and bad debts will increase from 1% to 2%. The company's required rate of return is 25%. Evaluate the proposal.

   [**Ans.** Increase in profit by ₹ 77, the proposal should be accepted]

Inventory Management

13

Chapter Outline

13.1 Introduction
13.2 Types of Inventory
13.3 Objectives of Inventory Management
13.4 Costs and Benefits of Inventory Management
13.5 Techniques of Inventory Management

13.1 Introduction

The term inventory refers to stock of goods that a firm maintains to facilitate the continuous production of goods and services. The inventories which include raw materials, work-in-progress and finished goods, are a vital part of nearly all business operations. Inventory is an important part of current assets of the firm.

According to Bolton, "the term inventory refers to the stockpile of the product a firm is offering for sale and the components that make up the product."

A firm should maintain an optimal level of inventories. The inventory management is very important in a firm as an error in setting inventory levels leads either to lost production or excessive carrying costs. The effective inventory management would enhance the profits of the firm. This is essential for overall objective of financial management to maximise the shareholders' wealth. Nowadays, firms use sophisticated computer systems to monitor the levels of inventory.

Inventory management is outside the mainstream of finance. It is under the operational control of production department and marketing department. However, financial manager is involved in several ways in inventory management.

13.2 Types of Inventory

A business firm has normally following types of inventories:

1. **Raw materials:** The raw materials refer to the goods which are to be converted into finished through the production process.
2. **Work-in-progress:** The work-in-progress refers to partially produced goods. Some units might have been just introduced, while others may have varying degree of the completion. The value of work-in-progress includes the cost of raw material, direct wages and factory overheads.

3. **Finished goods:** Finished goods refer to final products which are ready for sale. The products which have been produced but are yet to be sold come in this category.

13.3 Objectives of Inventory Management

The basic objective of inventory management is to maintain optimal level of inventory. In this context, the inventory management has to meet the two conflicting objectives:

1. **Minimum investment in inventories:** Both excessive and inadequate inventories are undesirable in a firm. Maintenance of excessive inventories in a firm will result in (i) unnecessary tie-up of the firm's funds and loss of profit, (ii) excessive carrying cost, and (iii) risk of low liquidity. The maintenance of inadequate inventories in a firm will result in (i) interrupted production, (ii) failure to meet delivery commitments.

   The aim of inventory management in firm should be to avoid excessive and inadequate level of inventory and to maintain optimal level of inventory for smooth production and sales operations. The optimal level of inventories in a firm will require the minimum investment in inventories while maintaining the smooth production and sales operation.

2. **Smooth and unhampered production and sales of goods:** The firm should maintain such a level of inventory that the smooth and uninterrupted production and sales are ensured. Inadequate level of inventories will lead to hampered production and sales of goods and in result, the firm may face the loss or lowered profits. This will create an obstacle in achieving the overall objective of financial management i.e., the maximisation of wealth of shareholders. On the other hand, by maintaining the excessive inventories the firm has to bear opportunity cost and the low level of liquidity. This will also cause a decline in profits. Finally, the objective of wealth maximisation will get defeated. Thus, a firm has to maintain the optimum level of inventories to have maximum return on investment in inventories. Consequently, this will help in achieving the objective of wealth maximisation.

13.4 Costs and Benefits of Inventory Management

Various costs and benefits are associated with the level of inventories in a firm. The firm should maintain the optimal level of inventories so that the costs can be minimised and benefits can be maximised. The costs and benefits of inventory management are explained below:

13.4.1 Costs of Inventory

The various costs associated with the maintenance of the inventory are given below:

1. **Ordering costs:** The ordering cost is the cost incurred by the firm in placing the order. The total annual cost of ordering is equal to the cost per order multiplied by the number of orders placed in the year. The fewer the orders, lower will be the ordering costs to the firm. Ordering costs are in nature of fixed costs like administrative costs—preparing purchase order, receiving and inspecting goods, recording the stocks, and transportation costs. These costs are fixed for each order. The ordering costs are inversely related to the size of inventory. For example, a firm requires an inventory of 1,000 units and the cost incurred in placing one order is ₹ 500. Then, if the firm places only one order (order size is 1,000 units), the ordering cost will be ₹ 500. Now, if order size is reduced to 500 units, then ordering costs will be ₹ 1,000 (₹ 500 × 2).

2. **Carrying costs:** These costs are incurred in maintaining the inventory. These costs are called holding or carrying costs. Two basic costs are associated with the carrying costs.
   (i) Storage cost: This refers to the cost of storing one unit of raw material by the firm. This cost is incurred in relation to rent of the warehouse, expenses incurred in the security of raw material, cost of insurance, handing costs, etc.
   (ii) Financing cost: This cost refers to the funds used for purchase or production of inventories. If the firm has to pay interest on borrowing funds used for the purchase of raw material, then such interest is also included in the cost.

   The total carrying cost is entirely variable and it rises in direct proportion to the level of inventories hold.
3. **Opportunity costs:** If the firm holds the higher level of inventories as compared to the requirement of the firm, it unnecessarily blocks the excess funds in inventories. These excess funds have an opportunity cost. If the excess funds have been invested somewhere else the firm would have earned some return on it.

The ordering cost and carrying cost are opposite forces. These costs together determine the level in the firm. A financial manager has to achieve a trade-off between the ordering cost and carrying cost.

13.4.2 Benefits of Inventory

The benefits arising out of maintaining inventory are explained below:

1. **Uninterrupted production:** The holding of inventories ensures continuous production of goods even if there is shortage of inventories in the market. If there is sudden higher demand of goods by customers, the firm can meet that demand if it maintains large stocks of inventories.
2. **Discount on bulk purchase:** If the firm purchases the raw material in large quantity, it can bargain for lower prices or discount on purchase. Similarly, if there is price rise, then the firm can make profit by selling the inventory procured at low prices at the increased prices.
3. **Meeting the competition:** By maintaining the sufficient inventory of finished goods the firm can meet the demand by the customers at right time. The firm can gain competitive advantage over its rivals by maintain its customer base.
4. **Goodwill:** The uninterrupted production and the timely supply of goods by the firm raises the goodwill of the firm in the market.

13.5 Techniques of Inventory Management

The objective of inventory management is to minimise the cost of inventory. Hence, appropriate techniques should be applied in managing the inventories in the firm. Two important techniques of inventory management are explained below:

1. ABC Analysis
2. EOQ Model.

1. ABC analysis. This technique is used when inventory is controlled on the basis of values of items. In this technique, various items of inventory are categorised into three groups of priority.

Then, managerial efforts are made to control the inventory in proportion to the priority. The high value and low volume items are included in category A, items with intermediate value are included in category B and the remaining items are included in category C. The categorisation of items has been explained below:

Category A: Items having high value and low volume are placed in this category. These items constitute only a small percentage of total inventory or volume, but they have very high share in total value of inventory.

Category B: The medium value items are included in this category. Their share in total value of inventory is almost equal to their share in total quantity of inventory.

Category C: The low value and high volume items are included in this category. The share of these items in the total quantity of inventory is very high, but their share in total value of inventory is very small.

An illustrative categorisation of inventory of a firm is given below:

Category of items	Basis	Share in total value	Share in total volume
A	High value, low volume	70%	10%
B	Medium value	20%	30%
C	Low value, high volume	10%	60%
Total		100%	100%

In the above illustration, category A items constitutes 70% share of total value of inventory, but their share in total volume of inventory is only 10%. The share of Category B items in total value of inventory is 20%, and their share in total volume of inventory is 30%. The category C items constitutes 60% of total volume of inventory, but their share in total value of inventory is only 10%.

ABC analysis is very important technique in controlling the inventory in a firm. However, it should be used with thoughtfulness as the items are categorised on the basis of their value and not on their relative importance.

2. Economic order quantity (EOQ) model. The EOQ model is used in a firm to find the optimal size of inventory. The optimal size of inventory is the order size which is placed every time. If more than optimal size quantity of inventory is ordered the carrying cost will be high. If less than optimal size quantity of inventory is ordered, the ordering cost will be high.

The EOQ model of determining the optimal order quantity that minimises the total cost of inventory is based on the following assumptions:

1. The annual consumption of inventory of the firm is known and is constant.
2. The ordering cost per order is fixed and is constant over the year.
3. The carrying cost of inventory per unit per annum is constant.
4. The consumption of inventory is uniform through the year.
5. The carrying cost and ordering cost are the only costs incurred on inventory procurement.
6. The inventory is supplied instantly.

The economic order quantity is calculated as given below:

If the ordering cost per order is fixed, the total ordering cost will be:

$$\text{Total ordering cost} = \frac{\text{Annual requirement} \times \text{Per order cost}}{\text{Order size}}$$

$$\text{Total ordering cost} = \frac{AO}{Q}$$

Where, A: Annual requirement of inventory

O: Per order cost

Q: Order size

The carrying cost will be based on average inventory.

$$\text{Average inventory} = \frac{Q}{2}$$

The total carrying cost will be:

$$\text{Total carrying cost} = \frac{Qc}{2}$$

Where, c: carrying cost per unit per annum.

As the order size increases, the total ordering cost decreases. On the other hand, as order size increases the total carrying cost increases. Thus, there is a trade-off between total carrying cost and total ordering cost as shown below in figure 1.

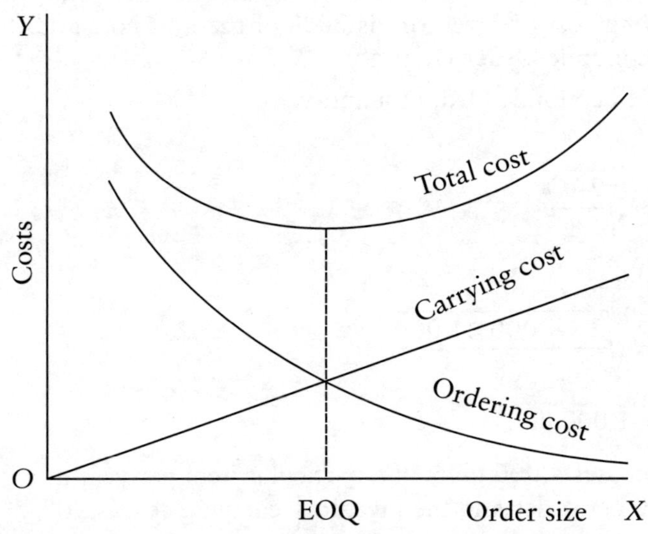

Fig. 1: Economic Order Quantity

The total cost will be minimum, where total ordering cost is equal to total carrying cost. Thus,

$$\frac{AO}{Q} = \frac{Qc}{2}$$

$$\Rightarrow \qquad Q^2 = \frac{2AO}{c}$$

And economic order quantity (EOQ) is:

$$EOQ = \sqrt{\frac{2AO}{c}}$$

Reorder point: The reorder point is that level of inventory at which an order is placed to replenish the inventory. The following formulae is used in calculating the reorder point:

Reorder point = Lead time × average daily usage + Safety margin

The lead time is the time taken in delivery of inventory after placing the order.

Example 1. The daily usage of inventory in a firm is 100 units. The goods are delivered by the supplier in 15 days after placing the order. The firm maintains a safety margin of 10 days. Find the reorder point of inventory of the firm.

Solution: The safety margin is calculated as given below:

Safety margin = daily usage × days

Safety margin = 100 × 10 = 1,000 units

The reorder point is calculated as given below:

Reorder point = Lead time × average daily usage + safety margin

Reorder point = 15 × 100 + 1,000 = 2,500 units.

Example 2. A company requires 4,000 units of a certain item per year. The purchase price per unit is ₹ 40. The carrying cost of inventory is 20% of the unit cost and the cost per order is ₹ 1,000. Compute the Economic Order Quantity.

Solution: Calculation of Economic Order Quantity,

We know that:

$$EOQ = \sqrt{\frac{2AO}{c}}$$

Substituting the values,

$$EOQ = \sqrt{\frac{2 \times 4{,}000 \times 1{,}000}{8}}$$

$$EOQ = 1{,}000 \text{ units}$$

Example 3. A firm purchases 4,000 units of a particular item per year at a unit cost of ₹ 40. The ordering cost is ₹ 1,000 per order and the inventory carrying cost is 20%.

(i) Determine the optimal order quantity and the minimum total cost including purchase cost.

(ii) If a 4% discount is offered by the supplier for purchase in a lot of 2,000 or more, should the firm accept the order?

Solution: (i) Calculation of Economic Order Quantity,

We know that:

$$EOQ = \sqrt{\frac{2AO}{c}}$$

Substituting the values,

$$EOQ = \sqrt{\frac{2 \times 4{,}000 \times 500}{4}}$$

EOQ = 1,000 units.

Evaluation of offer

Particulars	EOQ	Offer
Units per order	1,000	2,000
No. of orders	4	2
Purchase price per unit	40	38.4
Average inventory	500	1,000
Carrying cost per unit	8.00	7.68
Total Ordering cost	4,000	2,000
Total Carrying cost	4,000	76,80
Total Purchase cost	1,60,000	1,53,600
Total inventory cost	1,68,000	1,63,280

The total cost of inventory is least in case of 4% discount. Thus, the firm should accept the offer.

Example 4. A company requires 4,000 units of a certain item per year. The purchase price per unit is ₹ 20. The carrying cost of inventory is 20% of the unit cost and the cost per order is ₹ 500. You are required to:

(i) Compute the Economic Order Quantity.

(ii) What will be the total cost of ordering and cost of carrying inventories when 4 orders of equal size are placed?

Solution: (i) Calculation of Economic Order Quantity,

We know that:

$$EOQ = \sqrt{\frac{2AO}{c}}$$

Substituting the values,

$$EOQ = \sqrt{\frac{2 \times 4{,}000 \times 500}{4}}$$

EOQ = 1,000 units

(ii) Ordering cost = 4 × 500 = ₹ 2,000

Carrying cost = (1,000 ÷ 2) × 4 = ₹ 2,000

Total cost of ordering and carrying inventories = 2,000 + 2,000 = ₹ 4,000.

Example 5. A company purchases a raw material at ₹ 10 per kg. The company incurs a handling cost of ₹ 60 plus freight of ₹ 90 per order. The incremental carrying cost of inventory of raw material is ₹ 0.10 per kg. per month. In addition, the cost of working capital finance on investment in inventory is ₹ 0.30 per kg. per annum. The annual production of the product is 1,00,000 units and 5 units are obtained from 1 kg. of raw material.

(i) Calculate the Economic Order Quantity of raw material.

(ii) Advice, how frequently should order for procurement of raw material be made, assuming 360 days in a year?

(iii) If the company proposes to rationalise placement of orders on quarterly basis, what percentage of discount in the price of raw material should be negotiated?

Solution: (i) Economic order quantity:

Total ordering cost = 60 + 90 = ₹ 150

Carrying cost per annum = 12 × 0.10 = ₹ 1.20 per kg.

Cost of working capital finance = ₹ 0.30 per kg.

Total carrying cost = ₹ 1.5 per kg.

Annual requirement = 1,00,000 ÷ 5 = 20,000 kg.

We know that:

$$EOQ = \sqrt{\frac{2AO}{c}}$$

Substituting the values,

$$EOQ = \sqrt{\frac{2 \times 20,000 \times 150}{1.5}}$$

$$EOQ = 2,000 \text{ kg.}$$

(ii) Number of orders per annum = 20,000 ÷ 2,000 = 10

Frequency of orders = 360 ÷ 10 = 36 days

(iii) Calculation of discount

Particulars	EOQ	Quarterly orders
No. of orders	10	4
Order quantity (kg.)	2,000	5,000
Average inventory (kg.)	1,000	2,500
Total Carrying cost (₹)	1,500	3,750
Total Ordering cost (₹)	1,500	600
Total Ordering and carrying cost	3,000	4,350

Increase in total carrying and ordering cost = 4,350 – 3,000 = ₹ 1,350

Total purchase = ₹ 24,00,000

Thus, discount = (1,350 ÷ 2,00,000) × 100 = 0.675%

Hence, the firm should negotiate for 0.675% discount on all purchases if quarterly orders are placed.

Example 6. A company provides the following information:

The cost per unit of inventory is ₹ 4. Carrying cost is 10% of average inventory per annum. The fixed cost per order is ₹ 160. The number of units required is 20,000 per year.

You are required to calculate:

(i) EOQ

(ii) Total number of orders in a year

(iii) Total annual inventory cost at EOQ.

Solution: (i) Calculation of Economic Order Quantity,

We know that:

$$EOQ = \sqrt{\frac{2AO}{c}}$$

Substituting the values,

$$EOQ = \sqrt{\frac{2 \times 20,000 \times 160}{0.40}}$$

$$EOQ = 4,000 \text{ units}$$

(ii) Total number of order in a year = 20,000 ÷ 4,000 = 5

(iii) Carrying cost = 0.40 × 2,000 = ₹ 800

Ordering cost = 5 × 160 = ₹ 800

Total cost of ordering and carrying inventories = 800 + 800 = ₹ 1,600.

Example 7. The annual demand of raw material in company is 100,000 units. The ordering cost per order is ₹ 100. The annual carrying cost is ₹ 20 per unit. Calculate the total ordering cost, total carrying cost and total inventory cost, when order size is:

(i) 2,000 units

(ii) 4,000 units

(iii) 5,000 units

Also compute the Economic Order Quantity and total inventory cost at Economic Order Quantity.

Solution:

(i) When order size is 2,000 units, number of orders is 50.

Total ordering cost = 50 × 100 = ₹ 5,000

Total carrying cost = (2,000 ÷ 2) × 20 = ₹ 20,000

Total inventory cost = 5,000 + 20,000 = ₹ 25,000

(ii) When order size is 4,000 units, number of orders is 25.
Total ordering cost = 25 × 100 = ₹ 2,500
Total carrying cost = (4,000 ÷ 2) × 20 = ₹ 40,000
Total inventory cost = 2,500 + 40,000 = ₹ 42,500

(iii) When order size is 5,000 units, number of orders is 20.
Total ordering cost = 20 × 100 = ₹ 2,000
Total carrying cost = (5,000 ÷ 2) × 20 = ₹ 50,000
Total inventory cost = 2,000 + 50,000 = ₹ 52,000

We know that:

$$EOQ = \sqrt{\frac{2AO}{c}}$$

Substituting the values,

$$EOQ = \sqrt{\frac{2 \times 1,00,000 \times 100}{20}}$$

$$EOQ = 1,000 \text{ units}$$

When order size is 1,000 units, number of orders is 100.
Total ordering cost = 100 × 100 = ₹ 10,000
Total carrying cost = 500 × 20 = ₹ 10,000
Total inventory cost = 10,000 + 10,000 = ₹ 20,000.

SOLVED PROBLEMS

Problem 1. A firm purchases 2,000 units of a particular item per year at a unit cost of ₹ 20. The ordering cost is ₹ 50 per order and the inventory carrying cost is 25%.

(i) Determine the optimal order quantity and the minimum total cost including purchase cost.

(ii) If a 3% discount is offered by the supplier for purchase in a lot of 1,000 or more, should the firm accept the order?

Solution: (i) Calculation of Economic Order Quantity,

We know that:

$$EOQ = \sqrt{\frac{2AO}{c}}$$

Substituting the values,

$$EOQ = \sqrt{\frac{2 \times 2,000 \times 50}{5}}$$

$$EOQ = 200 \text{ units}$$

(ii) Evaluation of offer

Particulars	EOQ	Offer
Units per order	200	1,000
No. of orders	10	2
Purchase price per unit	20	19.4
Average inventory	100	500
Carrying cost per unit	5.00	4.85
Total Ordering cost	500	100
Total Carrying cost	500	2,425
Total Purchase cost	40,000	38,800
Total Inventory cost	41,000	41,325

The total cost of inventory is least in case Economic Order Quantity. Thus, the firm should not accept the offer.

Problem 2. A company requires 2,000 units of a certain item per year. The purchase price per unit is ₹ 30. The carrying cost of inventory is 25% of the unit cost and the cost per order is ₹ 1,000. You are required to:

(i) Compute the Economic Order Quantity.

(ii) What will be the total cost of ordering and cost of carrying inventories when 4 orders of equal size are placed?

Solution: (i) Calculation of Economic Order Quantity,

We know that:

$$EOQ = \sqrt{\frac{2AO}{c}}$$

Substituting the values,

$$EOQ = \sqrt{\frac{2 \times 2,000 \times 1,000}{7.5}}$$

$$EOQ = 730 \text{ units}$$

(ii) Ordering cost = 4 × 1,000 = ₹ 4,000

Carrying cost = (500 ÷ 2) × 7.5 = ₹ 1,875

Total cost of ordering and carrying inventories = 4,000 + 1,875 = ₹ 5,875.

Problem 3. A company purchases a raw material at ₹ 60 per kg. The company incurs a handling cost of ₹ 360 plus freight of ₹ 390 per order. The incremental carrying cost of inventory of raw material is ₹ 0.50 per kg. per month. In addition, the cost of working capital finance on investment in inventory is ₹ 9 per kg. per annum. The annual production of the product is 1,00,000 units and 2.5 units are obtained from 1 kg. of raw material.

(i) Calculate the Economic Order Quantity of raw material.

(ii) Advice, how frequently should order for procurement of raw material be made, assuming 360 days in a year?

(iii) If the company proposes to rationalise placement of orders on quarterly basis, what percentage of discount in the price of raw material should be negotiated?

Solution: (i) Economic order quantity:

Total ordering cost = 360 + 390 = ₹ 750

Carrying cost per annum = 12 × 0.50 = ₹ 6 per kg.

Cost of working capital finance = ₹ 9 per kg.

Total carrying cost = ₹ 15 per kg.

Annual requirement = 1,00,000 ÷ 2.5 = 40,000 kg.

We know that:

$$EOQ = \sqrt{\frac{2AO}{c}}$$

Substituting the values,

$$EOQ = \sqrt{\frac{2 \times 40{,}000 \times 750}{15}}$$

EOQ = 2,000 kg.

(ii) Number of orders per annum = 40,000 ÷ 2,000 = 20

Frequency of orders = 360 ÷ 20 = 18 days

(iii) Calculation of discount

Particulars	EOQ	Quarterly orders
No. of orders	20	4
Order quantity (kg.)	2,000	10,000
Average inventory (kg.)	1,000	5,000
Total Carrying cost (₹)	15,000	75,000
Total Ordering cost (₹)	15,000	3,000
Total Ordering and carrying cost	30,000	78,000

Increase in total carrying and ordering cost = 78,000 – 30,000 = ₹ 48,000

Total purchase = ₹ 24,00,000

Thus, discount = (48,000 ÷ 24,00,00) × 100 = 2%.

Hence, the firm should negotiate for 2% discount on all purchases if quarterly orders are placed.

Problem 4. A company provides the following information:

The cost per unit of inventory is ₹ 16. Carrying cost is 15% of average inventory per annum. The fixed cost per order is ₹ 960. The number of units required is 20,000 per year.

You are required to calculate:

(i) EOQ

(ii) Total number of orders in a year

(iii) Total annual inventory cost at EOQ. *(D.U., B.Com. 2015, N.C.)*

Solution: (i) Calculation of Economic Order Quantity,

We know that:

$$EOQ = \sqrt{\frac{2AO}{c}}$$

Substituting the values,

$$EOQ = \sqrt{\frac{2 \times 20{,}000 \times 960}{2.40}}$$

$$EOQ = 4{,}000 \text{ units}$$

(ii) Total number of order in a year = 20,000 ÷ 4,000 = 5

(iii) Carrying cost = 2.40 × 2,000 = ₹ 4,800

Ordering cost = 5 × 960 = ₹ 4,800

Total cost of ordering and carrying inventories = 4,800 + 4,800 = ₹ 9,600.

Problem 5. The annual demand of raw material in company is 10,000 units. The ordering cost per order is ₹ 200. The annual carrying cost is ₹ 10 per unit. Calculate the total ordering cost, total carrying cost and total inventory cost, when order size is:

(i) 100 units

(ii) 200 units

(iii) 500 units

Also compute the Economic Order Quantity and total inventory cost at Economic Order Quantity.

Solution:

(i) When order size is 100 units, number of orders is 100.

Total ordering cost = 200 × 100 = ₹ 20,000

Total carrying cost = (100 ÷ 2) × 10 = ₹ 500

Total inventory cost = 20,000 + 500 = ₹ 20,500

(ii) When order size is 200 units, number of orders is 50.

Total ordering cost = 200 × 50 = ₹ 10,000

Total carrying cost = (200 ÷ 2) × 10 = ₹ 1,000

Total inventory cost = 10,000 + 1,000 = ₹ 11,000

(iii) When order size is 500 units, number of orders is 20.

Total ordering cost = 200 × 20 = ₹ 4,000

Total carrying cost = (500 ÷ 2) × 10 = ₹ 2,500

Total inventory cost = 4,000 + 2,500 = ₹ 6,500

We know that:

$$EOQ = \sqrt{\frac{2AO}{c}}$$

Substituting the values,

$$EOQ = \sqrt{\frac{2 \times 10,000 \times 200}{10}}$$

$$EOQ = 632 \text{ units}$$

When order size is 632 units, number of orders is 16.

Total ordering cost = 200 × 16 = ₹ 3,200

Total carrying cost = (632 ÷ 2) × 10 = ₹ 3,160

Total inventory cost = 3,200 + 3,160 = ₹ 6,360.

THEORETICAL QUESTIONS

1. Write a short note on:
   (i) Economic order quantity. *(D.U., B.Com. 2016)*
   (ii) Reorder point for inventory. *(D.U., B.Com. 2012)*
   (iii) Costs involved in inventory management. *(D.U., B.Com. 2013)*
   (iv) ABC analysis of inventory control. *(D.U., B.Com. 2015)*
2. Explain EOQ and its importance. *(D.U., B.Com. 2009)*
3. What are the objectives of inventory management? How are they similar to the objectives of cash management? *(D.U., B.Com. 2010)*
4. What are the costs and benefits associated with inventory management? Explain them.
5. What is safety stock? What are the costs associated with safety stock?

PRACTICAL PROBLEMS

1. A company provides the following information:
   The cost per unit of inventory is ₹ 10. Carrying cost is 20% of average inventory per annum. The fixed cost per order is ₹ 100. The number of units required is 40,000 per year.
   You are required to calculate:
   (i) EOQ
   (ii) Total number of orders in a year
   (iii) Total annual inventory cost at EOQ. *(D.U., B.Com. 2015, N.C.)*
   [**Ans.** (i) 2,000 units; (ii) 20; (iii) ₹ 4,04,000]
2. A firm purchases 1,600 units of a particular item per year at a unit cost of ₹ 10. The ordering cost is ₹ 100 per order and the inventory carrying cost is 20%.

(i) Determine the optimal order quantity and the minimum total cost including purchase cost.

(ii) If a 4% discount is offered by the supplier for purchase in a lot of 800 or more, should the firm accept the order?

[**Ans.** (i) 400 units, ₹ 16,800; (ii) Total cost = ₹ 16,360, offer should be accepted]

3. A company requires 40,000 units of a certain item per year. The purchase price per unit is ₹ 10. The carrying cost of inventory is 20% of the unit cost and the cost per order is ₹ 200. You are required to:

   (i) Compute the Economic Order Quantity.

   (ii) What will be the total cost of ordering and cost of carrying inventories when 4 orders of equal size are placed?

   [**Ans.** (i) 4,000 units; (ii) Total ordering cost: ₹ 800, Total carrying cost: ₹ 10,000]

4. A company purchases a raw material at ₹ 50 per kg. The company incurs a handling cost of ₹ 300 plus freight of ₹ 300 per order. The incremental carrying cost of inventory of raw material is ₹ 0.75 per kg. per month. In addition, the cost of working capital finance on investment in inventory is ₹ 3 per kg. per annum. The annual production of the product is 1,00,000 units and 2.5 units are obtained from 1 kg. of raw material.

   (i) Calculate the Economic Order Quantity of raw material.

   (ii) Advice, how frequently should order for procurement of raw material be made, assuming 360 days in a year?

   (iii) If the company proposes to rationalise placement of orders on quarterly basis, what percentage of discount in the price of raw material should be negotiated?

   [**Ans.** (i) 2,000 units; (ii) 18 days; (iii) 1.92%]

5. The annual demand of raw material in company is 1,000 units. The ordering cost per order is ₹ 100. The annual carrying cost is ₹ 5 per unit. Calculate the total ordering cost, total carrying cost and total inventory cost, when order size is:

   (i) 100 units

   (ii) 200 units

   (iii) 500 units

   Also compute the Economic Order Quantity and total inventory cost at Economic Order Quantity.

   [**Ans.** (i) ₹ 1,000, ₹ 250, ₹ 1,250; (ii) ₹ 500, ₹ 500, ₹ 1,000; (iii) ₹ 200, ₹ 1,250, ₹ 1,450; EOQ: 200, ₹ 1,000]

Appendix 1

Delhi University Question Paper 2016
B.Com. (Programme), Semester V
Financial Management

Duration: 3 Hours | Maximum Marks: 75

1. (a) Briefly discuss major financial decisions with which a finance manager is confronted?
   (b) The role of finance manager has evolved overtime? Discuss.

   OR

   (a) What is annuity? Give three examples of an annuity.
   (b) Why time value of money is important in financial decision-making?
   (c) X financed a car by taking a loan of ₹ 4,00,000 at 10% p.a.. The loan is to be repaid in four equal annual instalments starting from the end of the first year. Calculate the amount of equal annual instalment.

2. A company is considering to purchase a machine. Two machines A and B are available each costing ₹ 50,000. Earnings after taxation are expected to be as follows:

Year	Machine A	Machine B
1	15,000	5,000
2	20,000	15,000
3	25,000	20,000
4	15,000	30,000
5	10,000	20,000

   You are required to indicate which of the machines would be profitable using:
   (i) Payback Method
   (ii) Return on investment method

   OR

A choice is to be made between two proposals which require an equal investment of ₹ 50,000 each and are expected to generate net cash flows as under:

Year	Project A	Project B
1	25,000	10,000
2	15,000	12,000
3	10,000	18,000
4	Nil	25,000
5	12,000	8,000
6	6,000	4,000

Which project should be chosen under:

(i) Payback period

(ii) Average rate of return method?

3. (a) Define "Leverage". What are the different types of leverages? Explain them.

(b) From the following information, calculate different types of leverages:

	₹ (in lakhs)
Sales	8,000
EBIT	1,950
PBT	950
Tax rate	40%

Variable cost is 70% of sales.

OR

(a) Distinguish between Net Income Approach and Net Operating Income Approach of Capital Structure.

(b) Companies U and L are same in every aspect except that U is unlevered and L has ₹ 20 lakhs of 8% debt. EBIT of both firms is ₹ 6 lakhs and tax rate is 35%. Equity capitalisation rate for U is 10%.

Calculate the value of each firm using M-M approach and cost of equity for L. Ltd.

4. (a) Write a note on Gordon's approach to relevance of dividend decision.

(b) ABC Ltd. is currently having 1,00,000 equity shares of the face value of ₹ 10 each. It is expected that company will have year-end net profit of ₹ 5,00,000. Due to recessionary conditions, the company expects 10% return on its investment in future. The equity capitalisation rate is 12%. Find out the market price per share according to Gordon Model under different payout ratios of 40%, 60% and 80%.

OR

(a) Explain the Modigliani-Miller hypothesis of dividend irrelevance.

(b) Earnings per share of ABC Ltd. is ₹ 10. The face value of its equity share is ₹ 100. Its rate of return on investment is 20%. Capitalisation rate for its risk class is 15%. Using Walter's dividend model, find out:

(i) The optimum payout ratio.

(ii) The market price per share if the payout ratio is zero.

(iii) The market price at a payout of 60%.

5. Compute the working capital requirements from the following details:

Budgeted sales	**30,000 units per annum**
Raw material cost per unit	₹ 8
Direct labour per unit	₹ 8
Overhead per unit	₹ 2
Total cost	₹ 18
Profit per unit	₹ 2
Selling price per unit	₹ 20

Additional information:

(i) Debtors are allowed 8 weeks credit.

(ii) Suppliers provide 5 weeks credit.

(iii) Raw material will be carried in stock for 4 weeks and finished goods for 2 weeks.

(iv) Factory process will take on an average 3 weeks.

Assume labour and overhead expenses to accrue evenly throughout the production cycle.

OR

Write short notes on the following:

(i) Operating cycle method of working capital.

(ii) Economic order quantity.

(iii) Evaluation of credit policy.

Appendix 2

Mathematical Tables

Table 1: Compound Value Factors for an Amount [$CVF_{(r\%, n)}$]

Period (n)	r, %														
	1	2	3	4	5	6	7	8	9	10	11	12	13	14	15
1	1.010	1.020	1.030	1.040	1.050	1.060	1.070	1.080	1.090	1.100	1.110	1.120	1.130	1.140	1.150
2	1.020	1.040	1.061	1.082	1.102	1.124	1.145	1.166	1.188	1.210	1.232	1.254	1.277	1.300	1.322
3	1.030	1.061	1.093	1.125	1.158	1.191	1.225	1.260	1.295	1.331	1.368	1.405	1.443	1.482	1.521
4	1.041	1.082	1.126	1.170	1.216	1.262	1.311	1.360	1.412	1.464	1.518	1.574	1.630	1.689	1.749
5	1.051	1.104	1.159	1.217	1.276	1.338	1.403	1.469	1.539	1.611	1.685	1.762	1.842	1.925	2.011
6	1.062	1.126	1.194	1.265	1.340	1.419	1.501	1.587	1.677	1.772	1.870	1.974	2.082	2.195	2.313
7	1.072	1.149	1.230	1.316	1.407	1.504	1.606	1.714	1.828	1.949	2.076	2.211	2.353	2.502	2.660
8	1.083	1.172	1.267	1.369	1.477	1.594	1.718	1.851	1.993	2.144	2.305	2.476	2.658	2.853	3.059
9	1.094	1.195	1.305	1.423	1.551	1.689	1.838	1.999	2.172	2.358	2.558	2.773	3.004	3.252	3.518
10	1.105	1.219	1.344	1.480	1.629	1.791	1.967	2.159	2.367	2.594	2.839	3.106	3.395	3.707	4.046
11	1.116	1.243	1.384	1.539	1.710	1.898	2.105	2.332	2.580	2.853	3.152	3.479	3.836	4.226	4.652
12	1.127	1.268	1.426	1.601	1.796	2.012	2.252	2.518	2.813	3.138	3.498	3.896	4.335	4.818	5.350
13	1.138	1.294	1.469	1.655	1.886	2.133	2.410	2.720	3.056	3.452	3.883	4.363	4.898	5.492	6.153
14	1.149	1.319	1.513	1.732	1.930	2.261	2.579	2.937	3.342	3.797	4.310	4.887	5.535	6.261	7.076
15	1.161	1.346	1.558	1.801	2.079	2.397	2.759	3.172	3.642	4.177	4.785	5.474	6.254	7.138	8.137
16	1.173	1.373	1.605	1.873	2.183	2.540	2.952	3.426	3.970	4.595	5.311	6.130	7.067	8.137	9.358
17	1.184	1.400	1.653	1.948	2.292	2.693	3.159	3.700	4.328	5.054	5.895	6.866	7.986	9.276	10.761
18	1.196	1.428	1.702	2.026	2.407	2.854	3.380	3.996	4.717	5.560	6.544	7.690	9.024	10.575	12.375
19	1.208	1.457	1.754	2.107	2.527	3.026	3.617	4.316	5.142	6.116	7.263	8.613	10.197	12.056	14.232
20	1.220	1.486	1.806	2.191	2.653	3.207	3.870	4.661	5.604	6.728	8.062	9.646	11.523	13.743	16.367

Table 4: Present Value Factors for an Annuity [$PVFA_{(r\%, n)}$]

Period (n)	r, %														
	1	2	3	4	5	6	7	8	9	10	11	12	13	14	15
1	0.990	0.980	0.971	0.962	0.952	0.943	0.935	0.926	0.917	0.909	0.901	0.893	0.885	0.877	0.870
2	1.970	1.942	1.913	1.886	1.859	1.833	1.808	1.783	1.759	1.736	1.713	1.690	1.668	1.647	1.626
3	2.941	2.884	2.829	2.775	2.723	2.673	2.624	2.577	2.531	2.487	2.444	2.402	2.361	2.322	2.283
4	3.902	3.808	3.717	3.630	3.546	3.465	3.387	3.312	3.240	3.170	3.102	3.037	2.974	2.914	2.855
5	4.853	4.713	4.580	4.452	4.329	4.212	4.100	3.993	3.890	3.791	3.696	3.605	3.517	3.433	3.352
6	5.795	5.601	5.417	5.242	5.076	4.917	4.767	4.623	4.486	4.355	4.231	4.111	3.998	3.889	3.784
7	6.728	6.472	6.230	6.002	5.789	5.582	5.389	5.206	5.033	4.868	4.712	4.564	4.423	4.288	4.160
8	7.652	7.326	7.020	6.733	6.463	6.210	5.971	5.747	5.535	5.335	5.146	4.968	4.799	4.639	4.487
9	8.566	8.162	7.786	7.435	7.108	6.802	6.615	6.247	5.995	5.759	5.537	5.328	5.132	4.946	4.772
10	9.471	8.983	8.530	8.111	7.722	7.360	7.024	6.710	6.418	6.145	5.889	5.650	5.426	5.216	5.019
11	10.368	9.787	9.253	8.760	8.306	7.887	7.499	7.139	6.805	6.495	6.207	5.938	5.687	5.453	5.234
12	11.255	10.575	9.954	9.385	8.863	8.384	7.943	7.536	7.161	6.814	6.492	6.194	5.918	5.660	5.421
13	12.134	11.348	10.635	9.986	9.394	8.858	8.358	7.904	7.487	7.103	6.750	6.424	6.122	5.842	5.583
14	13.004	12.106	11.296	10.563	9.899	9.295	8.746	8.244	7.786	7.367	6.982	6.628	6.303	6.002	5.724
15	13.865	12.849	11.938	11.118	10.380	9.712	9.108	8.560	8.061	7.606	7.191	6.811	6.462	6.142	5.847
16	14.718	13.578	12.561	11.652	10.838	10.106	9.447	8.851	8.313	7.824	7.379	6.974	6.604	6.265	5.954
17	15.562	14.292	13.166	12.166	11.274	10.477	9.763	9.122	8.544	8.002	7.549	7.120	6.729	6.373	6.047
18	16.398	14.992	13.754	12.659	11.690	10.828	10.059	9.372	8.756	8.201	7.702	7.250	6.840	6.467	6.128
19	17.226	15.679	14.324	13.134	12.085	11.158	10.336	9.604	8.950	8.365	7.893	7.366	6.938	6.550	6.198
20	18.046	16.352	14.878	13.590	12.462	11.470	10.594	9.818	9.129	8.514	7.963	7.469	7.025	6.623	6.259